Succeeding Postmodernism

Succeeding Postmodernism

Language and Humanism in Contemporary American Literature

Mary K. Holland

BLOOMSBURY

NEW YORK · LONDON · NEW DELHI · SYDNEY

Bloomsbury Academic

An imprint of Bloomsbury Publishing Plc

175 Fifth Avenue   50 Bedford Square
New York   London
NY 10010   WC1B 3DP
USA   UK

www.bloomsbury.com

First published 2013

Most of Chapter 2 has appeared in *Critique: Studies in Contemporary Fiction* 47.3 (2006):
218–42. The author has made substantial changes and additions for this book, and the first
section of Chapter 3 was previously published as "A Lamb in Wolf 's Clothing: Postmodern
Realism in A. M. Homes's *Music for Torching* and *This Book Will Save Your Life*,"
in *Critique: Studies in Contemporary Fiction* 53.3 (2012): 214–37.

Library of Congress Cataloging-in-Publication Data
Holland, Mary, 1970–
Succeeding postmodernism: language and humanism in contemporary
American literature / [Mary Holland].
pages cm
Includes bibliographical references and index.
ISBN 978-1-4411-3061-7 (hardcover: alk. paper)
1. American fiction–21st century–History and criticism. 2. Language and languages
in literature. 3. Humanism in literature.
4. Postmodernism (Literature)–United States. I. Title.
PS374.L29H65 2013
816'.609–dc23
2012038629

ISBN: HB: 978-1-4411-3061-7
ePub: 978-1-4411-2189-9
ePDF: 978-1-4411-5934-2

Typeset by Newgen Imaging Systems Pvt, Ltd, Chennai, India
Printed and bound in the United States of America

For Evan and Camden
who never let me forget what is real

Contents

Acknowledgments   viii
Introduction: Writing Postmodern Humanism   1

1   "Dead Souls Babbling": Language, Loss, and
    Community in *The Names* and *White Noise*   23

2   "The Art's Heart's Purpose": Braving the
    Narcissistic Loop of *Infinite Jest*   57

3   Recuperating the Postmodern Family: Mediating
    Loss in *Music for Torching* and *House of Leaves*   91

4   Joining Gravity: Making Language Matter in
    The Road, Extremely Loud & Incredibly Close,
    and *The Book of Portraiture*   129

5   "Set . . . softly down beside you": Poststructural
    Realism in "Octet" and *Everything Is Illuminated*   165

Conclusion: Metamodernism   199
Works Cited   203
Index   215

Acknowledgments

The argument of this book gathers ideas discovered at far-flung places and times over the past several years of my encounters with literature, collecting as well the influences of the many teachers, students, colleagues, and friends I have been lucky enough to discuss it with. I thank Vince Pecora and Kate Hayles for the rigor and insight that fostered the book's beginnings, and Chris Mott for helping me see where the book began at all. Endlessly, I thank Dennis Huston for showing me the life literature can lead to, and which led to this book. Perhaps this project began when Jack Zammito taught me, on my first day as a humanities student, to read literature exactly as Sontag would advise when I found her twenty years later.

To all the students who endured repeated deployments of these arguments, and helped me shape and sharpen them with their own astute questions, inventive readings, and contagious excitement about them, my deepest appreciation. Much of what I have come to in my criticism grew out of these fecund, challenging, and transforming interactions in the classroom. May it always be thus.

Early drafts benefited greatly from thoughtful feedback generously given by colleagues and friends, especially Andrew Higgins, who introduced me to Gumbrecht and is always up for a good talk about aesthetics; Jeffrey Fisher, who expanded my scope past postmodernism and many times lent his patient ear and eye; Kirsten Wasson, whose early response to a chapter convinced me I had a book worth finishing; and Stephen Burn, whose enthusiasm about my work told me I had one worth publishing.

I am enormously grateful to the United University Professions and SUNY for enabling the semester of leave without which this project might never have seen completion. Also, I thank the sisters at Linwood for providing the place in whose profound peace I worked on several stages of this book, as well as Tom Olsen and the New Paltz English department for allowing those indispensable retreats. *Dilige, et quod vis fac.*

Finally, my thanks to those whose support of various nonacademic kinds shepherded the rest of my life as it unfolded complicatedly around this book: my parents; extended family Eve and John; again and abidingly, Kirsten and Jeff; and my boys, Evan and Camden, who remind me why I care so much about the arguments I make in this book, and then remind me to stop arguing and go play.

Introduction:
Writing Postmodern Humanism

There is the irony that, in a sense, we are all humanists.
We experience the world as humanists, but this is not necessarily the way we theorize.

Madan Sarup[1]

In an intellectual climate of hyperperiodization, Benjamin's alarm clock resolutely ringing, it should come as no surprise that millennial arrival set off a clamoring about new ends and beginnings in theory and literature. A decade in and the twenty-first century does not disappoint: critics and theorists from feminist to political to comic, and certainly including literary, are declaring the end of postmodernism, and beginning, with however mountainous qualifications, to consider what is coming next.[2] The sheer volume of prose devoted to such a position indicates that something significant indeed is changing in art, culture, theory, and literature. And literature—no longer satisfied with reproducing the disaffected irony and language games that long caused readers to characterize postmodern literature as heartless and meaningless—makes its own vehement demand to be read and understood differently. But what exactly is changing? How may we most productively characterize these changes, and understand them in the context of the literature and theory out of which they develop? And does this moment of change really mark the end of postmodernism? This book addresses these questions by examining not just the literature and theories of the current century but equally those of the late twentieth century out of which they evolved.

Ian Watt has written that the novel grew out of new social conditions in which the autonomous individual prospered or failed by competing against others in social situations.[3] In 1996 Steve Tomasula augmented that argument, proposing that not only do literary modes and genres come about in response to social conditions and problems of the time, but also that our notion of what it is to be human shapes and creates the art of a time.[4] I want to extend that argument further in proposing that, in a time much defined by poststructural notions about signification, our notion of what language is, and how it works, and how humans stand in relation to it, dictates the kinds of literature we find in a period, the questions that literature raises about what it is to be human, and therefore also our notion of the human. That is, one way of understanding this literary shift is to say that American fiction in the twenty-first century looks, reads, and feels profoundly different from twentieth-century postmodern literature because it conceives of what language is and what it can do very differently. It displays a new faith in language and certainty about the novel's ability to engage in humanist pursuits that have not been seen clearly since poststructuralism shattered both in the middle of the past century. *Succeeding Postmodernism* identifies this dramatic evolution in twenty-first-century American fiction while locating its origins in a needed rereading of the fiction of the late twentieth century.

Essentially this book is interested in our changing ideas about the relationship between language and the human, and about uses of representation to depict the human in language. But in order fairly to consider how or whether such changes signal the end of literary postmodernism, we must first see clearly this relationship between language and the human in postmodern literature, and I will argue that we have not yet done so. Rather, we have often mischaracterized postmodern literature— especially fiction that takes as its starting point the language problems described by deconstruction theory—as unable to represent or care about the things that literature has traditionally cared most about: human relationships, emotional interaction with the world, meaning. It is the problem of language, the thinking goes, that the irreparable rift between signifier and signified—word and meaning—leaves language unable to represent meaningful affect, and literature that interrogates signification unable to care about the literary elements, like narrative arc and character development, that enable texts to construct meaning. Thus, we tend to read late twentieth-century literature as essentially antihumanistic, and with all the distaste that such a term implies. The first half of this book examines postmodern novels that struggle with just this problem of using "antihumanistic" language to signify affect, communication, and connection between human beings, especially within families. In its second half, beginning with Danielewski, it argues that novels of the first decade of the twenty-first century move from struggle to success, retaining the conviction that we are born into a linguistically determined world, while constructing new avenues toward meaning and meaningful human connection through signification and mediation themselves. These novels do so by redefining our concepts of what language is, how it works, and how fiction can harness it toward newly productive ends.

In making this argument, I concern myself quite intentionally with a particular facet of the highly diverse conglomeration of texts that comprise "postmodern" fiction,[5] as loosely defined by post-1945 periodization. Certainly other types of postmodern texts—less formally innovative, less thematically concerned with the problem of language and its practical implications—define their own battlegrounds and intersect with postmodernism, culturally and literarily, and what came before and perhaps "after" it, differently. As my interest here is the poststructuralist notion of the problem of language—the arbitrary, uneconomic relationship between words and things, signs and meanings, and the resulting absurdity of any notion of inherent, necessary, or universal meaning through language—this book focuses on a subset of postmodern (post-1945) literature that is really poststructuralist (language-obsessed) literature, a subset that leaves out much of what we call "postmodern" literature, including feminist and gender-study, ethnic, postcolonial, and cyberpunk, along with well-known postmodern authors like Jonathan Franzen and Richard Powers.[6] Watt's key observation about the traditional realist novel continues to hold true for today's rather untraditional novels: the novel and its form(s) arise in response to a social problem needing a solution. What an exciting thing it is to consider the ironic problem of how a novel, entirely made of language, might solve the problem of language itself. Language as solution to the problem of language: this proposition, which seems to threaten to collapse into tautology, instead fuels the argument of this book and those of the novels examined here. These novels do not try to escape the problem of language by reaching back to prestructuralist notions about language that deny that language is a problem, or by regressing to pre-postmodern narrative techniques, such as traditional realism, that hide the problem of language. Instead, this innovative portion of postmodern fiction absorbs poststructuralist assumptions about language, wrestles with the problems inherent in those assumptions, and proposes methods of solving those problems from within poststructuralism itself. And I would argue that these texts, and these assumptions, and the innovative adaptations to those assumptions, are what we see carried most forcefully and fruitfully out of the twentieth-century and into twenty-first-century literature, so that to chart the evolution from one to the other offers us the most meaningful way to read postmodern fiction and consider how our assumptions about and uses for fiction are radically changing right now.

Antihumanist and humanist language after 1945

In redefining specifically poststructural language as productive of, rather than anathema to, meaning, communication, empathy, and the relationships and communities that can result from such things, these novels assert most fundamentally a shift out of the antihumanism that had come to characterize postmodernism and postmodern fiction in the twentieth century, and into a new humanism that seems to be becoming characteristic of poststructural fiction of the twenty-first century. Until very recently (and perhaps even still, in certain academic circles), such a suggestion was thought to be paramount to heresy, or at least indicative of one's profound misunderstanding of poststructuralism.[7] But a slate of recent publications, such as Edward Said's 2004 *On Humanism* and Kwame Appiah's 2006 *Cosmopolitanism*, as well as related conferences and panels at conferences, such as the American Comparative Literature Society's "Humanism" conference in Princeton in 2006, begin to suggest a rethinking of the relationship between humanism and literature today.

The shock, opposition, even anger that often greets such a rethinking makes sense, however, in the context of the battle that has been going on in academia, stubbornly if with perhaps decreasing fervor in recent decades, since "theory" invaded the liberal humanist territory firmly staked out by English departments everywhere during the first half of the twentieth century.[8] Manifesting first in the 1960s as Marxist, psychoanalytic, linguistic, and feminist theories of reading that opposed the one-approach-fits-all view of liberal humanism, antihumanist theories of reading literature, much as antihumanist theories in general, sought to expose, excise, and remedy the faults of liberal humanism more broadly—the Enlightenment-born, individual-centered worldview—as they related to studying literature. Liberal humanism assumes an unchanging, wholly self-aware subject unaffected by exterior forces, a universal human nature, and a fully knowable truth we all agree upon; sees form as subordinate to content and therefore tends to be formally anti-innovation; detaches the text from historical, social, and political contexts; and keeps its values, and its ways of inculcating them, invisible. New theories of reading reacted against these inherited ideas by seeking to recognize the particularity, multiplicity, mutability, and conditionality of all things, ideas, and identities. The meeting of the -isms of the 1960s with new ideas about language and identity in the same decade from French thinkers like Derrida, Foucault, and Lacan led to the structuralist and poststructuralist theories that defined—and kicked off the full-fledged "civil war" of—the 1970s, the new historicism and cultural materialism of the 1980s, and then the theories of dispersal and eclecticism, such as postcolonialism and gender studies, of the 1990s.

All of these theories are in some way grounded in and an expression of the more generally antihumanist strain in philosophy that began with Nietzsche in the late nineteenth century and passed through Husserl, Heidegger, Foucault, and Althusser, among others, on the way to generating the poststructural linguistic theories of Derrida, de Man, and others during the postmodern period. In decentering thought, truth, and authority (Nietzsche), emphasizing our "thrownness" into a world/culture that shapes us without our consent and from which we are inseparable (Heidegger), viewing, like Nietzsche, truth as a function of power and dispersing it horizontally into the multitudes (Foucault), and describing the self as divided, even beyond Freud's tripartite division, because of its constitution by already self-divided language (Lacan), this philosophical strain of antihumanism sought to recognize a fundamental unknowability, particularity, and multiplicity in truth and identity that would end the marginalization, reductiveness, conservatism, and colonialism of humanist ways of thinking. Certainly such work needed to be done; such faults needed to be corrected, and antihumanism became the dominant paradigm for critics interested in finding in culture and in literature a more varied representation of what it means to be human than humanism allowed. It did the same for readers interested in encountering the text and its representations of the human as continuous with, rather than discrete from, the worlds and cultures in which they were created.

But, taken to extremes such as Baudrillard's theory of the hyperreal and related notions of the incommunicability, irrelevance, or, worst, nonexistence of meaning and real things, the antihumanist position on language and literature has amounted to throwing the baby out with the bathwater, in its failure to recognize that some of the goals and beliefs of humanism remain worthy and in fact crucial to the continued production of art and literature, and perhaps even to our continued humanity. Simultaneous with the 1980s heyday of theory, a rejection of theory began that only seems to wane, but not to end, as theory's own waning becomes increasingly apparent. Protesting extreme antihumanism's disavowals of truth in language and meaning in literature, the worth of subjective critique, and even the existence of reality itself, calls for a return to humanism in literature and in ways of reading literature sought and seek to remind us of what is at stake in literature and art, and must be at stake in order for the trajectory of art to be anything but terminal. Already in 1981, Charles Altieri was arguing the necessity of once again treating literature as a humanistic discipline by showing the limits of deconstructive thinking for literary meaning.[9] Criticizing antihumanist theories for valuing a text as concept rather than as a version of human experience, viewing the text as produced by language rather than by a human being called "author," and finding no place for affect in their signification-centered readings, Altieri raised a charge that has been echoed and evolved by many in the decades since. M. H. Abrams expanded this criticism when he diagnosed as antihumanist even self-proclaimed "anti-antihumanists" like Stanley Fish and Harold Bloom, whose deconstruction-based methods of reading against and wholly separate from authorship lead, he claimed, to the same dismal misreading of antihumanism.[10] Other critics began to propose solutions to the nihilism of antihumanism, which were often regressive,[11] or simply dismissive of the principles of poststructuralism itself.[12]

More recently, arguments for a return to humanism have begun to assert themselves not so much as counterarguments to a prevailing din of antihumanism but as unapologetic assertions of our inarguable need to work and think and write from the position of what matters, and, better, that there are things that do matter, things we can know and agree on. Kwame Anthony Appiah's sweeping *Cosmopolitanism: Ethics in a World of Strangers* (2006) begins by defending the necessity of notions of good and bad, right and wrong, and from that fundamentally anti-antihumanist position makes a humanist argument for considering what is true and right so that we can act morally to our fellow human beings, and thus improve the experience of every individual. Calling cosmopolitanism "universality plus difference,"[13] Appiah identifies his offering as essentially humanistic, but with a postmodern recognition of the need for multiplicity and uncertainty among people and ideas:

> We cosmopolitans believe in universal truth, too, though we are less certain that we have it all already. It is not skepticism about the very idea of truth that guides us; it is realism about how hard the truth is to find.... One distinctively cosmopolitan commitment is to pluralism. Cosmopolitans think that there are many values worth living by and that you cannot live by all of them. So we hope and expect that different people and different societies will embody different values. (But they have to be values worth living by.) Another aspect of cosmopolitanism is what philosophers call fallibilism—the sense that our knowledge is imperfect, provisional, subject to revision in the face of new evidence.[14]

His "universality plus difference" amounts to a kind of humanism plus humility, a basic shift that characterizes all of the postmodern humanism we are seeing in the twenty-first century.

The recent treaty on humanism by Edward Said, whose 1980 *Orientalism* made him famous and became a model for applying key antihumanist ideas to culture and literature, is in some ways even more noteworthy than Appiah's. Said acknowledges his theoretical shift in the first chapter of his *Humanism and Democratic Criticism* (2004), referring to a review by James Clifford of his groundbreaking critical work that pointed out what Clifford saw as an inconsistency between Said's avowed humanistic bias and the antihumanism of his subject and Foucaultian approach to it. Like Sarup's recognition of the ironically humanist experience of even antihumanists like Foucault and Althusser, Said's late-career *Humanism* can be read as an attempt to bring theory together with experience, and to assert that, in the end, it is our humanistic beliefs and impulses that must unabashedly guide our behavior and thinking. Calling Lyotard's critique of grand narratives "dismissive," Said also recognizes that human history contradicts theoretical foundations of antifoundationalism and antihumanism.[15] Like Appiah, Said asserts a nontotalizing, nonessentializing humanism that admits human fallibility, limitations in understanding, and difference. To readers, he offers a new humanist method of finding meaning in texts: "Close reading has to originate in critical receptivity as well as in the conviction that even though great aesthetic work ultimately resists total understanding, there is a possibility of a critical understanding that may never be completed but can certainly be provisionally affirmed."[16] To critics he offers a position from which to launch meaningful critique: "The task of the humanist is not just to occupy a position or place, nor simply to belong somewhere, but rather to be both insider and outsider to the circulating ideas and values that are at issue in our society or someone else's society or the society of the other."[17] All of his ideas about this humanism must begin, he asserts, in the "individual particular," a foundation that maps onto old humanism's investment in the individual, antihumanism's attention to the particular.

Such contemporary calls for humanism characterize exactly the baby that antihumanism discarded: literature's and theory's ability to be about something, to matter, to communicate meaning, to foster the sense that language connects us more than it estranges us, so that we can come together in ways that build relationship and community rather than the alienation and solipsism of antihumanistic postmodern literature. In this way, today's calls for a return to humanism aim to correct an extreme of antihumanism in much the same way that the rise of Enlightenment humanism aimed to correct a more original, perhaps Ur-antihumanism: however marginalizing and reductive humanism eventually felt to a twentieth-century culture grown enormously aware of the power of difference and the dangers of power, the importance of original humanism's disruption of the institution- and elite-centered middle ages can hardly be overestimated. But in overthrowing one manner of oppressive thinking, it caused another; twentieth-century antihumanism did the same. Today's critical, theoretical, and literary attempts to return to humanism through poststructuralism represent, in the context of two such monumental shifts, a more subtle course correction that aims to preserve the crucial new ground gained by antihumanism's decentering of authority and truth while retrieving then sustaining the progress gained by humanism 400 years ago.

While it is relatively easy to chart a shift back toward humanistic ways of theorizing through such publications as those listed above, it is far more complicated, and, I believe, illuminating to chart a similar turn from antihumanism toward humanism in literature, and that is one shift that this book seeks to demonstrate. Often depicting language as uncontrollable, inherently violent, and entirely other from human concerns and our ability to articulate them, many American novels of the 1980s and 1990s render societies as poststructuralists like Derrida, Lacan, and Baudrillard might have conceived them. The early works considered here, by Don DeLillo (*The Names* and *White Noise*),

David Foster Wallace (*Infinite Jest*), and A. M. Homes (*Music for Torching*), explore challenges to individual integrity and communication between individuals posed by such societies, often in the form of the narcissism and self-reflexive solipsism that seem equally to describe postmodern culture and language theory. Thus, these novels echo Christopher Lasch's critique that postindustrial culture has become dominated by the image, suggesting that society is a mediating machine for reproducing individuals driven by infantile desire. But what the characters desire most is freedom from desire: an escape from the suffering that attends immediate, unfiltered confrontations with life. Further, the novels illustrate the problem of narcissism as theorized by Freud, demonstrating that the ultimate danger of an image-based society lies in its tendency to construct a subject that can no longer direct its energies toward others. They do so largely through the rhetorical mode of irony, deploying it in opposition to the unmediated suffering their characters hope to avoid, and so narrowing the terms in which a literary escape from solipsistic disaffection might be imagined. But amid these blatantly antihumanistic depictions of how language works and does not work to build a humane world, these novels of the 1980s and 1990s struggle to use language to create and sustain meaningful relationships even within the maelstrom of the crisis of meaning that characterizes that literature and its culture.

Literature of the twenty-first century, however, converts repressed humanist struggle via antihumanist language into overtly sentimental deployments of language as an essentially humanist endeavor, as the last three chapters of this book argue. Mark Danielewski's groundbreaking *House of Leaves* (2000) constructs both individual identity and family through, not in spite of, its multiply mediated and hypertextual framework, meanwhile redeeming methods of inquiry and representation decreed useless by postmodern theory, like irony and psychoanalysis. Thus it departs radically from similarly aimed efforts to return to humanist interests such as individual identity and family like that of Homes, whose novel moves backward, to the comfortable assurances of traditional realism, in order to move forward out of antihumanism: *Music for Torching* can only conceive of saving its lost, disaffected characters through the morally and structurally conservative act of sacrificing an innocent child. But in the twenty-first century, we have seen a proliferation of novels that shift their foci toward the real, the thing, and presence, and away from the sign, word, and absence upon which earlier postmodern fiction fixated, as this book demonstrates using Cormac McCarthy's *The Road*, Jonathan Safran Foer's *Extremely Loud & Incredibly Close*, and Steve Tomasula's *The Book of Portraiture*. All of these changes contribute to the emergence of what I consider a new mode of realism, poststructural realism, that produces "reality effects"[18] not by repressing the machinations of fiction, as does traditional realism, but by making them visible via metafiction. This new literary strategy, illustrated using Foer's *Everything Is Illuminated* and Wallace's "Octet," uses self-conscious representation not only to return us to presence and the real, after decades of literature's obsession with the void, but also to remind us of the powerful ways in which acts of reading and writing impact the real world. Thus, these novels enact poststructuralism turned toward the ends of realism and humanism.

The temptation exists, amid a currently robust critical conversation about posthumanism, to categorize shifts away from postmodernism and even antihumanism as aspects of the posthuman. I see posthumanism, however, as a separate category of thought and literature altogether. One example of such categorization is Paul Giles's characterizing David Foster Wallace's work as "posthumanist" primarily because of its "traditional investment with human emotion and sentiment,"[19] and because of Wallace's often articulated opposition to liberal humanism. But I see the literary posthumanism as defined by N. Katherine Hayles,[20] upon which Giles bases his argument, standing in at least as much opposition to the work of Wallace and his like as in agreement. For while Wallace and other recent authors do much to "demystify the figure of the author,"[21] they do so in the interest of creating a present sense of the author, and in relation to the present, real reader, and very much not in the antihumanist interest of obliterating the author. Further, I would argue that merely to describe the "post-postmodern" shift in terms of a return to affect, created by an author for a reader, or, in Wallace's case, generated via a relationship between a reader and an author, is to acknowledge an essential humanism in these texts, in that affect is an essentially human quality requiring humans in relation to each other to house it. So the essential posthumanist quality of replacing the individual human with the faculty of computation, often spread out among and bridging humans and machines, does not account for this crucial shift toward affect and human feeling. On the contrary, in describing this shift in literature as a return to humanism through the methodologies of poststructuralism, I am neither pointing to a return to liberal humanism (with its assumption of the unified subject or universality of meaning) nor to a wholesale transcendence of the human into the information systems-based posthuman. Rather, I am proposing, more along the lines of Said and Appiah, that literature of the twenty-first century seeks to salvage much-missed portions of humanism, such as affect, meaning, and investment in the real world and in relationships between people, while holding on to postmodern and poststructural ideas about how language and representation function and characterize our human experiences of this world.

Signifying postmodern families

One finds pretty quickly that tracking literature's struggles to represent humanism simultaneously with poststructural ideas about language also means tracking literature's changing ways of representing families. To liberal humanists like Sanford Pinsker, for whom everything poststructural is inherently anathema to affect, meaning, and human connection, such a confluence must come as quite a surprise:

> Fiction is not finally made from other fictions but from the tougher, heart-wrenching business of defining oneself in the larger context of family. Postmodernist experimentation failed not only because its dazzling surfaces were hollow at the core, but also because its settings had no discernible address, its

characters' bones no flesh, and its families no force. If literature is once again to become a humanistic enterprise, it needs to imagine fully human beings, and I would argue that that requires fully human families.[22]

Inherent to this notion of mutual exclusivity between "postmodernist experimentation" and "fully human families" is the belief that investigating the nature of language and its impact on the contemporary world must come at the expense of exploring the nature of the human, as if these two realms, linguistic and human, themselves preclude each other. Yet, within the subgenre of language-obsessed postmodern American fiction, one finds not a lack of families or of moving contemplation of the family but rather a strong current of engagement with precisely the struggle that Pinsker denies: the struggle to define, create, and reconstruct family bonds from within the linguistic crisis that in many ways characterizes contemporary culture. And within this context, Pinsker's assumption of the inherent disconnect between language and the human becomes merely a reproduction of the anxiety about antihumanist language that such novels, I will argue, first articulate, then overcome.

The dozen or so texts examined here, both pre- and postdating Pinsker's appeal for a literary return to the family, center themselves in centerless worlds precisely on possibilities for family connections and for family as a context for constructing and understanding the self. And these novels do so, quite in opposition to Pinsker's concern, specifically in terms of the novelistic devices and the cultural context of mediation and ironic disaffection that breed those devices: they depict the crisis of family in an age ruled by the crisis of signification, and explore possibilities for the recuperation of family from within the culture of irony, simulation, and narcissistic self-reflexivity that attends contemporary notions of signification. These families "signify" and are "signified," then, in that they experience both the threat of dissolution and the promise of reconstitution specifically because of and in the context of these systems of signification and the cultural climate they engender, thus demonstrating a peculiar intimacy between familial and linguistic matters in our contemporary age, as well as a peculiar intimacy in the "signifying family."[23]

If this intersection between discourses of the family and of contemporary notions of language first seems counterintuitive, it is little wonder, for this pairing has received scant attention as of yet except to assert the assumption that one discourse precludes the other. In his rare critical consideration of it, Pinsker assumes that any engagement with family and humanism will necessitate a radical reorienting of the narrative concerns and techniques of postmodern fiction. He identifies a paradigm shift that

> carries us away from an older condition in which novelists operated, consciously or unconsciously, under the grip of family, and toward a new model in which novelists write under a very different sort of grip—namely, the grip of ideas. The result of this altered consciousness threatens to eradicate literary families altogether.[24]

Pinsker blames this shift on the literary and critical changes that grew out of the 1960s, which ushered in "radical reflexivity" (or "fiction about its own fictionality") and saw the transformation of the "Age of Criticism" (which formalistically considered "irony, paradox, myth, and symbol" as the building blocks of great literature) into the "Age of Theory," or "postmodernism." Though offering juicy bits for the grinding of critical teeth, these metafictions produced during our love affair with reflexivity, with thinking about thinking, strike Pinsker as most radical in their blatant omission of the human, feeling elements of fiction:

> The rub, of course, is that postmodernist fiction was often more fun to talk about than to reread, not only because its experimentations were often sterile, but also because its characters seemed so dehumanized. Families did not much matter because their connections failed to move anybody to love or hatred.[25]

While I find Pinsker's lyrical argument against the emotional sterility of much postmodernist American fiction, moving and often accurate, this book parts ways with his blanket assumptions about the state of the family in contemporary American fiction, by examining decidedly "postmodern" novels whose primary concerns bridge the considerable gap his essay describes between novels that concern themselves with "the grip of ideas" and those concerned with family.

Where these seemingly antihumanist novels surprise—and perhaps why their concerted engagement with traditional ideas like family and emotional connection have gone largely unnoticed—is in their sophisticated contextualizing of this "humanistic enterprise" within the discourse that Pinsker and popular notions of postmodernism believe to exclude such ideas. Pinsker anchors his notion of a humanist return on a backward-looking appeal to pre-postmodern literary genres and techniques; he places his very limited hope for the future of the literary family in "encouraging signs that a critical interest in social realism may be returning," and defines that "social realism" as the critically "déclassé" fiction of Bellow, Roth, and Updike.[26] This conservative hopefulness asserts that in order to create convincing, heartfelt portraits of families, writers must abandon their literary involvement with the contemporary ideas, cultural tendencies, and poststructural literary techniques that for them define the contemporary "realism" they must wrestle with through their writing. One of the novels considered here, A. M. Homes's *Music for Torching*, enacts a similarly nostalgic abandonment of its own postmodernist principles in order to secure some kind of recuperative valuing of the family. But the other novels examined in this book assert that the only way accurately to represent "fully human families" in the humanity-challenging reality of the late twentieth and early twenty-first centuries is to do so with full awareness of all the ways in which family suffers, endures, and remakes itself in that context.

Investigating the intersection between crises of signification and families is not the same thing as arguing for "family values," or for the nuclear family unit—which would not even be possible, since none of these families is in any way "traditional" and only one (in *Music*) is nuclear. But these novels do assert that contemporary culture negatively impacts families in many of the ways that contemporary social critics[27] recognize: through the manipulation, disaffection, and alienation perpetrated and encouraged by mediation, simulation, and consumption. Further, the novels suggest that these cultural consequences and reflections of contemporary concepts of signification work their destruction both on the level of the individual and of the family: by altering the lives of individuals, who in a culture of images and unfulfillable desire lose their senses of self and fulfillment that would allow them to extend themselves in meaningful relationships with others; and by reconstructing through mediation the family as reflection of the culture itself, the family as its own mediating machine. Then, the twenty-first-century novels examined here, as they turn their poststructural devices back to humanist ends, recuperate the family in the same terms in which the earlier novels condemned them, using the mechanisms of mediation, metafiction, and antirealism not to destroy the self, affect, and understanding but to construct them.

The "end of postmodernism"?

Does this shift in thinking about language and its ability to represent the human and the human family both in and out of literature constitute the "end of postmodernism"? Is a return to humanism, belief, and a model of language anchored in the real and constitutive of self, family, and community radical enough to insist a wholly new period must be upon us? Literary criticism over the past few years suggests that these are fair questions to ask, and demonstrates that many of us are asking them already.

"After postmodernism" has become a phrase widely and often enough used to merit its own issue of the journal *Twentieth-Century Literature* in 2007. In his introduction for that issue, Andrew Hoberek takes the by-now established position that literature emerging today is recognizably different from what we have come to define (variously) as "postmodern," then proposes ways in which we might approach our thinking about this new, "post-postmodern" literature. But this argument, like all other studies addressing the end of postmodernism, must first consider our inability to be simultaneously precise and fair when characterizing either the end or the thing we are ending. Citing, then critiquing, intellectual historian Minsoo Kang's audacious claim that we heard the "death knell of postmodernism in the US" on "June 18, 1993," with the release of the action movie *The Last Action Hero*—the popularizing of postmodernism's "standard devices" of irony, self-reference, and multiple reality destroying its status as a countermovement—Hoberek opens the issue by acknowledging then debunking the strong critical urge to place a period at the end of a phase of literature whose beginning and middle themselves continue to defy periodization.[28] Kang's provocative declaration about postmodernism's ending echoes a similarly bold, and perhaps similarly ridiculous, claim about postmodernism's beginning: at 3.32 p.m., on July 15, 1972, when the demolition of a public housing project in St. Louis marked the "failure of high modernism in architecture." Brian McHale cites this declaration by Charles Jencks as a stepping-off point for McHale's own argument about the beginning of postmodernism, which he concludes, with characteristic postmodern noncommittal, to have occurred not in 1972 but in 1966. More relevant and compelling here than the particulars of the debate about postmodernism's beginning is the fact that, even as skittish publishers of books and journals feed an apparently growing appetite for forays into the similarly commitment-phobic debate about the end of postmodernism, McHale, a central critic-architect of the postmodern, continues to hold a spotlight on the equally endlessly vexing question of "When Did Postmodernism Begin?"[29]

This simultaneity of bold declaration and tentative qualification, of predictions of ends and locations of beginnings, refigures the emergence of postmodernism itself. Stephen Burn opens his own astute "Map of the Territory" of waning postmodernism by observing that the word "postmodern" appeared in a critical book title one year *before* the word "modernist" did the same.[30] Similarities between the anxiety-ridden examinations of both birth and death dates and reasons for each are telling: as Jeremy Green convincingly claims as late as 2005, in the context of arguing for the period's end, "Postmodernism has yet to establish its own legitimacy."[31] Itself most consistently characterized by the indeterminacy it proposed as an essential shift out of modernism, postmodernism as a literary, cultural, and even historical period, more so than any other, comprises debate more than decree, its announced birth sparking protests against its existence (as seen from Altieri, Abrams, and others), its predicted death prompting disagreement and denial about its birth.

Such questions, integral to the period itself, about the nature and value of what postmodernism is or was are more productively addressed by a recent cluster of examinations of millennial American fiction than by the flashy proclamations of cultural critics like Kang and Jencks, with their pinpointed deathknells. In fact, in the same year in which Kang located the demise of postmodernism within the mainstream pop culture that had swallowed it whole, Green helped initiate a discussion about the waning of postmodernism's relevance and accuracy in describing contemporary American literature, and documented the ranging moments in which both leftist and conservative critics conceive of this death and the various terms in which they conceive it.[32] Stephen Burn adds dimension to this picture by focusing on the many knells that sounded throughout most of the 1990s, comprising objections to postmodernism by critics (such as in the "End of Postmodernism" seminar held in 1991 in Stuttgart), writers as critics (as in David Foster Wallace's groundbreaking interview with Larry McCaffery, and his essay "E Unibus Pluram: Television and U.S. Fiction," in a 1993 *Review of Contemporary Fiction*), and in literature itself (especially in work like John Barth's, which mocked that Stuttgart conference, in 1996). Burn mounts a compelling argument for locating the end of postmodernism as a way of writing and a way of thinking about writing specifically in the 1990s, thus clearing ground to establish his sense of what emerges as post-postmodernism in its wake.

In this way, the differing answers to the questions of what postmodernism is or was and when it might have ended offered by critics like Burn and Green, and even Kang and Jencks, act less as points opposed in a debate and more like points of light in a constellation whose increased population only sharpens the image they create. Points proliferate when we turn to the question of how to characterize what comes at the end and after postmodernism. Green's *Late Postmodernism: American Fiction at the Millennium* (2005) characterizes fiction of the 1990s in terms of its attempts to negotiate the problems posed particularly by what he calls late postmodern literature: loss of cultural authority, problematic definitions of the public sphere and its functions, uncertainty about the reading audience and the value of the novel, and the novel's fraught attempts to assert itself as valuable and useful in such a reading culture. Burn's 2008 examination of "American Fiction at the Millennium" also sees twenty-first-century literature as growing out of, and reacting to, problems climaxing in literature of the 1990s, but, like Wallace in his 1993 interview,[33] Burn blames the end of postmodernism more on the inherently self-destructive postmodern habit of self-referentiality than on an Oprah-versus-Franzen debate about the merits of literature within competing spheres of readership and literariness. Further adding critical weight to the growing sense that something changed meaningfully in American fiction of the 1990s is Samuel Cohen's 2009 consideration of that fiction, *After the End of History: American Fiction in the 1990s*, which starts with the by-now familiar anxiety over language's ability to do more than refer to itself, but expands out to consider the implications of such poststructural notions of language, and self-conscious uses of it in novels, asking how, or whether, the novel can participate in our making and understanding of history. Perhaps asserting the most substantial break from postmodernism, Raoul Eshelman in 2008 conceives of a post-postmodernism that is most essentially a post-postmetaphysics, identifying in contemporary transnational literature a "performatist" aesthetic that enacts a return to "specifically monist virtues," a repairing of the sign-thing split and a radical shift away from the poststructural gap that characterizes/d much of postmodernist literature.[34]

Three other contributions base their arguments for the "end of postmodernism" on the emergence of a "neorealism" or "dirty realism" at the end of the twentieth century, which, they assert, signaled the end of the efficacy of the metafictional and self-reflexive narrative techniques that so well defined the beginning of postmodernism, in the hands of authors like Barth, Pynchon, and Barthelme.[35] Robert Rebein made this argument as early as 2001, in his *Hicks, Tribes, and Dirty Realists: American Fiction after Postmodernism*; Neil Brooks and Josh Toth revived and extended the argument in their coedited volume, *The Mourning After: Attending the Wake of Postmodernism* in 2007, and in Toth's own *The Passing of Postmodernism: A Spectroanalysis of the Contemporary* in 2010. Not only do these latter two books share Rebein's investment in "neorealism" as the killer of postmodernism, but they also share each other's philosophical frameworks and considerable content, and employ evidence for the "end of postmodernism" posited by other books discussed above (especially Burn's). This extensive overlapping points to the curious way in which this sudden burst of "after postmodernism" criticism both presses forward and stalls out, as additions to the critical conversation follow upon each other's heels so closely as to have insufficient time to take account of each other. While Brooks and Toth's *The Mourning After* and Toth's *The Passing of Postmodernism* share the argument that postmodernism died in the mid-1980s (or in 1989, to be more exact[36]), only to be "mourned" (or perhaps, more accurately in Freud's lexicon, to produce neurotic melancholia) via "spectral" "repetitions" of the postmodern in the 1990s, Alan Kirby posits a more thorough break from postmodernism. In his very clever and convincing argument for *Digimodernism*, he calls this break a "cultural shift, a communicative revolution, a social organization," and, most importantly, "a new form of textuality" resulting from "the impact on cultural forms of computerization."[37] Describing "digimodernism" as characterized by texts that are evanescent, materially fluid, reliant on their technological status, always in the process of being made, renegotiating the relationships among author, viewer, producer, and writer, of anonymous and multiple authorship and therefore reinvoking authorship, Kirby's concept of what is happening "after postmodernism" stands in stark contrast to the "neorealist" picture offered by Toth and Brooks and reiterates that the multiplicity and indeterminacy that defined postmodernism clearly continue to define the "post-postmodern" period.[38]

The emergence over the past several years of (by today's count) eight books and a dedicated journal issue arguing that fiction and/or culture has changed substantially and generally enough to merit our consideration of a passing of postmodernism indicates quite clearly that we are seeing a dramatic critical shift in the way we read literature, in the nature of literature, or both. That these books and articles have been prominently published and widely read suggests that we are ready for these arguments in a way that I do not think we as a reading and critical community were only a few years before. Green, Burn, Cohen, Eshelman, Rebein, Toth, Brooks, and Kirby, among others, have all helped instigate and shape this examination of the shift with their investigations of late postmodern and post-postmodern literature in terms of its concepts and uses of history, language, authorship, and readership, producing an initial set of answers to the question of the end and legacy of postmodernism whose differing conclusions do justice to the plurality of the undefined period itself.[39] In this way, the defining characteristic of the period already survives the period's "death," "post-postmodernism" remaining as ontologically indebted to its ancestor as postmodernism is to modernism. The trick awaiting critics' awkward attempts at naming the offspring, and determining how in line it is with Derrida's Second-Coming prediction of the monstrous "birth . . . in the offing"[40] that would, for more than three decades, characterize postmodernism, will be to hone to fineness our understanding of the possible waning and wake of, certainly the dramatic changes within, postmodernism while preserving that defining plurality.

In this spirit, Andrew Hoberek provides context for the work being done by the "after postmodernism" issue of *Twentieth-Century Literature* and for the work we critics are doing in characterizing what comes after postmodernism. He cautions against making sweeping declarations about a literature that has barely begun to be born, statements that time, diversity of critical opinion, and continued production of representative works will certainly debunk. Perhaps most sobering to any heady attempts to define and label is his reminder that "the current state of fiction—in which postmodernism in the strong sense constitutes just one, no longer particularly privileged stylistic option among many—in fact resembles nothing so much as the state that followed the triumphant years of modernism."[41] That is to say, the early years of postmodernism were a mess—in fact we still can't agree on which years they were— and we would be foolish to think it any more possible to codify this emerging phase than it is to codify the one it is to bookend. The fact that so many contributions along these lines, including this one, spring up so soon itself suggests how very much the core of this new phase of literature overlaps with that of not only postmodernism but of modernism itself. When McHale considers the usefulness of the many and various recent single-year studies[42] in characterizing periods of literature, he questions the efficacy of such "annualization" ("the framing of the objects of study at the scale of one year rather than . . . a decade, a generation, or a century"), which lends the feeling of "*everything happening at once*, of the convergence of apparently disparate events,"[43] as if the dynamo has amped up the forces of history to an inhuman pace, the gyres are madly spinning. Clumsily trying to keep pace, we quicken the rate of analyses of periods we make increasingly short and nascently understood. Such haste might in part explain the divide felt in the academy between postmodern/twenty-first-century literature and earlier periods, and the curious, if not skeptical regard in which contemporary studies are sometimes held by scholars whose fields and debates about those fields have been centuries, not decades or years or months, in the making.

A bit less conservatively and a whole lot more productively, Hoberek instead suggests we recognize any identifiable change into the post-postmodern as not exemplifying "some singular, dramatic, readily visible cultural transformation" but rather as "grow[ing] out of a range of uneven, tentative, local shifts that in some cases reach back into the postmodern period and can now be understood in hindsight as intimations of a new order."[44] Certainly the recent projects by Burn and others contribute in just this way to what seems to be an increasingly urgent project of coming to terms with what is coming after postmodernism, with the diverse results Hoberek anticipated, and through a reaching back to the decade that preceded the turn. Indeed, all attempts so far to characterize the post-postmodern do so to some extent as Hoberek recommends, "look[ing] backward as well as forward, to consider what might have been taking place under our noses for some time."[45] In considering the fiction of (early) DeLillo, Wallace, and Homes as preface to examining the radically new fiction of Danielewski, Foer, Tomasula, McCarthy, and later Wallace, this book takes a similar tack. Rather than simply considering the noticeably new ways in which twenty-first-century fiction approaches the intersection between language and the human in terms of tone, structure, content, and form, this book examines that problematic intersection both before and after what we might consider a second postmodern turn, out of the antihumanism that quickly came to define the postmodern. It notes the fundamental antihumanist and poststructural assumptions that remain in place in such fiction—arbitrary language, multiplicitous and subjective truth, the defense of particularity and difference—while illuminating the humanist pursuits, of truth, critique, self-knowledge, and empathy, leading to community, that develop doggedly out of them. Such development is a final achievement of the potential offered by poststructuralism as a method for avoiding essentialism and universalism in the pursuit of knowing and expressing through language.

One needn't call this development the "success" of postmodernism, but several compelling reasons allow that choice. Repeatedly, those who pronounce the end of postmodernism base their claim on the fact that postmodernism, once the marginalized (and self-marginalizing) lovechild of avant-garde modernism and mid-century poststructural ideas about language, had by the 1980s become mainstream.[46] Having taken over popular culture and academia alike, becoming itself dogmatic, institutionalized, even hegemonic, postmodernism could no longer assert itself as that which denies universality and oppressive consensus. Toth goes so far as to say that postmodernism failed "because it *continued to speak*, because it continued to make and privilege *truth claims* about the impossibility of making such claims" and "*because it didn't die* as it should have."[47] Even more forcefully in a footnote, he asserts that "Had postmodernism been successful in its aesthetic endeavor, it would have ceased to move; it would have become absolutely silent."[48] This line of argument, popular today, asserts that postmodernism failed because its mandate that everything expressed in language be meaningless and "inaccessible"[49] became the cultural standard; that if this inaccessibility had remained marginal, "postmodernism" as a movement would still be viable. But viable for what, in what terms? What does it mean to equate the "success" of a movement with its inability to express anything meaningful, or to be accessible to most people? Why should we "mourn" the death of a movement whose aim was "inaccessibility," "elitism," and "increasingly emphatic insistence on . . . the utterly private nature of all discourse (or, rather, the futility of the social or public text)"?[50] If we define postmodernism as a movement of or toward silence, inaccessibility, elitism, and the futility of all acts of language, why not dance on its grave rather than write essay upon essay mourning it? The problem here seems to be with the way we define the thing we are mourning. What does it mean to say that a movement defined as futility has failed? Is that to say, rather, that it has finally succeeded?

In positing that newly humanist twenty-first-century literature might represent the success of postmodernism rather than its failure, I am suggesting that we might choose to understand postmodernism, even in the context of its poststructural ideas about language, as a movement that aimed and aims to do something meaningful using language, to ask and answer questions about what it means to be human in this world from the perspective of a postmodern culture and its attending poststructural notions about language. To do so is to understand postmodernism as a movement in a positive sense, as do many of the critics and theorists this book will explore (such as Sontag, Brown, Latour, and Gumbrecht), and it is to place it in the much larger context of our literary, scholarly, and human history of ideas since and before the Enlightenment in which every new movement of knowledge, thought, learning, and art has been in the service of applying new understandings of the nature of the human and of the universe, and more recently of language, to new ways of forwarding the same.

This positive concept of succeeding postmodernism rests on what is by now a well-accepted understanding of "postmodernism" more broadly, as a concept of the world and our place in it as impacted by cultural, historical, and philosophical effects of (late) capitalism, consumerism, image culture, loss of sense of historicity, awareness of the inescapability and definitiveness of subjectivity and perspective, attending issues of representation and the awareness that everything is in some way represented, consideration of the relationship between the real and the representation, effects of technology (the machine, the information age) on our understanding of that relationship, and on our understanding of the nature of the human. If we accept such a definition of postmodernism, then a separate question arises of how art, and for my purposes, literature and language specifically, reflects, questions, and responds to this period. One dominant strain of postmodernism in literature, which Toth and Brooks are right to point out became a dominant cultural response in general, is that of what I consider twentieth-century postmodernism: irony, language's futility, cynicism, disaffection, even straining into silence; solipsism and individuality over communal bonds; and loss of faith in language's ability to raise ethical or political concerns. But I see that response as one possible response in literature to the core assertions of the postmodern period, and to poststructural notions about the nature of language and what it can do; I do not see this literature of futility, solipsism, and silence as definitive of postmodernism itself. Rather, literature of the twenty-first century performs recuperative acts against silence and apathy, and does so from within the postmodern condition of image culture, subjectivity, and obsession with representation, and, more importantly still, in my thinking, from within the poststructural ideas about language that led earlier postmodern literature to end in silence and futility.

Literature today remains postmodern in its assumptions about the culture and world from which it arises, and remains poststructural in its assumptions about the arbitrariness and problems of language, and yet still uses this postmodernism and poststructuralism to humanist ends of generating empathy, communal bonds, ethical and political questions, and, most basically, communicable meaning. If we maintain the assumption that has held since the Enlightenment, that literature, along with art and science, emerges and compels us most essentially because it enables us to further our understanding of the nature of the world and the human and of the self in the world, then postmodern literature succeeds when it can remain fundamentally postmodern in its views of the world and of its own linguistic workings, while accomplishing these humanist goals for literature. Ultimately, then, *Succeeding Postmodernism* suggests, unlike the proliferation of "after postmodernism" criticism of recent years, that we are seeing not the end of postmodernism, but its belated success.

Notes

1   Madan Sarup, *An Introductory Guide to Post-Structuralism and Postmodernism* (Athens: University of Georgia Press, 1993), 76.
2   An inexhaustive search of "after postmodernism" criticism and theory yields abundant results in widely disparate fields: see Michael Ott on religion after postmodernism in *The Future of Religion: Toward a Reconciled Society* (Boston: Brill, 2007); Robert Samuels on automation in culture and technology after postmodernism, in *Digital Youth, Innovation, and the Unexpected* (Cambridge: MIT Press, 2008, Tara McPherson, ed.); Jonathan Harris on *Value, Art, Politics: Criticism, Meaning, and Interpretation after Postmodernism* (Liverpool: Liverpool University Press, 2007); theories of writing after postmodernism in *After Postmodernism: An Introduction to Critical Realism*, Jose Lopez and Garry Potter, eds (New York: Continuum, 2005); feminism after postmodernism in *Reclaiming Female Agency: Feminist Art History after Postmodernism* (Berkeley: University of California Press, 2005, Norma Broude and Mary D. Garrard, eds) and Marysia Zalewski's *Feminism after Postmodernism: Theorizing Through Practice* (London: Routledge, 2000); philosophy of history after postmodernism in Ewa Domanska's *Encounters* (Charlottesville: University Press of Virginia, 1998); *Capitalism after*

Postmodernism from H. T. Wilson (Boston: Brill, 2002); even *Comedy after Postmodernism*, by Kirby Olson (Lubbock: Texas Tech University, 2001). Taking a more holistic approach are *Theorizing Culture: An Interdisciplinary Critique after Postmodernism*, Barbara Adam and Stuart Allan, eds (London: University College of London Press, 1995) and Klaus Stierstorfer's *Beyond Postmodernism: Reassessments in Literature, Theory, and Culture* (New York: W. de Gruyter, 2003). Proposing whole new cultural models after postmodernism are Alan Kirby's *Digimodernism: How New Technologies Dismantle the Postmodern and Reconfigure Our Culture* (New York: Continuum, 2009), discussed later in this introduction, and Robert Samuels's *New Media, Cultural Studies, and Critical Theory after Postmodernism: Automodernity from Zizek to Laclau* (New York: Palgrave MacMillan, 2010).

3 Ian Watt, *The Rise of the Novel* (Berkeley: University of California Press, 2001 [1957]).

4 See "Three Axioms for Projecting a Line (or Why It Will Continue to Be Hard to Write a Title sans Slashes or Parentheses)," *Review of Contemporary Fiction* 16 no. 1 (1996): 100–8.

5 I use "postmodern" to refer primarily to the historical post-1945 period and its associated cultures of image, mediation, consumerism, technology, and so on, as best described by Jameson in his *Postmodernism, or the Cultural Logic of Late Capitalism*. I see "poststructural" as a more specific term, somewhat of a subset to postmodernism, referring to particular theories about language, the arbitrariness of the relationship between signifier and signified, and resulting changes in ideas about belief, truth, knowledge, power, and so on, that inform postmodernism, but not exhaustively. Or, as David Foster Wallace put it, "'Poststructuralist' is what you call a deconstructionist who doesn't want to be called a deconstructionist." See *Supposedly* (New York: Little, Brown and Company, 1997), 140.

6 This is not to say that texts concerned with ethnicity, gender, or politics are never also formally innovative or linguistically curious; Junot Díaz's *The Brief Wondrous Life of Oscar Wao* (New York: Riverhead Books, 2007) provides an excellent example of just such an intersection. I chose my literary texts simply according to which novels most effectively exemplify the uses of language that are core to my argument.

7 In early 2006, I presented a paper containing the main arguments detailed in Chapter 4, reading Foer's *Extremely Loud & Incredibly Close* as returning to belief and humanism via a new attention to materiality in language. It is a testament to how dearly we hold our critical ideas that a front of audience members, staunch old-school poststructuralism defenders, literally rose up against me to assert, with a verbal and physical aggression not normally seen in our heady conference spaces, that it is simply not possible to talk about poststructuralism, humanism, and belief in the same conference paper. Three years later, at the same conference, I was stunned to hear variations of my previously accosted argument, gingerly unfurled by critics reading late postmodern and contemporary literature in ways we had been taught were not possible. The considerable distance quickly traveled between those two sets of assumptions about literature argues that literature today operates differently than it long had been, making different arguments make sense.

8 This description of liberal humanism versus theory is largely informed by Peter Barry's nicely clear account of it in *Beginning Theory* (New York: Manchester University Press, 1995).

9   Charles Altieri, *Act and Quality* (Amherst: University of Massachusetts Press, 1981).

10 Abrams, "How to Do Things with Texts," in *Doing Things with Texts*, ed. Michael Fisher (New York: W. W. Norton and Company, 1989).

11 See Murray Bookchin's desire to "re-enchant humanity" in *Re-enchanting Humanity: A Defense of the Human Spirit Against Anti-humanism, Misanthropy, Mysticism, and Primitivism* (London: Cassell, 1995).

12 Adam and Allan's *Theorizing Culture* (London: University College of London Press, 1995) asserts that there is no postmetaphysics, there is no post-Freud, and poststructuralism offers no position from which critique is possible. Battersby's *Paradigms Regained* (Philadelphia: University of Pennsylvania Press, 1993) aims to "restore what poststructuralism discarded," but meanwhile asserts that humanism is anathema to theory, thus necessitating a flight from the tenets of theory in order to find a room for humanism. Meynell's *Postmodernism and the New Enlightenment* (Washington, DC: Catholic University Press, 1999) comes perhaps closest to seeking to renew humanism from within poststructuralism, rejecting the nihilism of postmodernism while searching for a way to find truth and good while still critiquing Western rationality as exclusionary. See also Robert Alter, *The Pleasures of Reading in an Ideological Age* (New York: Simon and Schuster, 1989); Helen Gardner, *In Defence of the Imagination* (London: Oxford University Press, 1984); James Gribble, *Literary Education: A Re-evaluation* (London: Cambridge University Press, 1983); George Steiner, *Real Presences: Is There Anything in What We Say?* (New York: Faber, 1989); George Watson, *The Certainty of Literature: Essays in Polemic* (New York: Harvester, 1989).

13 Kwame Anthony Appiah, *Cosmopolitanism* (New York: W. W. Norton and Company, 2006), 151.

14 Ibid., 144.

15 Said, *Humanism and Democratic Criticism* (New York: Columbia University Press, 2004), 10.

16 Ibid., 67.

17 Ibid., 76.

18 See Roland Barthes's "The Reality Effect," *French Literary Theory Today*, ed. Tzvetan Todorov (London: Cambridge University Press, 1982) and Jonathan Culler's "Convention and Naturalization," *Structuralist Poetics: Structuralism, Linguistics, and the Study of Literature* (Ithaca: Cornell University Press, 1975).

19 Paul Giles, "Sentimental Posthumanism," *Twentieth-Century Literature* 53, no. 3 (2007): 330.

20 See *How We Became Posthuman: Virtual Bodies in Cybernetics, Literature, and Informatics* (Chicago: University of Chicago Press, 1999).

21 Giles, "Sentimental Posthumanism," 329.

22 Sanford Pinsker, "Imagining the Postmodern Family," *Georgia Review* 48 no. 3 (1994): 515.

23 Whereas Henry Louis Gates, Jr, in *The Signifying Monkey* (New York: Oxford University Press, 1988) takes the idea of "Signifyin(g)" to a vertical axis in which signifiers point not toward signifieds or distinct concepts but to rhetorical figures and games, my interest in signification employs the more "standard" (or Saussurean) concept of a "chain of signifiers" extending horizontally in a metonymic displacement of meaning (48–9).

24 Pinsker, "Imagining the Postmodern Family," 508.

25   Ibid., 510–11.

26   Ibid., 513.

27   See Robert Inchausti, *The Ignorant Perfection of Ordinary People* (New York:
     State University of New York Press, 1991); David Cheal, *New Poverty: Families in
     Postmodern Society* (London: Greenwood Press, 1996); Judith Stacey, *Brave New
     Families* (New York: HarperCollins, 1990) and *In the Name of the Family* (Boston:
     Beacon Press, 1996); Edward Shorter, *The Making of the Modern Family* (New York:
     Basic Books, 1975); Zygmunt Bauman, *Intimations of Postmodernity* (New York:
     Routledge, 1992); Cynthia Carter, "Nuclear Family Fall-out: Postmodern Family
     Culture and the Media," in *Theorizing Culture*, ed. Barbara Adam and Stuart Allan
     (New York: State University of New York Press, 1995); and Christopher Lasch, *The
     Culture of Narcissism* (New York: W. W. Norton and Company, 1979).

28   Andrew Hoberek, "Introduction: After Postmodernism," *Twentieth-Century Literature*
     53 no. 3 (2007): 233–6.

29   McHale, *Modern Language Quarterly* 69 no. 3 (2008): 391–413.

30   Burn, *Jonathan Franzen at the End of Postmodernism* (New York: Continuum, 2008),
     3, citing these titles: Bernard Iddings Bell's *Postmodernism and Other Essays* (New
     York: Morehouse Publishing Company, 1926); Laura Riding and Robert Graves's *A
     Survey of Modernist Poetry* (New York: Haskell House, 1927).

31   Green, *Late Postmodernism: American Fiction at the Millennium* (Gordonsville, VA:
     Palgrave Macmillan, 2005), 24.

32   Ibid., 19–24.

33   "Metafiction's real end has always been Armageddon. Art's reflection on itself is
     terminal." See Wallace, interviewed by Larry McCaffery, "An Interview with David
     Foster Wallace," *Review of Contemporary Fiction* 13 no. 2 (1993): 134.

34   Eshelman's commitment to a repaired sign-thing gap makes his vision of
     post-postmodernism least useful in my opinion, since it is central to my reading of
     twenty-first-century literature's recuperation of affect and meaning that such literature
     can only successfully overcome the problems of language by using a language that is
     inherently problematic, rather than casting back to an early idealization of organic
     meaning. My insistence on a poststructural solution to our poststructural problem
     is, however, consistent with Burn's description of postmodern novels as "informed
     by the postmodernist critique of the naïve realist belief that language can be a true
     mirror of reality" (*Jonathan Franzen at the End of Postmodernism*, 20). Alan Kirby,
     in *Digimodernism*, criticizes Eshelman for what I would consider the evasiveness of
     "performativism" as well, in that it requires a misreading of postmodernism (41).

35   I will refer to, and argue against, the specifics of this "neorealist" argument in my last
     chapter on "poststructural realism."

36   Both books cite, in choosing 1989 as the death date for postmodernism, the deaths
     of Beckett and Barthelme, the rise of neorealist writers like Raymond Carver, Tom
     Wolfe's manifesto on the importance of traditional realism in literature, the rise of
     publications by religious thinkers, and, politically, the end of the Cold War with the
     fall of the Berlin Wall.

37   Kirby, *Digimodernism*, 50. Kirby presents some of the most exhaustive and clearly
     organized histories of "after postmodernism" criticism and the "post-theory"
     movement I have yet found, so that I have not reproduced them extensively here. See
     especially his chapter 1.

38 Of all the criticism I described, Kirby's concept of digimodernism (which I discovered just as I was completing this book)—its interest in the return of the author and changes in the materiality of texts, especially—comes closest to mine; in fact, I might have unknowingly written the literary application lacking in his book that focuses on larger cultural concepts. His sweeping cultural examination and my focused literary argument share at their cores broader ideas about poststructural applications bringing forth unironic author- and meaning-based texts.

39 McHale defines postmodernism as a "poetics of ontological plurality" in *Postmodernist Fiction* (New York: Methuen, 1987).

40 Derrida, "Structure, Sign, and Play," in *The Critical Tradition*, ed. David Richter, trans. Richard Macksey and Eugenio Donato (New York: St. Martin's Press, 1989), 971.

41 Hoberek, "Introduction: After Postmodernism," 234.

42 McHale, "When Did Postmodernism Begin?" These include, but are not at all limited to, Michael North's *Reading 1922: A Return to the Scene of the Modern* (New York: Oxford University Press, 1999), Peter Stansky's *On or about December 1910: Early Bloomsbury and Its Intimate World* (Cambridge, MA: Harvard University Press, 1996), Thomas Harrison's *1910: The Emancipation of Dissonance* (Berkeley: University of California Press, 1996), Hans Gumbrecht's *In 1926: Living at the Edge of Time* (Cambridge, MA: Harvard University Press, 1997), and Ann Hagedorn's *Savage Peace: Hope and Fear in America, 1919* (New York: Simon and Schuster, 2007).

43 McHale, "When Did Postmodernism Begin?" 394, 393 (original italics).

44 Hoberek, "Introduction: After Postmodernism," 241.

45 Ibid., 240.

46 This is the basis for the "end of postmodernism" arguments of Kang, Toth, Brooks, and Burn, among others.

47 Josh Toth, *The Passing of Postmodernism* (Albany: State University of New York Press, 2010), 109 (original italics).

48 Ibid., 178–9 n. 46.

49 Toth attributes this word to Huyssen.

50 Toth, *The Passing of Postmodernism*, 110.

"Dead Souls Babbling": Language, Loss, and Community in *The Names* and *White Noise*

"The world has become self-referring. You know this. This thing has seeped into the texture of the world. The world for thousands of years was our escape, was our refuge. Men hid from themselves in the world. We hid from God or death. The world was where we lived, the self was where we went mad and died. But now the world has made a self of its own. Why, how, never mind. What happens to us now that the world has a self? How do we say the simplest thing without falling into a trap? Where do we go, how do we live, who do we believe?"[1]

This is how one character in Don DeLillo's *The Names* (1982) describes the world in the late twentieth century, when everything refers to something else, even the formerly original world. Here and elsewhere in the novel, letter-obsessed characters ask, when everything signifies something else, can anything be in itself significant? Can the fate of the self be separated, or saved, from the fate of an infinitely regressing language? What gives the self meaning, and what *is* meaning in a world shorn from language? What does it mean for a human being to *mean*, to signify, to be significant?

Singh expresses the anxiety of a man who has been caught in the American culture machine: set amid a loosely knit community of transient Americans living and working in Greece, the novel depicts an America that has become emblematic of the information and technology culture that define the latter half of the century, its citizens all complicit, however unwittingly, in its mission of folding the rest of the world into its own ever-expanding system of mediation and reproduction. The mysterious and menacing events that surround these Americans—phones ringing twice, then stopping, charged stares in restaurants, and finally a botched shooting—reveal the sinister nature of their "bank" and "insurance" work, and the degree to which their presence on foreign soil is perceived as a threat or attack requiring equally forceful retaliation. One character explains this animosity toward Americans as a natural response to a nation whose physical and technological ubiquity have transformed it into "the world's living myth," so that the "function" of its citizens is "to be character types, to embody recurring themes that people can use to comfort themselves" (114): America's cultural dominance makes itself and its citizens a fiction in whose context the world, at times aggressively, defines itself. America becomes the simulation against which a "self-referring" world attempts to define itself as real.

The novel, written and set shortly after the Iran hostage crisis, envisions the dawning of a new kind of global terrorism perpetrated not by nations but by individuals or small groups whose largely anonymous actions against the perceived threat of American cultural, technological, and information-seeking invasions remain difficult to trace; the spread of an American web of "waves and radiation," therefore, produces not only new hordes of consumers of the American myth and its material products but also a new kind of resistance to that cultural web. Represented not only by underground aggressions toward individual Americans but also, eerily prescient of the September 11th terrorist attack orchestrated by Osama Bin Laden in 2001, by scattered, transient groups of (mostly) men living in caves and killing individuals in a mockery of this cultural machine, this untraceable threat to Americans as depicted in *The Names* defines not only the problem of the individual in a culture overtaken by mediation but also the problem of the American in the late twentieth century. With all national and individual identity, knowledge, and authority compulsively reproduced into mere images, and with only our own technologies of mediation to turn to in search of what has been lost, what possibilities are left for establishing a sense of self, of community, of what is real, of something meaningful that escapes this voracious identity-eating system? *The Names* attempts to suggest and critique possible answers to this question through character responses that range from reaffirming one's faith in a humanist language to accepting our culture of linguistic estrangement as a cautious defense against suffering. But it explores both of these options against the backdrop of another response that is as culturally compelling as it is ghastly in its extremity.

Singh attacks the problem of meaning in the contemporary world by joining a cult whose practices vigorously deny the possibility of meaning, instead asserting the absolute arbitrariness of systems of signification and the irreparable disconnection between symbols and things. The cult members murder by letters, choosing victims for the sole reason that their initials match those of the town in which they are killed. Certainly the cult represents the most extreme reaction in the novel to the problem of finding self and meaning in this linguistic and cultural uncertainty. But the cult's obliteration of the human being in the name of the symbol also represents the most extreme manifestation of the antihumanist nature of contemporary language and culture themselves.

We learn about this cult through the obsessive research of Owen Brademas, an archaeologist who works in the region of the cult and quickly discovers how closely his own interest in languages and letters parallels that of the cult members; his initial attempt to understand their behavior centers on a shared amazement at the lost link between language and the natural world: "I talked to them, Kathryn. They wanted to hear about ancient alphabets. We discussed the evolution of letters. . . . It's interesting to me, how these marks, these signs that appear so pure and abstract to us, began as objects in the world, living things in many cases" (116). Because the impulse to match sets of letters derives from a desperate nostalgia for a natural language, in which symbols mimicked the things they represented, even retaining in their shapes a mirror of the physical world, the cult's killings might seem to suggest an attempt not to deny the connection between signifiers and signifieds but to reestablish a new and ultimate method for connecting them. Indeed, the novel has often been read in just this way.[2] But such a reading does not consider why murder of a human being must stand in as this new connection, nor does it make sense in the overwhelmingly pervasive context of the cult members' desire to study and value words and symbols cut off from, not reconnected to, things.[3] Instead, I see the cult members as quite clearly performing that problem, so that they, and their most committed admirer, Owen Brademas, find this dehumanizing revisioning of language compelling not so much because of its linguistic implications—the troubling of signification and meaning—but because of the absolute disaffection, the shield from human suffering it allows them to construct. Owen and the cultists pursue the ultimate implications of what it means to live in a world in which unmoored signifiers assert their power over things, and in which human beings simply rank among those disempowered signifieds.

One of the novel's great strengths, however, is that the cult initially operates as a signifier seeking a signified, the sparse reports of its behavior floating about the region seeming to beg for reconstitution into a whole by interpretation. Therefore, the mystery surrounding the cult's practices constitutes an opportunity to examine and question meaning-making, language, and the decisions we make about both, through the eyes not only of the cult but also of Owen and his friend James. Perhaps not as language-obsessed as Owen but equally engaged in language as a livelihood, James has taken a job as a "risk analyst" based in Athens in order to be near his son Tap and ex-wife Kathryn, who works as a volunteer on Owen's archaeological dig on a small Greek island. Right from the start, then, Owen and James occupy profoundly different relationships to understanding language: Owen pursues ancient artifacts in order to understand the lives of the long dead and insulate himself from the living, while James adopts a life of writing and reporting only in order to be near and reconnect with the family he has all but lost. These two very opposite impulses, one toward alienation and the other toward human connection, presage the profoundly different ways that Owen and James will react to their knowledge of the cult.

So it is Owen who understands what James and Kathryn do not want to see: that the cult killings do not attempt to redeem our "fallen" language but rather express the cult members' denial of the loss inherent in a post-Babelian, or post-Adamic language. These killers "weren't repeating ancient customs, they weren't influenced by the symbolism of holy books or barren places, they weren't making a plea to Egyptian or Minoan gods, or a sacrifice, or a gesture to prevent catastrophe" (170). Rather, the cult's refusal to orchestrate the killings as ritual is a denial of linguistic loss—the loss of the connection between symbol and thing—which is itself a kind of denial of both social and linguistic surplus and of society's need to expend that surplus or siphon it off into some kind of totem. In his early theory of "effervescence" in *The Elementary Forms of Religious Life* (1912), Emile Durkheim posits such a surplus as a result of collective representations of knowledge that are greater than the sum of individual representations, an excess that for him becomes the source of both the social and the religious. Georges Bataille later theorizes the potlatch as first meaningless expenditure of this excess, then as purposeful expenditure in the service of a restricted economy in *The Accursed Share* (1967), while Claude Lévi-Strauss in *Introduction to the Work of Marcel Mauss* (1950) translates this social or economic surplus into a *linguistic* one that allows mediation between subjects and objects, and an inherent connection between words and things. The cult, however, in refusing to make its killing ritualistic or totemic in any way, poststructurally refuses to acknowledge that language can carry a surplus, and so seems to be trying to kill off the very human need—the need for language to be more than symbol, for it to contain and communicate the essence of a communal bond—that lies at the bottom of this surplus. Indeed, Mark Osteen refers to the cult's use of killing as "counter-sacrifice," in that it "turns subjects into objects with no intention of resacralizing them."[4]

The cult's eradication of the human in the name of the sign can be read as aligning with Heidegger's proclamation in the 1950 essay "Language" that language precedes the human.[5] In asserting the primacy of language over humanity, Heidegger at bottom asserts the antihumanity of language: "In its essence, language is neither expression nor an activity of man"; it is "not anything human."[6] Rather, language is the calling into being of both human and world; in the context of a disillusioned late twentieth-century-American culture, it rushes in to fill the vacuum left by the extinction of God. In *The Names*, however, language as brandished by the cult threatens the human not simply because it is entirely other from the human but because it expresses the absolute primacy of the abstract symbol over the physical thing. Each murder reduces the victim to a symbol, converting a human life into a trail of spoken and written reports of its death throughout the novel; the cult's choice of its victims only because their initials match those of the towns in which they are killed means that it allows only the victims' names or signs to signify. The killings, so "striking in design" (171), literally and figuratively *strike*— meaning both pound and excise—the human to elevate the symbol.

The novel dramatizes the extent to which disconnecting symbol from thing erases human body and human feeling by constructing both as conspicuous absences: in a novel whose various narrative thrusts revolve around a series of brutal and bloody murders, not one drop of blood is spilled "on screen."[7] This conspicuous absence of the novel's driving force speaks to the extent to which the cultists aggressively devalue and elide the visceral experience of killing and dying. For them, the murders are studiously intellectual acts, committed to make a linguistic statement for which the mess is not only beside the point but actually interferes with it: "The murders are so striking in design that we tend to overlook the physical act itself, the repeated pounding and gouging of a claw hammer, the blood mess washing out. We barely consider the victims except as elements in the pattern" (171).

This unmooring of the thing from the symbol—the removal of human body and feeling from linguistic signification—enacted by the cult illustrates one way of making manifest a concept of language that precedes and dominates the human world. In this context, the cult killings literalize Lacan's own formulation of those implications, his declaration that "the symbol manifests itself first of all as the murder of the thing." This statement comes as a culmination of his assertion of the primacy of the symbol: "It is the world of words that creates the world of things . . . by giving its concrete being to their essence."[8] As in Heidegger's essay, "Language," "Man speaks, then, but it is because the symbol has made him man."[9] Because Lacan defines words as "already a presence made of absence,"[10] this making of humanity by the symbol occurs through a process of loss: beyond creating the subject, the symbol also threatens it by obliterating the subject at its entrance into signification.

Lacan demonstrates this symbolic creation of subjectivity through loss and signification in his rereading of the *fort-da* game played by Freud's grandson. In it, he reads in the child's repeated tossing away and retrieval of the cotton-reel not just his "mastery" of the disappearance of his mother but his recognition in this disappearance, and in his desire for her return, of the possibility of his absence from himself:

> The ever-open gap introduced by the absence indicated remains the cause of a centrifugal tracing in which that which falls is not the other *qua* face in which the subject is projected, but that cotton-reel linked to itself by the thread that it holds—in which is expressed that which, of itself, detaches itself in this trial, self-mutilation on the basis of which the order of significance will be put in perspective.[11]

He sees in the reel and thread a model of self-division, a loss and retrieval of the self that mimics the process of signification. But in order to see these things in the reel, the boy can no longer see in it the original object he has lost and desired: his mother. Thus "his action destroys the object that it causes to appear and disappear in the anticipating *provocation* of its absence and its presence."[12] No longer missing his actual mother, the boy throws the reel for the pleasure of entering into loss and anticipating return, which for Lacan is the game of language itself. In this way, the *fort-da* game illustrates the same dynamic that obsesses the cult members, who devise their own murderous game to produce a similar satisfaction: they make a presence into an absence in a series of actions that generates meaningless repetition and pleasure in the anticipation of the next presence and absence. Like the boy, for whom the loss of his mother becomes incidental to the more compellingly compensatory pleasure of inserting himself into this pattern of loss and return, and hence into language, the cult commits murder not because the loss of the human being is significant but because in creating that loss it generates a pattern of repetitive loss in which the human being is beside the point. In other words, it makes of murder a language. As the boy's mother, or "the real," becomes unmoored from the reel that finally signifies only signification itself, the victim's body disappears from the novel so that only matching initials remain present to signify. In both cases, the process of signification—of losing and retrieving the object—takes precedence over the original object itself. The symbol murders the thing; murder becomes a language.

Derrida echoes this murderous inhumanity in his groundbreaking rethinking of the structure of the sign. Descending, by his own account, from Heidegger's linguistic formulations while disdaining the nostalgia for the origin inherent in them, Derrida's decentering of language proposes a theory of "interpretation, of structure, of sign, of freeplay" that "is no longer turned toward the origin, affirms freeplay and tries to pass beyond man and humanism."[13] This "passing beyond humanism" for Derrida amounts to a turning away from the definitively human need for presence, for origins, and for closed-off binary structures. His, then, is a theory of language that omits the human by omitting the human need for centers and closure; it is a human production of the inhuman, the antihuman, of a kind of language that will always remain beyond human understanding. Derrida acknowledges just this unfathomable contradiction—and the element of threat to the human inherent in it—in the vivid metaphor with which he ends the essay:

> Here there is a sort of question, call it historical, of which we are only glimpsing today the *conception, the formation, the gestation, the labor*. I employ these words,

I admit, with a glance toward the business of childbearing—but also with a glance toward those who, in a company from which I do not exclude myself, turn their eyes away in the face of the as yet unnameable which is proclaiming itself and which can do so, as is necessary whenever a birth is in the offing, only under the species of the non-species, in the formless, mute, infant, and terrifying form of monstrosity.[14]

What is "terrifying" about this "form" is that it is "formless"; what is "monstrous" about this "species" is that it is a "non-species." This thing that has been born is defined by irresolution and undefinability, by the threat of destruction it brings with its very creation. Adding to the terror of these binary-straining contradictions is the power of this linguistic beast to "proclaim itself," to assert its dominance over the human realm that must receive it. This, in fact, seems to be the essence of Derrida's metaphor of the monstrous baby: our human terror at being subject to a system of symbolization, at being powerless in the facelessness of it.[15] The striking threat inherent in Derrida's vision of decentered language, in fact, suggests that Derrida does not simply deviate slightly from Heidegger in this thinking on language but actually *reverses* Heidegger's central proclamation in "Language." For as Derrida describes it, language does not precede the world in order to create the human but potentially to destroy it.

We can read the transition from humanist to antihumanist language, then, in the context of the loss of the human element of language—the loss of the human need for connection between symbol and thing, and of the connection itself. In fact, the loss of the necessary connection between symbol and thing, the basis for this transition, comes about specifically because of the loss of the humanity of language. For, as Derrida asserts, language that is born of something entirely other than humanity does not rest on the central human need for closure, belief, meaning, and connection. It is exactly the loss, or refusal, of this belief in the necessity of connection between symbol and thing that defines poststructuralist language, the loss of knowledge defined by Lévi-Strauss as that which binds signifiers to signifieds.[16] In this way, our entrance into an antihumanist vision of language, through our cultural recognition, exacerbation, and reproduction of the disconnect that has always defined post-Babelian language, is the human creation of that which plagues and horrifies the human, the embracing of a theory of language that defies human nature by eliminating it as essential. Fredric Jameson, in "The Cultural Logic of Late Capitalism," describes one more way in which the human is threatened by a language in which symbols have taken precedence over things: in the "new depthlessness" posited by such theories of language, interiority as a model of human subjectivity becomes impossible, as does the notion of human expression of emotion. So the price of a world ruled by signifiers is the "waning of affect" that accompanies this destruction of traditional notions of subjectivity.[17] What is possible, perhaps primary, in a humanist concept of language, expression of human loss, becomes in the deadening experience of antihumanist language something quite different—loss of human expression. I will argue that it is this process of disaffection through embracing an antihumanist view of language that motivates the cult, and their most desperate follower, Owen, all along, and that it is the seduction of the promise of this disaffection that James must resist.

The cult's enactment of symbolic domination over human life illustrates its threat not only to the human individual—the murder victim—but to the human community as well, specifically in terms of disaffection. The cult structures itself around practices and values that are necessarily antisocial; even their own isolated community cannot finally sustain itself. The members derive no emotional connection through their shared love of the letter, demonstrated most poignantly when Singh seamlessly interweaves his respectful interest in Indian and Iraqi languages with his dehumanizing desire for the female cult member Bern:

> There are other alphabets to study in that area. I could go to the marshes. I'd take the woman except she's serious about starving herself. I'd like to fuck her everywhichway to Sunday or whatever the phrase. She's the kind you fuck with a vengeance, am I right? Each sound has one sign only. This is the genius of the alphabet. (295)

In fact, these killers come together in the name of an antihumanist system of signification as a retreat from communal demands, from the emotional involvement that such demands entail; they go so far as to divorce the act of murder itself specifically from the idea of family (202), and to commit it in a place, the desert, where "intended meaning is beside the point. The word itself is all that matters" (294). Ignoring the moaning, starving woman, the men prepare for their final killing with utmost analytic detachment, viewing their intended victim as "an empty body, . . . a receptacle for [his] own waste, . . . from the sigmoid flexure to the anal canal," and reminding Owen that "You know how it has to end," "It follows logically from the premise," and "It's a blunt recital of the facts" (302). Singh seems to have answered his own question, then—"How do we say the simplest thing without falling into a trap?"—by investing all value in a *system* of signification, or the "trap," rather than in any meaning or feeling that system might attempt to convey. Or put another way, his devotion to the cult suggests that he is not even asking the right question. For the cult skirts the problem of communicating meaning between people by eliminating the person from the system of language: the system they celebrate is, after all, insistently, murderously *inscribed*, victims pummeled with weapons bearing their initials, the written letter obliterating not only human body but also human voice.

Still, the novel offers another, contrary possibility for conceiving of and living with language, one based on human connection and knowledge of the self, articulated through the mingling of human voices. Most striking about the humanist thrust of a novel so deeply invested in demonstrating the inhuman effects of our contemporary culture is that *The Names* depicts this concertedly humanist concept of language, as pursued by James, not as a quaint example of a kind of language already discarded but as a real and necessary possibility that remains available to its characters, however problematically, even in a "self-referring world." Further, DeLillo presents these opposing methods of living in and understanding contemporary language and culture in the context of the possibilities for affirming or denying human connection, and more specifically, the possibilities for family, that each method brings.

Disconnection and disaffection: The language of denial

Defined from the start in terms of his "almost otherworldly" "pain" and "grief" (19), Owen Brademas finds in the cult's enactment of disaffection through antihumanist language exactly the balm he has been searching for through a lifetime of studying language. Owen responds to this pain by losing himself in meaningless patterns in language and the world, a fact we learn about him just after learning of his lifetime of pain, when Kathryn offers him, like a gift, a graceful moment of unplanned simultaneity she has recently witnessed: two motorcyclists roaring off in opposite directions at exactly the same moment (25). Later, Owen himself admits this devotion to pattern: "I've always believed I could see things other people couldn't. Elements falling into place. A design. A shape in the chaos of things. . . . I feel I'm safe from myself as long as there's an accidental pattern to observe in the physical world" (172). That both of these references to Owen's love for and reliance on design occur in the same context, that of his family, suggests this context is the source of his pain, the pain that pattern and design help him to escape. Kathryn tells her motorcycle story in order to rescue Owen from the subject of his family: "'I had an odd upbringing. My people were devout in not very conventional ways. . . .' Kathryn changed the subject for him" (24–5). And when asked how long he has felt the need for pattern to "feel safe from [him]self," Owen launches into a story about his boyhood experience at a Pentecostal church where his parents both spoke in tongues but he could not. It is this experience of failed speech, and so of the failure to connect with the family of the church and his own family, that propels Owen's quest for a written language devoid of mysterious meaning and painful emotional connections. And it is this conflict, between language as expression of affect and human connection, and language as disaffected pattern and alienation, that lies at the center of *The Names*.

Church began for him as an experience of light and connectedness to others, and one that even in his memory is filled with feeling: "It was a *memory* of light, a memory you could see in the present moment, feel in the warmth on your hands" (172, original italics); it was his "safe place." But his family's move to a Pentecostal church left him in a place where "there was nothing safe," that "let in everything but light," was full of "closed eyes" and a strange, "inside-out" language that cut him off from his parents: "His father fell away to some distant place, his mother clapped her hands and wept" (173). But as we will see from the novel's final chapter—Tap's own rewriting of Owen's alienation from this strange, compelling language—the pain Owen experiences as a child unable to speak in tongues also emerges from his inability to enter into the ecstasy of pure knowledge contained in this "inside-out" speech.

That his lifelong quest for security in patterned language results from this early alienation from the divine experience of glossolalia further links Owen's self-defensive reaction to the problem of language with the cult's. For glossolalia represents language that is, to the outside listener, no less incomprehensible than that celebrated by the cult—the difference being, of course, that speaking in tongues promises divine meaning to those who *believe* it is meaningful. Even Lacan appeals to glossolalia as a metaphor of language that masks or mediates meaning, however indecipherable the nature of signification.

In his groundbreaking essay, "The Function and Field of Speech and Language in Psychoanalysis," Lacan redirects Freudian study away from the contemporary interest in the Imaginary Order and toward what he considers the fundamental Symbolic Order, and concludes by exhorting his fellow psychoanalysts to recognize their task as primarily that of interpreting language: "Let him be well acquainted with the whorl into which his period draws him in the continued enterprise of Babel, and let him be aware of his function as interpreter in the discord of languages."[18] Lacan appeals to his peers to shift their focus from the ineffable, what the patient is not saying, to exactly what the patient does say; he reminds them that psychoanalysis is a practice premised on analyzed speech, whose only medium is in fact speech, so that the concepts and techniques that occupy psychoanalysts "take on their full meaning only when orientated in a field of language, only when ordered in relation to the function of speech."[19] The problem of the tower of Babel—site of confusion of the common language of humanity in order to preserve the absolute power of God—becomes the problem of psychoanalysis in the mid-twentieth century. And Lacan urges his fellow analysts to tackle that problem of tangled speech with faith that the mere attempt at interpretation will reveal, if not the "real" or real "meaning," some sense that "discord" somehow signifies. In this way, Lacan posits not that the signified no longer exists, or becomes permanently excised by the signified, but simply that accurate interpretation requires recognizing the disjunction between them. The cult's literalization of the symbol's murderous power over the thing, then, represents an extreme perversion of Lacan's theory of language rather than a simple reflection of it, as Owen's attraction to the cult reflects the extremity of his need to escape pain by engaging in language without belief. Incapable of this belief as a child, Owen found himself barred from the divinity of the language and immersed only in its meaningless babble. His decision to pursue the cult's radical insistence on written pattern devoid of meaning rather than a renewed faith in the human voice's ability to express significance represents a self-defensive turning away from the suffering of that early childhood trauma. For in the context of this novel, such a possibility for faith in spoken language exists—just not for Owen.

Indeed, DeLillo has expressed his own optimistic belief that a kind of meaning exists in the instances of glossolalia that abound in his fiction, and that he has observed in his own life. In a 1982 interview conducted while he was working on *The Names*, DeLillo mused about the possibility of a kind of pure, original language, devoid of the problems of signification that act as barrier between language and meaning in this "fallen world":

Is there another, clearer language? Will we speak it and hear it when we die? Did we know it before we were born? . . .

The "untellable" points to the limitations of language. Is there something we haven't discovered about speech? Is there more? Maybe this is why there's so much babbling in my books. Babbling can be frustrated speech or it can be a purer form, an alternate speech. . . .

Glossolalia is interesting because it suggests there's another way to speak, there's a very different language lurking somewhere in the brain.[20]

There is no mistaking the promise and optimism of this "purer," "dazzling" form of language in the glossolalia of Owen's childhood church: the preacher refers to it as "talk[ing] as from the womb, as from the sweet soul before birth," as "that babbling brook," as "child's play" (306). Those engaging in it are "in awe, exalted," and "knowing joy" (306). This idea of "knowing joy" is central to the "immense pleasure" of glossolalia, because it is a joy that comes from entering innocently into knowledge, as a child, without fighting against the barriers to knowledge erected by the system of signification in which that knowledge is conveyed. Thus glossolalia, and Tap's own written attempt to mimic its access to the "untellable" in the novel's final chapter, stands in as a third kind of language available, or frustratingly unavailable, to the characters in the novel. It is language that is not language, seemingly random and yet full of accidental pattern and meaning; it is language as celebrated by the cult but transformed by the addition of faith that such pattern expresses the divine. While James ultimately learns to recuperate a version of this prelapsarian[21] language through the writing of his son, Owen's unrecuperable loss, perhaps all the more painful because Owen discovered his inability to participate in the "child's play" of language while still himself a child, thrusts him into a lifetime of compensating for this loss through denial.

We begin to witness his mechanism of denial even as he describes his childhood encounter with glossolalia. When asked whether he spoke in tongues, Owen shifts from his affective description of the "hobbling chant, a search for melody and breath, bodies rising, attempts to heal a brokenness" to an analytical account of "learned behavior, fabricated speech, meaningless speech." James, perceiving the gap between the affecting experience lived and the "neutral experience" remembered, notes that Owen "measured what he was saying like a man determined to be objective" and "wondering in a distant way (or trying to remember) whether anything has been left out" (173). Clearly what has been left out is feeling, the emotional reaction to not being able to speak and so being left out of a community and estranged from his family, as well as the "immense pleasure" of accessing the kind of pure knowledge and meaning that glossolalia speakers enjoy. This emotional/pleasurable component of language, so appealing to and yet impossible for Owen on that day, reflects a kind of linguistic surplus that language as a fallen system of infinite signification in this novel absolutely cannot contain.[22] Rather than seek this joyful knowledge, Owen runs from the pain of the inability to enter into it by pursuing a language devoid of it—language where the symbol is all-important, and the mysterious and meaningful connection to things is absent.

The cult, especially the cell in India, provides the perfect opportunity for Owen to seek disaffected meaninglessness in pattern. As he travels toward the cult through India, he reads pattern and design everywhere he looks—"The cows had painted horns. Blue horns in one part of the countryside, red or yellow or green in another. People who painted cows' horns had something to say to him, Owen felt"—and sees in them "aspects of control" (278, 279). These patterns and "lists" are like a language to him, the language of India, which he studies not to find meaning but for the pure pleasure of learning its associations and patterns, the pleasure of grammar without signification. That this learning "seemed childlike . . . to Owen, the child again, made to learn a language, to think in lists" (284), reminds him and us that his attempt to acquire language is fuelled by the desire to heal the wounds of his early church experience, while denying the loss of that memory. So for Owen, India's promise of "control" is as important to his quest as are its offerings of patterns for deciphering; India is a place where he can immerse himself in written linguistic pattern while maintaining control and disaffection.

As the cult members depart to perform their final act of linguistic disaffection in the form of murder, Owen enters a silo and engages in his own equivalent of that act: the systematic disaffecting of his childhood memory of loss through language. Moments earlier, he had entered Bern's silo in an attempt to help her, and the scent of animal feed made him think, for the first time in 30 years, of the grain storage elevators of his childhood prairie town. In this moment, the silos become sites of affect, where the woman lies dying and the carefully suppressed memories of Owen's childhood come rushing back to him. His entry into a silo as the male cult members head toward a killing, then, marks his conscious decision to wrestle with his painful past as a rejection of the cult's murderous logic and a seeking of an alternative method of bearing language.

Once inside the silo and the memories it triggers, Owen revisits his past with the careful, calculating eye of a man for whom memory has become a defensive act; he conjures this memory not to *affect* himself but to aid in his *disaffection* of the aching past. His first thoughts of the silos of his youth center on their etymological origins ("see the Greek," he thinks). Once his thoughts wander to himself as a vulnerable boy in that landscape, and "the solitary church standing in weeds," we begin to encounter his self-monitoring: "It is necessary to remember correctly.... We want to get it right" (303). These are not the emotional reminiscences of a man lost in his past but the careful constructions of a man using his past for a purpose. Even when he begins to remember the fateful day of speaking in tongues, Owen does so from a position of distance and control. In fact, he does not so much remember the experience as he *imagines* it: "In his memory he was a character in a story.... He would recall exactly. He would work the details of that particular day" (304). He further separates himself from the emotion of the past by "remembering" the day from multiple perspectives, never allowing himself to inhabit fully the memory or its attending emotions: "(In his memory he is at the church, waiting, as well as inside the car, crammed between the door and a woman who smells of sour milk)" (305). He refuses to allow the memory to seep into his present life, imagining that "the bin was perfect, containing that part of his existence, enclosing it whole" (304).

When Owen lets that critical distance between his present and his young selves collapse, narrating the experience in the church through the mind of the boy, affect abounds. He is "spellbound"; he finds the preacher "startling, compelling." His mother is "in awe, exalted" (306). "The sense of expectation is tremendous. The boy is chilled. ... everything moves and jumps and lives"; there is "rejoicing" and the speaking in tongues is "beautiful" (307). But "in the bin," in retrospect and in his adult mind, Owen's view of the glossolalia becomes analytical. He marvels not at the rejoicing but at the "uses of ecstasy, see the Greek," defining ecstasy as "an escape from the condition of ideal balance. Normal understanding is surpassed, the self and its machinery obliterated" (307). He converts something beautiful and joyful into abnormality and self-obliteration, into "words flying out of them like spat stones," and "terrible holy gibberish." Alone in the silo, a woman dying nearby while the cult kills its last victim, Owen remembers glossolalia not as the magical, affecting language to which he was denied access but as the cold language of stones he would pursue his whole life, and as the violent, obliterating language pursued by the cult. Owen reveals both the conscious purposefulness of this act and the subconscious guilt it evokes when he connects his critical reconstruction of the past to his need for innocence in the present: "These early memories were a fiction in the sense that he could separate himself from the character, maintain the distance that lent a pureness to his affection.... His innocence depended on this, on the shapes and colors of this device he was building ..." (305). Here we see his conscious *choice* to remember instrumentally and disaffectedly; his clear sense of guilt at this act, and his analogizing of this memory act to the cult's stone-wielding concept of language, represents the guilt he feels for indulging in the cult's pursuit of disaffection through language.

It is this connection between the destruction of the vulnerable human body and voice and the vulnerability of human affect that links Owen to the cult killers. Ultimately he rejects the cult's murderous methodology, instead creating one that pursues linguistic disaffection while stopping short of the cult's violent endgame. So he ends up a man alone in a small room, into which he has "brought only the names, ... the correct number of objects, the correct proportions" (275), taking "conscious solace ... in things" (308), his studious insistence on disconnection—between symbol and thing, between himself and the world—harmful only to himself and his childhood memories.

Holding on to loss: The language of recovery

Contrasting with Owen, whom James sees as "a man in a room full of stones, a library of stones, tracing the shapes of Greek letters with his country-rough hands" (275), James learns an entirely different view of language through the course of his narrative that ultimately allows him to perceive "a human feeling ... emerge from the stones" of the Acropolis. After avoiding the mythic site for years, James finally finds that

> the Parthenon was not a thing to study but to feel. It wasn't aloof, rational, timeless, pure.... It wasn't a relic species of dead Greece but part of the living city below it. ... I hadn't expected a human feeling to emerge from the stones but this is what I found, deeper than the art and mathematics embodied in the structure, the optical exactitudes. I found a cry for pity. (330)

His changed reading of the Parthenon, from stony rationality to voice appealing to the many voices around it, signals a very different linguistic discovery—that language can be meaningful when it acts as a conduit of human expression and connection, regardless of the disjunction inherent in signification. The allusion to Nietzsche's Acropolis in *The*

Birth of Tragedy tempers the optimism of this vision with a reminder of the suffering necessary to create community through language.[23] Still, James reads the Acropolis as a modern-day tower of Babel that unites people through the shared cry, as the temple forged a community of sufferers in ancient Greece. So his is a decidedly humanist vision of language that worries about the possibilities of community in speech rather than the impossibilities of truth in letters and writing.[24]

DeLillo sets up this opposition between affected and disaffected, bonding and alienating signification with the cult's first appearance in the novel. "Tell James about the people in the hills," Kathryn suggests to Owen (26), but immediately James's thoughts intervene as he mentally follows his estranged wife to bed, imagining with great tenderness their intimate encounter. Owen begins to describe the cult's devotion to thingless symbols, but the novel alternates by paragraphs between Owen's narration and James's preoccupation with his wife and child in adjacent rooms. Next to the cult's insistence on eradicating the human body in the name of the symbol, DeLillo offers the possibility of sensing in symbol the lingering, almost physical presence of the human in the context of family and the familiar. Central to both these concepts of language are affect and its ability to bind us to others: for James, the fulfillment of family bonds and the suffering at the loss of them; for Owen, the need to deny and escape precisely this kind of suffering. These contrasting pursuits of language by James and Owen for the sake of maintaining or denying feeling and the human intimacies it enables point to the characteristic that is fundamental to them both: loss.

An antihumanist view of language as defined by Derrida and Lacan is structured according to loss, operating according to an absent center, an impossible "real," and denying the dialectical possibility of coming to subjectivity through mediation with the human other. This fundamental loss of the connection between symbol and thing, between word and meaning, is not only inherent in deconstructionist or antihumanist language but is actually *generative* of this language; it is a language born out of loss. But these structural losses generate a realm of loss in our human experience of the world that defies human need and understanding, not least of which is the "waning of affect," as described by Jameson, which accompanies this new subjectivity based on loss. The cult in *The Names*, then, dramatizes the fate of the human being in a world devoid of meaningful subjectivity and the ability to register and communicate emotion, in which human community becomes impossible.

Perhaps we can say of a humanist concept of language that it believes that language operates not according to loss but in the interest of preventing it, or at least of honoring and remembering unpreventable loss as part of the human experience.[25] According to a Hegelian understanding of mediated subjectivity (as well as Freud's basic concept of the self's development in the self and the other), language is a tool for human expression of thought and emotion that not only connects us to others but also allows the self to extend to the other in acts of self-creation.[26] This humanist idea of language, in which language is created by humans in the shared effort of coming to subjectivity, of creating selves and worlds, enables human relationships in defense against, and in the context of, acknowledged, human loss. DeLillo introduces his model of humanist language exactly in this context, of a connection that has been lost and that James wants to regain.

Speaking to his estranged wife with whom he struggles to reconnect throughout the novel and through his writing, James articulates the way in which words spoken between or about family conjure such closeness that they seem to negate the word-thing disconnect, seeming even to convert breathed words into tangible objects: "The subject of family makes conversation almost tactile. I think of hands, food, hoisted children. There's a close-up contact warmth in the names and images. . . . When children race out of rooms the noise of their leaving remains behind" (31). Despite the irreparably broken bond between word and physical world that Owen pursues and the cult celebrates, language flowing from family and the familiar offers a glimpse behind the mask of signification to a kind of meaningfulness represented by shared feeling, knowledge, and concern:

> This talk we were having about familiar things was itself ordinary and familiar. It seemed to yield up the mystery that is part of such things, the nameless way in which we sometimes feel our connections to the physical world. *Being here.* Everything is as it should be. Our senses are collecting at the primal edge. The woman's arm trailing down a shroud, my wife, whatever her name. I felt I was in an early stage of teenage drunkenness, lightheaded, brilliantly happy and stupid, knowing the real meaning of every word. (32, original italics)[27]

Here, James marvels at language's ability to move him into a realm of sensory indulgence and physical experience of another human being; through conversation, his estranged wife, "whatever her name is," becomes *present* to him again. This use of language to get beyond symbolic system absolutely opposes that of the "abecedarians," who view it *only* as symbolic representation: choosing victims for the sake of their initials alone insists that nothing besides the victim's initials can signify. But for James, language in the context of family reaches past names to "real meanings," bridging the distance between symbol and physical world. In conjuring physicality, this kind of language for James transports him from the intellectual language games of his adult mind back to the simple pleasures and absolute knowledge of his youth, his visceral understanding of the familiar making him feel like a drunken teenager. And it communicates exactly the truth and reality that factor as loss in Owen's concept of language. Rather than operating in the service of loss, James's deeply human-centered language conjures things that matter. James feels lost in the world not because of a fundamental loss at the heart of language but because of the very real loss of these familial connections that, as he signals throughout the novel ("They were my place, the only true boundaries I had," 49), had defined him and made his life make sense. Ultimately his linguistic quest is to refind his center and reforge these bonds through a language that makes those possible.

First, however, he takes a detour into disaffection in a desperate attempt to deny his loss. An early exchange with Tap insinuates the violence he has done to his son's writing, by changing the confused names (Mackintosh, Wellington, Ingersoll), and the violence inherent in written language:

> "Owen says 'character' comes from a Greek word. It means 'to brand or to sharpen.' Or 'pointed stake' if it's a noun."

"An engraving instrument or branding instrument."

"That's right," he said.

"This is probably because 'character' in English not only means someone in a story but a mark or symbol."

"Like a letter of the alphabet." (10)

James confronts this hint of menace and power every time he leaves his building in Athens and lies to the concierge about his destination to disguise his poor Greek. He worries that the lies are metaphysically disturbing: "What was I tampering with, the human faith in naming, the lifelong system of images in Niko's brain? ... Could reality be phonetic, a matter of gutturals and dentals?" (103). His recognition of his ability deeply to affect Niko by "tampering" with names reveals his belief in the power of language spoken between people to establish a shared experience of the world, a kind of shared reality. And using that power not to forge an honest bond but to protect himself by denying his own ignorance points to his willingness to exploit this power in much the same way the cult celebrates the murderous power of written language—to inscribe in the place of human connection a denial of suffering.

Indeed, when confronted with his own inability to solve an interpersonal problem or soothe pain, James often attempts to rename painful emotions in bearable words. Faced with a wife packing for Greece at the end of a troubled marriage, James lists his "27 Depravities" as he believes Kathryn would define them, then recites them at her repeatedly: "The oral delivery was a devotional exercise, an attempt to understand through repetition. I wanted to get inside her, see myself through her, learn the things she knew" (18). James names his failings and recites them in his wife's voice, as if by doing so he can make the accusations hers and therefore understand why she is leaving. But the list is merely an imposition of himself upon her, a cruel attack that he retrospectively recognizes as his "chief weapon of the period" (16). In Greece, he tries to use the same word-weapon against his son's fear when he finds Tap motionless and frightened, surrounded by huge, bobbing bees:

> They were beautiful, I said. I'd never seen bees this size or color. They gleamed, I told him. They were grand, fantastic.
>
> Raising his head now, turning. Did I expect relief, chagrin? As I held him close he gave me a look that spoke some final disappointment. As if I could convince him, stung twice before. As if I could take him out of his fear, a thing so large and deep as fear, by prattling on about the beauty of these things. (121)

James attempts to kill his son's fear and replace it with awe simply by calling the bees "beautiful" and "grand." But what James cannot yet see is that this renaming, like Owen's reconstructed memory in the silo, may seem merciful but is truly only killing, because it, like the lies to hide ignorance with the concierge and the lists to hide incomprehension of his wife, is at heart a denial.

His complicity with the cult's project of making the word visceral through violent denial of human vulnerability culminates in his simultaneously linguistic and bodily attack of Janet Ruffing, an American "bank wife" whose strangely detached belly dancing and objective analysis of it utterly fixate him. Most sinister about James's attraction to Janet is that he is seduced not by her dancing but by her disconnection from the dance and from her own body. His flirtation grows more urgent because of her lack of response, her staying at the club out of "sleepiness" (224), her "deadness of intent" (222). James claims to have been "deeply ... affected" by her "dancing, barefoot, in arm-length gloves," but the description of his response while she dances proves otherwise:

> She was all wrong, long and slender, a white-bodied bending reed, but the cheerfulness of her effort, the shy pleasure she found, made us, made me, instantly willing to overlook the flat belly and slim hips, the earnest mechanics in her movements. What innocence and pluck, a bank wife, to dance in public, her navel fluttering above a turquoise sash. I ordered another drink and tried to recall the word for well-proportioned buttocks. (220)

If he is "affected," it is in an intellectual way, a man giving credit to a sexless woman with the courage to dance badly, thinking of words like "innocence" and "pluck," thinking not about her buttocks but about the proper word to describe them. So his later description of her effect on him rings more true: "The way you sit here unmoved by our talking excites hell out of me" (228).[28] He is excited by the "lack of connection between [her] words and the physical action they describe, the parts of the body they describe," by the fact that, when she describes her dancing, her "voice [is] four inches outside [her] body." Like the cult members who are fascinated by language precisely because of this word-thing disconnection, but then insist on imposing a violent and dehumanizing connection by killing by letters, James is drawn to the disconnection between Janet's word and her body and yet is compelled to correct it: "I want to put your voice back inside your body, where it belongs" (228). But though his intent could be read as honorable—giving her a voice, linking her words to her body to approximate the kind of connecting language that he lauds earlier in the novel—in reality he copies the cult in method as well as intent: he asks her to recite words, to "use *names*" (228, original italics), not in order to connect with her but to take pleasure in her clear disconnection from herself and her own body. And he commits violence against her.

A few critics have read this scene in terms of the cult's linguistic logic, discussing James's infliction of words like "breast" and "tongue" upon Janet Ruffing. But, except for one, they ignore the cruel and violent ending that marks this scene as James's most concerted effort at trying out the cult's marriage of violence, language, and meaning. And even this critic, Matthew Morris, refers to the final forced sex as "rape or seduction." Further, Morris elides any emotional or bodily pain suffered by Janet by asserting that James's pushing himself into an unwilling woman "represents above all the real consequences of seemingly empty words," as if the most violent weapon used in this scene is language.[29] But the details of this moment of invasive and perverse human connection tell a very different story. Once James has extricated Janet from the club, he thwarts her every attempt to part company, responding to each of them with increasingly aggressive advances. He kisses her; she looks away. She says she wants to go down to where the taxis are; he "pull[s] her up higher past the cabarets" and holds her against the wall. She "grimace[s]" at him; he pushes her back into the wall, and when she again asks for a taxi, he thrusts his hand between her legs. She turns her head to the wall again. Eventually she even manages to run away, but he catches her and "mak[es] her bend slightly," lifts her skirt. She "whisper[s] with uncanny clarity, 'People just want to be held. It's enough to be held, isn't it?'," and he responds by "us[ing] [his] knees to move her legs apart." While he enters a capitulating, apathetic woman, "she seem[s] to be thinking past this moment, finished with it, watching herself in a taxi heading home" (229–30). Perhaps it is her apathetic capitulation he had wanted all along.

In this physical assault of Janet in the interest of enjoying both her disaffection and his own, James mimics the logic of the cult by first recognizing in Janet the primacy of words over any meaning or feeling and then reveling in the dehumanizing aspect of this symbolic primacy. That he finds words like "breast" and "leg" exciting precisely *because* of Janet's continued sleepy apathy, her complete disconnection from her own body, reveals that James's desire to "put your voice back inside your body" is not an earnest attempt to embrace her in a more humane, concrete kind of language—for such a shift on her part would destroy his sexual excitement—but an imperialist desire to assault her "unmoved" body with his urgent, empty words. Their encounter is therefore not, as Dennis Foster claims, a "disregard of the referential dimension of language" in a caring attempt to share with her a redeemed language,[30] but a wallowing in referentiality that propels James through this encounter with Janet, a desire to derive pleasure specifically from the disconnection between words and things, between a woman and her own body, and his own violent attempt to reunite them. Hardly a "positive personal connection" aimed at "renew[ing] his own faith in language's ability to evoke the inexpressible,"[31] this encounter with Janet is the novel's most sinister example of James's passing desire to inhabit *only* the expressible, only words.

We begin to recognize linguistic reorientation when James makes one Owen-like journey to cult territory to satisfy his curiosity about that "faith in naming"—but takes his young son, Tap, with him, thereby morphing an attempt to understand the cult's alienating concept of language into an opportunity to understand his son. In fact, Tap's childlike delight in Mani at the uncanniness of a weather report in Greek briefly unites father, son, and a virtual stranger in a communal appreciation of the wonderful oddity of the sounds of language, of babble, prefiguring James's own later discovery of feeling in the babble of voices at the Parthenon, and of the community enabled by it. Once James has returned from the trip, he recognizes his reason for taking Tap along—as a "safeguard" and "escape" (191) from his interest in the cult and its linguistic obsessions—and that "since the first of those island nights [he'd] been engaged in an argument with Owen Brademas" (191). Here, then, DeLillo defines the terms and stakes of the "argument" between James and Owen over concepts of language and their possibilities for significance, and reveals James's decision, despite ill-advised attempts at cult methods in the absence of his family, to locate meaning in the kind of affect—love for his son—that protected him from the cult.

Ultimately it is Owen's account of his attempt to share in the cult's alienating language that convinces James his devotion to the pleasure and pain of struggling toward human and family connection makes sense. After hearing Owen's story of the cult's murder and his own enbinned schism from language, family, and affect, James leaves him, "owl-eyed, in the room he'd been arranging all his life," and enters the streets "full of people and noise," pausing to relish the myriad sights and sounds and smells and "worlds" of the city. His pleasure at this movement from the pure rationality and asceticism of written language to the bustling, affective noise of speaking people reinforces his suspicion that "[he'd] been engaged in a contest of some singular and gratifying kind. Whatever [Owen had] lost in life-strength, this is what [James had] won" (309).

Back in Athens, he continues to be moved by this realization, struck by overhearing "two voices, that man and woman in plain rage, battling" (311), and yearning for quotidian details of his family's faraway lives. He decides "this is what love comes down to, things that happen and what we say about them" (312), and believes language is meaningful because his son, out of love for him, has shown him its meanings: "I found [Tap's] mangled words exhilarating. He'd made them new again, made me see how they worked, what they really were. . . . I thought he sensed the errors but let them stand, out of exuberance and sly wonder and the inarticulate wish to delight me" (314). And when James finally discovers the extent to which he is complicit with and threatened by the cultural system of signification in which he is a pawn—wondering whether the bullet that wounds his friend was (rightly or wrongly) meant for him, finding he has been betrayed by and betraying for the CIA all along—his thoughts come to the family and friends who move him. Finally, for James it is this knowledge of himself and of loved ones through language that the book is about:

> These are among the people I've tried to know twice, the second time in memory and language. Through them, myself. They are what I've become, in ways I don't understand but which I believe will accrue to a rounded truth, a second life for me as well as for them. (329)

This story is the work of a man who believes that language *can* mean by capturing the emotions that connect people to each other. What remains to be seen is, according to the novel's construction of this choice, how effective his choice can be in forming communities and reuniting his family.

Choosing a humanist view of language

Derrida is careful to clarify that the monstrosity of language and its immediate cultural implications result not from human "conception" but rather from a sort of "gestation" of history that unstoppably produces our "terrifying" contemporary concepts of language, the world, and our place in them. The two available "interpretations of interpretation, of structure, of sign, of freeplay"—one seeking to decipher meanings and origins and the other passing "beyond man and humanism"—he decrees "absolutely irreconcilable." Our human need to reach for meaning and order notwithstanding, he asserts, "I do not believe that today there is any question of *choosing*,"[32] that history has made a choice for us all. Crafted of systems of information, intrigue, and paranoia, and carefully set at a historical moment that saw America's entrance into international relationships newly threatening and threatened by transmission of these same cultural constructions of uncertainty, *The Names* also depicts the world as receiving, against its will and as a matter of historical course, this monstrous baby. But DeLillo, unlike Derrida, carefully injects choice into his vision of the decentered world by structuring his novel around several conscious and radically differing reactions to this crisis of language and culture, one of which does what is unthinkable for Derrida, in seeking "the inspiration of a new humanism." James indicates his humanist vision of language as choice when he reads Owen's encounter with the cult as a lesson that how he conceptualizes language determines what possibilities remain open for him: "This is what I was learning from the objects in the room and the spaces between them, from the conscious solace he was devising in things. I was learning when to speak, in what manner" (308). Indeed, he was learning *to* speak, that language spoken between human beings offers, he has come to believe, possibilities for knowledge and feeling that Owen's dedication to written letters refuses (in another distinction from Derrida).

DeLillo signals this element of choice formally as well, using first-person narrative to frame the entire novel as James's reaction to Owen's story of his cult experience, and structuring the novel in relation to the telling of that tale. After a short first chapter in which he introduces all of the terms he will eventually use to define the meaning of language—his love for his estranged family; the inherent violence of the letter; the looming symbol of the Parthenon, waiting to be translated one way or another—James introduces the man who will act as his counterpoint throughout the novel, and points ahead to the narrative moment that will allow him to come to that linguistic definition: "Show us their faces, tell us what they said" (20). This is the entreaty with which Owen later begins his own story of the cult's final killing, identifying himself as the "public storyteller" egged on by the "ragged mob" at his feet. Owen's invocation of this image as he begins his account of the cult reveals his own conscious construction of the events in a way that will lead him to the safety of his small room, just as his conscious reconstruction of the childhood day of not speaking in tongues led him to the safety of disaffection. James's repetition of this image at the beginning of his own narrative—this novel—alerts us that he is doing much the same thing, constructing his story in a way that will lead him to an understanding of language that works for him, in reaction to Owen's lonely view of language. James reframes his written account of this humanist search as the spoken, community-forming myth of the public storyteller.

The narrative also includes several moments of self-consciousness[33] to show us that these are *conscious* constructions: "I don't want to surrender my text to analysis and reflection," James informs us as he begins, thereby both denying the act of analysis in his writing and demonstrating the conscious decision-making and analysis that every narrative act requires. However much he, like Derrida, views his confrontation with language as emerging unstoppably from the world around him, the narrative's constant self-consciousness attests that James creates and constructs a carefully considered reaction to the problem of language with every linguistic nip and tuck. In several formal departures from first-person conventions, the novel cleverly reminds the reader of the humanist reaching and bias of our unreliable narrator. In one example, we watch Kathryn and Tap leave James and the island, James communicating both the distance that will stretch out between them and the connection that will remain by encapsulating memories of them in objects of the island house. As Tap waits on the dock to depart, "He asks [Kathryn] the names of things, ship parts, equipment" (134), and this shared interest in named things holds the family together as they prepare to split apart. But this example of words grown tactile in the context of families demonstrates less the sagacity of James's vision of language than his ability to impose that vision: James is not present as his family waits at the dock or heads out to sea. These connections through names and words occur only in his hopeful narrative mind's eye.

A similar formal trick later in the novel signals the aggressiveness with which his narrative shapes events into an optimistic vision of language. As James and Owen discuss the meaning of the cult's actions, in the context of Owen's childhood trauma and why it draws him to the cult, the narrative indicates James's adoption of Owen's ideas by absorbing them into itself. Quotation marks suddenly drop away so that the tentative conclusion reached in this conversation—"They are engaged in a painstaking denial. We can see them as people intent on ritualizing a denial of our elemental nature" (175)—seeps into the narrative voice, becoming not a possibility discussed by inquisitive friends but a reality known by the narrative, a merging of character and narration that suggests a kind of Bakhtinian dialogism. The first-person narrating voice commits such acts of identification repeatedly, learning things from the events it describes and then incorporating these lessons into itself, just as James does throughout the novel. His is a narrative voice modeling exactly the humanist concept of language he ultimately decides he can live with, a use of language that reaches out to others and brings them back into itself, always maintaining that bond between people, between the symbols they speak and write and the things of the world. Thus it suggests, also like Bakhtin, a heteroglossic orientation toward and dependence on others in the narrative, through which it becomes meaningful[34]— turning the man who would say of himself "I'm not a writer" (197) into the man who would write that narrative.

Finally, the novel points to our ability to choose how we respond to the problem of language by presenting the most important catalyst of James's choice—Owen's experience with the cult and his resulting withdrawal into alienated disaffection—in layers of construction. After imagining Owen as storyteller, James repeatedly reminds us that *he* controls Owen's story by reminding us of his role as narrator via brief interludes that wrench us back into the quotidian narrative present (in one example, James interrupts Owen's storytelling with Owen's own request for water, 285). In one of these interjections, James addresses such narrative construction directly, simultaneously denying and demonstrating narrative analysis as in his earlier disavowal of analysis: "'Do you realize what we're doing?' I said finally. 'We're submerging your narrative in commentary. We're spending more time on the interruptions than on the story'" (300). In this admonition, James as character guides Owen back to the "real" story while

James as narrator divulges the extent to which he controls all of the novel's storytelling. Then Owen's self-conscious reconstruction of his childhood trauma while in the silo is also James's, as is Owen's rhetorical flourish of ending his intimate account of the cult in the distanced third person. James's peppering of narrative self-consciousness throughout the novel and especially during this episode makes all of these acts of construction ultimately his.

But while the novel's construction of individual choice through self-conscious narrative construction argues for renewed faith in a humanist concept of language, it also undermines it. DeLillo's construction of this choice through a novelistic device that subsumes the rest of the narrative into itself might also frame James's story as an act of solipsism, and suggest that what seems a reassuring example of Hegelian mediation and self-discovery through the other is really just Derridean "auto-affection," in which the perception of growth through communion simply masks the always satisfying communion with the self.[35] James's humanist project becomes further undermined when we consider the ethnographic method by which he proceeds. For James's dogged and highly self-conscious narrative provides a studied and passionately human-centered amalgamation of the novel's many archaeological, anthropological, and ethnographic thrusts: as Kathryn obsessively digs for human artifacts, Owen travels the world in search of ancient, etched language, Tap investigates and records Owen's childhood, and James's many acquaintances participate in a vast American attempt to study, describe, and so exploit less powerful countries, James constructs this narrative as his own attempt to observe, understand, and make meaningful the human experience of language. Certainly in the larger context of the American colonialism of information and language systems perpetrated throughout the novel,[36] James's similarly ethnographic excavation of self-knowledge becomes suspect, and the novel's primary gesture of seeking the "inspiration of a new humanism" akin to the ethnographic thrust of Lévi-Strauss's *Introduction to the Work of Marcel Mauss* that Derrida so skewers in his "Structure, Sign, and Play." Perhaps the novel suggests that any linguistic act of choice in a poststructural age remains circumscribed by the monstrous solipsism of language in which it is articulated.

The only portion of the novel that remains free of James's narrative intervention, and thus free from his self-conscious efforts to construct a meaningful language, provides the novel's most compelling evidence of its humanistic reach despite the gaps and self-reflexivity inherent in language. The final chapter comes straight from Tap, unedited by James, and so represents language as it emerges from one who is innocent of the problem of language and the choices necessitated by that problem. If the Parthenon provides one possible frame for the novel, Tap's writing certainly provides another, more fitting one.[37] Tap's writing stands throughout the novel as a third way of coming to meaning through language, apart from the murders of the cult and the carefully recuperative narrative construction of James. From the beginning, his use of language is described as raw and intimate: "Flamboyant prose, lurid emotions. He absolutely collides with language" (32). His is exactly the kind of relationship to words to which James in his thoughts of language and family aspires—a *physical* one, in which words remain so tethered to the world they describe that Tap interacts with them palpably.

After his final, instructive visit with Owen, James rereads his son's pages and then understands why Tap's writing strikes him as so immediate and true:

> Nothing mattered so much on this second reading as a number of spirited misspellings. I found these mangled words exhilarating. He'd made them new again, made me see how they worked, what they really were. . . . His other misrenderings were wilder, freedom-seeking, and seemed to contain curious perceptions about the words themselves, second and deeper meanings, original meanings. (313)

These "spirited misspellings,"[38] far from spinning out into mere "wordplay,"[39] seem to me to move in quite the opposite direction—pointing not toward the infinitely regressing line of metonymic signification but to a real and particular thing that we thought had been lost. These misspellings in fact stem from Tap's innocent faith that some kind of connection between words and things remains, that language is inherently meaningful. His is the rare example of language that is not seeking a solution for its own inherent dissolution but that is, in its assumed wholeness, simply doing what it can to comfort a suffering man.

Tap tells the story of Owen's traumatic alienation from language in the Pentecostal church of his youth, a story of one boy's fall from innocence into the terrifying discovery that language stands between us and the world. In the story, Orville flees the scene of failed glossolalia and runs out of the church, into "the nightmare of real things, the fallen wonder of the world" (339). Critics consistently read this final line of the novel as Orville's "exclusion from the Eden of Adamic speech"[40] and his entrance into a postlapsarian language devoid of "transcendence" and "deep and abiding meaning."[41] Tap's rendition of Owen's suffering invites these readings—especially his description of Orville looking "in vane for familiar signs" (339)—while also suggesting something perhaps more specific about his understanding of Owen's childhood trauma by representing Orville's loss as a very *human* one:

> No where did he see the gentle prairie of his careless days. Lonnie Wright was long gone. He would have opened his door to any young wafe, even a bad one. There was no where to run but he ran. . . . Why couldn't he understand and speak? There was no answer that the living could give. . . . He ran into the rainy distance, smaller and smaller and smaller. This was worse than a retched nightmare. It was the nightmare of real things, the fallen wonder of the world. (339)

When Tap describes the "nightmare" of entering into a fallen language and a changed world, he does so primarily by describing the disappearance of the human element, Lonnie Wright, that had been so central to his Adamic experience of the prairie. Further, he frames the scene's end as a human loss, cleverly constructing Orville's retreat into the rain in cinematic terms that transform reader into audience watching the figure of a small boy disappearing into the distance.

But the nightmare for Orville, and which continues through a lifetime of language study for Owen, is a fantastic discovery for the young writer Tap, whose "spirited misspellings" and emotion-filled prose reveal the truth of that alienated child's experience more fully and accurately than James's or Owen's narratives ever could.

Tap in his innocent entrance into language *before* the fall provides the novel's most optimistic view of humanist language because of his fearlessness in the face of it. Neither a weapon against others nor a place to hide the self, language for Tap is above all a tool for human connection. He represents the churchgoers' experience of glossolalia in the same terms of physicality and immediacy that his father used to characterize the human-centered language of family and the familiar: "The strange language burst out of them, like people out of breath and breathing words instead of air" (335). But Tap demonstrates his faith in the redeeming power of language most strikingly by transforming the metaphor of young Owen's inability to believe in divine linguistic meaning into the undeniable physical reality of his character Orville. In a redemptive revision of James's anxious lies to the Greek concierge, Tap suggests that by changing the words he can heal Owen's traumatic childhood experience: urged by the preacher to "Get wet," to "Let me hear that babbling brook" (306), to enter the "river of language" which is God (152), Owen sat mute and powerless in the church as a boy, sat denigrating the power of tongues in the silo as a man. But Orville runs out into the rain.

Tap's powerful faith in writing is born of an innocence that is unavailable to adults in the novel's systems- and language-obsessed world. His story is a naïve enactment of exactly the linguistic immediacy toward which James's humanistic vision strives and falls short. "I'm not a writer. My son writes," James claims early in the novel (197). But it is the example of his son's guileless connection through language that causes James to *choose* to become the writer who will write this novel, who will articulate his own limited but hopeful humanist vision of language in the considerable shadow of his son's breathtaking linguistic accomplishment.

Fear of fear itself: Simulating disaffection in *White Noise*

Three years after *The Names*, DeLillo imagines a world so thoroughly permeated by mediation and simulation that in it, Singh's troubled speech about referentiality and James's paranoia about the disconnection between words and things would seem nonsensical, or naïve. Indeed, the growing dominance of the signifier that troubled the outlying cult members in *The Names* becomes blithely accepted by, even definitive of, culture at large and energetically celebrated by a new breed of academics determined to reinterpret the loss of the real as not threatening but exciting, freeing, and fun. *White Noise* gives us the world in the Information Age, awash in the ubiquitous output of technology as machines insistently and authoritatively communicate with us and with each other. In this sea of "waves and radiation," the human being witnesses, and participates in, the transformation of the nature of language from possible source of communication between people to entirely the domain of the machine, other from the human, and usable by a traumatized humanity only as a way to construct a bearable world through disaffection and denial. By expanding into American, academic, and domestic cultures *The Names*'s proposition about the damning consequences of living defensively and murderously by poststructural concepts of language, DeLillo's most famous novel intensifies that warning in ways that would characterize depictions of the problems of language and representation in fiction through the end of the twentieth century.

Murray and his pop culture colleagues model this survival technique for Jack, studiously (and under the sanction of the university) converting "real" world things—soda bottles, cereal boxes, Elvis—into artifacts, into art, by Warhol's ways of evacuating the interior and dismissing the authentic thing, constructing the simulation of an irrelevant real and then touting this "hyperreality" as primary. They also model the infantilization that will typify both critical and fictional depictions of American culture at the end of the twentieth century.[42] All single, childless men, the members of the pop culture or "American environments" department of College-on-the-Hill are ill-mannered, unkempt, baby-faced and socially inept, comforting themselves with the order and mastery of collecting and the inclusive clubness of their self-appointed nicknames and hierarchies of authority. In fact they've constructed their careers out of these extended adolescences, converting the "shiny pleasures they'd known in their . . . childhoods" into "formal method."[43] Competing in the lunchroom like boys puffing their chests on the playground, and throwing food at each other to defuse any moment of sincere disclosure, this clique of "smart, thuggish, movie-mad, trivia-crazed" (9) man-children suggests the sterility, aggression, self-indulgence, and emotional evasiveness that are the fate of a community whose members subscribe to the postmodern tenets of Murray Siskind. It also suggests, more sinisterly still, that disaffection and the elevation of the sign over the thing, and of the defended self over the connected community, are not the scarcely acknowledged ideology of a small, foreign, and marginalized band of crazies but are rather the slick, calculated message disseminated methodically and worldwide, and with inarguable power, by the unified low-high front of popular culture and the academy.

The novel offers one obvious etiology of adolescent regression and aggression by situating its insecure adults in a world whose technological changes have left them behind, creating an underclass of baffled adults at the mercy of their technologically savvy children. But Murray adds to this rather accidental explanation an intellectual argument for the benefits of regressing to childish ways, as evidenced by his teaching of cinematic car crashes. He explains his celebration of them in terms of their "American optimism," "the old 'can-do' spirit" of the constantly evolving technology required to manufacture increasingly realistic representations of increasingly complicated, and violent, things. He therefore finds their clean, true, "artless" "innocence" and "fun" far preferable to the "complicated human passions" that otherwise sullenly occupy films (132). Onto the dichotomy of representation and thing, DeLillo has in this novel added that of childishness and maturity, implying that for all of these pop culturists, and later for Jack, eschewing "complicated human passions" by embracing the world of simulation amounts to a simultaneous abandonment of adult responsibility for the real world, a theme that Wallace, Homes, and Danielewski will develop in multiple novels, interviews, and essays in the last decade of the twentieth century (see Chapters 2 and 3). As Murray instructs Jack throughout the novel in his theory of the new language of television and the supermarket, both of which require that we "look innocently"—harnessing the same willingness to confuse real and image that prompts young Wilder, crying, to touch his pixilated mother on the living room television screen—the eerily savvy and responsible children rush in to fill the vacuum left by the adults who have abandoned their adulthood.[44]

In these and many other ways, effects of this narcissistic, infantilizing society are most clearly evident in the family: unlike the geographically sprawling *The Names*, *White Noise* is concertedly domestic, and most concerned about the effects on the American family of the cultural and linguistic shifts charted internationally in the earlier novel. The novel repeatedly dramatizes Lasch's description of the attack of image culture on the family, in which "the picture of harmonious domestic life, on which the family attempts to model itself, derives not from spontaneous feeling but from external sources, and the effort to conform to it therefore implicates the family in a charade of togetherness" (172). At the mall, attempting to rebuild through consumption his (false) sense of his own largeness after being caught unmasked by his bemused colleague, Jack takes solace not only in his buying power but in the fact that that power aligns him with his consuming family, who "gloried in the event. I was one of them, shopping" (83). In the similarly technologically layered and mediated experience of drive-through eating, "half stunned by the dimensions of [their] pleasure," the family shares a "mood of intense concentration, minds converging on a single compelling idea" (232). But both mall and drive-through leave them wanting only to be home, alone, in their separate rooms, the family bond produced only in their shared desire to get away from the world, and then even to get away from each other. In his longest meditation on family in the novel, DeLillo defines the contemporary human family specifically through this mechanism of alienation through mediation and consumption, presenting the family as a collection of people united by nothing so much as their collective effort to define a family experience and even mythology out of ruthlessly recycled, processed, and largely inaccurate information: "The family is the cradle of the world's misinformation. There must be something in family life that generates factual error. . . . The family process works toward sealing off the world. Small errors grow heads, fictions proliferate" (81–2). This is the family as facet and henchman of the same postmodern culture of mediated information and delinked language that produces the cult and the consumer alike: family as mediating machine.

But though the two novels' cults of letters and of consumption result in the same twin casualties of the knowable self and the communicating family, from the same root cause of dehumanization, the deaths at their centers differ markedly. Death for Jack is the "whole huge nameless thing" (288), whose unknowability and refusal to be mastered catalyze all the dehumanizing conversions of "complicated human passions" into bloodless, "innocent" representations that define the book. Even before he has met and been mentored by the poststructural apologist Murray, Jack attempts to master his fear of death by converting one of history's most merciless and prolific killers, Hitler, into an academic topic, a department, an icon (prompting the wonderfully apt comparison by Murray to Elvis). Under Murray's tutelage, Jack learns to envy the fearlessness and magical thinking of Orest Mercator, too young to have a concept of death, and progresses to such horrific conversions of human suffering into harmless representation as he demonstrates when watching, "almost in appreciation," a burning woman from the insane asylum, whose unimaginable suffering he aestheticizes into a beautiful thing (239), and when he manifests Murray's theory of killers and diers by shooting Willie Mink. But Dylar provides the most pointed, perfect metaphor for Jack's desperate desire to escape his own suffering—fear of death—by converting it into a representation of itself. For Dylar does not promise to cure death, but only to combat the fear of death; the fact that Jack lusts after it even though one potential side effect of the drug is death itself illustrates how completely he fears the fear and not the death.[45] In fact, Dylar can be read as a metaphor for the novel's entire narrative thrust, in that Jack's desire to, like Murray, elevate the simulation to the level of the real is his equivalent of Babette's taking the drug: both want to rid themselves of affect, of the affect surrounding death, by making that affect inhuman—merely a chemical reaction in the human brain, or merely an infinitely receding trip along the signifying chain.

In converting fear of death into fear of fear of death—a malady that is not only once-removed but for which there is also, handily, a pill—Jack practices a technique that he will extend to other sources of suffering and loss in his life. Confronted with Babette's own paralyzing fear of death, Jack responds not with sympathy for her pain but with admonishment that she has abdicated her assigned role of bringing happiness and stability to his life (197, 199). Refusing to allow her to be who she is, Jack imposes his infantile need on her instead, calling her "Baba," taking refuge repeatedly in her breasts. He performs the same act of colonialism on his son Wilder, whom he loves for his innocence of language, his existence in an Adamic world equally outside systems of signification, "complicated human passions," and responsibility to others. When the boy cries relentlessly and inexplicably for hours, Jack never considers what suffering he might be trying to communicate but only hears "an expression of nameless things in a way that touched [him] with its depth and richness," an "ancient dirge," and the sacred record of some "holy place" (78, 79), transforming the child's "huge lament" from an agonizing experience of Wilder's inability to explain his pain into a satisfying encounter with the beauty of meaningless language.[46] Jack's later conversion of the terrifying fact of Wilder's tricycle ride across a busy highway into a thrice-removed tale, absent of all markers of emotional inflection, signals that his accomplishment of total dissociation from the suffering and death and fear of death of himself and those he loves is complete.

The distance between Jack's dead-flat narrating of Wilder's potentially fatal "child's play" and the redemptive prairie-building of Tap marks the vast difference between these two novels' ultimate attitudes about and hopes for the cultural and linguistic problems they demonstrate. Whereas Tap's exuberance invites hope that a humanist choice such as James's can salvage in our fallen world some of the constructive magic of prelapsarian language, the resolute disaffection, the absolute depthlessness of tone in the final chapter of *White Noise* leaves the reader—beyond unclear about what social critique the novel is willing to make—disoriented in the same void of meaningful inflection that Jack has so willingly built and entered. Novel's end finds and leaves him safely ensconced in the equally depthless image-world of the supermarket, surrounded by the only kind of truth, knowledge, and death—wholly apart from "complicated human passions"—that world will acknowledge:

> But in the end it doesn't matter what they see or think they see. The terminals are equipped with holographic scanners, which decode the binary secret of every item, infallibly. This is the language of waves and radiation, or how the dead speak to the living. (326)

So the final conversion of human emotion into disaffected simulation occurs when Jack at last acknowledges the lengths to which he will go to escape his own suffering: he accepts that language has become wholly the domain of the dead, and that "the dead" have become purely a matter of language and simulation—existing solely on "tabloid racks" as images completely divorced from the reality of death, and subsumed into the media-constructed "cults of the famous and of the dead." In resolutely eschewing the human, adult world of uncertainty and suffering and fear of death (like the grocery bag boy whose own resistance to the complexities of adult life he so poetically imagines, 281), he enters instead the perfect deadness of the machine world.

But these, the novel's final words, enact its final regression, its final repetition of all it seems to deny but that insistently haunts it throughout. For however staunchly Jack and the academics deny the "whole huge nameless thing" of death itself for the sake of the safety of simulation, something always remains, something real and inescapably painful, that quietly qualifies and critiques their insistent denial.[47] Despite its constant and increasingly urgent displacement of the real by simulation, the novel draws distinctions between "real," physical death and simulated death throughout. While Alfonse and his cronies fantasize death, SIMUVAC volunteers fake death, communities concoct rumors of death, televisions broadcast images of death, and computers at Autumn Harvest Farms print out starred indicators of future death, many characters in the novel actually die. Jack reads about one of these deaths, that of Mr Treadwell's sister, as part of what appears to be a daily perusal of the obituaries. This he narrates to us on the heels of his contemplative visit to the Old Burying Ground of Blacksmith Village, where he strains to read names and dates of actual dead people on stones, thinking, "Is there a level of energy composed solely of the dead? They are also in the ground, of course, asleep and crumbling" (98).

Watching the insane asylum burn, Jack confronts again these two kinds of death, real and simulated, when his appreciation of how *satisfying* the blaze is, how true to his childish expectations of it—the men in rubber boots and "old-fashioned hats," the "manned and trained" hoses, the "telescopic ladder," even a "Dalmatian . . . in the cab of a hook-and-ladder truck" (239–40)—gives way to his shock at the woman burning: "How powerful and real." When a "smell of acrid matter" reaches him, he understands anew what troubles him about the conflation: "An ancient, spacious and terrible drama was being compromised by something unnatural, some small and nasty intrusion. . . . It was as though we'd been forced to recognize the existence of a second kind of death. One was real, the other synthetic" (240). Here, synthetic (human-made, manufactured) death provides a material metaphor for the human-made simulations of death manufactured throughout the novel, a realization for Jack that the images of death we create, so innocuous and reassuring in the minds of Murray's colleagues, will prove as poisonous and deadening as real, embodied, "natural" death itself. This proves to be true in the aftermath of the fire, as father and son struggle together to understand and contain the horror they have witnessed. First touting the fire as an opportunity for father-son intimacy ("Fathers and sons seek fellowship at such events. Fires help draw them closer, provide a conversational wedge," 239), Jack later finds that talking about the fire only becomes another opportunity to evade and deny suffering, as did father and son while watching the blaze. For what they talk about when they talk about the fire, about the burning woman and the windows blown out, are the trucks, hoses, and ladders represented and perhaps even inspired by the fire-free fire-engine books of both Jack's and Heinrich's youths. The fire is indeed a "wedge" between them, enabling the kind of conversation that holds two mutually suspicious people safely apart, rather than bringing them together in shared recognition of a painful truth. Here, as in so many scenes of the novel, we find that the tragedy of the novel does not lie so much in the disappearance of the real—of real suffering, death, and anxiety about death—but rather in our inability to hold ourselves open to that real suffering that makes us human.[48]

Unlike in *The Names*, it is a tragedy unmitigated by glimpses of or options for ways out of it. True glossolalia does not exist in this novel, which offers no opportunities for the kind of redemptive language in which DeLillo expressed so much faith over years of interviews. Instead, babble only comes here from machines, as the utterance not of inspired human voices but of the dead and of meaningless white noise. The novel's opening chapter implies this transformation in babble's nature and potential, when it depicts the machine invasion of the once quiet town as the "dead souls babbling" of highway noise (4). DeLillo then illustrates the cultural systems behind such a transformation when he ends Jack's consuming spree with a description of shopping mall as tower of Babel:

> Voices rose ten stories from the gardens and promenades, a roar that echoed and swirled through the vast gallery, mixing with noises from the tiers, with shuffling feet and chiming bells, the hum of escalators, the sound of people eating, the human buzz of some vivid and happy transaction. (84)

Here, human voices mix with the drone of their machine world, forming a conglomerate "human buzz" whose meaning and purpose can only be expressed as a capitalist "transaction." This thorough mixture of human and machine describes how language has changed from *The Names* to *White Noise*: no longer something to be reckoned with, a problem of disaffection through signification to be resisted through faith in human relationships, now language *is* the machine world, is spoken by the machine world, creates the machine world in its arbitrary image, so that it can no longer sustain the human element of faith. Indeed, the German nun's bitter description of her "dedication" as "pretense," her simulation of belief, obliterates the earnest faith with which DeLillo ends the previous novel. Her equation of "fools, children," "idiots," "lunatics," and "those who speak in tongues"[49] as the keepers of truth and faith converts the promise of "child's play" into the selfishness and insanity of infantile magical thinking that destroys both family connections and possibilities for a larger community capable of producing anything but alienating apathy. Taken together, these novels are warnings of what we lose when we lose access to or belief in a language that can connect us to the real world, to ways of knowing, to each other, without imagining a way out of the predicament. This task of imagining a way out, and creating that way through fiction, is precisely the one that David Foster Wallace will undertake for himself and hope to be possible for all fiction, as he and other writers of the late twentieth century and beyond work, with varying results, to create fiction that both knows it is made of arbitrary language in a ceaselessly mediating world, and shapes out of that language the empathy, earnestness, human connection, and awareness of the real and of real suffering that early poststructural literature so methodically elided.

Notes

1 Don DeLillo, *The Names* (New York: Vintage Books, 1989), 297. Subsequent references will be parenthetically noted.

2 Paula Bryant, for example, asserts that the cultists kill "to attempt the binding of symbol and object into one-to-one correspondence through a terminal act of connection," in "Discussing the Untellable," *Critique: Studies in Contemporary Fiction* 29 no. 1 (1987): 19.

3 Thomas Carmichael reads the cult murders as an attempt to escape our fallen language: "Ritual murder and political assassination, DeLillo's fiction maintains, are always and also attempts to escape the prisonhouse of language, understood as all that which would undermine the illusion of an unmediated access to the real and the sound assumption of a coherent and stable subjectivity." See "History and Intertextuality in Don DeLillo's *Libra, The Names,* and *Mao II," Contemporary Literature* 34 no. 2 (1993): 214. This reading would suggest that these completely intellectualized killings *undermine* the problem of mediation and disconnection in language, rather than performing it, as I argue.

4 Mark Osteen, *American Magic and Dread* (Philadelphia: University of Pennsylvania Press, 2000): 129. The cult's killing in denial of this idea of linguistic surplus, a kind of deconstructive denial of an early twentieth-century theory of reanimating language after the fall, becomes even more interesting when contrasted with the blatant use of sacrifice at the end of A. M. Homes's *Music for Torching* (New York: HarperCollins, 1999), as Chapter 3 will discuss.

5 For a more extensive exploration of DeLillo's philosophical connections to Heidegger, see Bonca, who points out—and I would agree—that the chief difference between the two is that whereas Heidegger expresses absolute confidence in the presence of Being, DeLillo's fiction shows him to be "never less than racked with ontological doubt" ("Don DeLillo's *White Noise," College Literature* 23 no. 2 (1996): 41 n. 5. What I think is striking about this particular novel, however, is the extent to which that doubt is accompanied by, and often overshadowed by, concerted attempts to believe that language *can* still connect us to Being.

6 Martin Heidegger, *Poetry, Language, Thought,* trans. Albert Hofstadter (New York: HarperCollins, 2001), 194, 205.

7   Frank Volterra's description of the film he plans to make of the cult killings reveals
    a visual obsession and unself-conscious impulse to construct a representation of the
    cult that would make sense and meaning out of their behavior. It seems to be just
    this attempt to make meaning out of visual order that prompts another former cult
    member to point out the incompatibility of film to the method of the cult: "It is not
    a film. It is a book" (212). It is in fact *this* book, and must be a book, because what
    the cult is doing has little to do with the landscape and people that Volterra wants
    so badly to organize and everything to do with words. In this way, *The Names*, and
    particularly the cult, asserts itself, within a culture whose self-image is becoming
    increasingly filmic, as insistently of and about the printed word, much as *House of
    Leaves* will do nearly two decades later (see Chapter 3).

8   Jacques Lacan, *Écrits*, trans. Alan Sheridan (New York: W. W. Norton and Company,
    1977), 140.

9   Heidegger, *Poetry, Language, Thought*, 65.

10 Lacan, *Écrits*, 65.

11 Jacques Lacan, *Seminar, Book XI*, trans. Alan Sheridan, ed. Jacques-Alain Miller (New
    York: W. W. Norton and Company, 1981), 62.

12 Lacan, *Écrits*, 103 (original italics).

13 Derrida, "Structure, Sign, and Play," 970.

14 Ibid., 970–1 (original italics).

15 Derrida's metaphor points forward to a collection of other monstrous baby figures
    that disturb our contemporary cultural landscape, including the giant Infant in
    Wallace's *Infinite Jest*, which emerges as a symbol of the infantile narcissistic tendency
    that is produced by and along with our cultural waste (see Chapter 2). Other
    examples of monstrous babies in contemporary culture—also implying a similar
    threat of infantile regression to solipsism—include the ravenous, tantrum-throwing
    toddler in Martin Amis's *London Fields* (New York: Vintage, 1991); the misshapen
    product in an industrial town of an ill-advised union in David Lynch's *Eraserhead*
    (1977); and the giant infant encountered by an adolescent while being prevented from
    joining the adult world in Hayao Miyazaki's animated film *Spirited Away* (2001). This
    pattern raises the question of whether Derrida's monstrous baby metaphor implies a
    similar solipsistic risk.

16 See *Introduction to the Work of Marcel Mauss*, trans. Felicity Baker (London:
    Routledge and Kegan Paul, 1987). Lévi-Strauss's claim, as noted and critiqued by
    Derrida, that "language can only have arisen all at once" (59) assumes that "the two
    categories of the signifier and the signified came to be constituted simultaneously
    and interdependently, as complementary units; whereas knowledge, that is, the
    intellectual process which enables us to identify certain aspects of the signified,
    one by reference to the other . . . only got started very slowly. It is as if humankind
    had suddenly acquired an immense domain and the detailed plan of that domain,
    along with a notion of the reciprocal relationship of domain and plan; but had spent
    millennia learning which specific symbols of the plan represented the different
    aspects of the domain" (60). "Knowledge," then, is the human process of making the
    universe signify by understanding the relationships between signifiers and signifieds,
    by bringing them together in signification.

17 Camus also implicitly links disaffection with the unmooring of the human being from
    meaning, when he locates absurdity not in the universe but in the confrontation of
    the unreasonable world with "the wild longing for clarity whose call echoes in the

human heart." See "The Fact of Absurdity," in *The Myth of Sisyphus and Other Essays*, trans. Justin O'Brien (New York: Knopf, 1955), 16. In this early treatise on theater of the absurd, Camus hopes to reveal the illusion of reality—its apparent order and rationality—not in order to express apathy for the world's irrationality but to expose the true cause of the existential yearning for meaning and identity that makes us human. Christopher Lasch, on the other hand, reads the rise of theater of the absurd as an enactment of a pathological "longing to be free from longing" (241) and its attendant disaffection, which characterize the late twentieth century. (See Chapter 2 for an elaboration of these ideas by Lasch.)

18 Lacan, *Écrits*, 106.

19 Ibid., 39.

20 DeLillo, interviewed by LeClair, in "An Interview with Don DeLillo," *Contemporary Literature* 23 no. 1 (1982): 24–5. See also Anthony DeCurtis's interview of DeLillo in *Introducing Don DeLillo*, ed. Frank Lentricchia (Durham: Duke University Press, 1991).

21 Or, as Foster puts it, "an area where speech and the prelinguistic verbal meet, . . . the brain's speech-maker producing its stuff without any allegiance to a symbolic order, without reference." See "Alphabetic Pleasures," in *Introducing Don DeLillo*, ed. Frank Lentricchia (Durham: Duke University Press, 1991), 166.

22 Here is another way in which this novel's idea of language contrasts with Derrida's: with the loss of this kind of "pure," "original" knowledge comes the *loss* of joy, not the finding of *jouissance* in "freeplay."

23 See p. 146. I am indebted to Vincent Pecora for pointing out this allusion.

24 Osteen also reads James as arriving at a fundamentally optimistic view of language (139), as James learns to view it in terms of "obligations to Others," in a reversal of the "Orientalism" he and his American friends have practiced throughout the novel. But whereas Osteen insists that *The Names* expresses an untroubled view of language as open to possibility and radical, authority-free renaming (141), I will argue that, though it distinguishes itself in DeLillo's oeuvre as passionate about language as possibility rather than as weapon or closed room, this novel nevertheless remains troubled by the authorial solipsism that Osteen reads as overcome.

25 The stark difference between the end of *Everything Is Illuminated* and the end of its embedded novel provides an excellent example of these two different concepts of language; see Chapter 5.

26 See Martin Hegel, *Introduction to Aesthetics*, trans. T. M. Knox (Oxford: Clarendon, 1979).

27 Dennis Foster reads this passage, in "Alphabetic Pleasures," as evidence that "what DeLillo explores so remarkably in this book is the complicity between the physical texture of our daily, rationally pursued lives and the needs that persist from what [he calls] a 'prelinguistic' life." By "prelinguistic," Foster means "a use of language that functions without symbolic representation" (159), and he links all of the novel's characters under its rubric (159). But this facile comparison overlooks important differences in responses to language in the novel specifically in characters' engagement in "symbolic representation."

28 Here he is like Volterra, who loves Del for her "dull empty perfect face," a face devoid of affect, that "never changes, no matter how tired she is, how sick, whatever" (203, 204).

29 Matthew J. Morris, "Murdering Words," *Contemporary Literature* 30 no. 1 (1989): 123.

30 Foster, "Alphabetic Pleasures," 168.

31 Bryant, "Discussing the Untellable," 20–1.

32 Derrida, "Structure, Sign, and Play," 970 (original italics).

33 David Bosworth also notices this self-consciousness, but he interprets it in a very
    different—and damning—way: "At least three times, [DeLillo] has Axton, in his
    first-person narration, observe self-consciously that the reader will want less
    'reflection,' more fast-paced scenes and dramatic action. But to prediagnose the
    complaints of one's readers is not to cure them. And to pretend so is, ironically, to
    mimic the error of the book's own cult members, their fixation on the totemic power
    of language, the author relying on magic instead of performance, hoping that through
    the mere act of 'naming' his fiction's faults, he can, like demons, cast them out."
    Bosworth's central "complaint" is that the novel is "curiously static," that the ideas in it
    "are not developed so much as described . . . and described . . . and described again."
    See "The Fiction of Don DeLillo," *Boston Review* 8 no. 2 (1983): 30. I argue that
    DeLillo does quite the opposite, describing the cult's ideas about language precisely
    so that James's and Owen's may develop over the course of the novel in changing
    relationship to the cult's. Further, I argue that the self-conscious quality of the book
    operates not as the author's "excuse" for poor writing but the mechanism by which
    this development may unfold.

34 See M. M. Bakhtin's *The Dialogic Imagination: Four Essays*, trans. Caryl Emerson and
    Michael Holquist, ed. Michael Holquist (Austin: University of Texas Press, 1981).

35 For Jacques Derrida's explanation of "auto-affection" see his *Of Grammatology*,
    trans. Gayatri Chakravorty Spivak (Baltimore: Johns Hopkins University
    Press, 1976).

36 See Matthew Morris's "Murdering Words" for a cogent discussion of colonialist
    impulses in the novel.

37 Paula Bryant cautions us against viewing the novel's structure in terms of the two
    versions of the Acropolis that *almost* bookend the novel, thus dismissing the final
    chapter, in which Tap takes over the narration. For Bryant, the final chapter is an
    "open-ended, exuberant, unorthodox coda" that prevents a "neat, circular return
    to [the novel's] beginning . . . in a traditional modernist manner" by "shattering
    [the novel's] structure in order to jar the reader in the same way that its eccentric
    language formations shatter words themselves" (24–5). In the place of this static
    modernist revision, Tap's writing offers a vision of language as "impl[ying] multiple
    new beginnings," "perpetual regeneration," and "a back-and-forth motion between
    the chapter and the previous episode" (25); Bryant reads the novel's ending as
    offering language that opens into "wordplay," "multiplicity," and "uncertainty," in
    opposition to a nostalgic modernist discovery about what language can do. This
    description of language sounds a great deal like Derrida's description of language
    as freeplay, her conclusion about the novel a lot like Matthew Morris's: "we should
    enjoy language as we do music . . . the author has given us word play for its own
    sake" (124). And however much she praises the "reaffirmative" power of language
    (25), her characterization (echoed by Bonca and then Osteen years later) of the final
    chapter as a coda—distinct from the rest of the text in both form and intent—implies
    a discreteness between Tap's writing and James's that, I argue, opposes this chapter's
    narrative function. Also, we can read the final chapter as providing a kind of
    circularity of its own: almost immediately after DeLillo introduces the Acropolis as
    looming symbol in need of translation, James sits down with his son to talk about
    Tap's writing (9).

38 Two striking examples: during the speaking in tongues, one man is "realing" in the corner (335)—one thinks that perhaps he is "getting real"—while another "dumb foundedly tried to speak," perhaps finding that he is dumb in the process (338).

39 See Bryant, "Discussing the Untellable."

40 Foster, "Alphabetic Pleasures," 172.

41 Thomas Carmichael, "Lee Harvey Oswald and the Postmodern Subject: History and Intertextuality in Don DeLillo's *Libra, The Names,* and *Mao II," Contemporary Literature* 34 no. 2 (1993): 212; Paul Maltby, "The Romantic Metaphysics of Don DeLillo," *Contemporary Literature* 37 no. 2 (1996): 262.

42 Christopher Lasch's *The Culture of Narcissism* (1979) argues that changing modes of production, the rise of advertisement and consumerism, and image culture have resulted in the deterioration of both individuals' senses of self and of family bonds, leading to a lack of adult authority and an increase in infantile behavior. See Chapter 2.

43 Don DeLillo, *White Noise* (New York: Penguin, 1985), 69. Subsequent references will be noted parenthetically.

44 Examples include Heinrich narrating events to a crowd of eagerly listening adults during the Airborne Toxic Event (123); Denise making her family react once the warning sirens have begun (119); the jet-setting Bee quietly condescending toward her intimidated parents (97).

45 As do his admissions that what he longs to survive is not death but his "deep terrible lingering fears" of death, which signs are for him "deep and real" (DeLillo, *White Noise,* 198). Babette makes similar conversions of death into less terrifying representations of itself when she imagines it as "nothing but sound," or, "white noise."

46 Another particularly wonderful conversion Jack manages is the transformation of the man who gave Babette Dylar—and her unwelcome lover—into a bit of receding static he can turn off like an old black-and-white television: "Panasonic" (241).

47 DeLillo's ending on "the dead" cannot help but allude to Joyce's short story by the same name, and here I suggest that the constant theme of regression, and the disaffecting irony through which that regression operates throughout the novel, constitutes an allusion to the ironic recursivity of "The Dead" as well. See Vincent P. Pecora's *Self and Form* (Baltimore: Johns Hopkins University Press, 1989). Therefore, much as we might like *White Noise* to end with a return to the real dead that haunts the novel throughout despite the characters' denial of it, even this textual allusion to Joyce points only to more disaffection and irony. This reading differs from those of the novel's previous critics. Mark Osteen provides a brief summary of critical interpretations of this highly contested ending (*American Magic and Dread,* 190 n. 19), and offers the reassurance that, whether we find in it a search for new kinds of spirituality or an admonition of the failings of postmodern American culture, DeLillo's refusal to take a clear stance "signifies DeLillo's recognition of his own imbrication in white noise: he admits that there is no privileged position—or at best a fleeting and fluctuating one—from which to comment." So for him the novel's ending represents success in terms of its own mimicry of the inhuman ambiguity of the mediating machine. But the novel's undeniable allusion to all that its literary ambiguity and inhumanity cannot repress makes such mimicry, to me, much more a sign of loss than any implication of gain or success.

48   Or, it is a denial of what Heidegger calls "anxiety," an anticipation of one's certain death that proves constitutive of Being, or "Dasein." The novel's investment in anxiety about death has long been recognized by critics; in fact, Mark Osteen (echoing Thomas LeClair) points out that DeLillo's working title for the novel at one time was "The American Book of the Dead" (*American Magic and Dread*, 165).

49   DeLillo, *White Noise*, 319.

2

"The Art's Heart's Purpose": Braving the Narcissistic Loop of *Infinite Jest*

We come to David Foster Wallace's fiction through the lens of irony—a tricky, risky, at times damaging lens—because Wallace instructs us to, putting us and his fiction in a precarious position. Wallace was the rare sort of writer who penned not only fiction but manifestos for fiction, and *Infinite Jest* is a novel conceived in the fire of such a manifesto. We cannot help but read this novel in the context of the agenda Wallace so clearly and passionately articulated shortly before its publication, and consider its success in implementing that agenda. Perhaps we might most accurately say that *Jest* is inarguably a brilliant achievement in exactly the terms Wallace set for fiction. But, like *The Names* and *White Noise*, its success must be measured more by the intensity of its struggle than by any clear overturning of cynical postmodernism's structures and themes. For while *Jest* creates a world that is fully aware of the empty irony that defines it and causes its immense suffering, it does not imagine for its characters a way to eschew that irony for the earnestness Wallace championed. Further, its inability to overcome the irony of which it is conscious is largely due to the novel's failure to recognize and address the cultural drive toward narcissism that fuels and is fueled by that irony.

In a 1993 interview with Larry McCaffery and essay on television, David Foster Wallace characterizes his writerly position as a third- or fourth-generation postmodern novelist who has inherited a world of problems from his literary ancestors, most fundamentally in the form of irony.[1] Though it was "just what the U. S. hypocrisy of the fifties and sixties called for," irony has become, according to Wallace, "an end in itself, a measure of hip sophistication and literary savvy."[2] This fall from biting instrumentality into vapid mimesis of an intellectually dead culture is inescapable, Wallace points out, because of irony's exclusively negative nature: "It's critical and destructive, a ground-clearing. Surely this is the way our postmodern fathers saw it. But irony's singularly unuseful when it comes to constructing anything to replace the hypocrisies it debunks."[3] Having done its job—clearing the literary landscape and imagination of outdated assumptions about both art and the world—irony is left to chatter away in toothless self-reflexivity. Further, Wallace establishes a crucial link between irony and mediation that exposes exactly the self-reflexive loop he must escape if he is to make a difference in his novels. Irony, he claims, lost its critical teeth when it became the very "aura" that surrounds us,[4] a reversal of its predecessor, earnestness, that could occur only through the magical ubiquity of television.[5] It was television's adoption of irony as its dominant mode in both advertising and programming that ruined the constructive possibilities of irony, making it such an invisible part of our environment that it transformed from reactionary to the norm. The castration of irony is for Wallace an important example of the destructiveness of unconscious mediation—of the ability for medium to eclipse message: television destroys all authority and then replaces it with itself, so that whatever it transmits disappears in the shadow of the authoritative fact of its transmission. Irony, as television's regular rhetoric, becomes then no longer a tool either in- or outside its waves and radiation but only fuel for the mediating machine. How can fiction devoted to the same techniques of irony and mediation convey more than *its* medium?

Wallace's stated solution to the late postmodernist's quandary is to turn away from the ironic quicksand he inherited and back to the kind of writing his ancestors left behind—a return to emotion, earnestness, belief, and straightforwardness.[6] He strives to write fiction that demands its reader recognize its mediating voices and in so doing invites the reader to make an emotional investment in it. The only way to construct a novel that enables the reader to do this, according to Wallace, is for the author to demand the same painful emotional investment and reaching out of himself:

> It seems like the big distinction between good art and so-so art lies somewhere in the art's heart's purpose, the agenda of the consciousness behind the text. It's got something to do with love. With having the discipline to talk out of the part of yourself that can love instead of the part that just wants to be loved.[7]

Later, at the end of his interview with McCaffery, Wallace will go so far as to characterize the proper work of the contemporary writer as a kind of parenting, a cleaning up of the mess inherited from his raucous predecessors that implies a need for the authority and responsibility that postmodernism in general is happy to have gotten rid of. Through all of these surprisingly traditional tasks he assigns to the contemporary writer runs the same implacable current: the writer's need to forgo the solipsistic disaffection that had become identical with postmodern irony in order to reach out to his reader, and create characters that can reach out to each other in earnest connection as well.

But before he has even finished his manifesto, Wallace begins to demonstrate the difficulty of being earnestly other-directed in a culture defined by disaffected irony and self-interest. In the interview with McCaffery, he mocks his own sincere investment in writing with love—calling for an accompaniment of woodwinds, apologizing for being "sappy"—and worries about the unhipness of his "art's heart's purpose."[8] And rather than end his television essay on the near-lyrical vision of a next generation of postmodern writers willing to risk "sentimentality, melodrama. Credulity," Wallace resorts to a snide example of exactly the kind of "I don't really mean what I say" variety of irony he has criticized in this same essay: "Today's most engaged young fiction does seem like some kind of line's end's end. I guess that means we all get to draw our own conclusions. Have to. Are you immensely pleased."[9] The ironic uncertainty he expresses here in both content and grammatical evasiveness—with the missing final question mark—undercuts all the heartfelt assertions about selflessness and love that have come before. How can a writer, however well intentioned, survive his own unconscious addiction to irony? How can a society? Wallace will ask these questions through

Infinite Jest, with a predictably problematic answer. For his greatest accomplishment in the novel will be the construction not of a character strong enough to escape the ironic trap the novel has set but rather of one earnest enough to suffer the irony, and brave enough to struggle heroically to escape it, but still doomed, almost sadistically so, by a novel that does not overcome its own ironic ambivalence.

This ironic conundrum is particularly striking and stubborn because it persists in spite of Wallace's clear acknowledgment of it: "[T]his stuff has permeated the culture. It's become our language; we're so in it we don't even see that it's one perspective, one among many possible ways of seeing. Postmodern irony's become our environment."[10] He uses a remarkably similar metaphor to describe drug addiction in *Infinite Jest*, when Don Gately recalls a joke told by a longtime Alcoholics Anonymous veteran after newcomer Gately has raged against the program: "This wise old whiskery fish swims up to three young fish and goes, 'Morning, boys, how's the water?' and swims away; and the three young fish watch him swim away and look at each other and go, 'What the fuck is water?' and swim away."[11] That night Gately dreams of being in water "the same temperature he is" (449), signaling his dawning awareness of the treachery of an addiction so thoroughly permeating that one can no longer perceive where the addiction ends and the self begins. The fish joke diagnoses the problem of addiction; Gately's astute dream begins to move him from diagnosis to solution. Wallace's alignment of ironic disaffection with unconscious addiction through this metaphor shared by interview and novel suggests his hope that (quite in contrast to the evidence of interview and essay) a similar awareness that we are all swimming in irony may lead to our own growth out of it. So his creation of Hal Incandenza and Don Gately as characters in *Infinite Jest* who register the threat of irony and apathy and so struggle to swim against the tide indicates the novel's clear intent to enact Wallace's agenda for redemptive postmodern fiction. But Wallace does not seem fully to confront, either in this interview (or the many that came after the book's publication) or writing his novel, the difficulty of positioning himself outside of the society he consciously critiques, and the impossibility of successfully critiquing a society whose sinister and powerful underpinnings remain largely unacknowledged: not just destructive irony but the pathological narcissism that makes us feel, when we try to reach out to others through earnest communication, like fish out of water.

The problem of language as solution

In his interview with Larry McCaffery, Wallace speaks at length about his sense that Wittgenstein's work (in his late *Philosophical Investigations*) details our "tragic fall" into a language that contains us completely and yet keeps us forever disconnected from the world to which it is referring. What compels Wallace about Wittgenstein's philosophy, however, is not the "closed loop" of language in which we find ourselves trapped but Wittgenstein's later analysis of this linguistic trap as "the single most comprehensive and beautiful argument against solipsism that's ever been made."[12] Wittgenstein orchestrates this paradox, according to Wallace, by arguing "that for language even to be possible, it must always be a function of relationships between persons. . . . So he makes language dependent on human community." Rather than seem an untenable contradiction, this intimate human connection at the heart of a completely inhuman, self-contained linguistic system strikes Wallace as the great beauty of Wittgenstein's formulation, and one he accepts completely. It is this belief in the possibility, even the necessity, of human connection via a language that separates us even from the world we live in that allows Wallace to begin from a very different place regarding language than many of his contemporaries, even than DeLillo with his admiration for linguistic pattern: Wallace declares that "language and linguistic intercourse is, in and of itself, redeeming, remedying."[13]

The task remains for him to demonstrate, via his own linguistic construction, exactly how human beings find redemption and connect with each other through a fallen language. Part of Wallace's answer to this conundrum lies in his stated goal of using his fiction to create a relationship between author and reader in which both collaborate in creating a novel out of their shared empathy for the characters' suffering:

> We all suffer alone in the real world; true empathy's impossible. But if a piece of fiction can allow us imaginatively to identify with characters' pain, we might then also more easily conceive of others identifying with our own. This is nourishing, redemptive.[14]

Then he must find a way to invite and enable this readerly empathy and meaning-making strictly through language in opposition to the disaffecting and distancing tendencies of a language seen as broken and dehumanizing in much of contemporary literature.

Wallace communicates through *Infinite Jest* this invitation, even need for the reader to intervene in language and interpret or wrench it into meaning by presenting language in the novel as a distinct problem. It is a proliferating, out-of-control hydra that cannot be contained in the novel's 981 initial pages, spawning nearly 100 pages of footnotes, many of which themselves run several pages, as if chunks of the text continue reproducing beyond its own confines. Many of the footnotes simply define jargon and acronyms that invade the novel through the worlds of drugs and tennis, implying the incorporation of multiple, ever-fissioning vocabularies that require yet further appeals to language in a kind of delayed or receding act of interpretation. The scope of this linguistic reproduction as problem becomes clear when we consider that it is not only the culture of disease (junior-tennis training being consistently compared to and linked with drug addiction in the novel) that creates the proliferation, but that the same condition emerges from the culture of recovery: the Alcoholics Anonymous program presents itself specifically as an alternative *language* to that of addiction. It creates jargon for each of its core concepts, usually using a proper noun, signaling its attempt to remap the linguistic landscape of its lost adherents. In this way, AA provides one of the novel's many examples of ironically self-defeating cures: adrift and confused in a world whose language has become meaningless, these people who have lost their senses of self turn first to drugs as a way to forget the self and then to AA and its promise of a new language they can believe in. But its insistence that members follow the program even, and usually, *without* understanding it indicates that they have simply substituted for the nihilism of our crisis of signification an equally meaningless language in which they choose to believe.[15]

Thus, *Infinite Jest*, itself a linguistic creation, offers problematic language as solution to the problem of language, a linguistic house of cards requiring constant hands-on attention from any reader wishing to negotiate it. Certainly, part of our "share of the linguistic work"[16] that Wallace knowingly hands us is the job of containing the mess and cleaning it up a bit—of building a foundation to prevent the novel's imminent disintegration into babble. Indeed, the concept of "babble" operates quite differently in *Jest* than in the two DeLillo novels examined in Chapter 1. Hal's descent into monstrous babble at the end of his story, and at the beginning of the novel, introduces the novel as a long-winded, Shahrazadian use of language to stave off Hal's solipsistic death-by-babble. The wraith/Jim Incandenza, however, describes "aural realism" specifically as a kind of *productive* babble: "it was real life's real egalitarian babble of figurantless crowds, of the animate world's real agora, the babble of crowds every member of which was the central and articulate protagonist of his own entertainment" (835–6). The wraith/Incandenza believes that such babble honors our real-life multiplicity of voices more thoroughly than can any artistic construction that privileges certain voices at the expense of silencing others (making them into "figurants"). Wallace's reference here to babble "Or possibly *Babel*" (1076 n. 342) clearly indicates that the wraith/Incandenza believes his constructed babble to be exactly the kind of ecstatic, truth-filled language that DeLillo's novels first hoped and then failed to recreate. And critics of *Infinite Jest* have asserted that the productive babble of "aural realism" is precisely what Wallace has produced with his novel.[17] But I argue that, for all its multiplicity of voices, narrative strains, and perspectives, the novel reads more as a readerly intervention against babble than an indulgence in it. For it asks readers to make of the sequential multiplicity a coherent story by paying attention to *individual* voices at individual moments, to recognize unique human stories within the linguistic fray. Further critiquing the wraith/ Incandenza's faith in babble is the fact that Incandenza hoped to save his son Hal—to awaken him from the silent role of "figurant" he had chosen to play—specifically through an infantile experience of babble through the film *Infinite Jest* that, in the end, turned out to be more solipsistic death sentence than awakening.

Rather than positing a way back to meaningful infantile babble, then, *Jest* suggests that the only path to meaningful language is one in whose careful construction the reader painstakingly contributes. Which vocabularies and explanatory footnotes will we deem worthy of our careful attention? Which will we allow to fade into the textual blur? The novel's (and author's) refusal adequately to mediate language displaces the task onto the reader, whose exhausting attempts to, quite literally, come to terms with the entirety of the effusive text align her with the novel's own linguistic gatekeepers, Avril and Joelle. Faced with a world gone crazy in so many ways, their shared reaction is to exert control where they feel they can—over the very grammar of language, as we must do over nearly 1,100 pages of *Infinite Jest*.[18]

Language's constant assertion of itself as problem, then, insists that we attend to it in productive ways, *not* that we seek ways out of it. In fact the novel suggests quite clearly that such an escape is not possible. Catherine Nichols seems to me to misread redemption in the novel through just this avenue when she interprets *Jest*'s "linguistic grotesqueries" as examples of the novel's "aesthetic nonconformity"[19] to which we must attend in order to fulfill Wallace's claim that "any possible redemption requires first to face what's dreadful, what we want to deny."[20] But this reading assumes that attending to what is "dreadful" implies attending to what *escapes* language; Nichols goes so far as to locate the novel's greatest successes in overcoming the culture of irony in its moments when linguistic communication absolutely breaks down. For her, the most impressive evidence of the triumph of Hal Incandenza and Don Gately over the superficial, ironic, disaffected culture against which they struggle is their complete withdrawal from the culture's sanctioned symbolic order toward an inner earnestness and self-expression, which she characterizes as virtuous in the context of such a symbolically minded culture.

Nichols's reading here of the tyranny of the "symbolic order," together with her earlier claim that the novel points us away from linguistic transgressions in favor of the more revealing, unsymbolized "Otherness" of the novel, implies a Lacanian reading that valorizes the pre-Symbolic as site of the real that our culture has forgotten. But this equation of all coherent language with the masking, limiting "Law" that, for Lacan, prevents us from reaching the real, opposes Wallace's own stated commitment to language as operating through human connection to enact redemption. Indeed, even for Lacan, to escape the paternal "Law" of the symbolic order with its insistent Oedipalization—to attempt to approach the real that resides in the pre-Symbolic realm—means abandoning the language that has replaced one's desire for the mother in favor of an infantile state that eschews language for the pleasure of desiring the mother as self, of pure solipsism.[21] And it is here that Hal and Don end, completely cut off from the world and desiring only their own infantile fulfillment (as I argue below).[22] Celebrating this kind of solipsism in a novel whose main thrust throughout is its characters' struggles to escape the culture's various solipsistic traps (drugs, fame, entertainment, etc.), and whose author so passionately argues for the need to promote empathy and human relationships in fiction above all else, makes as little sense as celebrating an escape from the symbolic order that Wallace believes offers a path to redemption. Rather, it is his belief in language's ability to mean and forge human relationships—not in spite of the necessity of linguistic mediation but through it, as the novel demonstrates in the reader's recuperative work—that aligns the concept of language and healing espoused by Wallace and the novel with redemptive language as theorized by Freud, rather than the tyrannizing symbolic order of Lacan.[23]

In Freud's theory of the human mind and its ability (or inability) to interact meaningfully with the outer world, language, especially speech, serves as the primary tool for communicating and understanding that mind—understanding being inseparable from communicating—in an intimate process of growth and discovery that requires an earnest connection between two people, analysand and analyst. Though his concept of the "talking cure" evolved dramatically through the decades in which he refined and expanded his theory of psychoanalysis,[24] Freud never deviated from his core belief that one could only understand and cure him- or herself through expression of his or her fears and desires to a mediating other. But in his "Remembering, Repeating, and Working Through" (1914), Freud complicates the idea of the talking cure by declaring that the goal of the analyst must not simply be to make the unconscious conscious, but to make conscious the mind's unconscious *resistances* to conscious memory by allowing the patient to transfer his or her unconscious feelings onto the analyst. When he radically redefined his theory of the drives in *Beyond the Pleasure Principle* (1920), he implied a similar reworking of psychoanalytical method, or the talking cure: by establishing the pleasure principle as secondary to a more compelling, primary repetition compulsion (or death instinct), Freud discovered that it was not the unconscious that resisted traumatic memory but the *conscious* mind. Thus the analyst's efforts to help the patient work through traumatic memory consist of "procuring [from the resisting, conscious mind] the toleration of that unpleasure by an appeal to the reality principle."[25] The "talking cure," then, evolves into an attempt by the analyst to convince the patient to postpone feelings of satisfaction and repress his or her instinct to regress in order to attain that satisfaction, all in the name of the "reality principle" that asks us to put personal growth over our fear of unpleasure.[26] But what happens to this unpleasurable talking cure in a culture that programs its members to desire pleasure—in exactly Freud's sense of lack of excitation, or discomfort—over all else? How feasible is such an approach to understanding and healing the self through the pain of facing present and past trauma in a society that promotes, as its painless alternative, infantile regression to total fulfillment? This promotion of regression to infantile pleasure amounts to promoting the resistance that causes repetition compulsion rather than painful understanding. Thus the novel, which in its collection of storytelling voices, and especially in its AA subculture, can appear to attempt a talking cure, instead creates the looping repetition of narcissistic infantile regression that contains and thwarts the attempt.

Narcissism as postmodern despair

Everything that David Foster Wallace needed to know about the peculiarly postmodern angst of late twentieth-century-American culture he found on a cruise ship. In "A Supposedly Fun Thing I'll Never Do Again" (1997),[27] the eponymous essay in a collection examining absurdities and grotesqueries of American culture, Wallace embarks on a mission for *Harper's Magazine* to apply his quirky wisdom to a seemingly innocuous American experience. Instead, he gradually finds in the nonstop flow of staffers' servitude and guests' indulgence the secret to our very American brand of despair. In fact his essay and trip begin with a keen sense of despair, of the usual Modernist-existential sort; associating it with the ocean around him, he refers to it, á la Hemingway, as "primordial *nada*" (262). Accordingly, he reads the ship's ubiquitous "YOU ARE HERE" maps as reorientation not on the ships' decks but in the universe, as reassurance of the passengers' mere existence (264 n. 8). But when his despair only deepens and ripens over two weeks of uninterrupted self-indulgence, Wallace begins to understand that cruise ship culture breeds a particular kind of despair rooted not in existential angst but in the solipsistic narcissism of contemporary American culture: his need to validate his existence ceases when he learns, from the cruise, the superior reassurance of ceasing to need.

Wallace finds that the cruise line promises exactly this needlessness with its "authoritarian" advertising strategy, whose "near-imperative use of the second person" (267) dictates not only what readers will experience on the cruise but *how* they will perceive and interpret it. This promise to relieve the passenger of all obligation not just for orchestrating a good time but for having it as well Wallace calls "near-parental," an assumption of responsibility so absolute as to remove him as thinking adult from the entire experience. Indeed, Wallace realizes that infantilizing removal of responsibility for the self is exactly the point, is both sign and endgoal of the ultimate luxury of doing "*Absolutely Nothing*" (268, original italics):

> How long has it been since you did Absolutely Nothing? I know exactly how long it's been for me. I know how long it's been since I had every need met choicelessly from someplace outside me, without my having to ask or even acknowledge that I needed. And that time I was floating, too, and the fluid was salty, and warm but not too-, and if I was conscious at all I'm sure I felt dreadless, and was having a really good time, and would have sent postcards to everyone wishing they were here. (268)

What the ship promises with its obsessive desire to relieve the passenger of all decisions and duties that both stress and denote adult life is the chance to withdraw entirely from a world in which we owe ourselves to others and to indulge in one in which we must "do nothing" but satisfy ourselves. Thus its offer to "pamper" us implies, as Wallace cleverly points out, a promise to swaddle—or diaper—us in the bliss of the infant's narcissistic existence (261), as Wallace perversely swaddles *Infinite Jest*'s characters in the Year of the Adult Depend Undergarment. To some extent the ship fulfills its promise to mimic the mother's womb: Wallace admits that he sleeps marvelously on the heavy seas, for "in heavy seas you feel rocked to sleep, with the windows' spume a gentle shushing, the engines' throb a mother's pulse" (285). But ultimately he comes to understand that this promise to give us exactly what we want—freedom from all need—operates as the source of the ship's production of despair.

For after days of being almost forcibly gratified, cleaned-up after, and guided, Wallace finds himself looking longingly from his own island of luxury to a far superior and *more* luxurious cruise ship anchored nearby. In this longing he realizes the sinister result of his pampered days: he is desperately dissatisfied. Here, then, is the "psychological syndrome" that's got them all chatting like lunatics in the Lido Lounge—the longer they are indulged, the greater their dissatisfaction becomes, until "grievances that started picayune . . . quickly become nearly despair-grade" (315). So part of the problem lies in the promise that one can be truly, wholly, unendingly satisfied. But a more terrifying element of the problem is how very much we want to believe such satisfaction is possible—our willingness to believe the lie, our *need* to believe it, a need that Wallace identifies as a definitively American one: "the source of all the dissatisfactions isn't the *Nadir* at all but . . . that ur-American part of me that craves and responds to pampering and passive pleasure: the Dissatisfied Infant part of me, the part that always and indiscriminately WANTS" (315–16). Wanting alone, of course, poses no threat: we are born wanting; our insatiability is "a priori" (317). But despair grows out of our willingness to believe not just "a big one" told by the cruise company but "*the* Big One," the lie at the heart of a whole culture of despair: that "my Infantile part will be sated" (316, original italics). His is a postmodern, consumer-culture reworking of Modernist, existential despair after it has been thoroughly reshaped by the authoritarian hand of this floating model of contemporary society.[28]

Of course, the cruise ship as Wallace experiences it does not delineate a thorough microcosm of American society, but it certainly represents that portion with the consumer power to influence what we call American society. It is a self-selected collection of people whose main goals while on the ship consist of consuming (food, drinks, passive entertainment, material goods) and being done for, and whose desire for passivity extends to the willingness to be disempowered by the decision-making, care-taking staff of the ship. These are also people who have likely been drawn to the cruise experience by the same highly mediating and manipulative advertising materials that Wallace details in his essay: they come on the ship hoping to *become* the happy people in the ads whose images reflect for them the identity they lack in their real lives but hope to attain during the unreal life of the cruise. As such they are models of what happens in American culture when one submits to the promises of consumption, disempowerment, and mediation as avenues to selfhood and self-fulfillment: they become caught in the cycle of needing to consume and merge into media to compensate for social and individual identities they lack, then withdrawing further to deny that the craving continues. They are, in other words, a perfect model for the crisis of contemporary American culture as outlined by Christopher Lasch in *The Culture of Narcissism* and depicted by Wallace in *Infinite Jest*.

Though Lasch's social critique has failed to gain wide academic acceptance (his nostalgia for paternalism and tendency to confuse women and children in their need of it go a long way toward explaining why), his examination of narcissism in late twentieth-century-American culture proves useful in explaining the phenomenon of postmodern despair articulated so clearly in Wallace's cruise ship essay and demonstrated by his novel. According to Lasch, our epidemic of narcissism accompanies an epidemic loss of self, both arising out of our media age. He turns to Susan Sontag's description of the modern world as the "society of the spectacle" to point out our crippling dependence on images of the world to validate our realities, on images of the self to infuse us with a sense of selfhood (47–8).[29] In a society in which "our sense of reality appears to rest . . . on our willingness to be taken in by the staged illusion of reality,"[30] the theater of the absurd arose as an early artistic attempt to expose just this dependence on illusion. In a radical redefinition of "realism," playwrights such as Brecht turned Ibsen's formula on its head, forcing viewers to confront the structures of illusion in theater rather than working to make them invisible. For these writers, "the reality they wish to re-create in their works is that of illusion":[31] Brecht intended the *emfremdungs Effekt*, or alienation effect, of his productions to prevent viewers from being lulled into any comforting illusion of reality, instead forcing them to pay attention to the ideas and political content of his plays.[32]

This reversal of the tenets of realism prefigures exactly what Wallace maintains is one of his primary goals for fiction—exposing mediation to his readers as a representation of reality's multiple illusions, rather than using illusion to represent reality.[33] Lasch cites as societal consequence of this culture of reproduction, mediation, and the image the individual's "uncertainty about what is real."[34] It is a short step from losing a sense of reality to losing the sense that anything is significant, and one that Lasch makes as well as Wallace: Lasch warns of the same cultural and individual disaffection bred by a culture of mediation that Wallace, in his interview with Larry McCaffery (148), strives to banish with his own earnest writing. Also like Wallace in his essay on television, Lasch blames the culture of consumption enabled by a culture of mediation for exacerbating this disaffection, in that a culture of consumption "promises to fill the aching void" that it creates, and that it steadfastly refuses to fill.[35] Further, Lasch, like Wallace, blames the media and its accompanying consumer society for establishing television and other technologies of mediation as authorities that replace traditional paternal authorities, creating disaffected mothers and fathers as a consequence.[36] These similarities shared by Wallace and Lasch in diagnosing societal ills of the late twentieth century, spanning 1979 to 1993, build a remarkable alignment between a postmodern movement in late twentieth-century literature and a conservative social critique that, almost 25 years after its publication, has never gained acceptance in socially liberal academic circles. Such an alignment speaks both to the radicalism of Wallace's movement away from irony and unreflexive mediation in the context of contemporary literature and criticism, and the prescience of Lasch's social critique.

But Lasch's critique goes farther than Wallace does in the essay and interview that claim to establish an agenda—of writing earnestly to "*give* the reader something," and "to ask the reader really to feel something"[37] for his next creative work. While Wallace simply diagnoses the problem of entrenched irony in media and literature, Lasch critiques American culture as a whole in terms of his broader accusation of a crisis of liberalism. For Lasch, technologies of reproduction and mediation are just one cause of the problems that face Americans as they head into the "me" decade of the 1980s, and even then they are not so much cause as symptom of a much larger threat: the increased and destructive socialization of every facet of American life, and thus the attack on individual power, authority, and so selfhood. Flanks of this attack appear in many forms, of which mediation is one. But Lasch traces the roots of late twentieth-century culture to changes in modes of production that ushered in the century and began a transference of power to corporations and the state and away from the individual and families. The resulting loss of individual authority in relation to one's job, one's spouse or children, even one's ability to view the self and the world free from mediating images leads to a profound sense of loss—of selfhood, of connections to others, of the ability to situate oneself in the world. For Lasch, corporate demands, state dictate, and media and consumerist images rush in to fill that loss, leaving the individual completely dependent and childlike, infantilized.

Lasch's more expansive view of our culture of mediation and disaffection, then, allows him to consider and connect social forces and symptoms that escape Wallace's media-minded analysis in both interview and essay. Most fundamental to Lasch's critique, and most notably absent from Wallace's own, is the problem of narcissism as a central feature of modern American society that cripples individuals and prevents or poisons interpersonal relationships. Our thoroughly mediated world causes us obsessively to consume images of the self; the culture of advertising and consumption enabled by this mediation stimulate "infantile cravings" for fulfillment that can never be satisfied;[38] the destruction of paternal authority—or, more palatably, of our ability to believe in the authority of the individual—encourages the exercising of these infantile impulses and discourages intimate human interaction. Ultimately, Lasch declares, all we can feel is a "longing to be free from longing,"[39] the desire to escape this endless escalation of unfulfillable desire. This desire to be free from desire, Lasch recognizes, is really a desire to be the infant again, caressed in a womb of absolute self-fulfillment. Thus Lasch's analysis centers upon a cultural phenomenon that Wallace's pre-*Infinite Jest* critique elides: infantilizing narcissism as a central feature of modern American society.

An overused and overgeneralized word, "narcissism" as defined by Freud takes two significantly distinct forms: primary and secondary. Essentially the directing of libidinal energy back toward the self rather than attaching it to external objects, narcissism begins in the human infant as a normal stage of psychological development: the infant first expresses sexual (externally directed) instincts purely in the service of satisfying the ego-instincts. Therefore the earliest sexual object, or object of libidinal attachment, is the mother, she who satisfies all needs, and whom the infant perceives as part of him- or herself.[40] In desiring the mother, the infant is simply desiring the self, and existing in a closed loop of constant fulfillment that seems to flow from no external source. Once the infant perceives his or her separation from the mother, however, the "unassailable libidinal position" of absolute self-fulfillment is no longer possible. So Freud posits a "secondary" narcissism, in which adults who remain dedicated to the satisfaction of the self create an "ideal ego" out of all they value in themselves and extend their libidinal energy to that ideal. In other words, adult narcissists love others for reflecting what they perceive as best about themselves in an attempt to approximate that closed-loop bliss of infantile self-fulfillment that ego formation forces them to abandon.

Lasch expands this theory of secondary or pathological narcissism through the work of Melanie Klein, who locates in that early separation of infant from mother the rage and aggressivity toward the original libidinal object that later accompanies the adult's pathological recreation of the narcissistic state. Having internalized the feelings of disappointment and aggression first extended to the mother, the child feels threatened by them and so "attempts to compensate himself for his experiences of rage and envy with fantasies of wealth, beauty, and omnipotence." Not surprisingly, Lasch asserts that "intense feelings of emptiness and inauthenticity" accompany these images of greatness, a result of the ego's obsession with the inability of external objects to fulfill it.[41] Reading the pathology of the individual as the key to an entire society (a methodology modeled for Lasch by Freud himself), Lasch thus explains the shallow and endless cravings of a society based on consumption and mediating images through the impossible desires of the individual longing to return to the bliss of infantile narcissism.

Evidence of this desire, and of its pathologically compensatory adult narcissism, permeates *Infinite Jest*: It is the reason the residents at the Ennet House have become addicted to drugs, and the reason many of the residents at the Ennet Tennis Academy (ETA) play competitive tennis. So it is significant that, for all his careful commentary in interviews surrounding the novel on threats against our humanity lurking in contemporary American society, Wallace does not overtly grapple with the despair-inducing seduction of narcissism until his 1996 cruise ship essay.[42] It is as if two weeks of cruising enable him finally to articulate what shadowed his novelistic writing for several years, and to define what troubles, murkily, an otherwise comic novel. Whereas Wallace devotes constant attention in *Jest*, as in his critiques, to the problems of irony and mediation, infantilization and narcissism emerge in the novel not so much as problems consciously to be solved as a deadly undertow against which the novel struggles—and, as I read the novel, fails—to make forward progress. It is this unconscious stagnation in the culture of narcissism that ultimately prevents the novel from fully accomplishing the goals Wallace sets forth in his agenda for novelistic redemption: the nagging compulsion of narcissism, left unfaced and unresolved, quietly but insistently overwhelms the considerable bravery exhibited by the novel, its author, and its characters as they labor to recreate individual integrity and communal connection from their cultural ruins.

Critical treatment of the novel dances around the treachery of this narcissistic desire, while reading it primarily as a success in fulfilling Wallace's artistic agenda.[43] N. Katherine Hayles's argument, for example, acknowledges the psychological dilemma that I am exploring at the heart of the novel, by reading in the text repeated evidence of the "illusion of autonomy"—or our inability to fulfill ourselves completely —and the "fact of recursivity"—or our need to extend ourselves to others in order to function not just as a society but as sane and healthy individuals.[44] But rather than view recursivity as the novel's noble endgoal, I point out that this illusion of autonomy, so clearly and consciously dashed, as Hayles rightly claims, by instances of the "fact" of recursivity in the novel, still persists through narcissistic desire as an irrational, largely unconscious longing that relentlessly afflicts characters despite their attempts to deny or escape it. In this way, "recursivity" manifests not only as a method of escaping an illusion of our autonomous selves but also, and even more forcefully, as evidence of the destructive implications of a culture that counters the potentially solipsistic autonomy of the individual with the certainly self-obliterating invasion of the self via mediation. For in this culture, and in this novel, the extreme opposite of autonomy does not lie in healthy, life-enhancing relationships with the world and others but in the crippling, utterly solipsistic trap of *dependence*: it is not for nothing that the bulk of the novel's action occurs during "The Year of the Depend Adult Undergarment," and that virtually every attempt to resist externally mediating forces—whether drugs, coaching, or screaming cultural productions like entertainment and advertising—results only in further dependence. Therefore, even as Wallace struggles to create for his characters a way out of the cultural quagmire in which his novel places them, *Infinite Jest* instead depicts what happens when recursivity, through the society of consumption and mediation, becomes pathological—trapping one within the self rather than freeing one from it.

The legacy of pathological narcissism

The pathological recursivity of secondary narcissism presents as the novel's foundation, the sickness from which, historically, all else in the novel springs. Tucked seemingly randomly into the chronological disarray, the novel's temporally initial moment in fact establishes the pattern of parental selfishness that will poison generations in its relentless cycle: "WINTER B. S. 1960—TUCSON AZ" offers the childhood story of Jim Incandenza, Hal's father, through the impossible point of view of the man in such pain that he orchestrated a way to die by exploding his head in a microwave oven. The persistence of this voice from beyond the grave speaks to its undying effect on the boys it ushered into the world, which we see from the seeds of fears, abilities, and sure self-destruction that Jim's father passes on to them. Jim learns from his father that "You are going to be a great tennis player. I was near-great. You will be truly great," a dictate and obsession Jim passed on to Hal (*IJ* 158); he learns his phobia of spiders, which he passed on as a roach phobia to Orin; he learns to view drugs as an alternative to the pain of athletic performance; and he learns to pass these traits on to his own boys in the name of his own retrospective need to construct an accomplished self through the mirrors of his children, as Jim's father clearly attempts in this moment to do with him. Wallace's careful placement of this episode affirms, or foreshadows, its function as root cause in the narrative: it follows on the heels of the first account of Hal's rocketing explosion of tennis potential, and accurately suggests what awaits him on his way down.

Not only is the novel well aware of this cycle of narcissistic parental cruelty—depicting it as equally compelling and inescapable, if not more so, than the more commonly recognized cycles of drug addiction and physical abuse—but the children who suffer it and pass it on prove quite aware of it as well. The Incandenza boys make their own behind-the-scenes film of the world of junior tennis titled "Tennis and the Feral Prodigy,"[45] the title alone suggesting the paradoxical reality that prodigies are pathologically constructed, not born. Written by Mario and voiced by Hal, the film recreates the making of a tennis star, from keeping one's keys on the floor to nurturing that one great arm through constant ball-squeezing. But before a boy can get to these practices one other thing must happen; he must "[h]ave a father whose own father lost what was there" (173). Bringing far more bitterness to their documentation of their fathers' near-abusive attempts to reflect themselves in their lives are the boys at MIT, whose on-air performances of "Those Were the Legends That Formerly Were" convey both their keen awareness that their fathers' failures stand behind the abuse, and their own steadfast refusal to bow to that pressure.

Most troubling about this chain of abuse in which each father exploits his son in his attempt to reflect a reassuring image of himself is that ironic awareness itself cannot stop the cycle. After all, Jim's radical departure from tennis shortly after establishing ETA to build a career in filmmaking signals a profound attempt to separate himself from the thing that threatens to bind him, cruelly, to his sons. And his films themselves can be read as vehicles for exploring his destructive self-reflexivity. Most famously, *The Joke*, in which the audience finds itself faced only with an image of its watching self, and

The Medusa v. The Odalisque, in which these two mythological creatures battle using their reflections while characters in the audience become turned to gems and stone, explore the destructive narcissism and pathological recursivity of both filmmaker and film viewer. But the moments in his films of "unhip earnestness" (289) and "flashes of real emotion" (741) perceived by Joelle and Hal suggest that his work represents not Jim's unreflective reproduction of self-reflexivity but rather an exploration of the mechanisms that surround us with it and threaten to eclipse even these small attempts at earnest human connection.

However self-absorbed his films, this adult investigation of the child's experience is surely preferable to the unexamined transmission of it under the guise of bettering a new generation. For under Marathe's defense of the need for well-chosen belief, seemingly so wise and mature in comparison to Steeply's insistence on the American privileging of absolute freedom, seethes exactly this sinister presumption of a father's right to shape a child in his image: "How to choose any but a child's greedy choices if there is no loving-filled father to guide, inform, teach the person how to choose?" (320). Marathe's passionate defense of paternalism, so sane in the face of a country full of people willing to line up to view a film they know will destroy their minds in the process of rendering pleasure, reveals its narcissism once Marathe fully explains his concept of belief. He does so through the story of meeting his wife, in which he chooses to love her without knowing her and insists on giving his life to her after finding she is a victim of the Concavity, having no skull, no sanity, and far too many eyes, cavities, and leaking orifices. He chooses to love her to rid himself of "the old despair of before choosing" (780), and it is this model of self-reflecting "love" and "belief" that Marathe argues should be narcissistically passed down to America's children.

Of course, fathers are not the only perpetrators of this abuse, and Avril provides the novel's key model of the self-indulgent mother. Joelle remembers that "Orin described his childhood's mother as his emotional sun" (738), unwittingly providing the perfect metaphor for a woman who extends her emotional energy to her children only so that they could reflect it back to herself; in adulthood, Orin contrasts this innocent child's vision of his mother with a more savvy vision of her as "The Black Hole of Human Attention" (521). Hal describes the same selfish tendency when he notes that "to report any sort of need or problem is to mug her" (523).

And, true to form, Avril's central failure as a parent is her absolute inability to put her own needs aside in order to answer her children's. As foundational to the novel and its Incandenza narrative as Jim's recollections of his father is the story of Hal's eating basement mold, a defining family fable that reappears several times throughout the novel, most significantly in the episode that opens the novel but ends the story. In this account, always presented through Orin's mediation as a moment of intense dramatic import, Avril works in her garden plot in her obsessive-compulsive way, wearing layers of bags and plastic and a face mask to keep herself clean (an obsession that runs throughout the novel in ironic contrast to the constant seepage of waste going on all around her). Into the scene toddles a 4-year-old Hal carrying "a rhombusoid patch of fungus ... sort of nasal green, black-speckled, hairy like a peach is hairy ... a patch of very bad-news-type mold" (1042 n. 234), and when he declares,

"I ate this," the purpose of the scene becomes clear: not the trauma of Hal's eating mold but the trauma of Avril in her "perfect box of string" (1043 n. 234) dealing with her child's disgusting transgression.[46] She can bring herself to touch neither Hal nor the mold, running from him screaming while he follows her crying, until a neighbor finally arrives to take care of everyone. It is a formative memory for Orin, who repeats it in detail in response to questions about his family, as well as for Hal, who explains to the Arizona recruiters his utter incoherence and disaffection, the ruination of his mind, as "something I ate" (10). This "something" is both the mold of his childhood and the ruinous realization of his mother's absolute self-absorption revealed by that mold, as well as the DMZ we can assume he ingested shortly before this interview. Their conflation as the source of his destruction points to the link between childhood abandonment by self-absorbed parents and drug addiction that weaves its way throughout the entire novel.

The effects of this double-dose of narcissistic parents are clear for both Orin and Hal, though the sons develop in response to their parental experience in opposite ways. Orin learns to mimic the self-absorption he has been taught, becoming what one of his closest friends describes as "the *least open man* I know" (1048 n. 269, original italics)—a charge that could easily be extended to his father Jim. Meanwhile, his sexual penchant for young mothers—going so far as to ask them to scatter photos of their children around the room during sex—reveals both the roots of this need to validate himself by pretending to love others and his desperate striving to gain the mother's love he never received.[47]

But unlike Orin, rather than mimic his parents' pathologically narcissistic mediation of others, Hal remains stuck in the role of mirror that his parents had assigned him throughout childhood. Even as a toddler his "monomaniacally obsessive interest and effort, as if Hal were trying as if his very life were in the balance to please some person or persons" is such that he is alternatively diagnosed as suffering Attention Deficit Disorder and "Gifted"; in school he considers academic competitions "approval-fest[s]," later comparing the intense pleasure derived from correctly answering questions to the "pale sweet aura that an LSD afterglow conferred, some milky corona, like almost a halo of approved grace" (999 n. 76). Long before turning to the escape of tennis (also characterized as a form of "self-forgetting," 635) or finally of marijuana and DMZ, Hal has learned that pleasure comes most certainly from pleasing others and pathologically forgetting the self. Wallace illustrates this tendency to "self-forgetting" most vividly in Hal's perverted experience of grief therapy after finding the exploded head of his father, in which his sole purpose is to "empathize with the grief-therapist" and "deliver the emotional goods" that will please him (255, 254). Unable to mediate others but himself needing constant mediation from without, Hal remains caught in the same cycle of pathological recursivity that entraps his obsessively mediating brother Orin. It is no wonder, then, that Hal's dedication to "self-forgetting" should leave him in exactly the state that Lasch identifies as the vulnerable position of the narcissistic American: feeling a "huge hole" that is "going to get a little bigger every day until I fly apart in different directions" (785), a hole that he attempts not to fill—which seems impossible in a world made up of images and similarly hollow people—but to forget.

The cycle of infantile narcissism

Even more compelling than these specific examples of adult narcissistic behavior is the novel's argument that narcissistic culture remains terrifyingly inescapable because of the relentless, unprocessed infantile impulses that underlie adult narcissistic behavior. In other words, the novel compels and unsettles us not because it reflects an already self-consciously self-reflecting world, but because it paints as the underbelly of that world an unstoppable welling up of infantile suffering of which neither novel nor world is fully conscious or in control. Like Lasch, Wallace understands that, while the possibility of secondary narcissism has existed as long as humans have enjoyed and suffered their self-conscious independence from the world around them, this pathology only began to define an entire culture when that culture itself became a machine that reproduced for its members the need for and promise of infantile satisfaction.

Wallace's construction of a culture that both produces and experiences desire for infantile satisfaction through technological evolution echoes Lasch's interpretation of our experience of modern technology: in both novel and social commentary, our development of machines that make us increasingly dependent on their work, their products with their promises of fulfillment, and their contribution through massive reproduction to our image-based society, acts as a key catalyst of our feelings of infantilization and our *desire* for those feelings. The novel offers as its most biting example a history of the videophone, whose lifespan was cut surprisingly short by the very American obsession that bore it: our love affair with image. Wallace brilliantly illustrates through this vignette how easily a cultural need to indulge infantile fantasies trumps even our American fascination with technological advancement. For no amount of technologically induced pleasure gained by the new devices could make up for the profound loss of self-centeredness caused by them: "The bilateral illusion of unilateral attention [conveyed by a standard telephone] was almost infantilely gratifying from an emotional standpoint: you got to believe you were receiving somebody's complete attention without having to return it" (146). The videophone, of course, destroyed this illusion, and worse, forced callers to *pay attention* to each other, to reach out of their previously sightless, narcissistic wombs. Further, callers suddenly had to worry about how they appeared to each other. Their eventual response to these dilemmas, concocted, of course, through further technological advancements, consisted of altering their appearances to convey both the self-image they preferred to transmit and the illusion of their attention. First electronically altering their videophone images, then wearing high-definition masks to mimic on the phone their presentable appearances, they eventually demanded masks that improved upon their appearances (making them reluctant to show their real selves in public), and finally hid in their homes behind full-body representations of themselves. People whose need for absolute security in and approval of their inner-directed selves had been stymied by technological development turned back to technology to recreate wombs in which to hide.

Even the emergence of the novel's film cartridge technology and its eventual prominence came about because of the American desire to be fully in control of and satisfied by a technology that allowed the user to make all demands and be asked nothing in return. In InterLace TelEntertainment's ad campaign that finally killed off the already ailing "Big Four Broadcast Networks," the pitch to abandon network stations and even cable as highly "passive" entertainment experiences that dictated only a limited number of choices to the viewer ironically foreshadows the extreme passivity that this technology will engender in the lethal *Infinite Jest* cartridge, creating a society of individuals fixated behind closed doors on machines streaming entertainment designed to fulfill their every desire.

In the looping form that is characteristic of the novel, our need for infantile fulfillment both feeds technological evolution (as in the cases of the videophone and film cartridge entertainment) and is further *produced by* our own technology. Wallace offers as gross evidence of the culture's production of infantile needs the giant Infant spawned out of the looping, waste-fueled and waste-producing process of annular fusion in the Concavity.[48] Wandering the wasteland, "leaving scat piles as big as houses and keening for its lost parents,"[49] this monstrous, terrified and terrifying baby represents both the inconsolable pain and the destructiveness of the infantile needs this culture and its technology produce in their dictatorial, Frankensteinian ways. The cultural poisoning also registers in skull-less, extra-eyed newborns, forever trapped in the dependency of infancy, birthed in the fumes of a society's waste.

But lest the novel seem exclusively to blame technologies of modernization for this narcissistic bind, it cannily diversifies culpability by accusing the contemporary arts of popularizing the ironic culture that also leads to these infantile cravings: "[T]he lively arts of the millennial U.S.A. treat anhedonia and internal emptiness as hip and cool" (694). Further, the association of hip apathy with the cultural umbrella of the arts explains not only how a widespread perception of emptiness leading to infantile regression is produced, but also how this production simultaneously results in its own *denial*. For hipness implies a kind of "mature" resistance to feeling for oneself and others, so that all expression of human need and pain are seen as "infantile"; yet it is just this need to release oneself into the pure need of the infant that such hip emptiness encourages. Wallace seems to refer directly to his own assessment, in McCaffery's interview, of the dehumanizing problem of irony when Hal links cynicism with fear of infantilization in *Infinite Jest*:

> [W]hat passes for hip cynical transcendence of sentiment is really some kind of fear of being really human, since to be really human . . . is probably to be unavoidably sentimental and naïve and goo-prone and generally pathetic, is to be in some basic interior way forever infantile, some sort of not-quite-right-looking infant dragging itself anaclitically around the map, with big wet eyes and froggy-soft skin, huge skull, gooey drool. (694–5)

Registering here but not in Wallace's account of irony in his interview and television essay is the insidious way in which infantile, narcissistic need catalyzes the constant production of disaffected irony. Hal reveals here that hip cynicism actually operates as a way of masking our simultaneous desire and despise for what we're "really lonely for: this hideous internal self, incontinent of sentiment and need, that pules and writhes just under the hip empty mask, anhedonia" (695). This culture characterizes at every turn the thing it despises as infantile, "incontinent," full of need, while recognizing in the unmistakable reference to the monstrous infants that it is exactly this infantile need that it produces. Through this convoluted interdependence of insistent repetition and repression, Wallace depicts infantile narcissism as the disturbingly omnipresent element in a cultural machine whose constant denial ensures its troubling ubiquity.

Contributing to this sense of the culture's culpability in this vicious cycle is the fact that, in a novel filled with people both modeling hipness and craving infantile regression, only those who remain somehow outside or rejected from mainstream American culture perceive and consistently resist its pathetic state. Mario represents the novel's key critic of ironic culture, loving Madame Psychosis's radio show because "it is increasingly hard to find valid art that is about stuff that is real in this way" and noticing that "it's like there's some rule that real stuff can only get mentioned if everybody rolls their eyes or laughs in a way that isn't happy" (592). Marathe, legless and wheelchair-bound, offers the novel's other defense of earnestness, wondering "why the presence of Americans could always make him feel vaguely ashamed after saying things he believed. An aftertaste of shame after revealing passion of any belief and type when with Americans, as if he had made flatulence instead of had revealed belief" (318). But Mario's vast collection of physical deformities, extreme even in the context of widespread grotesqueries such as this novel's, means that he inhabits a thoroughly marginalized role throughout the narrative. And Marathe is Canadian, and even then a member of a self-ostracizing group, *Les Assassins des Fauteils Rollents* of Quebec, whose mission calls for complete separation not just from ONAN[50] (Organization of North American Nations, a union of America, Canada, and Mexico) but from their own country. So rather than celebrate—as Wallace does in his critique—those who resist the infantile fear of earnest emotion, and the desire to protect oneself from the "unpleasure" of pain, the novel only punishes them. Indeed, every character in *Infinite Jest* who struggles against a culture of narcissism—also the sweat-licking gym guru Lyle, and Gately in his final fight against the relief of medical drugs—suffers both emotionally and physically in ways that define him as grotesque and so socially unacknowledged.[51]

Therefore, as with any repressed and unacknowledged force, this craving for infantile satisfaction bubbles up compulsively throughout the narrative that denies it. Again and again, characters experience adult traumas through the unresolved pain of their childhoods, in the context of the original infant's trauma of discovering the parent's disappointing inability or refusal to provide total satisfaction. Not surprisingly, these memories of disturbed infantile states emerge, or resist emerging, as the adult struggles to process the more conscious secondary/pathologically narcissistic behavior to which that early trauma has led. Wallace in fact presents two key examples of depression—a condition as ubiquitous in the novel as addiction—specifically in terms of an adult's reaction to the infant's loss of total comfort and a sense of the self as complete (as in Geoffrey Day's early experience of the "large dark billowing shape [that] came billowing out of some corner in [his] mind," 649),[52] and as the child's horrific betrayal and abandonment by the parent (as is the case for the deeply repressed Bruce Green, 578). Most poignantly, the novel depicts the resilience of the dream of absolute love and fulfillment offered by infanthood and dashed by our entrance into adulthood by presenting, in one of the book's most startlingly earnest moments, a return to the safe haven of mother's love as our surest escape from the suffering of this world. For as Lucien Antitoi[53] endures the unimaginable pain of being skewered mouth to anus with his own broom handle by members of the AFR, his mind fills instinctively with "his mother's linen apron, her kind red face above his crib" (488); and when he mercifully emerges into death he "finds his gut and throat again and newly whole, clean and unimpeded," a newborn babe returning home and "sounding a bell-clear and nearly maternal alarmed call-to-arms in all the world's well-known tongues" (488, 489).

Clearly, then, *Infinite Jest* remains conscious of infantile narcissism as an inescapable element of contemporary culture. But though the novel argues unmistakably that our instinctive desire for infantile fulfillment both contributes to the pathological narcissism we fall into as adults and remains our unspoiled hope despite the impossibility of its fulfillment, the novel remains ambivalent about how best to treat this problem. The complex and pathos-filled scene in which Hal mistakenly attends a men's support group meeting best exemplifies the difficulty of dealing with the pain of our lost infantile fulfillment in a culture that both denies and reproduces that loss. In a rare expression of self-awareness that one might expect a novel full of unprocessed need to celebrate, Kevin Bain expresses his adult feelings of anxiety and loss explicitly in terms of infantile need: "'I'm feeling my Inner Infant standing holding the bars of his crib and looking out of the bars . . . bars of his crib and crying for his Mommy and Daddy to come hold him and nurture him. . . . And nobody's *coming!*' he sobs" (802, original italics). Though the men in the group, also clutching teddy bears to symbolize their Inner Infants, shower Kevin with empathy and, as the leader puts it, "nonjudgmentally listen to Kevin's Inner Infant expressing his grief and loss" (800), Hal feels nothing but ever-intensifying discomfort and then disgust at the sight of these middle-aged, middle-class men in their sweaters so earnestly emoting. On one obvious level, of course, Hal simply represents a cynical society's disapproval of this tiny subculture of earnestness. But when he mentally articulates his objection to the group's exercise he also reveals a reasonable critique of its oversimplification:

> All through his own infancy and toddlerhood, Hal had continually been held and dandled and told at high volume that he was loved, and he feels like he could have told K. Bain's Inner Infant that getting held and told you were loved didn't automatically seem like it rendered you emotionally whole or Substance-free. (805)

This critique exposes the group's core belief, in the sanctity and rationality of our need for infantile satisfaction, as the fantasy that it is—one that will not be fulfilled no matter how active we become, as the group leader teaches his members to do, in our pursuit of this fulfillment. And yet the tone of the scene remains mixed, conveying the very real and affective pathos of Kevin's pain as clearly as the rationality of Hal's objection.

The scene also reveals an ironic ambivalence about our ability to heal this need through the one method that seems in the novel to offer solace. For the therapeutic, talking-cure approach of the group, though uncomfortable for an outsider to witness, clearly works for the men involved—and yet in this case therapy also serves as part of the problem: Kevin felt abandoned as a child because his parents left "him and his brother with Hispanic nannies while they devoted themselves to their jobs and various types of psychotherapy and support groups." In fact, Kevin becomes completely abandoned at the age of 8 when his parents are crushed in their car by a "falling radio traffic helicopter on the Jamaica Way on the way to Couples Counselling" (803). Therapy and the talking cure here seem to offer cures as destructive as the disease they are meant to cure, simply because each of these cures contains the risk of narcissism.[54]

Significantly, the same looping pathology defines and so calls into question the culture of recovery represented in the novel by the Alcoholics Anonymous program. For, in equally powerful and less subtle ways than the Incandenza family, the novel's drug addicts, recovering and not, further illustrate the pathological recursivity of narcissism, in which narcissism operates as both cause and effect of their addictions. They, like Hal, are born of families for whom self-centeredness is a ubiquitous abuse, if the least of much worse abuses, and their turn to drugs comes out of the narcissist's ultimate need to escape a self that can no longer find sustenance in the world. In their absolute inability to put any need above their need to duck into the nihilism of a good drug binge, these addicts become for *Jest* the ultimate example of the solipsism of narcissism, and, in their physical and mental debilitations, the worst possible result of pathological recursivity, in which one is unable to extend oneself out of one's own head because others have extended themselves too far in. Or they are *almost* the most extreme example of the price of narcissism, as even their delusions and stink can't come close to the utter self-abandonment of the viewer of the *Infinite Jest* film cartridge. But theirs are only slightly milder versions of that mind-mediating drug: Wallace draws a careful relationship between the two, pointing out that "a drug addict's second most meaningful relationship is always with his domestic entertainment unit, TV/VCR or HDTP. A drug addict's maybe the only human species whose own personal vision has a Vertical Hold" (834). Filmed entertainment provides the addict relief from the burdens of self and others second only—until the release of the film *Infinite Jest*—to the mind-numbing effect of drugs: both serve the same addiction.

Then it is ironic that a collection of people defined by their solipsism should endeavor to cure themselves foremost through an appeal to empathy. The Boston Alcoholics Anonymous program as presented by this novel privileges above all else the sheer power of bringing sufferers together in order to connect with each other's pain. The Ennet House requires all residents to attend an AA or NA (Narcotics Anonymous) meeting every night, and encourages them to "sit right up at the front of the hall where they can see the pores in the speaker's nose and try to Identify instead of Compare. . . . *Identify* means empathize" (345, original italics). The narrative goes on to note, reassuringly, that identifying is easy, because "all the speakers' stories of decline and fall and surrender are basically alike, and like your own" (345). In fact, a core bit of the AA message, relentlessly repeated night after night by various speakers at the meetings, is that "You are not unique" (349), that all the stories hit the same narrative highs and lows with a good deal of suffering along the way, and that the member's job is not to figure out *his or her* story or *his or her* path to recovery but blindly to submit his or her will to the universal experience of the Program. So when the program asks its members to "Identify" with each other, what it really dictates they do is empathize with this standard story each member tells, with their own story, with themselves. In this way, the AA and NA programs ultimately ask not that members reach out to empathize with strangers but that they simply recognize in themselves their place in this infinitely repeating sameness, the recursivity of addiction. A perfect example of the solipsism members exhibit even as they believe they are progressing through a program of empathetic growth comes from Ken Erdedy's first meeting experience, when he withdraws from the concluding circle of eager hugging out of confusion and discomfort, only to be virtually throttled into expressing "empathy" by Roy Tony in all the terrifying "empathy" of his reform: "you gone risk vulnerability and discomfort and hug my ass or do I gone fucking rip your head off and *shit* down your neck?" (506, original italics). As solution to the solipsism of the story of drug addiction, the AA program provides an alternative to that addiction, an alternative way of forgetting the self: the Program as stand-in for the drug.[55]

Therefore, in the same way that the Incandenza family illustrates pathological narcissism as a cycle in which solipsists break out of themselves only to infect other people with their disease, the culture of both drugs and drug recovery unfolds as its own relentless cycle, both spawned and propelled by this narcissism, in which even earnest attempts to escape only lead back to new manifestations of the solipsistic loop. This pathological recursivity is the legacy, the novel seems to say, of our culture of pathological narcissism. That the conscious attempts in *Infinite Jest* to understand, escape, or heal from this legacy—Jim's films, Hal's tennis and drugs, the AA program— themselves inflict or indulge the same narcissistic tendencies suggests that something remains, unprocessed and powerful, that locks the characters in their closed loops.

Escaping the loop/escaping into the loop

Still, the novel has consistently been read by critics as most fundamentally a narrative of hope in the face of the depressed, addicted, self-involved future that the novel predicts for America. Valiant attempts by the novel's two main characters, Hal Incandenza and Don Gately, to develop in traditionally narrative ways toward self-awareness and community-mindedness form the basis of these readings. Certainly I agree that within the novel's context of compulsive narcissism, Gately's ability to transform from a drug addict so self-centered that he cannot bring himself to intervene in his colleague's gruesome torture, to a kind of den mother caring for other drug addicts, provides clear evidence of growth toward community-mindedness even in the midst of this suffocatingly solipsistic culture. But what I hope my exploration of the relentless pull of infantile narcissism will add to an assessment of the novel as a whole and of the key question of the development of Hal Incandenza and Don Gately is an awareness of the powerful ways in which this unprocessed pull toward solipsism ultimately *thwarts* any attempt to grow free of the clutches of a culture of narcissism.

Hal's nightmarish experience at his university interview that opens the plot and closes the story frames the pages that follow specifically in terms of a journey leading to Hal's utter detachment from the external world: Hal's last words in the story imagine an orderly in the hospital that will likely institutionalize him asking, "what's *your* story?" (17, original italics), and the "infinite jest"—or, as LeClair points out, "gest" or "story"[56] —is off and running. The classic version of the infinite "gest" is, of course, *The Arabian Nights* (also called, tellingly, *The Thousand and One Nights*), in which Shahrazad tells one story after another to postpone her death; in this sense, her story is also a "jest" or joke she perpetrates against her captor. The joke of this novel, then, lies in the fact that we know Hal is doomed to the solipsistic death of his pathological society from the moment we meet him, yet the novel defers our understanding of this culture and of this moment as long as possible, parsing out seemingly infinitely repeating examples of its recursive loop over more than 1,001 pages of Hal's "story," a story told, in essence, to postpone his own certain death.

Hayles points out that two "Bottoms" (citing AA-speak for the low point an addict hits before accepting the need to make radical changes) frame the novel's looping structure (694), and certainly Hal's animalistic performance in this scene is one. But the question remains whether his is a Bottom from which he can rebound, as the AA reference implies, or, as I will argue, one toward which the trajectory of the novel has been aiming all along, and out of which no amount of looping repetition will lift him. For his prodigious linguistic gifts—what the novel offers as one potential avenue for salvation, as does *The Arabian Nights*, in a culture collapsing into solipsism—have been clearly destroyed by the drug he has taken in his flight from the suffering of tennis and the sufferings masked by tennis; he can no longer write or speak coherently. Left without this gift, his one defense against the worldly stimulations to which he cannot respond is "[a] neutral and affectless silence" (9), essentially the pain of mimicking disaffection without the salve of expressed irony. Crouching in this pain, unable to communicate it and so heal from it, Hal succumbs to that greatest of all drugs, the call of the promise of infantile fulfillment and freedom from the pain of need, when he asserts in the ambulance that takes him toward institutions and away from the world of human discourse, "I have become an infantophile" (16).

In contrast to this clear, voluntary, and conscious descent into the unrecoverable Bottom of infantile narcissism, Don Gately's final narrative experience illustrates the threat posed by this ultimate drug even in the face of one's heroic attempts to oppose it. On one hand, Gately's extended hospital stay is a testament to his courageous *resistance* to the infantilized role inflicted upon him by medical staff and offered by the drugs that various doctors repeatedly encourage him to take. Though he experiences his medical incapacitation as physically infantilizing throughout, repeatedly referring to his railed bed as his "crib," Gately's thoughts (inexpressible because he has been intubated) indicate his constant struggle against the indignities inflicted upon him while he lies helpless in bed. Further, even in his disabled state he acts as confessor to a stream of visitors who narcissistically take advantage of his muteness to unburden themselves through guilt-ridden attempts at working through: Gately becomes, like Mario, one of those "damaged listeners" from whom "bullshit often tends to drop away" (80). He worries about who will make Ennet House's meatloaf, exhibiting the parental tendencies that drove him to defend the remorseless Lenz like one of his own children, with his life. He continues the work begun in sobriety of making conscious for the first time the formative traumas that led to his self-abandonment in drugs, centering on his mother and her beatings.

But stealthily interwoven with all these acts and thoughts of personal growth and caring for others runs the thread of infantile desire. Again and again he experiences his current suffering in terms of the terror and emotional need he felt as an abandoned toddler who, with plastic film bulging and receding over a hole in the ceiling above him, envisioned a "monstrous vacuole inhaling and exhaling" (809), ready to eat him alive. This infant's version of existentialism—terror of losing the self with the absence of the mother—plagues him throughout his illness with increasing frequency and urgency, eventually expanding into a dream/memory in which his mother is sucked out of existence by a tornado that the toddler Gately escapes by hiding in the dark expanse of the ocean. The projected allusion to Wallace's characterization of the ocean in "A Supposedly Fun Thing" as "primordial *nada*" is unmistakable; Gately, "no longer clear if he was little Bimmy or the grown man Don" (816), is haunted then and now by the loss of self implied and represented by his mother's abandoning of him. His earnest attempts to work through the trauma of this abandonment lead to an eerie channeling of the *Infinite Jest* film, in which he receives the apology of the film's mother as Death, the pure absolution of the mother's guilt for her son's pain; he enters the film's "milky filter" to become the baby and "asks Death to set him free and be his mother" (851). In this way, Gately experiences the film with its promise of infantile fulfillment as one possible solution to his infant's experience of loss.

While Gately's journey in the hospital bed certainly emerges as his struggle between these two competing impulses—toward emotional maturity and reaching out to others, and toward infantile regression to self-absorption—the final moments of his narrative suggest that the seduction of infantile narcissism proves irresistibly compelling. First, he experiences two "wakings," once into a memory of the Bottom experience that drove him to recovery, in which he witnessed, through a drug-induced stupor, the torture of a colleague; and finally into his dream/memory of his mother's total abandonment of him. Rather than signal the kind of heroic "awakenings" one would hope for at the end of a struggle such as Gately's, these ironic wakings instead void any notion of heroic transformation. For his waking into the memory of drugs, fear, and suffering is really a waking into the memory of the merciful unconsciousness brought by the drug "Sunshine": rather than recalling the drug indignantly, as the source of his inability to come to his associate's aid, Gately remembers it as "delicious" and "obscenely pleasant" (979, 981), a welcome escape from the horror being staged around him. Thus Gately's return to this memory does not even represent a neurotic (and necessarily doomed) attempt retroactively to prevent its trauma by generating the anxiety that was initially lacking, as Freud theorizes the repetition compulsion in *Beyond the Pleasure Principle*,[57] but merely his repeated indulgence in the mind-numbing pleasure of the drug itself. In this way, his "waking" into this memory functions as an alternative to taking the drugs offered by his doctors as an escape from suffering—heroic in its small way, perhaps, but indulging the infantile desire to escape the pain of the world all the same.

In his memory, the drug certainly fulfills this purpose: as he had felt like a toddler "reach[ing] in the dark for the bars of his playpen" while bingeing on Dilaudid with Fackelmann before Bobby C arrived, he later enjoys the comfort that the drug's infantilization brings in the midst of the horror of Fackelmann's eyes being sewn shut, transforming the man in charge of the misery into the parent who will protect him: "C was going to protect Bimmy Don from the bad floor's assault" (980). And the last thing he sees before exiting this memory is a mirror coming at him, in it "a reflection of his own big square pale head with its eyes closing" (981) into the drug's reassuring apathy and solipsism. His "waking" from this self-abandonment is no more promising, for it only underscores the reason for drugs' attraction during the binge, and for his return to that memory while suffering in the hospital. For he "comes to" out of the drug stupor and into his memory/dream of childhood abandonment, "flat on his back on the beach in the freezing sand, and it was raining out of a low sky, and the tide was way out" (981). Providing Gately's narrative end as well as the novel's actual end, this image of the abandoned child full of fear and need indicates what remains most true and present for both individual and culture, regardless of attempts to deny or resist that fear and need.

Uniting Hal and Don in their regression toward infantile narcissism—and, to my mind, further underscoring the novel's insinuation that this regression seriously thwarts all attempts to overcome cultural irony and apathy and the narcissism that underlies them—is an ominous, inexplicably shared mental quest for the ultimate narcissistic drug of the *Infinite Jest* film. While Gately, in a fevered stupor, "dreams he's with a very sad kid and they're in a graveyard digging some dead guy's head up and it's really important" (934), Hal envisions, on his way to the hospital, "John N. R. Wayne . . . standing watch in a mask as Donald Gately and I dig up my father's head" (16–17). Most interesting about this mysterious intersection between the two main characters are the narrative implications brought by the *Hamlet* motif that unites them. Having run quietly through the novel in connection to the film (whose title, obviously, references the play's gravedigger scene), the *Hamlet* allusion becomes, through these characters' shared desire, a final suggestion of narrative departure from the classic Oedipal journey of progressive enlightenment in favor of a looping descent into solipsism. For just as the underlying Oedipal story of *Hamlet*—a son overcoming his love for his mother to avenge his father and secure his rightful adult identity as king—gets hijacked by young Hamlet's increasingly complex acting out of his own self-obsessed needs, so does any potential Oedipal narrative of linear progress from infantile satisfaction to mature separation into an other-directed self become derailed by this lethal film. We see this displacement of the promise of Oedipal struggle and personal growth by the desire for regression to infantile solipsism not only in the persistence of infantophilia in Hal's and Gately's ends, but also, quite cleverly, in this desire that finally brings the two characters together—their desire to dig up Jim Incandenza's headless body, and so the film that was buried with him in the head's stead. For it is the *film*, with its promise of absolute satisfaction as infantile love, that both are after; not even Hal Oedipally pursues the head of his father, choosing instead the film that has taken its place.

This film represents the novel's core expression of the closed loop of infantile narcissism, its lethality stemming from its irresistible offer of the opportunity to both inhabit the longing-free space of infanthood and receive an apology for the original trauma of having to leave that space. In this way, the film does *not* function simply as a representation of the experience of infantile narcissism that the culture craves: it offers, rather, the experience of being a knowing adult, already separated from the mother and suffering from that separation of longing and loss of self in a culture that only exacerbates that suffering, and receiving the apology that could ease the suffering. It provides an attempt to reproduce the experience of infantile fulfillment without the anxiety that will lead to later pathology, to bypass this experience of original loss and free the viewer to enter adulthood without the burden of the resentment and inconsolability that send him or her looping back into narcissism.

Jim Incandenza seems to intend that his final film accomplish exactly this kind of healing, as he explains (via the wraith) to Don Gately:

> [H]e spent the whole sober last ninety days of his animate life working tirelessly to contrive a medium via which he and the muted son could simply *converse*. . . . His last resort: entertainment. Make something so bloody compelling it would reverse thrust on a young self's fall into the womb of solipsism, anhedonia, death in life. A magically entertaining toy to dangle at the infant still somewhere alive in the boy, to make its eyes light and toothless mouth open unconsciously, to laugh. To bring him 'out of himself,' as they say. The womb could be used both ways. A way to say I AM SO VERY, VERY SORRY and have it *heard*. (838–9, original italics)

The wraith notes that Jim hopes most fundamentally to bring Hal out of the infant's mute solipsism and *into* the symbolic order, reconnecting him to the larger world. But even in this description we find the same ambivalence of intentions that shapes the inescapable loop of this novel: while claiming that Jim sought primarily to "bring [Hal] 'out of himself,'" the wraith characterizes Jim's method as one that seeks to make Hal "unconscious," to bring him to life by putting him in the position of the unthinking, pleasure-filled infant. One could argue, to save the father from the accusation of intending to harm his son, that his mistake lay in believing that speaking to his son via the mute solipsism into which he had descended would allow him finally to hear his father, perhaps freed from the Oedipal resentment that accompanies one's exit from that solipsism. But the film's wake of destruction testifies that, to the adult plagued by longing and loss in this culture of irony, mediation, and narcissism, more compelling than hearing that apology and joining the adult community is the chance to remain the blissfully entertained infant. Thus the film, itself endlessly looping, reproduces the closed loop of infantile narcissism, the repetition compulsion in which all characters are stuck as they yearn for the infant's comfort, unwilling to endure the pain, or unpleasure, necessary to break out of it.

Families in the loop

Wallace's demonstration of the problem of narcissism through the Incandenza family and the families of the addicts who circulate through and around Ennet House argues strongly that this desire for solipsistic satisfaction, born in every psyche but inflamed by contemporary culture, is a disease that runs in families, is generated and spread by families, only to feed back into the culture that forced its spread. One clear bit of societal evidence of this disease—apart from the abundance of evidence of narcissistic abuse that buzzes restlessly inside individuals' heads—lies in the proliferation of abandoned children that litter this text, as in virtually all of the novels examined in this book. In a strikingly rare critical recognition of the importance of family in this family-driven novel, LeClair characterizes *Jest* as "a profound cross-class study of parental abandonment and familial dysfunction."[58] Indeed, both ETA and Ennet House seem to comprise almost exclusively the abandoned: at ETA, some parents drop off their children without even stopping, throwing gravel as they speed away (519); parents of boys injured in the Eschaton debacle travel to the academy to complain to the school's headmaster then forget to check on their children before heading home (1046); boys entertain each other in the locker room by trading stories of being forgotten by their parents (628). And virtually every addict in the novel, whether recovering or not, carries a backstory of being abandoned by parents (Treat, Green, Krause), or themselves abandoning their children (Ruth van Cleve), or both.

Hayles relates this cultural problem of abandoned children more specifically to society's resistance to the recursivity that defines it, citing annular fusion's production of the giant Infant as evidence of "how the illusion of autonomy poisons family relations, creating failures of communication so extreme they become tragic."[59] I have made a similar argument for the destructiveness of solipsism, or "the illusion of autonomy," but I also read in the culture's *pathological* recursivity the repetition compulsion of narcissism; this reading implies the somewhat more troubling conclusion that the culture's recursive loop operates not as a model for human connection but as structural evidence of the havoc wrought by our inability to resist the seduction of narcissism. In either case, the novel clearly demonstrates that at the core of this disease of solipsism lies the destruction of the family bond.

Once again, Wallace's novel echoes the social critique of Christopher Lasch, who also places the family bond at the center of a web of dysfunction created by and creating the culture of narcissism:

> The psychological patterns associated with pathological narcissism, which in less exaggerated form manifest themselves in so many patterns of American culture—in the fascination with fame and celebrity, the fear of competition, the inability to suspend disbelief, the shallowness and transitory quality of personal relations, the horror of death—originate in the peculiar structure of the American family, which in turn originates in changing modes of production.[60]

Leaving aside the slippery question of causality, which morphs throughout his critique, Lasch's assessment of the fate of the American family in contemporary culture essentially argues that parents disenfranchised by increasingly powerful and invasive techniques of reproduction and state authority find themselves with little to give their children, and thus lose their ability to bond with them; it is essentially a condemnation of pathological recursivity in which the absolute loss of autonomy actually *prevents* our bonding with others. As outside forces take increasingly central roles in shaping families, parents—and then children—experience a "striking lack of affect,"[61] and families mold themselves into an ideal of normality that is emotionless. As demonstrated in the novel, the decline of parental authority also "encourages the development of a harsh and punitive superego based largely on archaic images of the parents, fused with grandiose self-images," and produces oscillations of self-esteem characteristic of narcissism;[62] these fluctuations in self-image, of course, lead to increasingly desperate attempts to reassure the self and satisfy one's longing for fulfillment. Thus "the culture of consumption in its central tendency . . . recapitulates the socialization earlier provided by the family";[63] family and culture collude in their encouragement of unfulfillable longing, a collusion made possible by the fundamental brokenness of the family unit.

But the real power of this novel lies not simply in its ability to demonstrate so convincingly the destruction of family by our culture of narcissism, or its participation in that culture, but in its ability to demonstrate that the consequences of that family destruction reverberate far beyond the family unit. Hayles's exploration of family destruction—in relation to the larger processes of recursivity and annular fusion that fuel both the novel and the culture of the novel—reveals the vast implications of family breakdown. By pointing out the destruction brought to the entire nation by the film meant to operate as father-son bond, Hayles strongly argues that "the radiating consequences make clear that the scale of the problem exceeds family dynamics, encompassing international politics and ecological crises as well as the socio-economic enactment of abjection that killed television."[64] Thus the novel's use of the family to illustrate the perpetuation of the cycle of narcissism and its constantly destructive effects as both microcosm of and participant in a larger American and even international culture that shares its narcissistic disease, much as Lasch explores family dynamics as both causing and suffering from the larger American culture, forces us to face the problem of the contemporary family as central and fundamental, and as something that we cannot afford to ignore.

For his part, Wallace sees the broken contemporary family as emblematic not only of our larger cultural problems but even of his more specific concern of the American *literary response* to those problems. In what seems a startling non sequitor at the end of his interview with McCaffery, Wallace describes his frustration with his literary inheritance from postmodern writers enthralled with the empty, self-reflexive wit of irony as the teenager's eventual irritation with his marauding friends in the absence of his parents: "For a while it's great, free and freeing, parental authority gone and overthrown," but then " you gradually start wishing your parents would come back and restore some fucking order in your house." *Infinite Jest*, with its parodic meditations on apathetic irony and rampant mediation, clearly emerges as Wallace's responsible response to the realization "that parents in fact aren't ever coming back—[that] *we're* going to have to be the parents."[65] "Being the parent" in this novel means reaching outside oneself and taking responsibility for oneself and others as they negotiate the seductive cycles of narcissism in which everyone takes a wild ride. It is the alternative to succumbing to that narcissism, the only one that seems to offer a method for making and maintaining human relationships in an intensely infantile and solipsistic world. The novel, like Wallace's cruise ship critique, proceeds according to this binary of infant and parent, positing transformation from one to the other, however halting and imperfect, as evidence of individual growth: Gately's paternal responsibility for his fellow addicts at Ennet House proves his heroic advancement out of the infantile solipsism of drug addiction; Incandenza's attempt to move his son out of "anhedonia" and into the symbolic order indicates his hope that Lacanian growth out of the preverbal imaginary and into language, the "Law of the Father," can save him. The novel even describes Hal's final, devastating decision to choose infantophilia as a turning away from adult responsibilities to others, from the paternal head, by replacing the paternal head he pursues with the infantilizing film.

Then it is perhaps most ironic that this novel earnestly pursuing parental authority never manages to produce an unqualified care-taking parent or functional family. The closest we get to the emergence of adult authority from the chaos of childish indulgence comes from Don Gately's significant transformation from selfish drug addict to selfless janitor and guardian for other recovering addicts. But the progress he makes ultimately magnifies the deadly power of our constitutional and cultural craving for infantile narcissism when he turns his back on this adopted parental role to duck into the pain-free security of his own infantile entertainment. Of course, the characters' inability neatly to complete a progressive narrative arc does not necessarily signal the *novel*'s inability to make of character struggles a meaningful societal critique. But when the psychological and cultural limitations from which the characters suffer and through which they are defined equally shape and bind the world and structure of the novel, no room for critique remains. Don Gately in all his triumph must also be seen as complicit with and inescapably limited by the culture in which he is stuck—and in which the looping novel is stuck—and whose recursive structure his own pathological recursivity mimics. Certainly Wallace's agenda as stated in his interview with McCaffery indicates that constructing this novel as critique of exactly these mediating social and cultural force is in fact the primary way in which he intends to invoke a new kind of parentalism, or paternalism, with *Infinite Jest*. But finally the novel's obsessive structures of repetition, proliferation, and deferral mark it as not establishing an external stance from which that society might be critiqued.

I have argued that, given the inescapability of the drive to infantile self-satisfaction that permeates this novel, regardless of its near-heroic attempts to break free from its culture of disaffection and irony, *Infinite Jest* captures American society after the party is over and while everyone is standing around waiting for parents will who never come: the selfish chaos no longer feels like fun, but no one has yet grown up enough to clean up the mess. Wallace has gamely jumped into the fray, perhaps through the character of Gately, knee-deep in filth but unable single-handedly to stave off the wave of waste and suffering that bears down upon his fellow orphans. Committed to the imagist agenda of reimposing boundaries between the real and the fictitious,[66] he has instead created a world in which even the most self-aware and well-intentioned character finds solace in the infantile retreat that blurs the boundary between self and world. Indeed, Wallace has managed in *Infinite Jest* the patricidal liberation of eliminating one key purveyor of self-reflexive schlock, Jim Incandenza, but has left in his place through Incandenza's final film an ill-guided and failed attempt at healing whose cleanup attempt only begets more solipsistic mess. It still remains for Wallace to create a new paternal head to right the transgressions of the one he has exploded.

Notes

1   Wallace repeated and expanded upon these ideas about the problems of postmodern American fiction and his proposed solutions in many interviews after this one, though in a less focused and easily quotable manner: see David Lipsky's *Although of Course You End Up Becoming Yourself* (New York: Broadway Books, 2010) and Stephen Burn's *Conversations with David Foster Wallace* (Jackson: University of Mississippi Press, 2012).

2   Wallace, interviewed by McCaffery, "An Interview with David Foster Wallace," 147.

3   David Foster Wallace, "E Unibus Pluram," *Review of Contemporary Fiction* 13 no. 2 (1993): 183.

4   Here he identifies the "aura" that fixates Murray before the Most Popular Barn in America in *White Noise* as not the missing Benjaminian aura of authenticity, but as what has replaced it: irony itself ("E Unibus Pluram," 170–1).

5   This is exactly the paralyzing binary view of irony that is exploded by Michael Roth in *The Ironist's Cage* (New York: Columbia University Press, 1995) and Linda Hutcheon in *A Poetics of Postmodernism* (New York: Routledge, 1989). See Chapter 3.

6   Wallace, "E Unibus Pluram," 192–3.

7   McCaffery, "An Interview with David Foster Wallace," 148.

8   Ibid., 148, 149.

9   Ibid., 193.

10   Ibid., 147–8.

11   David Foster Wallace, *Infinite Jest* (New York: Little, Brown and Company, 1996), 445. Subsequent references will be noted parenthetically.

12   McCaffery, "An Interview with David Foster Wallace," 143.

13   Ibid., 137.

14   Ibid., 127.

15   The program's ironic participation in a system of linguistic reproduction and inscrutability that in part leads to the addiction that creates need for the program does not necessarily invalidate the program itself. Gately acknowledges this paradox in terms of the "infamous Boston AA cake analogy." His AA counselor reminds him that belief and understanding have no effect on a cake mix: "if he just followed the childish directions, a cake would result" (466, 467). Gately demonstrates his faith in the value of the incomprehensible program when he passes this advice on to other new members who are struggling with it.

16   McCaffery, "An Interview with David Foster Wallace," 138.

17   See especially Thomas LeClair, "The Prodigious Fiction of Richard Powers, William
     Vollmann, and David Foster Wallace," *Critique: Studies in Contemporary Fiction* 38
     no. 1 (1996): 32; and Catherine Nichols, "Dialogizing Postmodern Carnival," *Critique:
     Studies in Contemporary Fiction* 43 no. 1 (2001): 15.

18   Avril establishes the Militant Grammarians of Massachusetts, or MGM (an ironic
     alternative to the entertainment studio bearing the same initials), which sends
     corrective missives to "advertisers, corporations, and all fast-and-loose-players with
     the integrity of public discourse" (995 n. 51); she completed her undergraduate
     Honors work on "the use of hyphens, dashes, and colons in E. Dickinson" (1005
     n. 110). Strikingly similar to Avril (which may help to explain Orin's intense and
     likely Oedipal attraction to her), Joelle also finds her thoughts often monopolized
     by grammatical rules and transgressions; the penchant for grammatical errors in
     AA-speak is what most vexes her about the program (366).

19   Nichols, "Dialogizing Postmodern Carnival," 6.

20   McCaffery, "An Interview with David Foster Wallace," 136.

21   Lacan makes this argument that language replaces the original desire of the mother
     through his rereading of Freud's observation of the *fort-da* game, as I have detailed in
     Chapter 1.

22   A fact that Nichols not only admits but lauds, claiming that Hal restores his "personal
     agency" by "turning the self inside-out rather than suppressing it beneath deliberate
     artifice" (13).

23   Marshall Boswell implies as much when he reads the novel as a critique of Lacan's
     language-based concept of identity, in his *Understanding David Foster Wallace*
     (Columbia, SC: University of South Carolina Press, 2003). Boswell's chapter views
     the characters' suffering at their perceived emptiness, and their addiction-driven
     attempts to fill/escape it, as Wallace's warning of what happens when we erroneously
     view ourselves as constituted via linguistic construction. Written shortly before
     Understanding appeared, my argument reads the novel along similar avenues but
     toward a slightly different end: not as a critique of a way of theorizing subjectivity but
     as a diagnosis of what happens to individuals in a culture that exacerbates the very
     real problems of self-constitution that Freud and Lasch describe.

24   See *Studies in Hysteria*, with Josef Breuer (1895), *The Psychopathology of Everyday Life*
     (1901), and the famous cases of "The Rat Man" (1907) and "Little Hans" (1908), all
     in *The Standard Edition of the Complete Psychological Works of Sigmund Freud*, trans.
     and ed. James Strachey (London: Hogarth Press, 1953).

25   Sigmund Freud, *Beyond the Pleasure Principle*, trans. and ed. James Strachey (New
     York: W. W. Norton and Company, 1961), 21.

26   Ibid., 7–8.

27   David Foster Wallace, *A Supposedly Fun Thing I'll Never Do Again: Essays and
     Arguments*. (New York: Little, Brown and Company, 1997). Subsequent references will
     be noted parenthetically. Originally published in *Harper's Magazine* as "Shipping Out,
     or the (Nearly Fatal) Luxuries of a Comfort Cruise" in January of 1996.

28   Wallace transfers his own sense of the child's total security in his pre-Copernican
     universe to a nostalgic Hal when he wanders alone the early-morning halls of the
     Ennet Tennis Academy: "I wondered briefly whether it was true that small children
     believed their parents could see them even around corners and curves" (864). Wallace
     again recognizes the instinctive attraction of childish selfishness and self-satisfaction
     in "Getting Away from Already Pretty Much Being Away from It All," also in

Supposedly, in which he reports on the Illinois State Fair from his perspective as erstwhile resident of the Midwest (89–90).

29 Lasch, *The Culture of Narcissism*, 47–8.

30 Ibid., 87.

31 Ibid., 88.

32 Brecht's *emfremdungs Effekt* can be traced to Shklovsky's idea of *ostraneniye*, or defamiliarization, which he elaborates in his essay "Art as Device," in *Theory of Prose*, trans. Benjamin Sher (Normal, IL: Dalkey Archive Press, 1991). McCaffery, in fact, invokes the term "defamiliarization" in his interview with Wallace (138), clearly implying a similarity between Shklovsky's concept and Wallace's desire to expose to his readers the illusion of reality so that they might better grasp his novels' social critiques.

33 Such defamiliarization is also what the "wraith" in *Infinite Jest* proposes—and so what both Jim Incandenza's films and the novel itself strive to do, as the wraith can be read as representing both Incandenza and Wallace himself.

34 Lasch, *The Culture of Narcissism*, 90. Here Lasch cites Erving Goffman's *The Presentation of Self in Everyday Life* (New York: Doubleday, 1959), 56, comparing Goffman's assessment of absurdist characters to the "theatrical approach to existence" that "reenters daily life."

35 Ibid., 72.

36 Ibid., 170, 175.

37 McCaffery, "An Interview with David Foster Wallace," 148, 149 (original italics).

38 Lasch, *The Culture of Narcissism*, 143.

39 Ibid., 241.

40 Sigmund Freud, "On Narcissism," in *The Standard Edition of the Complete Psychological Works of Sigmund Freud*, trans and ed. James Strachey (London: Hogarth Press, 1953), 88.

41 Lasch, *The Culture of Narcissism*, 39.

42 Several interviews collected in Burn's and Lipsky's books verify that Wallace completed *Infinite Jest* before researching and writing his cruise ship essay. Further, in none of the interviews so far collected in which Wallace explains his thinking about the novel does he specify infantile narcissism as a problem the book wrestles with. Instead, when asked why he wrote the novel, he repeatedly answers that he "wanted to do a book that was sad" (*Conversations* 55; also 59 and 81). The most specifically he defines this "sadness" is as "what it's like to live in America around the millennium" (59) and as being "essentially miserable" "at a time when our lives are more comfortable and probably more full of pleasure, sheer pleasure, than any other time in history" (55).

43 Boswell's reading in *Understanding* is a notable exception. For what I consider more problematically optimistic readings of the novel, see Timothy Jacobs's "American Touchstone," *Comparative Literary Studies* 38 no. 3 (2001) 25–31; Catherine Nichols's "Dialogizing Postmodern Carnival: David Foster Wallace's *Infinite Jest*"; and LeClair's "The Prodigious Fiction of Richard Powers."

44 N. Katherine Hayles, "The Illusion of Autonomy and the Fact of Recursivity," *American Literary History* 30 no. 3 (1999). Similarly, Stephen Burn reads the novel's refusal to close and resolve as "Wallace's greatest bequest to the writers who come after him," which is "his conception of the novel not as an isolated object, but as a node in a connectionist network, always striving to reach beyond itself" in *David Foster Wallace's* Infinite Jest: *A Reader's Guide*, 2nd edn (New York: Continuum,

2012), 75. His reading of the novel as network node derives from a compelling wealth of systems—mythical, historical, scientific, and philosophical—Burn locates in the novel's allusions.

45 In doing so, the boys also mimic their father's self-obsessive tendency to mediate his own life by remaking it as film, in further evidence of his pathologically recursive narcissism; many of the episodes described in Jim's vast filmography are filmic retellings of events contained in the novel.

46 Wallace extends the cruelty of Avril's obsessively self-interested limitations to Mario as well: he was "involuntarily incontinent" to his early teens, but his mother never once cared for these needs: she "couldn't handle diapers" (768).

47 At the same time, Avril's sexual preferences speak to her own (most likely unconscious and clearly pathological) desire to extend herself to her sons: when Pemulis comes upon her and Wayne in a sexual encounter in her office, Wayne, a tennis player, is dressed like Avril's football-playing son, and Avril wears the costume of Orin's girlfriend Joelle, a cheerleader.

48 For a discussion of the "recursivity" of annular fusion as central metaphor for the novel's refusal of individual autonomy, see Hayles's article.

49 Hayles, "The Illusion of Autonomy and the Fact of Recursivity," 689.

50 To Hayles's note of the masturbatory implications this acronym lends to the international organization it describes (685), I would add that the image of onanism also signals the intense narcissism that permeates the culture of this novel far beyond political practice, as well as, perhaps, the masturbatory technique of the novel itself.

51 Wallace critiqued his tendency to punish earnestness when discussing his first novel: "I tend only to be able to have people say stuff that I think is serious if I'm simultaneously making fun of the character. I think that's a weakness" (in Burn, *Conversations*, 9–10). He also criticizes his own family's constant mocking of serious matters, finding the habit, as an adult, "kind of a slimy way to approach things" (in Burn, *Conversations*, 13).

52 This thing in its horrible "shapelessness" recalls DeLillo's description of the Airborne Toxic Event in *White Noise* as a metaphor for death and the existential crisis that attends our recognition of death's threat. Significantly, what appeared in DeLillo's novel as an external, technologically produced threat forcing individuals to react by denying and fleeing the real/death, becomes in *Jest* a force that originates in the mind, so the flight becomes one from the self.

53 Antitoi's name marks him as part of a culture of narcissism, suggesting he is "anti-you."

54 In this reading I deviate radically from LeClair's favorable comparison of the novel to an AA meeting rather than to the *Infinite Jest* film, a comparison that implies that the novel enacts the real-world honesty of multivoiced "radical realism" rather than the "single-voiced, seductive and possibly destroying" solipsism of the film cartridge ("The Prodigious Fiction of Richard Powers," 34). At an AA meeting, one person speaks while the others strive to listen empathetically, creating by definition one speaker in a room full of figurants. The novel, however, *does* resemble the wraith's philosophy of "radical realism," being composed of a stream of voices, often without accompanying listeners: even the reader cannot assume to be their constant audience, for how astute is one expected to stay over nearly 1,100 pages?

55 My reading of the AA program as illustrative of the pathological recursivity that permeates the novel opposes the commonly held critical view of the program, which

reads AA as an earnest and unironic depiction of one successful mode of healing in the novel. Certainly I would not dispute the novel's clear assertion that the program "works," especially for a character like Gately, despite the abnegation of understanding and autonomy required of its members, so that in the end the novel's depiction of the program is strongly ambivalent. But at least as striking as its success in helping members overcome addiction is the deeply ironic way in which the AA program achieves its success—is, in fact, its own complicity with the pathological recursivity from which these addicts are trying to escape. For a reading of the AA program as completely unironic, see especially David Morris's "Lived Time and Absolute Knowing: Habit and Addiction from *Infinite Jest* to the *Phenomenology of Spirit*," *Clio* 30 no. 4 (2001): 375–415, in which he argues that AA's irrational approach to healing addiction enacts a needed return to religious community. More highly nuanced treatments of the AA program as a tentative or partial solution to the problem of the novel appear in Hayles's "The Illusion of Autonomy and the Fact of Recursivity" and LeClair's "The Prodigious Fiction of Richard Powers."

56 LeClair, "The Prodigious Fiction of Richard Powers," 35.
57 Freud, *Beyond*, 21.
58 LeClair, "The Prodigious Fiction of Richard Powers," 32.
59 Hayles, "The Illusion of Autonomy and the Fact of Recursivity," 689.
60 Lasch, *The Culture of Narcissism*, 176.
61 Ibid., 170.
62 Ibid., 178.
63 Ibid., 181.
64 Hayles, "The Illusion of Autonomy and the Fact of Recursivity," 692.
65 McCaffery, "An Interview with David Foster Wallace," 150 (original italics).
66 Wallace, "E Unibus Pluram," 173.

3

Recuperating the Postmodern Family: Mediating Loss in *Music for Torching* and *House of Leaves*

Mark Danielewski's *House of Leaves* (2000) succeeds exactly where Wallace's ambitious *Infinite Jest* stalls out—in redeeming language and the family unit through the culture of mediation that threatens both through the end of the twentieth century. Like Wallace's novel, *House of Leaves* is at heart about a film, or a series of films, which depict both individual and family at the mercy of the nihilism of forces of mediation and simulation; and like *Infinite Jest*, *House* remains insistently about the written word and the author's project of redeeming it. But whereas Wallace's attempts to solve the problem of language and signification through language led to deadly loops of solipsism that destroyed the families and individuals he hoped to save, Danielewski constructs a funhouse of mediating images that reflects distorted images of the self not in the solipsistic loop of self-reflection but as part of a project of reconstructing individual and family identities.[1] In so doing, *House of Leaves* recuperates a model of the family from within postmodernism and reclaims a notion of meaningful written language through the written word. Further, *House of Leaves* puts the family and the domestic setting at the center of its attempts to redeem language more so than any other novel examined in this book, by intimately connecting the problems of the family and the crisis of language through one foundational symbol—a house that resists signification. Thus, the novel suggests both the dire implications of the crisis of signification on the family, and that the domestic space might provide the context in which to address this crisis: family and the home provide both impetus and mechanism for redeeming language. The innovation required for this success in redeeming language through reconstructing the family, and vice versa, becomes particularly clear when set against another, almost exactly contemporaneous novel that also places the crises of signification and culture squarely in the context of the domestic: A. M. Homes's *Music for Torching* (1999), which also uses the house as central symbol of these crises, but cannot maintain its postmodern structure while imagining a way out of them.

Sacrificing to save the family in *Music for Torching*

Music for Torching begins as a yuppie couple, vaguely unsatisfied with their materially full but spiritless suburban lives, burns down their own house in a briefly invigorating kind of potlatch, or act of conspicuous waste.[2] In willfully turning an implement of suburbanness, the barbecue grill, against their own home, husband and wife feel an excitement, aliveness, and purpose that have eluded them in the numbing predictability and safety of suburbia. One of the novel's great accomplishments is that it never defines the horror against which they strike out with this act, though one senses that in the decidedly conspicuous act of burning the house they are to some degree turning consumption upon itself. In this way, the novel feels haunted throughout by Edward Albee's *A Delicate Balance* (1966), in which a family finds itself invaded by neighbors who are suddenly too terrified to return home; the terror in the play remains pointedly nameless—"WE WERE FRIGHTENED . . . AND THERE WAS NOTHING"[3] —but present and palpable nonetheless. Albee's play masterfully captures the impact upon the domestic setting of exactly the enormous social and cultural changes that DeLillo depicts on a much broader scale in his novels—the proliferation of language, information, technology, and reproduction, and the resulting lack of anything originary and stable, like meaning, truth, and reality—by crafting at its center a terror that is a nothing, that is an absence, that is only and exactly a lack. At one point in *Music*, Paul alludes to a similarly nameless domestic fear: "Paul doesn't tell Elaine that he's aware that almost anyone else would think it's a perfectly lovely Saturday but that he's scared, absolutely petrified, and he doesn't know why."[4] Though never explicitly invoked, Albee's play with its eerie sense of futility in the face of inarticulable horror provides the dominant tone of Homes's novel, despite its surface of ironic apathy and cheeky absurdity. In fact, when I questioned the author about this similarity between Albee's play and her novel, Homes enthusiastically revealed that she had in fact written the novel with this play in mind.[5]

This undefined lack plagues the materially rich protagonist parents of *Music* as they struggle with feelings of emptiness and longing in their beautiful house filled with beautiful things—and two lovely sons. One finds right away that it is the sons who are most conspicuously forgotten, most strangely unable to move the parents or provide the affective fullness they so clearly lack, especially the younger Sammy, whose tender pleas to his parents for help go unheard throughout the novel. This family relationship once again provides a perfect example of the dysfunctional family as outlined by Lasch: the father, Paul, finds himself emasculated by a bureaucratic job he does not know how to perform while Elaine, the mother, has lost herself to a homemaker's role that she finds equally beyond her grasp; lacking their own senses of purpose and personhood, the parents seem to have no stable identities through which to form bonds with their children. Instead, they take solace in consciously infantile acts in which they reject their parental nonidentities in favor of mimicking the rebelliousness of adolescence. One suspects that this adolescent behavior brings them a great deal of comfort, in that it is the closest they can get to a kind of authenticity, an acting out of exactly how lost and unformed they feel. As in *White Noise*, such behavior necessitates that the children occupy the role of responsibility vacated by the adults. But quite unlike DeLillo's novel, the children here are not admired for their surpassing knowledge and abilities, but rather become invisible to their needy and self-occupied parents. From the beginning, then, the children in *Music for Torching* operate as a sign of loss, of what has been present but has been forgotten. And it is exactly this loss that ultimately differentiates *Music* from Albee's *Balance*, in that the death of one child at the end of the novel finally converts the parents' indefinable lack into a specific and terrible loss they can grieve.

Also quite unlike *White Noise*, and most of DeLillo's other novels, *Music for Torching* is not on its face about slippery systems of signification or deadening technologies of mediation. And yet the novel conveys exactly the loss of self and of the ability to feel that plagues DeLillo's characters in their media-saturated states, as well as the difficulty of constructing lives they can live with: *Music* illustrates the terrifying void of family life once America's nexus of waves and radiation has become so ubiquitous as to be invisible and silent. In *Music*, home as a nurturing nest for the family is a construct requiring exhaustive maintenance work. Of her own efforts to maintain even her dysfunctional family, Elaine says simply, "I can't do it anymore" (19), just before kicking over the grill that will light her house on fire. Meanwhile the one Cleaveresque family on the block, the Nielsons,[6] where children write skits to perform after dinner and everyone gets a favorite dish on Wednesdays, garners bitter mocking and suspicion from Paul and Elaine: they call the Nielsons "shape shifters" (55), implying something necessarily monstrous about such familial perfection. Indeed Mrs Nielson turns out to be an enthusiastic lesbian who introduces Elaine to a silver-studded leather dildo harness as her dryer buzzes dutifully in the laundry room. Such sly conversion of the 1950s housewife to dirty-talking lesbian adulteress insists that by the late twentieth century, images of happy nuclear families can only operate as covers for the shocks and even grotesqueries that lie beneath (as memorably filmed in *Blue Velvet*, 1986, and more recently in *American Beauty*, 1999[7]). Finally it is this sense of suburbia as false and painstakingly constructed that resonates most thoroughly with DeLillo's nightmarish vision of a world composed solely of waves and radiation: Paul and Elaine's experience of suburbia reflects the shockwaves of the shattering of epistemological certainty that rocks Jack's world. Having already accepted that nothing original or authentic exists anymore, Paul and Elaine slip into the ironic detachment that accompanies the terror of living in a world where nothing is real, including one's own behavior or its consequences.

For Paul and Elaine, then, it is *hard* to be an upstanding adult, virtually impossible to be a helpful and caring parent. Striking out against their house, central symbol of the demands upon them of the domestic, is only the beginning. This act of self-sabotage begins a pattern of self-indulgent and risky behavior aimed at waking them up from the *ennui* that engulfs their lives: while having sex, Elaine cries to Paul "I'm so bored it's not even funny" (15); this pathetic cry becomes a refrain throughout the novel for both of them. In response to this boredom they attack not just the house but themselves and each other, in vain attempts to make themselves feel again. Both begin affairs—Elaine with Mrs Nielson and Paul with both a friend's young mistress and the mother of one of Sammy's classmates—while seeking other physical intensities as well. Most extreme of these is their two-day binge on crack cocaine, which is the central event of Homes's 1990 short story "Adults Alone," in which she first introduced this family, and which is an indulgence Paul and Elaine remember with great longing in this novel. Other more aggressive acts insinuate the violence that bubbles just under the surface of their ultrasafe lives and that will burst forth at novel's end to affect them once and for all. The novel opens with Elaine gently slicing open Paul's neck with a kitchen knife after a neighborhood dinner party, an enactment of her own sadistic fantasy: "If I wanted to kill you, I would just go like this," she says as she pulls the knife across his skin (4). Later, Paul wounds himself by acquiescing to a genital-area tattoo, at the urging of his borrowed mistress, and admits to Elaine that "I thought it would wake me up—like electroshock" (243).

The direct result of such exploits is the increasing infantilization of both parents: Paul becomes lost after suffering the tattoo and must catch a ride home with a neighborhood father, then requires a hired babysitter to watch him while he recovers from the infected tattoo; Elaine whines to her mother that "I want to be the child" as her mother helps daily with cleanup of the fire-damaged house (261). Like the self-centered parents of Lasch's critique, they are so busy attending to their own childish needs that they completely ignore the very real needs of their children, farming them out to various neighbors and friends as they indulge in reckless and selfish behavior. And though the narrative with its transgressions and disjunctions seems appropriately unconventional for a domestic novel at the end of the twentieth century, its conventionality lies in the price these two must pay for their childishness at the end of the novel, and in the clear warnings of this price that coexist throughout the narrative with the carelessness of its two protagonists.

The horror and awful earnestness of that horror which end the novel change the tenor of the story so utterly that they force the reader back through the narrative, searching for the thread that led to that final, cataclysmic event: Sammy, the 9 year old whose innocence and vulnerability practically shimmer through the dullness of his parents' lives,[8] shot in the head at school by his schoolmate and playmate Nate. Though prescient of the spate of school shootings that would rock the country within months of the novel's publication, this unimaginably terrible event, broadcast to watching school officials and parents by a police robot, almost reads as a cheap shock of an ending—until we return to the novel and *pay attention* to Sammy's expressions of concern that pepper the novel throughout. Then we find that nearly every chapter contains a warning: Sammy cast as victim when his brother Daniel ties him up in a game of "hostage" (38); Sammy sweetly quoting his favorite line from *Bambi*, which his brother calls *Waiting to Be Road Kill* (85); Sammy begging to come home from Nate's house, where he stays after the fire, and sobbing when Nate waves good-bye (all ignored as his father fantasizes about playing house with Nate's mom, his own long-term mistress) (152); Elaine perceiving in a rare unself-centered moment that Sammy seems "a bit strange," but doing nothing about it (187); Nate shooting Sammy-as-rhino in the school play (221); Sammy, on the morning of his death, claiming that Nate is moving, then admitting he made it up (317). Taken together, these moments depict an innocent boy feeling threatened and scared and unable to articulate that threat; they depict parents given every indication that something is wrong but giving none of their attention to figure out what that might be.

Chapter 10, which precedes the chapter containing Sammy's death, seems to present a circular ending that will restore order and offer readers relief with the chance for a new beginning: the neighbors come by for a housewarming party to celebrate the repaired house and give Elaine and Paul a Weber grill, "the real thing," as if to insure no further "accidents" by acknowledging the flimsiness of both their previous barbecuing equipment and their hold on happy suburban life. Indeed, once their friends have gone, Paul and Elaine finally seem to grasp that their "boring" suburban lives carry the potential for life-saving community:

> In the end, the goal is to be left with something: a spouse, children, even parents if you can manage it. The goal is not to be left alone, not to be left old, poor, and on the street. Everyone thinks it could happen to them, everyone worries that they might drift so far from reality as not to be welcomed back—think of bag ladies, men living on steam grates, the Montgomery boy. Everyone secretly knows that it's something that could happen at any moment—an error or an accident.
>
> Paul and Elaine are left alone with the grill. (311–12)

With this new appreciation for the frailty of their grasp on community in mind, the grill becomes a liability, something to be lidded in a clear gesture of protecting their newly valued house. This transformation of grill from instrument of liberating potlatch to potential threat against their homestead signifies the profound change the house itself has undergone—from burden and threat to Paul and Elaine's individual abilities to fulfill their selfish desires, to sacred protector of the family. Shortly after the party this newly united family appears, assembled for party cleanup, and Elaine ensures that the unity will continue: she hands new alarm clocks to the children "like gifts,"[9] set for seven when they will reassemble for a hearty, home-cooked breakfast: "She's determined to have tomorrow go right" (312). And finally, she breathes deeply into the neck of her younger child as she tucks him in, absorbing the beauty and sweetness that have, for the course of the novel, eluded her. She says a prayer for his safety.

Looking back, one can't help but wish that Homes had stopped with this tenth neat and redemptive chapter. But instead she adds the odd number 11 in which she defies all the possibility for peace and recovery just offered. The day starts well—with a pancake breakfast under the "shiny" mail-order bulbs Elaine has bought just like supermom Pat Nielson; Elaine and Paul finally take steps toward improving their lives in adult ways (Elaine visits a career counselor; Paul refuses another date with the sadistic mistress). But all the self-help they can muster can't stop the horror they set into motion when they burned their own house and sent Sammy to live with the violent Nate. In this way, the narrative absolutely blames the parents for their child's death, not simply through their inaction but through the one action that launched the narrative and displaced their son. Even Sammy, exiled from the house during the weeks of cleaning because of his severe asthma, recognizes this fact, claiming "This is the house that hurt me" in a vague accusation (268). Ultimately, it is the struggle to define homes and families that kills him: when Nate's mother pleads with her son via police robot that "Everyone wants to go home and watch TV. Don't you want to go home?" Nate responds, "I'm not going home . . . no one is going home" (351). Then his final words before shooting Sammy—"Get out of my house"—suggest that his anger and violence toward Sammy have been motivated by a desire to protect "his" house all along (352). After all, it is Sammy's father who is conducting, none too subtly, an affair with Nate's mother. Nate's final order to Sammy, delivered with gun in hand, elicits the image of a man protecting his property—both from the boy who has invaded his family home and the police robot that has just invaded this classroom he has commandeered. They are the words of a boy wanting to protect his home like a man, trying to do, in the wrong way, the one thing that none of the adults in this novel has given much thought to. Finally, in one more heartbreaking role reversal, it is Sammy's older brother Daniel who reacts to the shot, raging into the face of the gun-wielding Nate before carrying his dying brother out of the building. The novel's ultimate warning seems to be that this is what may happen when apathetic adults fail to define and protect their homes and families: left to the unreflective and clumsy actions of children, and of parents behaving like children, what sorts of families will emerge?

Sammy's death, then, is the punishment his parents endure for their negligence and the price they pay for the possibility of a new beginning. Sammy is a sacrifice. In this way his death is by definition meaningful, just as it is meaningful in that it finally provides an object for his parents' vague sense of domestic dread. Sammy's death, and the raw emotions surrounding it, provide the earnestness and affect that have been absent from the novel to this point. The sudden arrival of these qualities in a book filled with ironic disaffection is all the more striking because the novel at this late point finally thrusts us into the technological and consumerist world that DeLillo's characters know so well: television news cameras construct the incomprehensibly terrible event into a "story"; the police attempt a technological intervention—a robot sent to negotiate with Nate—that fails except to broadcast the horrible moment of Sammy's wounding to his watching parents; Nate's mother tries to convince him to come out of the school where he is holding Sammy hostage by promising a trip to FAO Schwartz where "I'll buy you anything you want" (345). Even Nate's behavior smacks of television and film intervention: just before taking Sammy hostage, he points his gun at Sammy and says "I'll show you what history is"—devoid of explanatory context—and then grabs the "little girl" next to him and kisses her (337), as if reenacting filmed scenes that have accumulated, uncomprehended, in his head. At this late point in the novel, Homes seems finally to condemn the media in her accusation of the parents: of course it seems impossible to construct home as a safe haven when the media constructs a world full of meaningless violence and equally meaningless narratives, and whose only fulfillment comes from simulation and consumption. In the midst of all these attempts to control the unfolding events through mediation and consumption, Sammy's gruesome wound ("'Did they find the eye?' someone asks," 354) stands as a horribly insistent reality that necessitates exactly the earnest attention and emotional reaction that Sammy has been denied throughout the novel. It forces a reexamination of the home, of the domestic, of parental roles, and it forces an acknowledgment that our culture that breeds violence while devaluing parental responsibility requires this reexamination. That Sammy's death comes in the name of the home suggests that the home has become a dangerous place, one that does not protect us from the ills of the world but that takes these ills inside it and turns them against us. The home is no longer a haven from culture (as social critics like Robert Inchausti, David Cheal, and Christopher Lasch claim for society at large) but rather a reflection or constitutive element of the culture industry from which it was meant to protect us—equally deadening, equally murderous.

In this way, the narrative arc of *Music* is much more traditional—more realistic than postmodern—than that of *Balance*, for while Albee's play ultimately resolves its domestic drama (somewhat) without ever defining the terror that sent the neighbors packing, Homes's novel deliberately caps its sprawl of loosely related quotidian events with a decisive event that brings the narrative meanderings to a halt and finally puts a name and face on the terror that has haunted their lives. For alongside their suburban angst, the very real possibility of losing a child, a parent's worst nightmare, has existed all along, and in readable ways: one senses when reencountering these moments, sickly, that we are meant to comprehend the mounting danger, to read the signs that Sammy's parents, too preoccupied with their own selfish needs, cannot. So when the call comes, and when the shots are fired, they do not surprise us but rather neatly become the terrible thing that Sammy has feared all along, and to which all of his hints have pointed. For the reader, then, Sammy's death is the signified for a novel's worth of signifiers, a closed sign-thing relationship that makes meaning and sense out of a narrative that had previously proceeded according to lack of the same. In an equally conservative way, his death functions similarly for Paul and Elaine, bringing them together over his dying body that finally eclipses the nameless terror that to this point has motivated them through the narrative: the novel's final words, Elaine's, are, "It's over" (358).

With that strikingly blatant declaration of closure, the novel reveals the degree to which these two conservative transformations depend on each other. Paul and Elaine may reconcile, but only because this death has also transformed the narrative structure and content of the text: it replaces nameless lack with specific loss; it replaces the postmodern potlatch of conspicuous consumption with which the novel began with meaningful sacrifice, and it renders readable and meaningful a narrative that, until Sammy's death, seemed pointless and episodic. The conversion of disaffected individuals into grieving parents comes as a shockingly traditional ending for what had been a banally postmodern narrative, a recuperation of sorts in its return to both closure and affect. Tellingly, when Homes agreed to my characterizing the novel as conservative, and as a kind of morality play, she admitted that one impetus for continuing to write about Paul and Elaine past the limited short story "Adults Alone" was that she "didn't approve of the characters and what they were doing."[10] In order for this novel to become a morality play in its finale, it must reach back into its discontinuous narrative and plot a newly meaningful narrative development that offers Sammy's consistent pleas and tears as counterpoints to Paul and Elaine's apathetic exploits. It does so by reaching back in another, larger way to a pre-postmodernist narrative convention of sacrifice whose inherent system of morality and meaning-making transforms the entirety of the novel into a progression of readable signs, culminating neatly in a powerful event whose consequences bring everything into focus, and thus confounding every readerly expectation established until the moment of sacrificial conversion. Transforming potlatch into sacrifice, a slippery chain of signifiers into a statically signifying thing, and fragmented narrative into a through-line to meaning, the novel's ending is shocking for the same reason that it satisfies: against the expectations generated by the novel to that point, it allows us to find the book meaningful. Ultimately, *Music* offers a kind of painful, backward optimism. It constructs a world containing enough inherent moral measure that parents who behave as Elaine and Paul do must pay.[11]

Appearing first as a work-in-progress on a website in 1997, then once again online as a work in the process of publication in 1999, and finally as a published print book in 2000, *House of Leaves* began life as a crossover phenomenon that captivated web and print readers alike;[12] over a decade after its print publication, the novel continues to exist in and generate a genre-blurring space that one can only call hypertextual.[13] Even the book's print form insistently questions and redefines the idea of the novel: unlike any book printed before it (but now in a fair bit of similar company), it features text running up and down margins, flowing backward, and defining "windows" through which text from the adjacent page "leaks"; uses color ("house," in any language, appears in blue,[14] and some editions use red for struck passages and "minotaur"); preserves pages of "stricken" text; and employs multiple fonts to distinguish at least three narrative voices. This multiplicity of narrative voices indicates the key way in which the novel insistently defies novelistic convention through narrative structure as well as print form, refusing to provide a central narrator or narrators around which the rest of the text can be organized. Rather, the novel offers an Escher-like[15] lattice of authorial construction in which each author implies the other with no possibility of an original source:[16] one character writes an academic analysis of another's series of films exploring the mysterious house; another comments upon this found academic analysis in footnotes that are quickly taken over by the commentator's own self-exploratory story; and "editors" comment upon both academic writer and his commentator—constructing a three-tiered narrative structure that becomes further complicated when characters within these narratives seem to bring their own powers to bear on the text.[17] Finally, the novel continues to assert itself as vehemently nonlinear and immune to definitive interpretation through its content as well. It tells the story of a house that measures larger on the inside than on the outside, where compasses do not work, and whose spaces grow and shrink randomly and without warning, so that the house is, above all, a space with no center, a physical model of centerlessness.

If ever there was a postmodern novel, this is it; it virtually screams to be read as a novel grappling with the concepts and troubles of postmodernity. But ultimately it is not the novel's insistent postmodernity, its defiance of conventional novelistic devices, narrative construction, and subject matter that make this book remarkable at the "end" of the postmodern age, but rather its surprisingly conventional appeal to exactly the emotion and psychological depth that much of postmodernity had long jettisoned. For through this novel about a house, and book, as manifestation of the problems of language and family in the postmodern age, in which men become lost and families are torn apart, emerge two stories of reconciliation and personal growth made possible only through experiences of the impossible house. Both of these stories are conceivable only within the context of mediation and simulation that defines the house; one of them—a young man's attempt to come to terms with the house as academic writing, an attempt that leads him to come to terms with his grief over the childhood loss of his mother—charts a classic narrative arc of psychoanalytical discovery through confrontation with unprocessed trauma. So it is the simultaneous coexistence of models of poststructuralism and of psychoanalytic "working through" via language that, for me, defines the most interesting impossibility of this text. In this way the novel enacts a kind of return of affect and psychoanalytical working through that postmodern literature and theory have largely repressed. For it is not only loss that lies at the center of this novel but grief for that loss, and once the novel discovers that, once it turns from disaffected academic representation to the raw grieving of individuals, it reads less as unmoored hypertextuality than as an almost conservative remembering of the feeling individual in this hypertextual world. Thus *House of Leaves* remains as invested as *Music for Torching* in recuperating the earnestness and emotional connection that have been lost in this age of constructed realities, gnawing lack, and detached irony, and so in reimagining a successful nuclear family. But unlike Homes's largely reversing recuperation, *House* remains rooted in the sprawling uncertainty of hypertext, where nothing is exactly real or original and identities are wholly constructed, and yet creates *within* that impossible space a place for affect, earnestness, subjectivity, and family that cannot be ignored.

Unheimlichkeit and the family

As in *Music for Torching*, the house in Danielewski's novel operates not as refuge from the threats of the outside world, but as an embodiment of those threats that bring the dangers of the crisis of signification to bear upon the vulnerable members of the family. Notably different in this case, however, is the house's existence specifically as a representation of this crisis and so as a threat to the family from the very beginning. Appearing 15 years after Jack struggled through his conversion to postmodern epistemological uncertainty, *House* unfolds long after this destabilization took place and takes it as its most basic premise, one that encompasses everything else the book constructs: its wildly unconventional print form and fractured narrative structure immediately signal this context. Danielewski acknowledges his entrance into an already well-established fray of linguistic instability when he describes his work as "not so much an experimental novel as . . . what comes *after* the experiment,"[18] citing the groundbreaking techniques of Mallarmé, Sterne, Cummings, Hitchcock, and Kubrick as predecessors whose work allows his own to operate within an already established linguistic crisis rather than defining it. This description of the novel suggests that Danielewski envisions its intervention in exactly the terms in which I read it as succeeding—as neither description nor response to cultural and linguistic crisis but as that thing that Wallace aimed to produce in his fiction—as an example of "*then* what do we do?"[19] So the house that the Navidsons encounter appears immediately and unmistakably as a direct representation of the crisis of signification: centerless, directionless, infinite, random, meaningless, monstrous—a house whose absent center is occupied by a nothing that can, and does, kill. Further, Zampanò's dating of the house in <u>The Navidson Record</u> at least back to 1607 Jamestown[20] suggests, as insistently contemporary novels like DeLillo's *White Noise* and Homes's *Music for Torching* do not, that this crisis of signification and its potential consequences are not new products of our contemporary culture of technology, information, and mediation, but rather have always lurked, waiting to be discovered, and that our role is not chronicling and understanding it but learning to adapt and survive inside its treacherous space.

Like Homes, Danielewski depicts the transformation of the house's function from safe haven to threat, in this case by differentiating from the outset between the film Will Navidson intended to make about his new house and the one(s) that eventually resulted. In a declaration of intentions that opens *The Navidson Record* film, Navidson draws a clear line between the dangers of the external world—"gunfire, famine, or flies"—and the "outpost" of their home. Zampanò, too, sets up the family's entrance into the house as a battle against loss, introducing Navidson as having been abandoned young by a departing mother and dying father, so that he enters the house (as Johnny Truant enters the text of the *House*) as a child of loss seeking some sort of recovery. Zampanò also establishes a compelling backstory for this filmic effort at family composition, revealing that the troubled relationship between Navidson and his longtime companion Karen has prompted Navidson to turn "reconciliation into a subject for documentation" (10). Perhaps further contributing to Navidson's characterization of home as domestic haven from the warring factions of the external world is the fact that it is this divide that has caused the couple's estrangement. For Will, a photojournalist renowned for venturing into dangerous territories to capture his award-winning shots, moving into this house in Virginia marks his simultaneous entrance into domesticity and exit from an adventurous career. His language in this introduction indicates that he knowingly pits one against the other, choosing the safety and solidarity of home over the personal risks and fulfillments of his professional life; as Zampanò tells us, "abandoning photography meant submitting to loss" (23).

But all of these intentions for the house as family protector become rapidly overturned as the film progresses. Two months later, the Navidson family[21] returns from a four-day absence to find the first in a series of increasingly troubling and impossible changes in their house. Zampanò initially describes (crediting others) this "spatial violation" as "uncanny," noting its German translation as *unheimlich* and Heidegger's own examination of "uncanniness" as a feeling not just of the anxiety of Being but also of "not-being-at home" (*Nichtzuhause-sein*) (24). Johnny's footnote (which provides the translation of Heidegger) makes great fun of the translated passage ("which only goes to prove the existence of crack back in the early twentieth century"), but, academic sniping notwithstanding, the overlap between the anxiety of Being and the anxiety of being "unhome-ly," or not at home, provides an excellent context in which to read the oddities of the house and their effect on the people who experience them. For it is in the anxiety of not-being-at home, of experiencing the home as an uncanny place, that people begin to feel the oddities of their own selves. "In their absence, the Navidson's home had become something else," and it is this transformation from home-ly comfort to unhome-ly anxiety that drives the remainder of *The Navidson Record*—and that reverses the strong intentions with which Navidson began the film. In other words, it is the destruction and destructiveness of *home* that puts both individual inhabitants and family relations at risk.[22]

Significantly, the first "spatial violation" that converts the home to the uncanny occurs specifically as a violation against the family unit: Navidson and family return from their trip to find that a new closet has appeared *between the parents' and children's rooms.* The addition symbolically and physically establishes the pattern that will intensify as the house changes in increasingly drastic ways. With each spatial mutation of the house, each assertion of its existence outside the realm of reason and measure, the family will be further torn apart. This initial change also foreshadows the very real physical threat the house will pose to the family:

> Oddly enough, a slight draft keeps easing one of the closet doors shut. It has an eerie effect because each time the door closes we lose sight of the children.
>
> "Hey, would you mind propping that open with something?" Navidson asks his brother. (40)

As the adults become increasingly obsessed with trying to understand the impossibilities of the house, with coming to terms with its crisis of signification, the children become increasingly alienated, so that the mystery of the house reproduces the parent-child disjunction of *Music for Torching.* Again we see the children ordered out of the house, so that they "drift farther and farther out into the neighborhood for increasingly long spates of time" (56). Even when they are inside, the house ensures their alienation from their parents, engulfing Daisy and Chad in a new, larger hallway that broadcasts the children's playful chatter back to their parents as echoes signifying nothing so much as their immediate absence. The structural changes also directly pit house against family by awakening the photojournalist in Will while igniting the homesteader in Karen: "If he goes in there, I'm outta here. Kids and all," declares Karen (62). But once the house begins to change—once it becomes *unheimlich*—the house no longer represents domestic possibility for Will but rather the risk and adventure he had given up for the sake of that domesticity.

The inevitable explorations of the house that proceed in spite of these signs of family risk begin to generate more representations of the disjunction that both is the house and is produced by the house, in terms of family disconnection. Zampanò notes that even the form of the short film "Exploration #4" reflects this disconnection, never allowing more than one person in the frame for long stretches of time: Navidson, at least retrospectively, is aware enough of the house's estranging consequences to edit a film that can convey them. But the children seem most affected because most forgotten. As in *Music*, the novel gives clear signs of their distress, as in their ominous drawings of consuming blackness. But again, the parents' selfish concerns dominate, so that "Karen's inability to concentrate on them ... soon drives both children away" (315). The children put themselves to bed, drawn back downstairs later by the commotion to confront alone the bleeding Wax and dead Jed. The one adult who attempts to take action on behalf of the children—Teppet Brookes, Chad's suspicious teacher—bursts in heroically at the scene of the exploration, then "fails to utter even one word or offer any sort of assistance" (317), leaving minutes later, so that "the children are once again abandoned" (319).

As if to indicate the novel's desire to condemn Will and Karen for their narcissistic detachment in the face of the house's epistemological uncertainty, *House* offers evidence that at least one narrative voice contemplated punishing these neglectful parents as *Music* punished Paul and Elaine:

NOTE # [illegible] CHAPTER XIII:

Perhaps I will alter the whole thing. Kill both children. Murder is a better word. . . . Let both parents experience tht [*sic*]. [Let] their narcissism find a new object to wither by. [illegible] them in infanticide. Drown them in blood.

Presented as a note on hotel stationary, typed in red ink and partially obscured by drops of red ink or blood, this editorial comment greets the reader in a frontispiece collage of textual artifacts that sets the stage for the novel before any of the novel's more coherent text begins. It thus prepares us not only for the themes the novel will take up, but also for the highly mediated way in which the novel will render those themes. The note expresses an editorial idea as a possibility, ultimately rejected in the proper novel, but included here all the same; its idea to kill the children to punish the adults is both excluded from and included in the novel. And it is a rejected/accepted novelistic device credited to no one and everyone. It seems to come from Zampanò, supposed author of the Navidson story, and yet bears the cryptic mark "MZ 2,147," which could refer either to the novel's real author, Mark Z. Danielewski, or again to one of his creations, Zampanò (whose other names we do not know). But of course the possibility also exists that Johnny, whose character has amassed and edited Zampanò's The Navidson Record, shaping this narrative with his own personal comments that ultimately take control of the academic analysis, could have written this note (as well as everything else attributed to Zampanò); that the note is typed in Courier, the font used for Johnny's footnotes throughout, further argues this possibility.[23]

In any case, what the note does clearly do is contemplate making a decided, immediate, and conventional restorative act, as did Homes, that would convert children to meaningful sacrifices and end the mystery of the house once and for all. Instead, both children are saved, through the less impactful sacrifice of Will's brother Tom, and the novel continues from this point to generate several hundred more pages of *unheimlich*ness within which the Navidsons must learn to unite as a family. The introductory note also establishes quite bluntly what the pattern of family estrangement as a result of the house suggests more subtly: it tells us, from the start, *what is at stake* in this crisis of signification that masks itself as an esoteric intellectual game—our lives, the lives of our children, and the security of our families. And it prepares us to encounter the house in this postmodern age as a battleground.

Recuperation through remediation

Perhaps because *House of Leaves* begins with the effects of a shattered epistemological security well in place, this novel ultimately manages to construct comfort in exactly this epistemological chaos—using the mediation and simulation that define it to redefine human agency, emotion, and connection. One might say that this novel is *at home* in its chaos, finding in its infinite energy means for growth and regrouping. Making a home from the *unheimlich* is exactly what the Navidsons (and their commentator, Johnny Truant) ultimately do. For as surely as the house begins to tear the family apart, in the end the strength of the family bond becomes the only thing that can successfully fight the voracious boundlessness of the house. During both the initial "Exploration A" and the more extensive "Exploration #4," it is the children who sense what is going on in the bowels of the house, and whose cries Navidson follows home like breadcrumbs, and memories of whom keep him, during the almost fatal Exploration #5, *present* in this house that swallows things like buttons as soon as one stops thinking about them. At the end of that last Exploration, it is the reunion of Karen and Will that defeats the house by physically undoing it: beginning in her children's room, Karen enters the engulfing house as it expands into the nothingness that has replaced the wall bearing her children's nightmarish drawings, looking for Navidson. She finds him, curled up like a baby,[24] after which the house "dissolves" around the couple, leaving them in the warm front yard (524). When it reappears it is a normal house again, a clear reversal of the *unheimlich*ness that has pursued the family for so long.

The last chapter presents the newly reunited Navidson family, Will and Karen finally wedded, in their new, completely normal house in Vermont, depicted as a homey home in Navidson's film by the "simple, warmly lit shots" that capture mother and child in the maternal act of hair braiding, as well as "hundreds of photographs" of the happy family. In fact, "Every room, stairway, and corridor supports pictures of Karen, Daisy, Chad, and Navidson as well as Tom, Reston, Karen's mother, their friends, distant relatives, ancient relatives" (527). This new house wears its photographs of happy family members like an armor: the house is *constructed* of family, its walls, halls, and staircases bound by the images of family solidarity, so that family becomes the force that defines the house and refuses to allow any *unheimlich* shapeshifting. As in *Music for Torching*, harsh prices have been paid for this solidarity: Navidson has lost an eye and a hand; Karen has fought breast cancer; Tom is dead. But unlike Homes's novel, *House* remains firmly rooted, or rootless—the novel's last page refers to the Nordic mythological tree yggdrasil, whose "roots must hold the sky" (709)—in its context of hypertextuality and mediation. The Navidson Record's ending brings no sense of neat novelistic closure—instead offering Navidson's parting shot of the Halloween ghouls, of the movement of "nothing," and of "darkness sweep[ing] in like a hand" (and here Zampanò's description of the film's final moment echoes the darkness that swept in to kill Holloway during "Exploration #4") (528). And it is followed by nearly 200 pages of further mediating material: appendices, photos, an index that creates its own fictions, all further constructing and reconstructing what has come before. Still, the recuperation of family in this final chapter is undeniable and powerful, and properly couched in the labyrinthine context of mediation that both threatened and finally enabled it.

This final representation of the family's victory over the house—its ability to define its own stable sense of home, as Navidson had intended to do at the beginning of the film—through the symbol of family *images* reminds us that the power to redefine both the self and the familial bond amid the chaos of a wholly unknowable world has lain strictly in mediation all along. N. Katherine Hayles makes this argument in her *Writing Machines* when she reads the novel as constructing subjectivity not in spite of or behind but through remediation.[25] As a key example of construction through remediation she offers the sequence in The Navidson Record in which Karen finds Will throwing away a clump of her hair. Hayles points out that "the layering here is already four-fold," with Navidson editing the film of this supposedly real event, Zampanò viewing and recreating the film in language, the reader encountering that verbal description of the film, and finally a (fabricated) critic interpreting the scene. "As the meanings proliferate, Navidson's relationship with Karen became similarly multilayered and complex, combining disregard with tenderness, jealousy with regret, playful resistance to her chiding with a deep wish to recover what he has thrown away." In this way, "the subjects . . . are evacuated as originary objects of representation but reconstituted through multiple layers of remediation."[26] This reconstitution of the subject and of intimacy through remediation, I argue, further enables a recuperation of emotional connection and so of family bonds, through not only technological remediation but also the multiple mediation of strategies of meaning-making that those technologies struggle to represent.

After all, it is the *film* (and actually a film within a fictitious film) that Karen constructs about Navidson, "A Brief History of Who I Love," that prepares her to reconcile with him, and so enables her to return to the house and rescue him from his final exploration. Her film progresses from Navidson's childhood to his photojournalism and ends with a loving shot of him playing in the snow with Chad and Daisy; in so doing it traces Karen's new understanding of the care and humanism of the man she loves and the father of her children. Zampanò specifies that this revelation comes about purely through the acts of mediation involved in making the film:

> The diligence, discipline, and time-consuming research required to fashion this short—there are easily over a hundred edits—allowed Karen for the first time to see Navidson as something other than her own personal fears and projections. She witnessed for herself how much he cherished the human will to persevere. She again and again saw in his pictures and his expressions the longing and tenderness he felt toward her and their children. (368)

By understanding the philosophical connection between the work that kept him away from her and his love of his family, and by coming to this understanding through doing the mediating work herself, Karen learns to accept Will's photojournalism as a fundamental part of his identity, and as the same drive to foster and represent human connection that, she now understands, he contributes to his family. Her film recuperates Will specifically by redeeming his mediating work.

Karen includes in her film a revelation with profound implications for both Will and his work when she shows "the world" that Navidson has feelingly named his most famous photograph with the hand-lettered "Delial." She exposes such a privacy in direct confrontation with the censure that the photograph had brought to Will, a censure the novel conveys with typically mediated "real-world" impact: the novel's "editors" point out in a footnote that the photograph called "Delial" is "clearly based on Kevin Carter's 1994 Pulitzer Prize–winning photograph of a vulture preying on a tiny Sudanese girl who collapsed on her way to a feeding center," and that the shot brought accusations of "gross insensitivity" which, soon after he won the Pulitzer, led to Carter's suicide. Here Danielewski cleverly allows Carter's real self-loathing to leak into the novel and attach itself to his character Will Navidson. Navidson himself expresses this guilt, finally, in a letter he writes to Karen just before embarking on the nearly suicidal final exploration. That his obsessive and self-deprecating thoughts about Delial take up nearly half of the letter indicates the degree to which this guilt symbolized a larger self-doubt that led him back into the house, where he goes searching for something he has lost. The letter also reveals that what he has lost has been lost through mediation, by specifying that "Delial"—notably enclosed in quotation marks even on the back of the photograph, so that the word becomes more a titling of the *picture* than a naming of the girl—haunts him because he has made of her an image, a mediating transformation that is clearly in this case a kind of murder:

> But the photo, that's not what I can't get out of my head right now. Not the photo— that photo, that thing—but who she was before one-sixtieth of a second sliced her out of thin air and won me the pulitzer though that didn't keep the vultures away ... the real vulture was the guy with the camera preying on her for his fuck pulitzer prize. (392)

Even his attempt to remember the girl is doomed to fail, as he can only even remember her as "Delial," his own representation of an image of a girl. However, Karen's loving filmic attention to this photo—to both the image and his attempt at humanizing it through naming it—represents not Will's failure to save the human but his earnest attempt to do so. It is a (filmic) remediation of his (photographic) mediation of the girl that, if it cannot save the girl, at least can recuperate the humanity of the man.

Finally, Karen places this reconstruction of her husband squarely in the context of her reconciliation with him through the transformation of the house into a livable space. For Zampanò describes her film as "the perfect counterpoint to that infinite stretch of hallways, rooms and stairs. The house is empty, her piece is full. The house is dark, her film glows. . . . On Ash Tree Lane stands a house of darkness, cold, and emptiness. In 16mm stands a house of light, love, and colour. By following her heart, Karen made sense of what that place was not" (368–9). Her making sense of Will and his work, then, transforms the endlessly mediating house into a house that makes sense, once again demonstrating the intimate connection between the production and healing of the house's *unheimlichkeit* and its inhabitants' own anxieties about themselves and each other.

Similarly, Will's film about Tom constructs a reconciliation through remediation that is only possible in filmic retrospect. Zampanò notes at the end of the transcript of Tom's Hi 8 video footage, taken during Exploration #4 while Tom waits alone for days at the impossibly deep end of the sinking stairwell, that this portion of *The Navidson Record* reveals painstaking editing used by Will to craft an homage to Tom, who is dead by the time Navidson makes this film (274). In editing "Tom's Story," Navidson transforms the brother he had long accused of selfishness, laziness, and excessive drinking into a brave explorer and caring brother whose first priority was the welfare of Navidson's family. This reconstruction allows Navidson, who had before the saga of the house hardly spoken to his twin brother for years, to include Tom's pictures in the family collection of his new home. Zampanò also reflects Navidson's careful construction of "Tom's Story" in his written representation of it, typesetting "A Short Analysis of Tom's Story" like a composed poem, confined to one visually arresting page on which each line is perfectly centered.

But then of course Zampanò is no stranger to mediation and construction. Johnny, his editor in *Pale Fire* style,[27] points this out from the beginning, asserting in his introduction to The Navidson Record that "Zampanò's entire project is about a film which doesn't even exist," "most of what's been said by famous people has been made up," and that most of the books listed in Zampanò's own footnotes are "fictitious" (xix–xx). But Johnny also understands Zampanò's point in creating The Navidson Record, and my point in holding up Karen's and Will's films as examples of recuperation through reconstruction: these blatant constructions find their power to create agency and assert earnest emotional connection not in spite of their fabrication but because of it. As Johnny puts it in his introduction, "The irony is that it makes no difference that the documentary at the heart of the book is fiction. Zampanò knew from the get go that what's real or isn't real doesn't matter here. The consequences are the same" (xx). Zampanò ensures that we get this point by undermining his own narrative at every turn, not only filling his manuscript with "false quotes [and] invented sources" but also inserting the "greatest ironic gesture" of all, "love of love written by the broken hearted," and a book about "light, film and photography" written by a man who "was blind as a bat" (xxi). All the while Zampanò demonstrates, through his fabricated The Navidson Record, the power of fabrication to generate earnest connection.

Ultimately Zampanò's use of unapologetic textual fabrication for recuperation demonstrates its validity most vividly in his own life. When he is first discovered, dead and alone in a musty, cat-infested apartment, Zampanò is an image of pathos: "'Eighty fucking years old, alone in that pisshole,' Lude had told [Johnny] later. 'I don't want to end up like that. No wife, no kids, no nobody at all. Not even one fucking friend'" (xiv). Johnny too seems pained to think that "Zampanò had no family." But his attitude about the man changes right around the time that he discovers Zampanò's penchant for fabrication, when he realizes that Zampanò, like his book, was not as he appeared. He was "a very funny man," and he wasn't always alone—because of the book. Rather, he had "numerous readers visiting him during the day" (xxi), and writers who took dictation, with names like "Béatrice, Gabrielle, Anne-Marie, Dominique, Eliane, Isabelle and Claudine" (xxii). These women clearly spent considerable time with him, for they knew him well enough to provide the descriptions of him that crowd Johnny's introduction. Having admitted "there is no greater comfort in my life than those soothing tones cradled in a woman's words," Zampanò used his constructed film and his book on that film to construct a sort of family of women around him. Finally, Danielewski extends the lengths to which his character Zampanò might go to create through textual construction a family for himself by adding to Zampanò's journal this comment about creating his own son:

> Perhaps in the margins of darkness I could create a son who is not missing; who lives beyond even my own imagination and invention; whose lusts, stupidities, and strengths carry him farther than even he or I can anticipate. (543)

The connections here to Johnny Truant are unmistakable: his "lusts, stupidities, and strengths" are all recorded "in the margins" of The Navidson Record as footnotes. Further, this entry is labeled September 21, 1970, and Pelafina reveals Johnny's birthdate in one of her letters (592) to be June 21, 1971—exactly nine months after Zampanò muses about creating a son. It is this kind of creation from within, characters spawning other characters, that situates *House of Leaves* inescapably in a vortex of mediation. And whether we indulge the fantasy that Johnny created Zampanò, Zampanò created Johnny, or Pelafina created both[28]—this being only a sampling of the possible narratives of construction that the book variously pursues and undermines— what remains true is that interdependent narrative constructs all work toward creating and recreating family: Zampanò birthing a son, Pelafina reconnecting with her son, Johnny remembering and representing his mother.

This lattice of interlocking narrative constructions—a lattice that extends in all directions, with no beginning or end—points to the fact that people and interpersonal connections are not merely constructed or mediated in this novel but are reconstructed and remediated: not only does Zampanò construct the entirety of The Navidson Record, but Johnny reconstructs it when he organizes and interprets the mess of notes that Zampanò leaves behind. Johnny describes the fragments he finds as "illegible," "impenetrable," "burnt," or "obliterated," and admits to having no clear idea of Zampanò's ultimate intentions for the document (xvii). Therefore, Johnny's recovery of this text can only be read as a vast mediation and fabrication of Zampanò and his ideas, one to which the reader must continue to contribute. Or Zampanò mediates himself by constructing Johnny as his editor. Or Pelafina mediates herself doubly by constructing herself as Zampanò and her son as her own remediator. However it may be or not be, the narrative structure insists on this process of multiple construction and mediation as not only the context for the novel but as the only source of creation of the novel and within the novel.

Tellingly, this process of reconstitution through remediation is repeated during one of the most central moments of familial recuperation in the novel, at the end of the tragic "Exploration #4." Titled "The Escape," in the main text of The Navidson Record but referred to as "The Evacuation" in an earlier footnote (#265), the waffling in descriptive title already reveals the degree to which this event becomes remediated. Even the fact that the event garners its own section and title, when almost all others in The Navidson Record, no matter how crucial, blend seamlessly into the main text, points to the section as a construction within a construction. Right away Zampanò introduces the fabrication theme that is inherent in the sequence: Tom builds a furniture barricade to block the door to the ominous hallway, and one of Zampanò's imagined critics comments that Tom's construction greatly resembles the stage in a theater (339); when the barricade begins to sink with the dissolving floor, Zampanò wryly comments that "the devouring of one theatre of the absurd leads to another" (343). Indeed, considering how Zampanò describes the sources for this text, it is difficult to view these events as much more than theater. He tells us that no cameras are positioned outside the house to capture the considerable action that he reports occurring there, and that the cameras running inside wind up producing "incomprehensible" images (316 n. 265). In later (and separate) interviews, Reston and Navidson admit that the captured images are "incompetent" and "inadequate" (343, 344): they are only made comprehensible, as Zampanò asserts, by Navidson's "brilliant" use of "stylistic discrepancies" to "drive home the overwhelming horror and dislocation experienced by his family" (316 n. 265).

Adding to the layers of remediation is the fact that much of what Zampanò reports descends from these two interviews (344), "The Reston Interview" and "The Last Interview," both of which were conducted long after the events they describe and quoted nowhere in their entirety; as such they represent highly subjective reconstructions of an already highly mediated film. And even *within* this layer of remediation comes another, for some of what Reston reports, namely Navidson's witnessing of the death of Tom, describes an event that *he did not see*. Zampanò explains this remediation as purposeful and meaningful:

> By relying on Reston as the sole narrative voice, [Navidson] subtly draws attention once again to the question of inadequacies in representation, no matter the medium, no matter how flawless. Here in particular, he mockingly emphasizes the fallen nature of any history by purposefully concocting an absurd number of generations.... A pointed reminder that representation does not replace. (346 n. 308)

Navidson's silence on the death of his brother, and his forcing another to tell the story in a doubly mediated way, acts narratively to recuperate the loss of his brother as a real event that cannot be represented; it acts to protect the humanity of the brother he has refound from the potentially destructive act of representation. Only through remediation can the narrative communicate Navidson's need to salvage his brother and the degree to which their highly mediated relationship represents a successful family recuperation.

What Zampanò does not point out, however, is that every act of familial recuperation that occurs in this central scene emerges from the same circumstance of remediation. For it is Reston who describes, in his interview, how Navidson ran into that "closet space intervening between parent and child" to save Karen. At one point Reston reminds us that he is reporting Navidson's impression of this moment of reconciliation: "*supposedly* she calmed down as soon as she was in his arms" (341–2, emphasis added). Daisy's rescue, too, comes to us remediated: the "darkness and insufferable limitations of the Hi 8s" cause Zampanò to rely heavily on the Reston Interview for this entire final scene in the kitchen in which Daisy is saved and Tom lost (346 n. 308). Zampanò's description of the proliferation of black ash on the walls and of what "we hear Tom [say]" further suggests that none of this representation is a straight description of a videotape but is further remediated by the testimony of the absent Reston. What Navidson, professional mediator, asserts here with his silence on the subject of the physical salvation of his family, and what Zampanò then demonstrates by conveying these recuperations through at least five layers of mediation, is that the truth of these events *is* unrepresentable as single acts of mediation, and yet through this process of multiple remediation the significance and emotion of the moments of family salvation and loss can be communicated, and have been communicated in this novel. This strategy validates mediation through remediation: the very self-consciousness of the multiple layers of mediation allow meaning and earnestness to emerge unspoiled by the taint of invisible manipulation, so that what was once considered inherently false and courting detachment from reality becomes, through multiple acts of mediation, one step in the successful representation of emotional experience leading to interpersonal connection and the recuperation of families.

Remediation as "working through" to grief

In the same way that multiple acts of mediation redeem each individual act, the novel's all-encompassing context of narrative remediation recuperates individual narrative strategies. One of the strategies redeemed by its containment within the *House's* matrix of mediation is the psychoanalytic process of "working through" that leads the trauma victim out of the repetition compulsion of melancholy and into the recuperative process of grief. Whereas the Navidson family (and Zampanò's academic analysis of it) demonstrates the process of recuperation of emotion and familial bonds through remediation of inscription technologies, Johnny Truant's reconstruction of Zampanò's text—in which the "monster" in the labyrinth becomes the mother he has lost but has been unable to grieve—depicts recuperation of a traumatic past through his own psychoanalytical remediation of that story. For Johnny, this traumatic understanding, generated through the same process of remediation that unites the Navidson family, becomes an essential part of his ability to come to terms with loss and so remember the mother whom trauma had obliterated. By integrating Johnny's psychoanalytical process of working through so thoroughly into the mediation matrix that defines the novel, Danielewski legitimizes this recently maligned metanarrative as a valid meaning-making method even within our postmodern culture.

Johnny's footnotes to <u>The Navidson Record</u> create a virtual blueprint to Freud's theories of "working through" traumatic experience to escape the trap of melancholy and emerge into conscious, healing grief. In his "Remembering, Repeating, and Working Through" (1914), Freud recommends psychoanalysis as a technique for making unconscious memories of traumatic experience conscious so that victims of trauma can break free from the compulsion to repeat traumatic experience as a substitute for conscious memory. Key to recognizing elements of this unconscious traumatic memory are the victim's dreams, which (Freud asserts here and throughout his writing) contain experiences, often from childhood, that have been neither forgotten by the patient nor consciously understood. Key to making these experiences conscious and so understanding them is transferring the unconscious memories into a conscious realm that is separate from and so safe for the self. Freud focuses on the patient's transference of his or her unconscious feelings onto the analyst, who may then make them conscious so that the patient can "work through" these now-conscious resistances to memory.[29] Johnny transfers his unconscious trauma onto his reading of The Navidson Record in a similar act of self-alienation from unbearable emotion that leads to self-understanding.

Johnny's exploration of his traumatic past through reconstructing The Navidson Record demonstrates recuperation by becoming conscious specifically of grief. One year after publishing "Remembering, Repeating, and Working Through," Freud extends his theory of working through unconscious suffering to the crippling experience of melancholy by identifying the problem of melancholy as that of unconscious suffering of loss that must be consciously worked through ("Mourning and Melancholia," 1917). In this account, he describes melancholy as a reaction to the loss of a loved one resulting in "a profoundly painful dejection, cessation of interest in the outside world, loss of the capacity to love, inhibition of all activity, and a lowering of the self-regarding feelings to a degree that finds utterance in self-reproaches and self-revilings, and culminates in a delusional expectation of punishment." What interests him about this list of symptoms is that it also describes the more transient and less damaging experience of mourning, save for the central addition of feelings of self-loathing. Freud deduces from this difference that, whereas in mourning one experiences the conscious loss of a loved object, in melancholia one experiences "an object-loss which is withdrawn from consciousness," since the melancholic confuses the unconscious object-loss with an ego-loss in an unconscious identification with the lost object. The result of such ego-loss is an impoverishment of the ego, leading to the self-reproach Freud finds characteristic of the melancholic—and which the reader cannot help but find characteristic of the initially melancholy Johnny, whose behavior while reading The Navidson Record clearly echoes Freud's description of melancholia: "This picture of a delusion of (mainly moral) inferiority is completed by sleeplessness and refusal to take nourishment, and—what is psychologically very remarkable—by an overcoming of the instinct which compels every living thing to cling to life."[30]

But Johnny's concerted effort to make conscious his unconscious traumatic past accomplishes more than merely rescuing him from the self-loathing of melancholy. In the context of the novel's larger project and its attention to the threats presented to the individual by the culture of mediation that *House of Leaves*, like *Infinite Jest*, recreates, his psychoanalytic "working through" enables the even more crucial escape of the habit of narcissism that this culture creates, and that *Infinite Jest* creates without escaping. For Freud's paper on mourning and melancholy is notable not merely for distinguishing between these two reactions to loss but also for its further development of his notion of narcissism. Ultimately, Freud differentiates between mourning and melancholy specifically through the element of narcissism: while the mourner escapes interminable grief and self-reproach because he or she maintains a strict division between the self and the lost object, the trap of melancholy results from the sufferer's "narcissistic identification with the object," which represents a "*regression* from one type of object-choice to original narcissism." This regression makes of melancholy a "pathological mourning."[31] Like the cycles of pathological narcissism that entrap the characters of *Infinite Jest* because they would rather regress to a painless infantile state than endure the suffering of their present lives, the pathological mourning of melancholy initially presents for Johnny as a regressive narcissism that promises to shield him from the reality of losing his mother. Such melancholic regression demonstrates the unsurprising fact that it is easier to suffer the self-controlled pain of self-reproach than to acknowledge the uncontrollable, unstoppable pain of losing another, of in fact losing *the* Other who has created one and against which one has shaped one's life. Johnny's journey, then, carries him away from the narcissism that encompasses the world of *Infinite Jest* by forcing him into the conscious recognition and emotional experience of profound loss that those in Wallace's world regressively defend themselves against.

Johnny's comments on <u>The Navidson Record</u> reveal from the beginning that an unknown traumatic subtext lies at the heart of his interaction with Zampanò's book. In his first intrusive footnote, in which he admits having changed Zampanò's "heater" to "water heater," Johnny also finds that something unsettles him about the story of his exploits he has told the previous night: "It's like there's something else, something beyond it all, a greater story still looming in the twilight, which for some reason I'm unable to see" (15). A few days later, he senses something lurking in his peripheral vision as he works in the tattoo parlor, something clearly associated with Zampanò's book because of the "scent of something bitter & foul" that accompanies it. This scent, a recurring image for Johnny, links his obsession with the book to the emotional charge he associates with his first reading of Zampanò's writing: "If I had to give it a name, I think I would call it the scent of human history—a composite of sweat, urine, shit, blood, flesh and semen, as well as joy, sorrow, jealousy, rage, vengeance, fear, love, hope and a whole lot more" (xvi). He turns to find nothing but a deserted corridor, "or was it merely a <u>recently</u> deserted corridor? this thing, whatever it had been, obviously beyond the grasp of my imagination or for that matter my emotions" (27, original emphasis). He does, however, get a clear sense of what the thing is:

> Before I turned, it felt exactly as if in fact I had turned and at that instant caught a sight of some tremendous beast crouched off in the shadows, . . . ragged claws slowly extending, digging into the linoleum, even as its eyes are dilating, beyond the point of reason, completely obliterating the iris, and by that widening fire, the glowing furnace of witness, a <u>camera lucida</u>, with me in silhouette, like some silly Hand shadow twitching about upside down. (27)

His sense that the thing lies beyond the grasp of his emotions identifies it as a traumatic remnant of which he has not made conscious sense; his vision of it as a beast clawing the linoleum, and converting him into a kind of "hand shadow" through the glow of its eyes, indicates that Johnny has identified this traumatic remnant with Zampanò's beast, which gauged the floor next to his body and later causes Tom to make hand shadows in defense against his own fear. Further, the "ragged claws" identify the beast here and elsewhere with Johnny's mother, Pelafina, who has told Johnny in a letter that she had "long, ridiculous purple nails" when he was a child and she was taken away from him (630).

The beast is further associated with Johnny's mother in this passage through his reference to the *camera lucida*, which Barthes made famous as a (failed) method of mourning—specifically of mourning the loss of his mother. He asserted that the photograph could *not* signify, could not in fact capture the essence of its subject in any meaningful way, instead producing only a "flat" reproduction that, because it could not convey a memory, actually blocked memory.[32] This photographic failure to penetrate the subject accounts for Barthes's use of the term *camera lucida*—referring to the prephotographic technology in which one drew an object according to its projection on paper through a prism—rather than *camera obscura*, to communicate the superficiality of the reproduced image. Because of this limitation, Barthes found that the photograph could not help him mourn his mother: "The Photograph—my Photograph—is without culture: when it is painful, nothing in it can transform grief into mourning."[33] Johnny's reference to the *camera lucida* suggests that, at this point in his psychoanalytic working through, the essence of his grief—the loss of his mother—remains inaccessible to him. It also implies his need to come to terms with the person he has become because of that loss, as created by the glare of the beast's/his mother's photographic eyes. Though it will be many months before he makes the explicit connections from his traumatic hauntings to the beast in the house and finally to his mother, Johnny at this moment unconsciously understands that what he is trying so hard to see is a vision of his mother, and of himself as seen through his mother's eyes: who is the man that this monstrous mother has created?

The next time Johnny encounters this beast in the tattoo parlor, he begins to experience traumatic self-alienation, or his own uncanniness: he feels he is falling apart. But this time the encounter with the beast comes as a *textual* assault: letters and words attack "like artillery shells. Shrapnel, like syllables, flying everywhere. Terrible syllables. Sharp. Cracked. Traveling at murderous speed" (71). His flight from this word-beast results in his landing in a sea of spilled black ink, so that for a moment he thinks he has disappeared in a "dissolution of the self" (72). Only the purple ink that has splattered on his face and arms defines his presence. Hayles reads this moment as the novel's best example of the "borderland between the metaphoric and the literal, the imaginary and the real" where the beast exists, the two inks defining Johnny in terms of both presence and absence.[34] But the passage also connects Johnny's presence and his absence in terms of his mother, the black ink representing her words and letters that came to him like weapons over the years, and the purple, as Hayles points out, representing the nailpolish she claims to have worn on the day she tried to kill him. She is the source of both his creation and his destruction, simultaneously through her words.

Once he has forged this connection between the beast of <u>The Navidson Record</u> and his own maternal haunting, he grows increasingly involved in the book, beginning to think that "questions about the house will eventually return answers about myself" (297). The sense of control over the book with which he began reverses into his belief that he depends on the book for his survival, that he has been created by it, so that he is a construct of fiction (326): "There's only one choice now: finish what Zampanò himself failed to finish. Re-inter this thing in a binding tomb. Make it only a book" (327, original emphasis). Thus his mediation of The Navidson Record, presented as a remediation of an already highly mediated academic analysis, proceeds as a conscious attempt to reconstruct a self he can live with.

True to psychoanalytic form, Johnny experiences an unconscious working through of his childhood trauma in the form of a dream before he is ready to face his past consciously. He records this dream, and seems to experience it, alongside a section of The Navidson Record detailing competing psychoanalytic explanations for Navidson's return to the house in Exploration #5, along with competing analyses of three dreams described by Navidson shortly before that solo trip. In this pretentious context, Johnny's dream lies in stark contrast, pulsing with raw emotion and uninterpreted connections backward and forward into the narrative he has been constructing. Zampanò's long-winded academic analysis might warn us against imposing theoretical or psychoanalytic interpretation onto Johnny's dream elements, but the textual evidence of these connections to both his own narrative and Zampanò's becomes undeniable.

Johnny dreams he is in a "deserted kitchen" shimmering with "stainless steel"; when he visits his childhood house months later, he uses both images to describe the kitchen there (505). He is attacked by a "drunken frat boy," who has been identified earlier in The Navidson Record as Theseus, killer of the minotaur, in an updated version of the minotaur myth (110–11 n. 124), thus placing Johnny in the position of the minotaur. He notices his hands look melted, now being only "the thin effects of skin which have in fact been dipped in boiling oil," and so recalls the accident in which his mother spilled boiling oil on him when he was 4 years old. But this time his entire body and face become deformed as a result: he now resembles the minotaur, a boy who has been abandoned by his family. The frat boy turns into a series of women who try to kill him—women who appear to be maternally caring for him even as they cause him pain—until he realizes he is monstrous now; it is *his* claws and teeth that are "long and sharp and strong" (403–5). His mother has deformed him, abandoned him, then transformed him into the exiled minotaur, but because of the pain she has inflicted he can strike out against her if he chooses: in his dream, Johnny faces the pain of his mother's abuse and uses it to take control of his future. Shortly after this dream, Johnny sells his mother's locket, along with his first letter to her lodged inside it, and decides to set off on a journey of self-discovery to "quiet the [s]ea" inside him. It is a sea of pain begun by his mother's first wounding of him—the burning-oil accident, which produced "Oceanus whirls" (506) on his arms—that he seeks to calm, an action made possible by the transformation he experienced in his unconscious working through of his dream.

In the course of his journey he realizes that, though his questions of the book and its house do return answers of himself, ultimately he is investigating the wrong house and "tracing the wrong history" (502). At this point he sees that "My mother is right before me now," and he leaves the Navidson history behind to visit the asylum where his mother lived and died and the house where she was taken from him. He wanders the labyrinthine halls of the hospital and stands in the spot where his parents' kitchen once was, site of the original wounding and birth of the "Oceanus whirls," and finds "something, hiding down some hall in my head, though not in my head but a house, . . . perhaps by the foyer, . . . incessantly flicking its long polished nails" (506); here he conflates the site of gruesome scene in "The Escape" with the site of his mother's leaving. Following his preparations to take control in his dream, Johnny then goes through a transformation from victimized, deformed boy at the center of a maze to the monster who stalks the labyrinth, fantasizing that he murders Gdansk Man and plans to rape Kyrie while killing her: "I will become, I have become, a creature unstirred by history, no longer moved by the present, just hungry, blind and at long last full of mindless wrath" (497). This transformation from victim to raging perpetrator, enabled by his return to his childhood home and the memories it holds, serves as the climactic end to Johnny's journey; his entry into wrath leaves him unable to remember any of the journey that has come before.

But once he has reread his journal entries, he continues his journal with an entry that divulges the key to the house, to his house, an entry that reads to us as a method by which he decodes all that has come before. As he writes this entry he remembers that his mother never did strangle him, and that "his own dark hallway"—his equivalent to the Navidson hallway—was a "brightly lit" foyer in which his mother was forced to leave him. The "roar" in this hallway was not the monster of the house, or his father's reaction to Pelafina's strangling of him (as she claimed in her letter), but his mother's own screams as she was torn from her child. Johnny now understands that his 7-year-old's incomprehension of the moment turned his mother's leaving, and his mother herself, into a traumatic cipher, leading to his traumatized disaffection: "I grew to insist on her absence, which was how I finally learned what it meant to be numb. Really numb. And then one day, I don't know when, I forgot the whole thing. Like a bad dream, the details of those five and a half minutes just went and left me to my future" (517)—that is, until he rediscovered those "five and a half minutes" in "The Five and a Half Minute Hallway" that began the Navidson adventure. In this discovery, Johnny converts the nothing that haunted the Navidson labyrinth into a something: "Of course there always will be darkness but I realize now that something inhabits it" (518). The beast, once liminal, an absent presence, becomes in Johnny's reconstructed memory something equally ethereal and shapeshifting but nonetheless real, the sign of a real loss, of the loss of his mother.

Having declared in the beginning that "we all create stories to protect ourselves," he ends this journal entry, as he begins and ends his portion of the novel, with a story. Such bookending suggests that all that has come in between comprises the "protective" story he has spun.[35] In this final story, an ill-formed baby sustained by machines is finally released into death by his mother's love. Johnny offers it as an ultimate act of healing by attributing it to the doctor he claims to have met while visiting Seattle, an imagined stay during which his journal entries chart physical and mental recovery that culminate in his telling statement that "I'd forgotten my mother" (508). Having remembered the real trauma in order to let it go, he is free to create a story in which his mother finally lets go of him, and the suffering child dies—a story in which the

"Oceanus whirls" of his scarred arms become the "tiny fingers curled like sea shells" of the baby, his "sea" grown calm.

My argument so far has been that the clarity of the psychoanalytic encoding of Johnny's story demonstrates that we are to read this character as experiencing a psychoanalytic "working through" of his traumatic past via writing. But more ambitiously, the novel as a whole encourages us to read Johnny's story in this way through narrative structure and its mediated narrative strategies. First, Johnny frames the entirety of *House of Leaves* as a journey of discovery that begins with a haunted house and ends, for him, with his discovery of exactly what is haunting that house, as we see from the structure of chapter XXI: the seemingly disjointed sequencing of his journal that occupies that chapter reveals itself to be Johnny's method of shaping his own writing and Zampanò's to produce this narrative of psychological self-discovery. Early on October 31, 1998, after he has completed his journey to his childhood house but before he has understood what it means, he writes the introduction to the novel *House of Leaves*, in which he casts the experience of reading the novel as personally revolutionary ("you'll suddenly realize things are not how you perceived them to be at all. For some reason, you will no longer be the person you believed you once were," xxii) but cannot yet assert any of the answers he has found. His portion of the novel ends with his entry written later that same day, in which he finally understands what the "hallway" means to him. That he ends not with the chronologically last entry but with the one in which he remembers and lets go of his mother's haunting defines his story precisely as a working through to grief through his mediation of The Navidson Record. Therefore, he presents his story *not* as a story of coming to terms with this horrible absent presence, with the nothing at the heart of the Navidson house, but of putting a face to that nothing, making it a something, and so turning the horrifying lack into a loss he can grieve. His is a conversion of the terror of the crisis of signification into the pain of an individual suffering a loss he can accept and learn to live with.

Even the seemingly chaotic sequencing of his journal entries in chapter XXI supports this psychoanalytic reading, for Johnny tells us, after he has returned from his journey and suffered the self-obliterating transformation into "mindless wrath," that his only way to reconstruct and understand the journey is to reconsider his own writing:

I must remember.

I must read.

I must read.

I must read. (498)

Next, he presents the journal entries detailing that journey, ending in the narrative's present with his revelation-filled October 31st entry: thus the entries take us from his psychotic break, back through the discovery experience that caused it, and then to his understanding of it. By occurring not in the order in which they were written but in the order in which he reread/reencountered them in his quest for self-knowledge, the entries assert that it is only through consciously reconsidering and rereading his written past that he could reach such an understanding. His past is necessarily key to his understanding of his present, and of our understanding of his reading of this book, and his mediation of it.

The "editors" of the book, the most "exterior" of our mediating narrators, agree, encouraging us to read Johnny's story, and his reading of Zampanò's story, through the lens of his troubled past:

> Though Mr. Truant's asides may often seem impenetrable, they are not without rhyme or reason. The reader who wishes to interpret Mr. Truant on his or her own may disregard this note. Those, however, who feel they would profit from a better understanding of his past may wish to proceed ahead and read his father's obituary in Appendix II-D as well as those letters written by his institutionalized mother in Appendix II-E.—Ed. (72 n. 78)

They offer this helpful suggestion during Johnny's description of his attack by letters in the tattoo parlor, when he begins to associate the absent monster of the house with his forgotten mother. We will have no way of spying this association unless we have already finished the book—or read, as they suggest, the relevant appendices. This necessity of knowing Johnny's personal history in order to understand a thread of the novel *House*, and even in order to read the Navidson family's encounter with the house in the multilayered way on which the book insists, validates exactly a kind of reading—psychoanalytical, individually subjective—that our culture of multiple mediation claims to invalidate. In fact, this psychoanalytic reading is a *necessary* part of the structure that encompasses *House of Leaves*, as Johnny's journey enables much of the remediation that defines the book. Here we find the "depth model" disparaged by Jameson[36] in the service of a larger network of undifferentiated mediation and interdependence.

Johnny's dream of his transformation from trauma into grief in terms of his transformation into the minotaur—not just any mythological minotaur, but the one that inhabits Zampanò's narrative and so haunts the Navidson house—also establishes that it is this psychoanalytic process of "working through" that troubles both the Navidsons' labyrinthine crisis of signification and Zampanò's attempt to analyze and subdue it. Zampanò introduces the minotaur into the novel in chapter IX—"The Labyrinth," according to his "Possible Chapter Titles" listed in his Appendix A; this is the beast that haunts both house and *House*. But Zampanò quickly deviates from the standard myth of the minotaur, which he details in his main text as "a creature born from an illicit encounter between the queen and a bull." Zampanò offers his own theory of the minotaur in an elaborate footnote that immediately reveals his own discomfort with the topic: he has banished his musings on the meaning of the minotaur below the footnote line.

Deviating tellingly from the traditional myth, Zampanò imagines the minotaur as not half man, half bull, or simply a man with the head of a bull, but "a man with a deformed face." He then converts the sinister story of a father, King Minos, imprisoning his monstrous son and sending youths to kill him, into the sentimental tale of a tormented father who, unwilling to reveal publicly his deformed son but unable to harm him, places the boy in a labyrinth designed to contain him without the cruelty of bars. The domestic drama inherent in this revised version of the minotaur becomes even clearer when Zampanò describes a play that he claims was written based on his own "published thoughts on this subject." In the play (*The Minotaur*, by Taggert Chiclitz), "the Minotaur is a gentle and misunderstood creature," and King Minos a deeply conflicted father whose affection for his son produces "guilt and sorrow [that] incenses him to no end." Still, he is able to overcome his disgust at his son's deformities and develops a deep "paternal love" for him over the course of the play. When Theseus, whom Chiclitz describes as a "drunken, virtually retarded frat boy," "hacks the Minotaur into little pieces," the King's confliction between private paternal love and public persona thrusts him into a pathetic experience of simultaneous repression and loss: he "publicly commends Theseus," tears streaming down his face for his lost son, tears the public misreads as a "sign of gratitude" (110–11 n. 123).

What Zampanò asserts with his revision of the minotaur myth, and then tries to erase by striking the text, is that the "monster" that haunts the labyrinth is *not* merely a liminal creature of meaningless but is, or at least is also, the specter of a traumatized individual suffering a personal tragedy of loss. At the heart of the labyrinth and of the house is a family drama, a domestic crisis that demands attention as surely as does the crisis of signification that he and his fictitious explorers pursue. Clearly Zampanò believed this family crisis, this individual loss, was capable of recovery, as the play based on his ideas about the minotaur turns on its affective father-son reconciliation. But the play also reveals Zampanò's deep discomfort with this notion of family recovery, ending not with the father's public embracing of the son but with his painful repression of both his love and loss of his son. Finally, Zampanò—through his own remarks and his invention of Chiclitz's play—envisions the minotaur as a symbol of repression, as he admits in his comment on the labyrinth (110 n. 123). In fact, he is so insistent on this interpretation that he represses all material on the minotaur from his text, striking through it as if to erase his desire to read the haunting of the house as psychological trauma capable of some sort of healing. His attempted excision of the minotaur material thus becomes a sign of the need of the discourse of signification—the monster of meaningless that haunts the house—to repress the discourse of psychoanalytical healing. In this novel, it is a repression of the latter discourse that enables the former to maintain its absent center.

Then it is no wonder that it is Johnny, who has begun his own process of working through from the start, who revives this psychoanalytic heart of The Navidson Record and of the labyrinth. He keeps it present in the text and then himself embodies the minotaur narrative in the dream that leads to his own psychoanalytic healing, and to the healing of his own relationship, previously marked by abandonment and injury, with his mother. Therefore, his mediation of Zampanò's repressed psychoanalytic myth of the minotaur keeps this psychoanalytic possibility alive and at the heart of both The Navidson Record and Johnny's story, repressed by one and recuperated by the other. That Johnny constructs his own recovery into grief through mediation of a narrative repressed by Zampanò—and recuperates that repressed narrative at the same time— argues most strongly for the interdependence of the discourses of psychoanalytical working through and the crisis of signification: in this novel, each is born of the other.

Finally, what is most striking about Johnny's story is not simply that it is contained within a context that claims it is no longer possible or valid, but that this psychoanalytic element emerges as the most compelling element of the novel. The reader's first response to the novel, which is initially structured on the page in the familiar style of academic prose (important information in the main text, peripheral information exiled below the footnote line and back into the appendices), is to read the novel as the story of Will Navidson and family. Yet almost every reader I have encountered, including students, critics, and the thousands who have registered online their insightful responses to the book, begins to experience the book as the story of Johnny Truant. Johnny's story is so successful at its recuperation of affect and subjectivity, in other words, that his is the story that sticks with the reader after the *House* has finally been navigated. The book demonstrates the way in which his story bursts in upon the academic analysis of The Navidson Record by allowing Johnny's footnotes to overtake the main narrative in chapter XXI, for the first time becoming the featured text, with no intrusions by The Navidson Record.

According to the "editors," his story actually justifies the novel's printing. In the Foreword, the editors introduce *House* by pointing out that the first edition did not contain chapter XXI, Appendix II, Appendix III, or the index: both chapter XXI and Appendix II tell the main portion of Johnny's story, through his journal entries and his mother's letters. Johnny also points out in a footnote that these additions enabled the publication of the whole:

> To date, I've counted over two hundred rejection letters from various literary journals, publishing houses, even a few words of discouragement from prominent professors in east coast universities. No one wanted the old man's words— except me. (20)

According to the novel, Zampanò's story about liminal being and the nothingness at the heart of the crisis of signification could not compel publishers to take up his story. But the addition of Johnny's personal struggle with his own crisis of signification, one that *was* solvable in an old-fashioned recuperation of self and affect, did. His psychoanalytical journey, then, illustrates not only the resilience of a poststructurally disparaged narrative mode in this context of pure remediation, or the ironic need of this remediation matrix for that quaint strategy, but also the heart and soul of a book whose poststructural structure denies that such things exist.

Postmodern irony enabling postmodern families

There is a kind of irony at the heart of any argument that credits one discourse with the recovery of another that it has defined as obsolete. But it is a productive kind of irony. Offering the possibility of this return of the psychoanalytic journey—and so of affect and personal growth—from within the mediation that situates the novel so squarely in a postmodern and poststructural context argues for the viability of these concepts within contemporary culture. It also allows *House* to remain firmly in its genre-blurring novelistic context rather than forcing the kind of recuperation through narrative conventionality that *Music* requires. In this meaningfully ironic way, the novel provides space for an alternative to a postmodern insistence on ironic disaffection and meaninglessness while still declaring that it is those forces that continue to define our cultural reality in twenty-first-century America. Thus it offers an escape route that begins and ends on the inside of the mediation funhouse—a Möbius-strip structure that recalls the book's ultimate moment of circularity, when Navidson burns, page-by-page, a book in order to read it, a book that turns out to be this book, *House of Leaves*.

House of Leaves appeared in print in March of 2000, shortly before our wry, ironic American culture would face its own real-life version of meaningless destruction in the World Trade Center attacks on September 11, 2001. The over 3,000 deaths, coming, at first glance, out of nowhere, were so immediately incomprehensible and horrible at the same time—so traumatic—that we quickly heard cries from many of our nation's newsmakers of the "end of the age of irony."[37] But just as quickly came a flurry of irony apologists who asserted that irony would return to its rightful place before we knew it, reigning over the twenty-first century it had ushered in. They were right.[38] One commentator aptly characterized the death-of-irony proclamation as "a 21st century update of the regrettably mistaken maxim that there could be no poetry after Auschwitz."[39] It was as if those who predicted the end of irony wished for the same kind of simple reversal that *Music* attempts to enact—one that does not process the tragedy from inside the culture in which it is contained, but rather wishes to undo the context that leaves us unable to process that tragedy.

But this thinking is marred not just by a logical flaw—the belief that an undesirable product of culture can be changed by wishing away the culture that created it—but also by a shortsighted understanding of irony. When Graydon Carter and others wrote irony's obituary, they were working from the widespread popular understanding of irony as a state of detachment and disaffection, a lack of concern for "serious" things concerning the real world, and a preoccupation with images, consumption, media, and all the other products of our simulation culture. Beyond describing the American experience of the twenty-first century, this view of irony also represents a key theoretical view of postmodernism, as defined by Fredric Jameson (and as lamented by David Foster Wallace). In this view, neither the past nor the present is accessible except as simulation, so that meaningful art and commentary are no longer possible; parody, for example, must be replaced by the meaninglessness of pastiche, a random recycling of the past. Further, this constitutional superficiality means that subjects themselves become incapable of containing or expressing any emotional reaction to the state of meaninglessness in which they find themselves. Irony therefore becomes impotent, incapable of making qualitative judgments about the world—about the difference between what we encounter and what we expect—and so capable only of expressing our apathetic mockery of the simulated world in which we live.

This is exactly the kind of irony that seemed so appalling to many in the wake of the World Trade Center attacks on 9/11, an event which, though described repeatedly as looking "just like a movie" by traumatized witnesses groping for the comfort of anesthetized simulation, did not represent but *was* a horrifyingly real rupture of spaces and bodies. In the presence of such an insistently real event, ironic detachment and an apathetic contemplation of the disconnection between words and things seem monstrous. It is also the kind of irony expressed by the characters in *Music for Torching* and many (especially early) DeLillo novels;[40] I have argued in Chapter 1 that the characters in *White Noise* deploy exactly this kind of irony specifically in opposition to, or defense against earnestness, because *they do not want to care*. But it is precisely this ironic disaffection that elements of American art and culture seem in the twenty-first century to be trying to reverse. Of the "end of irony," Tim Cavanaugh commented that "deadpan japery isn't the cause of disaffection but the result."[41] As long as we are a culture defined by simulation, in which nothing *is* but merely *seems*, irony—at its core an acknowledgment of this is/seems disjunction—will define us. So is there a way to recuperate irony? Can irony both acknowledge the disjunction at the heart of our culture and care about what that disjunction means?

The concept of constructive irony is a fundamentally modernist one. Paul Fussell, in his seminal *The Great War and Modern Memory* (1975), defines "modern understanding" as "essentially ironic; and . . . originat[ing] largely in the application of mind and memory to the events of the Great War."[42] Here we find irony not being banished by but arising out of the enormous disjunction between expectation and reality brought on by the unprecedented horrors of World War I. Further, irony for Fussell promotes understanding, in that it cements memory: Fussell argues through numerous well-documented examples that it was exactly the ironies (truths countering expectations) of the war that caused soldiers to remember details they would have otherwise forgotten, and to wrestle these memories into some sort of understanding. This understanding was a strangely new one, as Michiko Kakutani points out when writing of Fussell's book in the context of contemporary calls for the "end of irony": "Inadequate in the face of that war's slaughter, traditional moral language gave way to double-entendres, sardonic humor and chill expressions of sang-froid. Everyday events began to mean their opposite." Still, the doubleness and wordplay that this irony produced spoke to an essential truth and mourned a cultural loss—the loss of innocence and of a world of expectations. This is the modern, earnest irony that another critic of the mid-twentieth century, World War I era describes: "The ironist is ironical not because he does not care, but because he cares too much."[43]

From this modernist formulation of productive irony we can take the lesson that proposing a solution to the morass of ironic disaffection that late twentieth-century postmodern culture has produced necessitates escaping the binary of irony/earnestness that so many twentieth-century postmodern novels reproduce. It requires defining irony not as an impediment to communication and expression but as a productive tool for both. Linda Hutcheon brings this idea of a caring, meaningful irony into the context of postmodernism in her *A Poetics of Postmodernism* (1989). A cornerstone of her politics of postmodernism, and that differentiates hers from Jameson's postmodernism, is her contention that meaningful parody *is* still possible, a contention that simultaneously revives a postmodern concept of irony: she defines contemporary parody as "repetition with critical distance that allows ironic signaling of difference at the very heart of similarity," which "enacts both change and cultural continuity." Directly countering Jameson, she claims that "to include irony and play is *never* necessarily to exclude seriousness and purpose in postmodernist art." Irony in this context becomes what allows us to make distinctions between past and present, and what allows us to make those distinctions meaningful in art. Hutcheon also asserts that, far from leading to personal apathy and social disconnection, parody and its accompanying irony can aid in the building of textual communities: "parodic double-voicing of heterogeneity is not just a device which allows contesting assertions of difference. It also paradoxically offers a textual mode of collectivity and community of discourses which has proved useful to both feminism and postmodernism."[44] This is an irony that works from within the boundaries of multivocal, heterogeneous postmodernism to generate meaning and build textual communities.

Michael Roth similarly proposes a "deprivileging of irony" as his solution to the "ironist's cage" in which we have become trapped in the late twentieth century. The cage comes about when we lose faith in the possibility for positive change that allows irony to function as a positive call to action: in order to argue for social change we must "preserve a clearing in which [ironist critics'] readers can reconnect to a project of political action. When this clearing can no longer be maintained, the ironic form comes to have an extraordinary privilege."[45] Roth demonstrates this process of ironic encaging through the social criticism and theory of Kojéve, Foucault, and Derrida, all of whom have, according to Roth, abandoned the Hegelian tradition of criticizing in the name of offering a more "true" philosophy, and instead only offer ironic acknowledgment of the untruths we cannot escape: traditionally, "the newest philosophy exposes the limitations—the bars on the cage—of his or her predecessors. We are urged out of the cage by someone who can see in. However, in the ironic trashing of this tradition, all that a philosopher can offer is a description of the *inside* of the cage."[46] Therefore, for Roth "it is not irony itself (a form that makes possible important types of criticism, play, and tolerance) but its privileging that has become problematic."[47] Certainly the novels of DeLillo and Wallace examined in Chapters 1 and 2 illustrate the profundity of the damage to individuals and society that such ironic privileging can do. But novels can imagine a way out of the ironist's cage they have helped to build, by using irony as Hutcheon and Roth encourage us to do: by dethroning irony as our reigning rhetorical mode of responding to contemporary culture, and allowing it to function as one device among many—including such pre-postmodern concepts like earnestness, belief, and psychoanalytically defined subjects—in an attempt to reimagine contemporary culture and its rhetorical modes as methods of constructing meaning and connection rather than mocking their impossibility. This is exactly how irony works in *House of Leaves*.

Academic criticism acts as the most pervasive and pointed object of parody in the novel, while offering a model for recuperation through ironic remediation. Academia and its exactitude receive plenty of direct mockery from Johnny, who habitually satirizes Zampanò's critical pretensions and shares his habit of tasking unaccredited

women, largely recruited from bars, to translate and transcribe important passages of
The Navidson Record. But the novel's form most blatantly illustrates its simultaneous
obsession with and derision of academic writing. Danielewski presents the novel
essentially as an academic analysis accompanied by one reader's interpretive footnotes,
but this academic form becomes quickly subverted in several significant ways. Not
only is the study's subject of inquiry, *The Navidson Record*, fictitious, but Zampanò's
appeals to academia to verify his concocted subject matter are equally false: he
undermines the veracity of not just one project but of the whole academic system in
which it is a part. Even the index reflects not an objective categorizing of the study but
an entirely new fiction in and of itself. Finally, Johnny's vividly earnest and affective
story most profoundly undermines the genre of academic analysis, in that the novel's
most compelling material exists not in its main text but in its footnotes, enacting a sort
of reversal, even a hijacking, of the structure of the academic essay.

One scene in the novel provides an effective example of how the novel brings form
and content together in its critique of academic analysis. Karen Green's film, "What
Some Have Thought," in which she consults a wide variety of "experts" for explanations
of the house, exists in the novel as a partial transcript, discredited from the start by the
mysterious gestation that colors every text in the novel as fictitious.[48] In it, each scholar/
thinker/artist—ranging from Camille Paglia, Stephen King, Harold Bloom, Stanley
Kubrick, and Derrida, to less famous doctors, architects, and engineers—interprets
the film from his or her own perspective, so that comments on the house's impossible
physics, psychological effects, filmability, bestselling potential, and misogynistic
impulses appear side by side, with no mediating commentary from Karen, Zampanò,
or Johnny. Laid out before us in this unanalyzed way, these competing interpretations
offer a model of what the novel as a whole accomplishes with its mediated structure:
all interpretations, all readings, seem equally valid and invalid[49]—each one taken
alone seeming plausible and interesting, but taken together, suddenly ridiculous in the
sheer magnitude of possible readings. In this way, the novel as a whole is structured
to resist criticism, being so shot through with contradictions and impossibilities, so
determined to present its multiple facets as equally possible and interdependent, that
most assertions about the book can be easily contradicted simply by a slight shift in
perspective. And yet, in perhaps its most basic inherent contradiction, the novel *invites*
criticism, in fact *demands* it, presenting itself as a code to be cracked, if only the reader
should give it proper scrutiny.[50]

This critique of academic criticism demonstrates the kind of meaningful parody
by way of irony that Hutcheon posits as one of postmodernism's strategies for
meaning-making. *House* does not merely repeat academic criticism as a laughable
pastiche but places it within its larger context of decentered remediation in which it,
like everything else, is both true and false. But within this parody of criticism one
subnarrative emerges that in turn mediates the parody: Karen's film begins and ends with
the comments of "Leslie Stern, M. D. Psychiatrist," an unmistakable gesture of closure for
a film that otherwise moves from speaker to speaker haphazardly. In her introductory
and concluding remarks, Stern answers Karen's questions about the meaning of the
house by asking "What do you think it means?," thus turning Karen's abstract question

about the house's crisis of signification into a question of personal meaning-making. The similarity between the privileging of this psychoanalytic perspective within the film's larger parody of criticism and the privileging of Johnny's psychoanalytic journey within the novel's larger context of remediation is unmistakable. Thus, irony in *House of Leaves* is transformed from debilitating detachment to instrumental narrative technique in two distinct ways: it defines for academic criticism a new function within the context of a postmodern world; and it exists within a mediating framework that insists it is one useful technique for meaning-making among many. Another, it posits, is psychoanalytic reconstruction. *House of Leaves*, then, offers in literary form an answer to the problem of the ironist's cage as Roth imagined it: the deprivileging of irony.

Finally, we can say that *House of Leaves* understands what *Music for Torching* does not, and what Wallace had been theorizing and striving toward in his fiction for a decade: that in order to propose a viable possibility in this twenty-first-century culture of the reemergence of some sort of earnestness and meaning—an antidote to the destructiveness of ironic detachment—that possibility must arise within the ironizing and mediating culture itself. Efforts such as these by Wallace and Danielewski to repurpose the postmodern tools at hand stand behind the cornucopia of affect-oriented, unapologetically humanist poststructural fiction that is coming to characterize literature of the early twenty-first century, as it constructs textual spaces in which it can make present not just the self and empathy between selves but also belief, truth, and the real.

Notes

1   Interestingly, Allen Ruch opens his review of *House of Leaves* with a description of an Ocean City funhouse as metaphor for Danielewski's novel. This analogy bears striking resemblance to a 1996 sociological study that reads families in funhouses as constructing individual and then family identities via shared responses to the distorted images encountered there. See Jack Katz, "Families and Funny Mirrors: A Study of Social Construction and Personal Embodiment of Humor," *American Journal of Sociology* 101 no. 5 (1996): 1194–238.

2   In describing the couple's burning of their house as a "potlatch," I use the term as Bataille did in early work such as that collected in *Visions of Excess: Selected Writings 1927–1939* (Minneapolis: University of Minnesota Press, 1985; trans. Allan Stoekl), to signify purposeless consumption or expenditure, or consumption not in the service of a larger economy of sacrifice. Such a use of the term contrasts Bataille's later definition, as in his 1967 *The Accursed Share* (New York: Zone Books, 1991; trans. Robert Hurley) of potlatch as a rational act in the service of a restrictive economy requiring a certain amount of sacrifice. This distinction is crucial to a reading of *Music for Torching* as structurally recuperative, as I read the act of burning the house as a wholly irrational and purposeless enactment of the meaningless consumption that this thoroughly bourgeois society encourages, whereas the death/expenditure of Sammy at the end of the novel ultimately reinterprets this postmodern narrative of meaningless consumption as a restrictive economy in which the sacrifice of a son

can make meaning for his parents, and all of the novel's heretofore pointless signs can signify. In moving from potlatch to sacrifice, the novel moves from postmodern indeterminacy to realist logic, from meaningless lack to meaningful loss.

3 Edward Albee, *A Delicate Balance* (New York: Penguin Books, 1997), 49.

4 A. M. Homes, *Music for Torching* (New York: HarperCollins, 1999), 273. Subsequent references will be noted parenthetically.

5 Conversation with A. M. Homes (Hammer Museum, Los Angeles, CA, July 24, 2002).

6 This family's name marks it as constructed by and constructing media production itself, suggesting that its members represent the media consumers whose opinions dictate the Nielsen ratings that have shaped television programming since the induction of automated monitoring of media consumption in the early 1970s. Homes's telling naming indicates the extent to which in her novel the family has absorbed the forces of mediation that presented such a distinctly separate and clamorous backdrop against which individuals struggle in *White Noise*. The name "Nielsen" even suggests that the family members *want* to be absorbed into media: the Nielsen Media Research company acknowledges its seductive power when it lists, as the first "FAQ" on its website, "How do I become a Nielsen family?" ("Nielsen Media Research," accessed December 31, 2003, www.nielsenmedia.com).

7 Similarly, Gregory Crewdson's photography exhibition in New York City in 2002, "American Standard: (Para)Normality and Everyday Life," collected images from the 1960s to the 1980s that "tell ambiguous tales of violence and alienation in meticulously ordered surroundings." See Ariella Budick, "Beyond Appearances in Suburbia," *Los Angeles Times*, July 10, 2002.

8 Thus he is much like Wilder, whom Jack and Babette loved for exactly this innocence, his existence before the threshold of the difficulties of modern life.

9 In the context of the previous night's grilling party, these gifts come from Elaine as a meaningful opposition to her earlier gesture of potlatch.

10 Conversation with A. M. Homes (Hammer Museum, Los Angeles, CA, July 24, 2002).

11 For an extended exploration of A. M. Homes's unique blend of morality, realism, and postmodernism in both her *Music* and *This Book Will Save Your Life* (New York: Penguin, 2006), see my article "A Lamb in Wolf's Clothing," *Critique* 53 no. 3 (2012): 214–37.

12 For the publication history of *House*, see N. Katherine Hayles's *Writing Machines* (Cambridge: MIT Press, 2002) and Eric Wittmershaus's "Profile: Mark Z. Danielewski," *flakmagazine*, accessed June 18, 2003, www.flakmag.com/features/mzd. html.

13 Coined by Ted Nelson in the 1960s, "hypertext" can be most simply described as writing that is nonsequential, allows the reader to make choices in constructing a narrative structure, and provides links among various points in the narrative or text. A partial list of fan sites devoted to discussing, decoding, and generally enjoying *House of Leaves* includes sites at houseofleaves.com, fanpop.com, joblo. com, and markdanielewski.info; of course, a *House of Leaves* fan club exists on Facebook.

14 Hayles compares the use of the color blue in this novel to the blue screen technique used in film, in which blue signifies a present absence, a "backdrop onto which anything can be projected," so that when the novel binds in a blue box a list of all that is *not* in the house, "the text is attempting to project into this space the linguistic signifiers for everything in the world, as if attempting to make up through verbal

proliferation the absolute emptiness of the House as a physical space." See Hayles, "Saving the Subject," *American Literature* 74 no. 4 (2002): 795–6.

15 The novel invokes this analogy, making several references to Escher's images as examples of self-reflexivity. Johnny further complicates this already complicated image by suggesting that "pages 30, 356 and 441, however, kind of contradict this. Though not really" (113 n. 133).

16 Danielewski urges his readers to resist the desire to impose clarity and order on a narrative structure that consciously denies both by asserting repeatedly the impossibility of privileging any one narrative voice over the others. See Larry McCaffery and Sinda Gregory, "Haunted House—An Interview with Mark Z. Danielewski," *Critique: Studies in Contemporary Fiction* 44 no. 2 (2003): 99–135 and Hayles, *Writing Machines*.

17 Danielewski underscores the text's authorial circularity by crediting the book to his characters on the title page, which reads, "House of Leaves by Zampanò with introduction and notes by Johnny Truant." Danielewski's name appears in the possessive only, on the page opposite this title page.

18 McCaffery and Gregory, "Haunted House—An Interview with Mark Z. Danielewski," 106 (original italics).

19 McCaffery, "An Interview with David Foster Wallace," 147 (original italics).

20 Mark Danielewski, *House of Leaves* (New York: Pantheon Books 2000), 413–14. Subsequent references will be noted parenthetically. For clarity's sake, I will refer to the film created by Will Navidson as *The Navidson Record*, and the academic book written about this film (and about Navidson's other films) as The Navidson Record throughout.

21 I use the somewhat inaccurate term "Navidson family," though it elides Karen Green's last name, simply to avoid burdensome prose.

22 This link between family trauma and the signification-resistant house also emerges as the origin of the novel: Danielewski has recounted in more than one interview that the haunted-house story of *House of Leaves* grew, through rejection by his father and recuperation via his sister, out of a short story titled "Redwood." Interviews also reveal the extent to which his vision of the shapeshifting house reproduces childhood struggles to ken an emotionally unstable father, and a traumatic tour with his father of a bullfighting school, his description of which closely resembles the hallways of the monstrous house (see especially McCaffery and Gregory, "Haunted House—An Interview with Mark Z. Danielewski," 103–5, 110–16).

23 Wittmershaus reveals, in a profile of Danielewski, that the author chose fonts for his various characters carefully: Times for Zampanò, Courier for Johnny (because he is a "courier of sorts"), Bookman for the editors and Dante for the title page. "And the reason those names came about wasn't purely haphazard," Danielewski says ("Profile: Mark Z. Danielewski").

24 The rebirth imagery here is hard to miss. But it is significant in that Navidson, *through* his journey into the house and its crisis of signification, transforms himself from a child of loss into one being born into a newly united family. The infantile imagery also resonates with the story with which Johnny Truant leaves us, about a defective baby being sustained by an elaborate technological interface—a representation of this book—until he is finally freed into death by his mother's love. Johnny, too, lets go of this loss that has defined him by heading straight into the jaws of lack, into the labyrinth of the book.

25 In "Saving the Subject," Hayles defines "remediation" as "the representation of material that has already been represented in another medium" (781).

26 Hayles, *Writing Machines*, 114.

27 Danielewski claims never to have read *Pale Fire*. Equally provocative is his comment that "I'll admit to being influenced by Wallace even though I haven't read any David Foster Wallace, because I believe we are often just as influenced by writers we do not read as we are not influenced by those we do" (McCaffery and Gregory, "Haunted House—An Interview with Mark Z. Danielewski," 114).

28 Hayles points out the possibility that Pelafina could have created both Zampanò's narrative and her son's commentary when she examines some of the ways that the novel allows "apparently distinct ontological levels [to] melt into one another": a portion of Pelafina's letter dated April 5, 1986, can be decoded to reveal the question "My dear Zampano who did you lose?" (615); and a small check mark, which Pelafina had instructed Johnny to insert in the lower right corner of his next letter if he received her letter intact, appears in the lower right corner of page 97—part of The Navidson Record. Both of these ruptures in narrative structure allow the author of one narrative, Pelafina, to enter into and even create other narratives in the novel ("Saving the Subject," 801–2).

29 Sigmund Freud, "Remembering, Repeating, and Working Through," *The Standard Edition of the Complete Psychological Works of Sigmund Freud*, trans. and ed. James Strachey, vol. 12 (London: Hogarth Press, 1953), 149, 154.

30 Sigmund Freud, "Mourning and Melancholia," *The Standard Edition of the Complete Psychological Works of Sigmund Freud*, trans. and ed. James Strachey, vol. 14 (London: Hogarth Press, 1953), 244–6.

31 Ibid., 249 (original italics), 250.

32 Roland Barthes, *Camera Lucida*, trans. Richard Howard (New York: Farrar, Straus, and Giroux, 1981), 91. I am indebted to Carol Viers for pointing out to me this association between *camera lucida* and mourning.

33 Ibid., 106, 90.

34 Hayles, "Saving the Subject," 789.

35 Johnny's healing "story" of finding and ultimately letting go of his grieving self contrasts significantly with the "story" of endless deterioration and loss of self that is Hal's in *Infinite Jest*.

36 See Fredric Jameson, *Postmodernism, or, the Cultural Logic of Late Capitalism* (Durham: Duke University Press, 1999), 12.

37 See Michiko Kakutani's "The Age of Irony Isn't Over After All," *New York Times*, October 9, 2001.

38 See, for example, Lena Sin's "Hey Pop Culture Mags—We Still Need You," *Thunderbird: UBC Journalism Review* 4 no. 1 (2001), accessed July 25, 2003, www.journalism.ubc.ca/thunderbird/2001–02/october/magazines.html. [currently unavailable]

39 See Tim Cavanaugh's "Ironic Engagement: The Hidden Agenda of the Anti-Ironists," *Reasononline*, accessed July 25, 2003, http://reason.com/0112/co.tc.rant.shtml.

40 Eerily, the DeLillo novel that captures perhaps best the kind of ironic detachment in an unreal world that we see in *Music* is his *Players* (New York: Vintage, 1977), in which one character's sense of numbness in an overwhelmingly technologized world is symbolized by her working in the enormously impersonal World Trade Center, for a firm called the "Grief Management Council" (18).

41 See Kakutani, "Ironic Engagement."

42 Paul Fussell, *The Great War and Modern Memory* (Oxford: Oxford University Press, 1975), 35.

43 Randolph Bourne, "The Life of Irony," *Youth and Life* (Freeport, NY: Books for Libraries Press, 1967), originally published in *Atlantic Monthly* 111 (March 1913), 120.

44 Linda Hutcheon, *A Poetics of Postmodernism* (New York: Routledge, 1989), 26, 27, 67.

45 Roth, *The Ironist's Cage* (New York: Columbia University Press, 1995), 148.

46 Ibid., 156 (original italics).

47 Ibid., 161.

48 Karen claims to have sent these experts a 13-minute compilation of footage from the house, yet Zampanò reports that whatever version of that film appeared in *The Navidson Record* disappeared before the film received wide release by Miramax (which Johnny tells us it never did). Johnny adds that no one from the transcript would verify that the film had ever been made.

49 The novel also discredits these interpretations by uniting the interviewees in their highly inappropriate lustful advances toward Karen.

50 The online discussion boards filled with nonacademic readers inexhaustibly teasing out the intricacies and narrative possibilities of the book speak to the novel's insistence on its own decoding; Hayles has compared this quality of the book, and this particular kind of decoding-mad reader, to contemporary video games and their addicted players (conversation October 22, 2002). The book elicits its invitation to decode in many ways, including its interdependent narrative structures that require constant back-and-forth reading to be constructed. But it also tantalizes the reader with encoded messages that appear in completely unexpected places.

4

Joining Gravity: Making Language Matter in *The Road, Extremely Loud & Incredibly Close*, and *The Book of Portraiture*

A sudden proliferation in the decade or so since *House of Leaves* of earnest, even "sentimental"[1] novels both steeped in poststructuralist notions of representation and aiming for various kinds of recuperation allows us in recent retrospect to view the groundbreaking work of Wallace and Danielewski as catalyzing a shift in tone and purpose that seems thoroughly to be occupying twenty-first-century literature. This chapter, and the one following it, will argue that fiction in the twenty-first century suggests a wholesale change in how it, and we, think about language, its role in our lives, the things it can accomplish, and therefore the vitality and usefulness of fiction itself. It does so primarily by reasserting the primacy of the real and the thing, language's own materiality and ability to impact the material world, and so the intimate interdependence between things and the systems of representation we use to interact with them, and a renewed faith in signification's ability to affect the real in positive ways. The shifts charted in the first three chapters all aim toward this new reality of twenty-first-century literature in that they both prophesy the shift and participate in its eventual achievement. While literary criticism has so far not acknowledged precisely the shift that this book describes, both criticism and theory of the past decade have registered a change in our ways of thinking about literature that runs alongside and perhaps intersects with the changes I am documenting here in literature.

I will argue for that shift in part through attention to changes in novelistic *form*, and intersections between form and content—form as once again implying content—in another agreement with Hoberek and his call to "adduce specific aspects of fictional form that both occur across a range of contemporary writing and depart in some way from postmodern norms."[2] Most obvious and immediately striking about the novels examined here, and the type of contemporary novel that I find most effectively accomplishes this humanist reappropriation of poststructuralism that so many contemporary novels seem to strive toward, are innovations in form in terms of textuality, or the ways novelists arrange words, and images, on the page. Like *House of Leaves* before them, Foer's *Extremely Loud & Incredibly Close* (2005) and Tomasula's *Book of Portraiture* (2006) use visual elements alongside linguistic ones, incorporating photographs, drawings, and sketches of paintings. They also set type in a variety of concrete ways in order to indicate actions, settings, and/or larger events, much as

Danielewski does in the action sequences of *House of Leaves*; in *Extremely Loud*, for example, words run together in increasingly tiny font to suggest the overlapping writing of a man running out of journal pages ("I want an infinitely blank book and the rest of time," writes Thomas Schell[3]). Tomasula's *Book* goes so far as to vary the colors of its pages, employing shades of ecru growing increasingly light as the book's sections move through time from the beginning of alphabetic history to the present or near future; Foer's novel uses red ink to represent one character's fondness for correcting errors in print, a trait that, once established, allows the novel to signify using ink alone the only time in the novel when a grown son encounters through reading and proximity his otherwise absent father. And also like *House of Leaves*, Foer's novel prefaces all parts of the novel proper, including title and copyright pages, with photographs that gesture to and suggest interpretations of events contained in the novel, implying—like the author-inflected copyright pages of Dave Eggers's *A Heartbreaking Work of Staggering Genius* (1999) and various books by Wallace, including *Consider the Lobster* (2005)—in less ominous fashion than *House of Leaves* that the textual world of the novel cannot be contained by the covers of the book, that text and physical world overlap—and that one must read each to read the other.

Such a collage or amalgamating approach to textuality makes manifest a similar quality in these novels' narrative construction. They incorporate a multiplicity of voices to tell the various, intersecting, and at times competing stories that comprise them, each story employing its own setting in time and place, its own voice, its own style. And yet part of the work being done that both marks it as an outgrowth of modernism and postmodernism and yet also distinguishes it as doing something different than both occurs by way of this multiplicity of voices, which work not independently of each other, their combination signaling cacophony and discord more than the euphony of message (as in, most famously, *The Waste Land*, or even the purposefully disjointed narrative of a high postmodern text like *Gravity's Rainbow*), but rather require the presence of the others to come together in a harmonious and meaningful way for the book as a whole. Thus the novels tend to present themselves as puzzles, together with the puzzle's implicit implication that the pieces promise to deliver more than the sum of their parts if properly placed in relation to each other. Already, through form alone, we can see these novels inviting acts of meaning-making that can seem quite at odds with twentieth-century notions of postmodernism and poststructuralism.

Not all fiction of the twenty-first century looks like this, of course, but much of it does, and I believe it is the most exciting and ambitious fiction of the past decade that tends toward these extreme innovations in textual and narrative form. My main goal in drawing attention to such novels in the context of characterizing twenty-first-century fiction is to suggest that these obviously "nontraditional" novels, which deviate so visibly from our expectations of what a novel is, do so in the service of getting closer to doing the work that we expected fiction to do before the postmodern turn. That is, in amplifying postmodern and poststructural narrative techniques in extreme ways, these novels reach back beyond postmodernism to do quite unabashedly the things that fiction was known and expected to do before our postmodern-era notions of language caused us to doubt whether anything made of language could do anything at all.

As these novels continue the shift executed by *House of Leaves* toward harmonious multiplicity in narrative voice and emphatic use of form in the service of content, they also continue and intensify a mechanism seen more subtly in that novel: the merging of language and the material world, the recognition and use of the materiality of language, in direct opposition to the "'dematerialization' that became typical of postmodernism,"[4] and that marks a real sea change in language-obsessed literature. Further, they do so in the service of humanist concerns that novels which elevate form over content, as Wallace mourns in his 1993 interview with McCaffery, for the most part jettison. In so doing, they transform what has been widely perceived as an antihumanist concept of language—poststructuralism—into a vehicle for humanism and realism. Ultimately, such a surprising shift forces us to reconsider the relationships between our concepts of language, reality, and the human.

Reasserting the real: *The Road*

Cormac McCarthy's *The Road* illustrates perhaps most powerfully and extensively this turn back to the real, to asserting the importance, significance, and primacy of the material world over the image, idea, and representation. Published in 2006, and followed by a film version only three years later, this novel opens with a waking from nightmare into reality, a reality so vividly bleak, terrifying, and dehumanizing as to make the waking hardly a kindness.[5] This is a novel that is about its landscape as much as it is about any character or idea; indeed one might say its landscape *is* its idea, in the way that Crane's sea and open boat are as vivid as his suffering correspondent. At the same time, the setting of this novel is much more than idea—and this is why it seemed born to be translated into a visual medium—in that it is not our ideas about this world that matter, but only the facts of the land themselves. Not even the facts but the pieces, the objects, the things in it. McCarthy spends a great deal of time describing the land and the sky, the absence of color, the ashes, the burnt trees, the corpses, the horizon always unchangingly gray in evocation of the ever-expiring world of Beckett's *Endgame* (1957): "Gray—gray—GRAY!" thunders Clov, when asked, again, to describe the view from the unreachable window.[6] As in that genre-busting play, the man and the boy in McCarthy's curiously unpostmodern postmodern novel inhabit a world trapped in its death throes, a "late world"[7] that seems both already dead and not quite done dying. As in *Endgame*, changes do happen—the two reach the ocean, and someone does die—but not to any clear progress or purpose.[8] Rather, the point of the novel becomes the pair's survival of the seemingly endless repetition of events that threaten both their lives and, more importantly, their humanity. Faced with the horrible literalization of the practical reality and moral challenge of David Mitchell's *Cloud Atlas* (2004)—"eat or be eaten"[9]—both man and boy find that every facet of their experiences, pragmatic and philosophical, ethical and moral, is determined simply and mercilessly by the physical conditions in which they live. Shot through with a subtle awareness of the late world's mistaken belief in the primacy of ideas and images over things, *The Road* becomes a cautionary tale for a preapocalyptic people who still have time to relearn to value the things we have before we only know we had them by their loss.

The waking that begins the tour-de-force opening paragraph of the novel is immediately curious in that it charts a passing only from sightlessness to sightlessness, the blindness of the beast in the man's dream, its "eyes dead white and sightless as the eggs of spiders" (3–4), prescient of the fate of the world into which the man wakes: "nights dark beyond darkness and the days more gray each one than what had gone before. Like the onset of some cold glaucoma dimming away the world" (3). The threat and the point here, in the man's nightmare and in his nightmarish reality, is not what can be seen via illumination, or the vision/dream in the man's head, or even the vista of the scorched earth he "glasses"—rarely does McCarthy use a verb implying operable eyes—several times a day. Rather it is the earth itself, the *things* of it that must be attended to, constantly: the earth itself is the "granitic" beast that haunts his dream. This sightlessness continues throughout the book, emphasizing its theme of absence of vision/illumination, while also establishing the importance of loss, the loss of living things once there to be seen, of useful things once there to be enlisted for the purpose of staying alive, the simple acceptance of the importance and reality of the presence of things and the indisputable knowledge that some things are good and worth having, and make a difference. Thus this novel quickly grounds itself in the earth rather than in dreams, but also in a certainty and knowingness and determinability, and in the importance of *presence*, that is rare in novels in and since postmodernism. It does so, in its backward, ironic, postmodern and poststructural way, by asserting the *absence* of all of these good things and forcing us to contemplate the devastation brought by such a loss.

The novel quickly asserts, then repeatedly reiterates, the presence (or former presence) of the forms, centers, and systems of order inherent in the universe that poststructuralism and novels informed by its thinking stalwartly deny. Early in the narrative, as if in response to the pattern of "those nights" whose "blackness . . . was sightless and impenetrable. A blackness to hurt your ears with listening," the man meditates not only on the void he stumbles in but also on the organizing frames, networks, and patterns begotten in and provided by the earth, whose faint presence he can still feel, however weak and dim they have become:

> He rose and stood tottering in that cold autistic dark with his arms outheld for balance while the vestibular calculations in his skull cranked out their reckonings. An old chronicle. To seek out the upright. No fall but preceded by a declination. He took great marching steps into the nothingness, counting them against his return. Eyes closed, arms oaring. Upright to what? Something nameless in the night, lode or matrix. To which he and the stars were common satellite. Like the great pendulum in its rotunda scribing through the long day movements of the universe of which you may say it knows nothing and yet know it must. (15)

As in the dream of the "granitic" beast, here the "autistic dark" animates and even personifies the void that the man struggles to navigate, its "autism" implying some more fully understandable, expressive, hospitable, and orienting natural state—former or elsewhere, but existing—measured against which this one might be particularly confusing. The man demonstrates his knowledge, perhaps memory, of some such more easily navigable state by entering into it and keeping himself "balanced" and "upright" within it, as if to remind himself of the systems of orientation working within his own body ("vestibular calculations in his skull"; "arms oaring") and of communication between his body and the organized world ("upright to what?"). His strong sense of a something contained deep within the earth ("lode") or encompassing the earth entirely ("matrix") that physically *holds* him in relation to the earth and to the other bodies of matter around him—like gravity, which, in essence, resides both in the earth and outside it; or like a magnetic center, such as the North Star—demonstrates his continued sense, even in this radically altered and seemingly senseless world, that some organizing, sense-making pattern or system remains and contains him.

This passage also introduces another theme that will become common in this novel and in others I will examine in these last two chapters, which is that of our unstoppable compulsion not just to feel or even understand such systems of order and sense, but to *write* about them. Here the narrator—or the man; their voices blur throughout the novel—refers to the man's response to this organizing principle not as a primitive urge but as an "old chronicle"; the voice then invokes the Foucault pendulum to connect this organizing force, moving in a completely predictable, pattern-making way, to the act of "scribing," the pattern itself becoming the thing inscribed, as if the earth through its systemized existence writes its own meaningful chronicle every day.

Whereas the novel is ambivalent about the usefulness of writing in the world, a point to which I will return later, the man's and the narrator's perceptions and appreciations of these organizing forces in the world remain unshaken throughout the novel. Every registering of loss becomes an opportunity to appreciate the beauty and meaningfulness of the whole that preceded the loss:

> Once in those early years he'd wakened in a barren wood and lay listening to flocks of migratory birds overhead in that bitter dark. Their half muted crankings miles above where they circled the earth as senselessly as insects trooping the rim of a bowl. He wished them godspeed till they were gone. (53)

The birds die off because they have no place to migrate to, the earth having become everywhere uniformly inhospitable, and yet their now-useless migratory "crankings" point to a previous machinelike precision in a world in which such patterned behavior allowed them to live. The coming extinction of the birds points not just to how much is lost with the disruption of these physical, earthbound patterns of orientation, but also to how much is lost with the loss of the things themselves.

Later in the novel, the man and boy encounter a man coming into the forest to "take a crap" who presents in every way as a threat to their lives and humanity. He looked "like an animal inside a skull looking out the eyeholes," with "a beard that had been cut square across the bottom with shears and he had a tattoo of a bird on his neck done by someone with an illformed notion of their appearance" (63). The inaccurate tattoo implies that the loss of the accurate image of the bird comes with the loss of the bird itself, then connects that loss—of life on the planet, and of our ability properly to represent that life—to the clearly reduced humanity of the man. After the loss of the image comes the loss of the words and names themselves, which we see soon after this encounter, as the narrating voice feels the world narrowing to an increasingly small pool of things and ideas and words to represent them:

> He tried to think of something but he could not. He'd had this feeling before, beyond the numbness and the dull despair. The world shrinking down about a raw core of parsible entities. The name of things slowly following those things into oblivion. Colors. The names of birds. Things to eat. Finally the names of things one believed to be true. More fragile than he would have thought. How much was gone already? The sacred idiom shorn of its referents and so of its reality. (88–9)

In this world, the existence of the idea, the word, and the name depends solely upon the existence of the thing itself, in direct opposition to the murderous logic followed from Heidegger through Lacan and Derrida into a postmodern novel like *The Names*.

The Road takes this reversal as far as it can go, creating a world whose things hold in existence not only the ideas and words that derive from them, but even the Word itself, the sacred and the idea of the sacred inhabiting the things that express them. McCarthy implies such a causal connection through a subtle formal echo that ties the godforsaken status of the world, established in novel's opening, to its myriad later material losses: "Gray. Silent. Godless" (4) becomes, when man and boy reach the anticlimax of the barren ocean, "Cold. Desolate. Birdless" (215). The replacement of Godlessness with birdlessness in this trinity suggests that the experience of the latter confirms the former, the loss of God following from the loss of material proof of God's existence, the loss of the things themselves implying the loss of their implied creator.[10] As with the birds, McCarthy seems to create a landscape so godforsaken not to argue the absence of God but to point to the travesty lying in God's wake, the inhuman horror of the world revealing how very much humans need God to be humane. Thus the novel finds a place for godliness in a thing of the world, in the boy. In fact, the first thing the man thinks of the boy and one of the first thoughts we encounter is that "the child was his warrant. He said: If he is not the word of God God never spoke" (5). The boy is, for the man, word and spirit made flesh, a perception supported throughout the novel not only by the father's often sacred visions of the boy but also by outsiders, such as the old man, Ely, who asserts "There is no God" and yet, when he sees the boy, thinks he is an angel (170, 172). Similarly, just before dying the father looks at the boy and sees that "there was light all about him . . . and when he moved the light moved with him" (277). As the boy contains God so does the earth contain the sacred, "the salitter drying" from it implying the extraction of the spirit from the scorched earth like water from salt flats (261). Without rehearsing anew a reading that has been well established by other critics, I touch on the theme of the boy's embodiment of the sacred to connect that reading to the novel's larger framework in which all ideas, all words, including the sacred, are held in the things that together make up the world.

And, as we see with the birds, it is *things* that make up this world and signal its wholeness and health, and the health of its systems for organizing those things. The organizing principles are nothing without them. McCarthy's "creedless shells of men tottering down the causeways [this word grown morbidly ironic] like migrants in a feverland" are no better than the directionless birds, "creedless shells" implying that the men are so physically undone as to provide inadequate frameworks for carrying the weight of a creed: they simply cannot support belief. This passage continues:

> The frailty of everything revealed at last. Old and troubling issues resolved into nothingness and night. The last instance of a thing takes the class with it. Turns out the light and is gone. (28)

Again connecting the problem of men harboring belief with the problem of things harboring categories of ideas and words, here the novel suggests that "creed"—belief, respect, ethics, and morality—is a kind of organizing category, like classifications and the names that distinguish them, and is just as dependent on the health and existence of the world's things—things creating the categories, like language, that contain them, not the other way around.

The novel ends with its most powerful assertion of this reversal of the poststructural creed of language preceding the human, word (and representation, in the case of Baudrillard) preceding thing, in a paragraph that is backward-looking in multiple ways. This end begins with "once," as if for a moment to end with a fairy-tale beginning that might lead to a better end. It then evokes, through a third mentioning of brook trout—unavoidably associated with Christian iconography as well as, more specifically, Hemingway's famous deployment of it in short stories like "Big Two-Hearted River"—a modernist ethos of known things, and of knowing things through the world of objects: fishing as a contemplation of the sacred. Then it describes those trout with an attention to their objecthood that is thorough and definitive, addressing us readers in the second person. After a novel's worth of suffering, these things hold all we need to know, as the boy originally held everything for the man:

> Once there were brook trout in the streams in the mountains. You could see them standing in the amber current where the white edges of their fins wimpled softly in the flow. They smelled of moss in your hand. Polished and muscular and torsional. On their backs were vermiculate patterns that were maps of the world in its becoming. Maps and mazes. Of a thing which could not be put back. Not be made right again. In the deep glens where they lived all things were older than man and they hummed of mystery. (286–7)

The uselessness of the patterns on the fish echoes the uselessness of the maps loved by the man when he was a boy—"everything in its place. Justified in the world" (182)—and of the 100-year-old brass sextant, "the first thing he'd seen in a long time that stirred him" (227), which he leaves in its corroded box on the foundered sailboat. But the sextant moved the man because, like the memory of the fish, it testified to the sense the world once made, a sense that could be mapped and measured—and held and smelled like moss, because the things of the world contained it.

The tragedy of the novel is that all of humanity is widowed to those sense-making things, the most significant things that have been loosed and lost from those absent things being meaning and order themselves. In this way the late world of *The Road* resembles the derelict world of so much postmodern literature in that it is made up of absence, everything that remains living in the gap, but with the crucial difference that this voided world is distinctly *abnormal* here (though by what means, human or nature, we never know): *The Road* does not, Beckett-like, dramatize the suffering that is the human condition; rather it suggests the suffering that will become our condition if we forget how to be human. The novel therefore must remember a time before this, when people were humane and nature allowed them to be, in order to assert the value of the lost things to which this absence points, even while the man works to obliterate his memory out of pain in the face of the same. Most of the painful memories he fights to suppress involve his wife, whose photo he eventually abandons in his commitment to surviving the present by preventing distraction by the siren of the past. But even then, he knows, and the novel insists, that changing or destroying the memory cannot touch the truth of the thing being remembered: "He thought each memory recalled must do some violence to its origins. As in a party game. Say the word and pass it on. So be sparing. What you alter in the remembering has yet a reality, known or not" (131). Here, and elsewhere, the novel asserts the unalterable primacy of things, and of a truth before representation whose representation cannot alter it, and also (perhaps therefore) an anxiety about the usefulness of any act of representation.

If representation is entirely dependent on the thing, and the thing can die, what is the point of representation? Who is to say there is any truth in it? Certainly the immortality of the representation over the thing was part of the *jouissance* that swept early postmodernism and helped produce the giddy, carefree tone of so much written in the 1960s and 1970s.[11] But underneath the play and gags lies a bitter dread—laughter in the face of the abyss, or of the bomb—that sours the fluff. *The Road* in many ways reverses this approach, grounding us in ashes and the mortality of the thing: "All things of grace and beauty such that one holds them to one's heart have a common provenance in pain. Their birth in grief and ashes. So, he whispered to the sleeping boy, I have you" (54). The light brought then by the boy is piercing in comparison, and the "breath of God" that "was his breath yet though it pass from man to man through all of time," as the woman at the end tells the boy, is a lightness that is in no way unbearable (286). Still, the question of the role of representation in a world made of things and not by words remains. If—as the man himself understands, in relation to his memories of his wife—the representation can deny the real, even though the reality itself remains untouched, what is the point of representing, through memory or through writing?

In his bleaker moments, the man sees none, wanting to leave the dying earth to end its own pendulumlike chronicling. Confronted with the bulging corpses of hundreds of water-logged books in a ransacked library, he comprehends the uselessness of one world's representations in the context of an altogether different world: "He'd not have thought the value of the smallest thing predicated on the world to come. It surprised him. That the shape which these things occupied was itself an expectation" (187). Later he contemplates the uselessness of constructing his own chronicle: "Do you think that your fathers are watching? That they weigh you in their ledgerbook? Against what? There is no book and your fathers are dead in the ground" (196). As his admission of the futility and endlessness of their journey increases, he mocks to himself the very idea of the chronicle:

> What time of year? What age the child? He walked out into the road and stood. The silence. The salitter drying from the earth. The mudstained shapes of flooded cities burned to the waterline. At a crossroads a ground set with dolmen stones where the spoken bones of oracles lay moldering. No sound but the wind. What will you say? A living man spoke these lines? He sharpened a quill with his small pen knife to scribe these things in sloe or lampblack? At some reckonable and entabled moment? He is coming to steal my eyes. To seal my mouth with dirt. (261)

In this time of mounting despair, his realization of his own imminent nonexistence, coupled with the disappearance of all tools for scribing, makes pointless whatever he might record. Notably it is not the absence of an audience that makes the act of recording ridiculous, but rather the absence of the one who recorded and the things used to record. Once he is gone, what matters what he might have written? Once the world he lived in has passed, what matters how it was represented? Like the library books written in days long gone, the man's chronicle seems to him equally irrelevant to a world that never knew him.

The novel's devaluing of the written word, however, ultimately opposes its valorizing of memory. In fact, the man orders himself to remember, both his wife and the world as they lived before the endtime. Focusing on the pleasurable memory of touching the tops of her stockings through her dress, he holds onto that memory in defiance of the universe in which she is absent: "Freeze this frame. Now call down your dark and your cold and be damned" (19). Moved by the color of a forest fire, he orders himself to "Make a list. Recite a litany. Remember" (31). Finally, the boy's godly goodness allows the man once again to unite memory and chronicle. Tended by his boy bathed in light, he thinks, "Look around you. . . . There is no prophet in the earth's long chronicle who's not honored here today. Whatever form you spoke of, you were right" (277). As the father nears death, uses of "he" grow increasingly indeterminate,[12] bleeding the father into the boy as the narrator and man have blurred into each other throughout the novel. When the woman at the end connects boy to father through the breath of God, the novel constructs the continuity necessary for the continued relevance of this and all chronicles. It is a relevance born of the body, carried in the breath, and passed from person to person and world to world, the meaningfulness of the message reconstructed anew in each body that carries it. In this way, one way to read the "fire" that the man carries and hands off before his death to the boy is as this moving thing the man once ordered himself to remember, and as the act of memory itself, of carrying a thing beyond itself via re-presentation, but one that cannot be accomplished by the word alone but requires living bodies—boys, men, trout in the stream—to harbor it.

How does a novel, made of language, solve the problem of representation, reverse the loss of the thing? *The Road* attempts to do so by using language to render things on which every act of language depends, simultaneously proving the powerlessness of representation in the face of lost determining things and the power of particular acts of language, passed from body to body, reader to reader, to say so. In the end the primary thing carried is belief, belief that centers and systems remain though particular things do not, that organizing principles and frameworks remain ready to be fleshed with meaning—belief that the word continues to appear and move through bodies. Perhaps most striking, then, about this poststructurally aware novel is that it offers itself to us as inarguably allegorical, its particular events casting grand general principles about the relationship between humanity and the physical world, and the relationship of both to acts of signification. Thus it is a poststructurally minded novel that flouts one of the early tenets of postmodernism, asking us to dig beneath its seemingly simplistic surface and language for lurking profundities, and thereby enacting exactly the kind of "depth model" and "grand narrative" that Jameson and Lyotard define as dead in the postmodern period. Redeeming and reconfiguring allegory for poststructural purposes, *The Road* marks a repurposing of pre-postmodern narrative techniques much as *House of Leaves* did with psychoanalytic discourse, both of these novels beginning from the poststructural divide between word and thing, but then enlisting language to heal the gap by offering a vehicle for self, memory, and humanity. Also like *House of Leaves* (and like *Endgame*, for that matter), *The Road* anchors its quest for meaningful ways of living in and chronicling an already-derelict world specifically in the context of family.

> There were times when he sat watching the boy sleep that he would begin to sob uncontrollably but it wasn't about death. He wasn't sure what it was about but he thought it was about beauty or about goodness. Things that he'd no longer any way to think about at all. (129–30)

The sentiment expressed by the man here is beyond rationality, explainable only by the fact that the boy is his, has come from his body. It is impossible to read *The Road* and imagine any relationship other than parent-child having the strength and integrity to support the enormity of the burden placed upon it by the narrative: what other "thing," in the absence of most everything else, could contain the worth and beauty of the world, and so assert the continued primacy of the real, against the relief of the dream? One imagines Pinsker reading this novel with great pleasure.

Reading matter(s): Materiality and/versus cognition in language

This return to the importance of things and the value contained in them in literature accompanies a resurgence of interest in thingness in theory. Such simultaneity suggests that contemporary literature takes this particular new tack not in response to theory, a move for which twentieth-century postmodern literature has been criticized, but in response to the same, or similar ideas about, and frustrations with, earlier literature that have motivated writers in the twenty-first century to create literature differently and critics to write differently about it. But it would be a gross oversimplification to infer that any return to the prominence or primacy of the thing in literature and in theory comes as a simple move away from a postmodern age defined exclusively in terms of the sign. Rather, postmodernism has in some ways always been defined as both sign- and thing-obsessed. When Steve Tomasula, in 1996, described his understanding of a current crucial shift in how literature conceives of itself in relation to contemporary culture and therefore how it proceeds in the postmodern period, he did so specifically in the context of the shift in language that has occurred, culturally, critically, and literarily: "the world of things has become a world of signs."[13] Ten years later his novel *The Book of Portraiture* would imagine the impact of that shift from thing to sign on letters and on the human. Any astute reader of post-1945 fiction and criticism, not to mention theory running through Heidegger, Lacan, and Derrida, would easily agree with Tomasula's assessment that most basically postmodernism has enacted a shift toward the sign. And yet, as Bill Brown, central author of "thing theory" in the early twenty-first century, reminds us, Baudrillard himself, proponent of the thing-destroying hyperreal, points out as early as the 1980s that "just as modernity was the historical scene of the subject's emergence, so postmodernity is the scene of the object's preponderance." The materialist Walter Benjamin also recognizes the importance of thingness in the experiments of the modernist surrealists whose resistance to modernity's insistence on the subject/object, people/things distinction would become a defining aspect of postmodernism, describing these surrealists as being "less on the trail of the psyche than on the track of things."[14]

How can an age be dominated by both the sign and the thing? While superficially seeming to express an impasse or opposition, these notions of a sign- versus object- or thing-based postmodernism[15] point to a period largely shaped by its interest in the slippery *relationship* between sign and thing, or the lack thereof, and therefore our anxiety about the ease with which each seems ever able to dominate and perhaps wholly displace the other, so that systems of signification once believed to produce meaning merely result in ribald signs or desultory things. After the fear that signs and things have lost their intimacy with each other comes the sick suspicion that language, which is supposed to join them together and allow us to interact with the world and with each other, has been likewise gelded, forestalling all intellectual and emotional inquiry and expression, and human connection, that language before the postmodern turn was presumed to make possible. These anxieties about what language and literature can do and how they can allow us to participate in the human community are at the heart of vexed postmodern ideas about the relationship between signs and things.

In April of 2003, Bruno Latour gave a lecture at Stanford[16] that distilled and amplified those concerns that had been sporadically and more tentatively voiced by a variety of critics ever since the poststructuralist age of theory, criticism, and literature began. Citing current widespread and extreme examples of egregious results of poststructural thinking—such as public tolerance of arguments against the mountain of evidence for global warming, and Baudrillard's sickening attribution of the more than 3,000 deaths in the World Trade Center attacks to our own capitalistic nihilism, as if ideology itself flew into those buildings[17]—Latour considers the contemporary consequences of last century's postmodern turn, which has by now resulted in a critical inability to agree on anything, and thus the inability to mount any meaningful critique. The problem has shifted, according to Latour, from "an excessive confidence in ideological arguments posturing as matters of fact" to "an excessive *distrust* of good matters of fact disguised as bad ideological biases." Powerfully, he reminds us that the goal of poststructuralism was "never to get *away* from facts but *closer* to them, not fighting empiricism but, on the contrary, renewing empiricism."[18] Such a statement implies that poststructuralism hoped to be not a way to abandon empirical sight, evidence, measurement, and judgment, but rather a new lens, mechanism for measuring, and methodology for judgment, with which to accomplish the same goals toward which productive critique—and so reading and writing, as most post-Enlightenment understandings of them would have it—have always strived. Also implicit in his recognition of the failure, or more accurately, exhaustion, of current uses and examples of poststructuralist thinking is the need for another new set of lenses and measuring devices to do what those implemented so far have not succeeded in doing. As modernity created and deployed the new lens of empiricism, so must postmodernity fashion not eddying language games but a method of turning poststructuralism toward empirically meaningful and productive ends.

Forty years earlier, near the start of the postmodern period Latour's speech aimed to help end, Susan Sontag made a similar argument about poststructural postmodernism that demonstrates the now-commonplace notion that "each style or movement contains within it the seeds of its own obsolescence."[19] For her 1964 essay "Against Interpretation" both espouses the poststructural notions of art and critique that were then only beginning to be born, while also and already warning against the extremes to which we have seen them taken, less and less productively over the decades since. Sontag's initial position in the essay would become a standard poststructural one, an argument against the kind of reading, such as a Freudian or Marxist one, that "excavates" a text in order to find its "deeper meaning" or "latent content," destroying the text in the process of maintaining exactly the form/content, interior/exterior, surface/depth binary that Jameson would later criticize as "depth models" of interpretation, in the service of building the sweeping "master narratives" later decried by Lyotard. It is no coincidence that her critique of these "elaborate systems of hermeneutics, aggressive and impious theories of interpretation"[20] extends from the same problematic form/content, interior/exterior binary that contemporary, poststructurally minded critics of interpretation[21] question, or that Sontag objects to such binary-building methods of interpretation for reasons very similar to those for which contemporary critics object to ways of reading and theorizing texts, as will be discussed below.

It seems that at the start of postmodernism and at its putative end, we have been struggling with the same problems: how to read the text in a way that recognizes and employs all of its signifying dimensions; how to see the text apart from our narcissistic interpretive impositions on it; most essentially, how to experience the text as a thing in itself rather than as only the inferior shadow image of a "real" world whose supposed supremacy takes precedence over it. For Latour as for Sontag, the poststructuralist notions of the irrevocably divided sign and thing pose as much promise for new ways of reading art as they do danger of reconceiving of both text and reading in meaningless ways: postmodernism at the end of the twentieth century really hadn't solved much at all. Or it did what all literary movements do, in solving some problems (naïveté about the capriciousness of language, and perhaps of existence itself) while proving inadequate to others (the difficulty of harnessing capricious language to say meaningful things about the capriciousness of existence).

Now, at what many consider the end of the postmodern age, when we are pondering the efficacy of its poststructural methods, how interesting to find these problems and concerns persisting in our ideas about reading and writing, about making and appreciating art. I see two strands of critical and theoretical approaches to literature today, expressed throughout the period, that are in line with this anxiety about how we conceive of the text, and that are beginning to characterize a new phase of literature in the twenty-first century, as well as new ways of thinking about and reading literature. One is an approach that has come to be called "thing theory," whose proponents (most notably Bruno Latour and Bill Brown) urge a return to paying attention to things and thingness, not just the social constructs we create using them. The other, related approach, absent so far from discussions about "post-postmodern" literature but crucial to it in my estimation, calls for a return to an understanding of reading that privileges one's embodied experience of the text and of the text in the material world, by literary and cultural critic Hans Gumbrecht in his 2004 *The Production of Presence: What Meaning Cannot Convey*.

These approaches to reading and theorizing literature share, in the largest sense, an emphasis on the material world in reaction to the perception that deconstruction and poststructuralism, and their impacts on our ways of reading, have gone too far in shifting our attention from the thing to the sign. This shift toward the primacy of the sign, goes the thinking of both these contemporary theories and their predecessors in the poststructural postmodernist period, results in thinking and literature that seem not to have meaning as their goal, much less empathy or connection between human beings within the literature, between literature and reader, or between literature and writer. As such, these theories are also reactions against constructivism—the sense that the social and textual constructs built in the name of things are more real and important than the things themselves, that we in essence construct things through signs. They are also a reaction against literary metaphysics—against our insistence on turning our attention to the ideal, the image, and/or the representation (the resilience of metaphysics being even more apparent in the postmodern period than in the Enlightenment), and instead, they strive to understand not ideas of thingness but things themselves, and (especially for Gumbrecht) to keep the physical world present, to be moved by it and to move within it in a way that the bloodlessness of poststructural, postmodern literature seemed to leave entirely behind. In examining these theories of thingness, however, we find how difficult it is to keep things at the center even of thing theory.

In 2001, *Critical Inquiry* published a special issue on "Things," in which Bill Brown introduced what became a relatively widely known "Thing Theory" and other critics applied it in various ways to literature. He points to a longing for experience of things in the world through the twentieth century in art and literature (though his examples come from the post–World War II period), and to a resurgence in the 1990s of theoretical attention to things, and to bodies in Hal Foster's *Return of the Real* (1996). At first, citing A. S. Byatt's thingophilic doctoral student in *The Biographer's Tale* and

Michael Serres's defiantly Lacan-reversing "*Le sujet naît de l'objet*," Brown seems to differentiate himself from these other, constructivist theories of thingness, which purport to be about things themselves but really are concerned with how encounters with things define subjects (material culture studies), how representations of things obscure the things they point to (Foster), or the liminality of all things, including bodies, in representation (Butler). But ultimately Brown's "thing theory" becomes another theorizing of the thing in which "thing" becomes more word or idea than, well, *thing*.

For how are we anymore talking about objects in the world that affect the world materially when Brown defines the thing as a liminality between the nameable and the unnamable, as what is "excessive in objects," as that which represents both the particular and the general category—especially when he points out that even the physical thing is wholly indeterminate, a "swarm of electrons"?[22] Indeed, Brown places his theory in the tradition of the aforementioned explosion of thing-oriented theories of the 1990s, which he identifies as a return to ideas about objects from the 1920s (in early architects of the modernist twentieth century such as Benjamin, Bataille, and Mauss), an avant-garde modernism that resisted mainstream modernism's dichotomy between objects and subjects. Thus his theory of the thing as existing in and between both subject and object is in line with this avant-garde that became the dominant postmodern treatment of subjects and objects as caught in an interdependent dialectic. His theory of thingness, that is, describes not an abandonment of core poststructural principles about language, representation, objects, and subjects, but an expression of those principles toward the end of thinking about things and how they get inevitably caught up in language and its principles. Consequently, Brown sees the problem of the thing as the problem of the thing being represented, that the thing always comes at us as a sign first, which is how it must enter into subject-object relations; things always feel "belated," "victims of the word," when we want them to feel and be primary.[23] *Il n'y a pas de hors-texte.*

Interestingly, Brown (along with others who theorize thingness, such as Hal Foster) derives his ideas about the impossibility of the object to remain, unread by a subject, only a thing, in part from art in the postmodern period that presents objects doing just the opposite—asserting pure objecthood refusing to be read as signs. As example he uses works by Claes Oldenburg, whose art since the 1960s has "re-created, with relentless consistency, the iconic objects of everyday life." And yet, the dominant effect of constructing such aggressive objecthood is that

> the grossly mimetic character of the work draws attention to the discrepancy
> between objectivity and materiality, perception and sensation, objective presence
> (a fan, a Fudgsicle, a sink) and material presence (the canvas, the plaster of paris,
> the vinyl), as though to theatricalize the point that all objects (not things) are, first
> off, iconic signs. (A sink looks like a sink.)[24]

These works of art *seem* to be expressing, in another repetition of modernist aesthetics in postmodern ideas about objects, Leo Stein's recognition of thingness apart from an object's function in a system of signs: "Things are what we encounter; ideas are what we project."[25] Yet, read by Brown, these art objects slide once again into the subject-object continuum into which so many other theories absorb the thing: "'this is art that . . . shows how weary that world has become of all our projections,'" he writes, paraphrasing art critic Rudolf Arnheim, then adds, "If these objects are tired, they are tired of our perpetual reconstitution of them as objects of our desire and of our affection. They are tired of our longing. They are tired of us."[26] Projecting onto the object our own anxiety about turning it into a sign, this reading of these art objects personifies them, swallows them into our system of understanding the self/subject by appropriating objects, makes objects into yet another piece of the subject, and disallows their objecthood—disallows the objecthood of works of art whose aggressive purpose is to assert only objecthood. The problem here, it seems, is not in things themselves but in *what happens when we read things*. Put another way, Brown's anthropomorphizing reading of these works of art that are themselves objects "grossly anthropomorphized"[27] illustrates how art converts the material (canvas, plaster of paris) into the signifying object that, once read, becomes the sign-indebted thing. The thing is the object read.[28]

Thus, part of what Brown seems to be saying in the end is that things can never be free of the signs we read them as, and he seems to be demonstrating that we are not capable of theorizing things in themselves, only in theorizing our readings of things, and how we represent them, so that we therefore cannot allow them to be things— much less objects—in themselves. The problem comes in the act of representation, theorizing, itself. We might *encounter* a thing as a thing—the paper that cuts our fingers, the falling nut that bops our heads[29]—but we can only think, talk, and write about things as the representations they become the moment we consider them in all of the contexts we bring to bear on them. The problem in grasping *thingness* in language is that every thing ceases to be a thing in language. Brown demonstrates a version of this dilemma in reverse when he cites a more recent work by Oldenburg, *Typewriter Eraser* (1999), a "pert," "rigid," "bright," and enormous invocation of an object that has been itself wholly erased by digital technology, whose power is "to dramatize a generational divide and to stage (to melodramatize, even) the question of obsolescence." When such an object evokes the child's response of "What is that thing supposed to be?," it points to the object's dependence on external, subject-imposed frames of reference to give it meaning outside of its mere materiality. But also, as Brown points out, it reveals how stuck the thing is in these imposed meanings that reduce it to its role in satisfying human need. "Released from the bond of being equipment, sustained outside the irreversibility of technological history, the object becomes something else"[30] —that is, one supposes, some thing whose uselessness brings it closer to being art.

But at the same time, the object's dependence on such frames of reference in order to become an identifiable thing also means that its meaningfulness and relevance to a human world is equally dependent on those precarious, transient frames of human reference: "How, Oldenburg's objects seem to ask, will the future of your present ever understand our rhetoric of inscription, erasure, and the trace?"[31] This is exactly the question raised about the value and meaningfulness of inscription and representation in a world shorn of relevant contexts by *The Road*; McCarthy's sodden library books are, for its novel's future generations, Oldenburg's *Typewriter Eraser*, as is the man's unwritten chronicle. *The Road's* focus on lost things is an attention to a world of both objects lost and objects made unreadable, unthinged.

Then one way of thinking about the thing-oriented literature of the early twenty-first century is as a response, and perhaps answer, to this problem of theorizing thingness. For literature, a thing itself made entirely of words/signs, always and already/only existing in the realm of representation, can only invoke the thing via, and as, representation. To say that literature is newly interested in things and the real is to say that it is interested in new ways of representing things and the real so that we might experience them as real things, which is to say that a new kind of mimesis, a new method of linguistic *trompe-l'oeil*, is being posited by novels interested in readers' contemplating thingness via, not naïvely in lieu of, representation. Which is to posit, as I will explore more fully in the next chapter, a new kind of realism that goes (at least) one layer further than traditional realism, using representation not simply to produce "reality effects" of the real, but rather to produce representation so obviously and multiply removed from the real as to open up a space into which the real seems to flood in. This is the problem and opportunity I see in postmodern fiction's treatment of things, the material, and language as it first represses the real to acknowledge the murderous primacy of representation (*The Names*), then points to the real as the thing being represented by the machinations of representation (*House of Leaves*), and now, in twenty-first-century literature, places things once again center stage to contemplate a world in which we might experience their primacy, while also foregrounding the struggle to experience the thing and keep it present through language. Central to these novels' methodology in making us aware of thingness, and of its role in our understanding of ourselves and the world, is our awareness of our role in *reading* these texts, and in reading things.

As Brown points out, "every decade [of the twentieth century] has its thing about things"; attention to thingness, in literature or theory, was not an invention of the twenty-first century. In fact, Sontag framed, even at the beginning of the postmodern period, the problem of hermeneutics- and sign-based concepts of literature and art in terms of the eclipse of the thing. Essentially, in warning against the dangers of the depth model of interpretation, in which "excavation" of a text's "meaning" wholly ignores the formal structures being excavated, Sontag is reminding us to remember that the text itself is a thing in the world, not simply a delivery system for content, and that we must encounter it as such; we must encounter art as things. In this way her theory of texts and reading aligns with an artistic impulse toward gaps, absence, and silences running at least from Mallarmé into postmodernism (one thinks of Beckett's disembodied mouth in *Not I*), as well as with the drive toward stubborn objecthood enacted by visual artists like Oldenburg. Both of these approaches try to escape the limits of the word that seems to ask only to be interpreted and therefore changed. Sontag instead values "transparence" in reading and criticism, which for her "means experiencing the luminousness of the thing in itself, of things being what they are."[32] Critics may achieve such transparence, Sontag argues, first by redefining what art is and what is important in art: they must pay attention to the *form* of the art, and recognize its own material existence as a thing in the world.

These ideas about what art is and how best to understand what it means lead to two ideas about the nature of reading: that we must approach the text as material object, with all of our senses—"We must learn to see more, to *hear* more, to *feel* more"[33] —experiencing it as a thing in the world that affects our embodied selves, quite apart from any interpretations we might press upon it; and that any other approach that aims primarily at interpretation or excavation of meaning actually *changes* the text. Thus Sontag implies that the text exists as a *thing* independent of our interpretations of it, and that it can be most authentically known if "experienced" in an "erotics" of art— treating the art as sensory thing—rather than in a "hermeneutics" of art—treating the art as a code to be cracked, and thus translated into something else entirely. Reading for Sontag requires experiencing the form and thingness of art as integral to its content or meaning.[34]

On the other hand, and at the other "end" of postmodernism, we find a critic like Walter Benn Michaels arguing exactly the opposite of Sontag, and yet in a way that can seem to center on a cause quite similar to hers, and to McCarthy's thing-driven *The Road*. In his 2004 *The Shape of the Signifier*, Michaels argues that reading the signifier as a material thing, affecting the world and creating affect in the reader, leads only to the meaninglessness of the text, in that such a method privileges the reading subject over the written text, the subject's unique experience over the integrity of textual ontology. Though targeting Paul de Man (who, says Lindsay Waters in his review of the book, Michaels presents as "Satan incarnate," a claim that is certainly bold but not terribly exaggerated), essentially Michaels is arguing against a generally poststructural way of reading a text, which allows for multiple readings based on the reader's affect-based encounter with the text in conjunction with infinitely moveable language. In his mind, it is a problem, and a grave error, to believe that the subject changes the text by reading it: his idea of what a text is and what it means to read a text rests on the assumption that the text holds one meaning, intended and conveyed by the author, knowable by the reader (upon "proper" reading), which the reader can understand or not, agree with or not, but cannot influence. For him, a text's meaning comes solely from its encoded, interpretable content, not from the subject position of its reader or the text's structure or material form. The reader, however affected by the text, has no effect on the text.[35]

In his incisive review of the book, Vincent Pecora points out substantial logical flaws in Michaels's audacious argument, criticizing Michaels's logic in pillorying poststructural ideas about reading as reinforcing "identity politics" most powerfully when he points out that Michaels defines race, culture, and religion as merely "identities" separate from "beliefs" and "ideas," and therefore, "ideologies."[36] Further, Pecora exposes a false and damning binary Michaels sets up between one type of reader, wholly logical, who ignores the "valuable . . . inconsistencies of the human imagination," and another, wholly artistic, who "refuse[s] to acknowledge that poems and art really cannot convey *experience* per se without *representing* . . . interpretable meaning."[37] That is, Pecora rightly sniffs out an insistent sign-thing split inherent in Michaels's staunch juxtaposition of "ideas" versus "experience" as mutually exclusive to each other, which results in a reading of reading on Michaels's part that denies the informing necessity of both. But Pecora's biting critique notwithstanding, the fact of Michaels's argument, and the need of the critic to argue against the materiality of the sign in order to preserve the meaningfulness of texts of all kinds, speaks to an undeniable anxiety about what literature is today and how it asks to be read, on top of his more explicitly expressed anxiety about how we as critics theorize reading and language.

From the interesting perspective of an editor who has seen a lot of theory and criticism come and go, Waters conceptualizes Michaels's theory as fundamentally not only anti-poststructuralist but also antiaesthetic, which is to say, one that views the text as composed solely of *ideas* and not at all of *form*.[38] He places Michaels's antimateriality, antiaffect, anti-poststructural argument in a history of literary criticism and theory (though pointedly referring to Michaels's work as "pseudo-theory") that have marshaled forces in reaction to Sontag's early postmodern appeal for aesthetic, experiential, and material appreciation of art. A return to ideology, Michaels's theory of what texts are and how we should read them is, according to this reading, little more than a defense of the critic's and reader's right—more, *responsibility*—to interpret the text from the naïve assumption that it exists only to transfer one meaning, fully expressed by the author and wholly knowable by the reader, and knowable without much attention to the form in which the ideology comes.

For those readers, critics, and academics who have long seen postmodernism, and especially poststructuralism, as a childish assault on meaning, knowledge, and our comfortable belief in language's flawless ability to communicate both, such a theory of texts and reading must be welcome, as if those parents to whom Wallace alludes at the end of his 1993 interview have finally come back and set things to right, reimposing productive boundaries in which meaning can arise. But what is interesting about this Sontag-Michaels schism, which seems neatly to bookend the beginning and end of postmodernism, is that Sontag was defending boundaries and integrity in texts and acts of readings too. The difference lies in what each critic sees as the source of that integrity. Whereas for Michaels, the unchangeable thing in the text (the thing unchanged by an act of reading) is its core idea, or ideology, or the intention of the author, for Sontag that unchangeable thing is the text itself as an object of art, comprising meaning *via* a form that reading cannot change and in fact depends on. Different readers' affective experiences with the piece of art therefore result in different understandings and meanings from the text, but the text as a "form of content" (Waters) retains its integrity. The crucial difference, then, in how these two critics and schools of thought about the nature of texts and reading view the work of art comes from how they theorize the importance, or lack thereof, of the text's materiality and form, and how that materiality and form do or do not participate in the text's production of meaning.

One might assume that such a vociferous argument launched by a leading literary critic such as Michaels attests to the great success of Sontag's project, that literature must have widely achieved this attention to its own materiality in order for it to push Michaels to mount such a defense against it. On the contrary, I will argue that, while Michaels's antiaesthetic argument clearly responds to the persistence of poststructural theories about literature and art through the end of the twentieth century, despite various backlashes against "European" theory in the 1980s and beyond, *literature* is only now, in the twenty-first century, beginning to attempt and achieve the kind of productive use of materiality as an avenue toward meaning—through attention to thingness in literature in relation to acts of signification, and in harnessing language as material in meaningful ways—that Sontag called for as postmodernism, as most accounts have it, began.[39] And critics and theorists today, Hans Gumbrecht with his *The Production of Presence* chief among them, are only beginning to imagine ways of conceiving of literature that productively marshal that materiality, despite a long false start in twentieth-century postmodernism that often produced the kind of literature and ideas about reading and about literature against which Michaels has been repeatedly drawn to argue. Uniting all of these examined poststructural interrogations of the relationship between signs and things, by Sontag, Latour, Brown, Gumbrecht, and Pecora as he critiques Michaels, is an insistence on the vital role played by the thing—the material object, and our experience in the physical world—in signification, not as a thing that supplants the sign in a repetition of the same destructive binary that modernism and postmodernism have been striving to erase, but as a crucial element of systems of signification and meaning-making that early poststructural ideas and literature largely forgot.

"The Production of Presence" in *Extremely Loud & Incredibly Close*

"What do you have to think a text is to think that pages without any writing are part of it?" asks Michaels of Susan Howe's concern that 86 blank pages were left out of both major editions of Puritan minister Thomas Shepard's *Autobiography*.[40] That Howe further points out as meaningful the need to turn the manuscript of the *Autobiography* upside down to read part of it appalls Michaels even more. In direct opposition to Michaels's contempt for valuing space, orientation, and other textual oddities as meaningful, many novels of the early twenty-first century ask exactly the opposite question: how do you read pages of sparse, strangely formatted, variously colored, or, yes, at times absent text in the context of a novel? For certainly recent novels present us with just such tasks for reading. Given his definition of the readable text as an immaterial, somewhat transparent device for transmitting the knowable intention of the author to the passive reader, in a recognizable, conventional way, it is probably safe to say that Michaels would not even call Jonathan Safran Foer's second book a novel. A reader with different ideas about what a text is, how it works, and what it means to be a reader might call it one of the most successful examples of poststructural humanism—and of postmodernism—we have seen yet. Like *House of Leaves*, it does not look much like a traditional novel, and certainly not like traditional realism. But rather than seeing its innovations in form, textuality, and resulting narrative technique as differentiating it from the genre of the novel, in the context of critical and theoretical ideas about how fiction works dating back at least to Sontag, we can read this novel and others like it as presenting such formal innovations in order to force us to pay attention to form, to consider the materiality of the text as integral to the text's ability to mean, and to require the reader's active participation in the construction of that meaning.

Like Danielewski's textually groundbreaking novel, *Extremely Loud & Incredibly Close* (henceforth, *ELIC*) redefines our notion of novelistic form from its first page, greeting us with images before the title page, as if, in an immediately hypertextual moment, the novel has broken loose from its proper confines and begins to bleed into the real world, the world in which we are reading. Further, the first image is of a keyhole: the book comes at us as a lock requiring a key, as a puzzle to be solved, explicitly through images as well as writing. And so the novel gets accused of being "all artifice and no substance" in its use of multiple media,[41] and has been repeatedly skewered for its use of a real photo of a man falling from the burning World Trade Center in a "flipbook" that ends the novel.[42] Such resistance to a novel that is so clearly engaged in exactly the linguistic, epistemological, and ontological issues foregrounded but certainly not created by postmodernism suggests an anxiety over what is happening to the genre as a whole, as the novel stretches to accommodate the questions in a poststructural age. But even the formal changes in this novel—heavy use of images and photographs, most obviously—are really only an intensification of strategies already in place in our literary tradition. After all, illumination via illustration has been going on for at least a half millennium, in texts like the Gutenberg bible in the fifteenth century, Blake's radical reworking of that text in his own "diabolical bible" in the eighteenth, and works by Twain and Dickens in the nineteenth, to name a very few.[43] Certainly postmodernism, with its explicit exploration of the operations of signifiers, has used images with new energy and purpose—consider the central and yet ultimately enigmatic muted postal horn that recurs throughout *The Crying of Lot 49* (1965), and William Gass's own playful romp through the meeting of word and (nude, photographed) body in *Willie Masters' Lonesome Wife* (1968)—but not without predecessor. Further, *ELIC* is not at all alone in its own time in incorporating image and formal and material innovation into its narrative strategies; rather it, like *House of Leaves*, is part of an emerging twenty-first-century tradition/trend of mixed-media literature[44] and ekphrastic literature[45] that identifies one of its central concerns as literature's relationship to images and to art, and to how we make art, through both word and image. So not only does it have its roots in a long tradition of literature that incorporates image, but it has its branches and leaves in an emerging tradition of literature that incorporates image specifically to interrogate and demonstrate how we represent things. This change in uses of the image means that *ELIC* uses pictures/drawings/photos/textual elements differently than Twain or Dickens, not to accompany the text but to help produce it.

Mark Haddon's recent novel, *The Curious Incident of the Dog in the Night-Time* (2003), provides a clear example of this kind of use of images: when its first-person autistic narrator shares with us, at the beginning of the novel, the chart of faces showing emotions like happiness, sadness, fear, and surprise, the novel announces that it is about his, and all of our, difficulty reading the world. The 9-year-old narrator of *ELIC*, Oskar, does something similar: young and naïve, he can't accept the loss of his father, or understand his own reaction to that loss. Unable to comprehend a world in which men can fly planes full of people and jet fuel into buildings full of people and meltable steel, he longs to sew everyone birdseed shirts, or put us all in his endlessly large pocket to keep us safe from the sufferings that lurk indiscriminately in the world. In this way the child narrator, with his limited language and knowledge, reflects the helplessness we all feel when confronted with meaningless suffering. Not surprisingly, contemporary novels exploring such limits of language and comprehension are often narrated by people whose faculties are in some way limited: children, autistic children, traumatized adults, or physically or emotionally wounded adults. The use of images and other textual elements reflects the struggle necessitated by these attempts to understand and communicate, and suggests that we need to marshal all tools, including pictures, and to wrench language, textual layout, and even the genre of the novel itself into new forms in order to do so. This is one large way in which I see *ELIC* and novels like it as an intensification and culmination of not only postmodernism, but also of modernism, still responding to Eliot's call in 1921 to make literature *"difficult,"* to produce, as Johnson said of the metaphysical poets, "heterogeneous ideas . . . yoked by violence together."[46] *ELIC*, with its gathering of heterogeneous voices, mixed media, and textual and visual allusions, dislocates us from the ease of a singular story and narrator, and forces us to rearrange all of its pieces of language into meaning.

But despite its seeming oddities in form, this novel also extends the line of literature reaching far back beyond the postmodern turn, in that it does the same kind of work that novels have always done: it assembles fraught pieces into a smooth story, in order to make meaning, to salve, to allow for growth and positive change. In fact, in many ways, this book is about meaning itself—that it exists and is the proper subject of fiction, even fiction that looks as surprising as this does, and questions so profoundly our abilities to make meaning. Coming after decades of bleak, often nihilistic literature that seemed to be about nothing at all, *ELIC* enacts the continued relevance of meaning in literature. It belies the common accusation that contemporary literature, so self-absorbed in its medium, had lost its message. It is also about learning to believe again after our worlds have been shattered—by the attacks on the World Trade Center, and by theoretical attacks on the usefulness of language—and we are, like Oskar, children at the brink of a new kind of knowledge and belief, after having everything we knew and trusted as real and true exploded, made suddenly and irrevocably absent.

We know right away that Oskar suffers most poignantly from the loss of his father in the World Trade Center attacks of September 11, 2001. His father's absence, and the very real and also psychologically symbolic absence of his body, haunts Oskar and motivates him on his quest for present answers throughout the novel. But a less specific and yet more terrifying absence also consumes Oskar, and lies beneath and around his grief for his absent father: the absence of bedrock belief and knowledge, of common ground to stand on, of something foundational holding up the world. Oskar signals his existential angst early in the novel, when he recounts a story that describes the nature of the universe for him, from Hawking's *A Brief History of Time*:

> One of my favorite parts is . . . where Stephen Hawking tells about a famous scientist who was giving a lecture about how the earth orbits the sun, and the

sun orbits the solar system, and whatever. Then a woman in the back of the room raised her hand and said, "What you have told us is rubbish. The world is really a flat plate supported on the back of a giant tortoise." So the scientist asked her what the tortoise was standing on. And she said, "But it's turtles all the way down!"

I love that story, because it shows how ignorant people can be. And also because I love tortoises. (11)

Oskar's two reasons for loving this story tell us important things about him: first, calling the woman's turtle-based explanation of the universe "ignorant" signals Oskar's own more sophisticated understanding that nothing in fact supports the earth, or the sun, or anything—that we, as all objects in space, float unanchored and ultimately ungrounded. Second, Oskar's innocent love of tortoises (much like his later, ill-labeled love of "pussies," 190) reminds us that, however sophisticated his grasp of this existential dilemma of groundlessness, he is still a child, whose raw need for guidance in a groundless universe reminds us of our own. The turtle story also foreshadows what Oskar will learn along the way of his quest, one that does not lead him to any relevant knowledge about his father but does cause him to meet, befriend, and even introduce to each other many loving people: Hawking's orbiting earth and sun remind us that every body in the universe, whether human or planetary, is held in place only in relation to each other—that's what gravity is. Hawking's final letter to Oskar best articulates the novel's major theme that, in the face of groundlessness, what we have to hold on to is each other. He writes:

The vast majority of the universe is composed of dark matter. The fragile balance depends on things we'll never be able to see, hear, smell, or touch. Life itself depends on them. What's real? What isn't real? Maybe those aren't the right questions to be asking. What does life depend on? (305)

ELIC is an attempt to turn that unknowable dark matter into things that matter, to fill our contemporary emptinesses, to create common ground to stand on by defining things we depend on and by deciding to depend on each other, as Oskar finally decides to depend on his mother, from whom he has been estranged since losing his father.

In fact, the novel connects Oskar's realizations about meaning and belief specifically to the renewal of his love for his mother, implying that it is this act of relearning to depend on his mother that allows him to reach a more mature, and, as he says, "complicated" understanding of the world:

Even though I'm not anymore, I used to be an atheist, which means I didn't believe in things that couldn't be observed. I believed that once you're dead, you're dead forever, and you don't feel anything, and you don't even dream. It's not that I believe in things that can't be observed now, because I don't. It's that I believe that things are extremely complicated. (4)

In describing, at novel's opening, his changed ideas about belief in this way, Oskar is quoting his own description at the end of the book of a transforming experience with his mother that has led him to his new belief, thus linking one to the other:

I probably fell asleep, but I don't remember. I cried so much that everything blurred into everything else. At some point she was carrying me to my room. Then I was in bed. She was looking over me. I don't believe in God, but I believe that things are extremely complicated, and her looking over me was as complicated as anything ever could be. But it was also incredibly simple. In my only life, she was my mom, and I was her son. (324)

As Hawking redefines the central question we should be asking from "what is real?" to "what does life depend on?," Oskar, and the novel, revises the question of "how do we know things?" to "how do we *believe*?"

This revision marks a noteworthy accomplishment—meaningful growth and change—in a novel whose central preoccupation is interrogating our methods of knowing and asking *how* and whether they work and whether we can really know anything for sure. The first chapter, besides illustrating Oscar's growth into belief, also introduces the problem of what and how we know. It does so through Oskar and his father's final, unfinished "Reconnaissance Expedition" (their version of a scavenger hunt) begun when his dad simply presented him a map of Central Park, *sans* clues. Directionless but determined, Oskar proceeds to dig things up all over the park, plots their locations on the map, and then searches the random points for his father's enigmatic message:

The dots from where I'd found things looked like the stars in the universe. I connected them, like an astrologer, and if you squinted your eyes . . . it kind of looked like the word "fragile." Fragile. What was fragile? Was Central Park fragile? . . . I erased, and connected the dots in a different way, to make "door." . . . I had the revelation that I could connect the dots to make "cyborg," "platypus," and "boobs," and even "Oskar." . . . I could connect them to make almost anything I wanted, which meant I wasn't getting closer to anything. (10)

Here Foer uses the image of constellations as analogous to our methods of meaning-making, pointing out that the meanings we build by connecting our dots are as individual, un-universal, unreal, and changeable as pictures in the sky imagined by people long dead. Who looks up at night and sees a bull, an archer, a dragon, until she has been told to see them, by people—like the ancient, sky-mapping Greeks—in whose lives such figures had meaning? This image insists that it is the *person* who makes things meaningful, according to the way she connects the dots she chooses to connect, according to the culture in which she lives—*not* the universe itself, not the stars. Then the novel proceeds to examine our ways of connecting dots, of making meaning out of such light and dark matter, most concertedly through acts of language. As in this initial celestial image of randomness and misunderstanding (we never do know what the father intended for Oskar to do with the map), the book is largely concerned with the limits and problems of language as a means of making and communicating meaning.

The book's use of photos and images implies these limits, suggesting that some things, both beautiful and horrible, are beyond words, like the flight of birds that marks Mr Black's awakened hearing (166–7), or the falling man who reappears throughout the novel and stands for so much of what Oskar cannot bear to express but longs to comprehend (62, as well as the final repetition of the image that ends the book). Other images that speak directly to the failure of language are the tattooed "yes" and "no" on the hands of Oskar's grandpa (260, 261), who has lost the ability to say every word, beginning with "Anna"—his life's great love, lost in the Dresden bombing—and ending with "I," the ability to articulate the self, as if the loss of one has led to the loss of the other. No longer speaking, he becomes a man who writes as constantly as he does futilely: he writes on bedsheets that are washed and daybooks that get stuck in clocks and bathtubs; he writes a letter every day to his son, but sends instead the empty envelopes to the boy's mother; he writes a final letter so impossibly endless that not enough pages exist to contain it, and it can only eradicate itself in overwriting.

Oscar's grandmother takes the futility of language even further, "typing" her life story on hundreds of pages that remain blank as she presses only the space bar (176). She also raises the question about language that the novel strives most earnestly to answer: having failed to tell her beloved sister Anna that she loved her on the night before the bombing, Oskar's grandma asks, in her last letter to her grandson, "how do you say I love you to someone you love?" That is, how do we say huge, true, meaningful things and have them remain true, not somehow reduced? How can words ever be enough?

Oskar's struggle throughout the book to represent for himself, and for us, the trauma of losing his father—and more specifically, of not picking up the phone when his father called in his last moments—illustrates most painfully the impossibility of capturing in words something as complex and inarticulable as such a loss. His attempt requires photos, letters to strangers, his scrapbook *Stuff That Happened to Me*, the journal we seem to be reading, all to document a search for the lock to fit a key that in the end has nothing to do with his lost father. Foer pithily captures this failure adequately to represent the extremes of life's experiences in words when Oskar, playing an association game with his therapist, can answer the word "happiness" only with the word "happiness." Oskar has set up a tautology, happiness equaling only happiness, a thing representing only itself and thus leading nowhere but back to itself, becoming meaningless. This linguistic tautology comes on the heels of some of the book's most powerful examples of the problems of communicating in language, in a chapter that is therefore thematically central to the novel and comes, not surprisingly, structurally in the novel's exact middle as well (page 187 of a book of 356 pages, if you count the final repeated images, which, *contra* Michaels, I absolutely do).

In this chapter (called "Happiness, Happiness"), Oskar plays for his class an interview of a witness of the bombing of Hiroshima, who recounts how scores of people died inhumanly, one of them her own daughter. But never does the woman directly answer the questions posed to her. When asked to describe the iconic images that have come to represent the bombing to those of us who did not experience it, the mother describes her search for her daughter instead. For her, the bombing could not be reduced to the "mushroom cloud," or "black rain"; these words and images were not her truths (188). Hers was her real daughter, melting in her arms. Next, Oskar illustrates how the atomic bomb burned away dark matter while leaving white, by holding up a piece of paper whose letters had been removed. The page he uses for this demonstration is one he loves so much from *A Brief History of Time*, and when he looks at his classmates "through the story of the turtles," Oskar asks them and us to ponder the connection between the erasure of language and the erasure of the human (190).

But despite all of its examples of the limitations of language and problems of communication, ultimately *ELIC* is most interested in proving what language *can* do, that it does impact the world in positive ways and bring us together. It recognizes that, as a novel, its only or primary tool for turning what Hawking calls "unknowable dark matter" into things that matter, for constructing ground to stand on, is language— which is fine, because the novel also understands that as humans our only or primary tool for doing these things is also language, limited though it may be.

Then one large way to read the novel is as a process of first creating vast emptinesses—or acknowledging the many emptinesses that exist in our contemporary lives—and then beginning to fill them. On the night before his death, Oskar's father tells him a story in which a fictitious sixth borough floats away, leaving a hole in New York City and creating gaps between lovers separated by the secession; Oskar represents this gap in his scrapbook with a photograph depicting the vast emptiness in the heart of the city, an emptiness that echoes the true loss of the World Trade Center and all of the lives in it (60–1). In fact, each major character at some point describes feeling a hole in his or her center that longs to be filled. Most strikingly, the novel fills these emptinesses with language, letters, and words that it insists exist physically, and materially. The grandpa's tattooed "yes" on one palm and "no" on another is one example of this material language, his body speaking for him: when he leaves his wife, she wants to "slap him with his words" (306). When they meet, he already mute and talking through writing, she cries his words when he uses a page of his writing to wipe her tears (31). The boy who will not tell his mother of his father's final voice message before the towers fell converts these last words via Morse code and colored beads into a bracelet so that she wears her husband's words around her wrist (35).

In the novel's most meaningful act of transforming material words into something that matters, the boy and his grandpa dig up his father's empty coffin and fill it with decades' worth of letters the grandpa had written but not sent to his son. Even the grandson's need to dig up the coffin marks the novel's conviction that meaning and connection can come from the absence at the heart of language: Oskar digs up the coffin he knows will be empty "because it's the truth, and dad loved the truth," the truth that "he's dead" (321). It is an absence more than a presence that he needs to find and face. But it is an absence he wants to fill, and the satisfaction with which both father and son to the lost man fill his empty coffin with letters that are never to be read suggests one more characteristic of language's materiality—as something that matters—as it functions in this novel: it brings meaning not in spite of its potential meaninglessness but because of it. Here, as in many other instances in the novel, it is the *fact* of signification/communication between people itself that matters, that becomes matter, a matter that can fill the emptinesses that lurk within and open up between us.

It takes all of these acts of language, a panoply of texts and voices, to convert this novel from one that interrogates the limits of meaning-making to one that makes meaning despite the limits of language: Oskar's many pictures and journals; the grandpa's letters every day to his son, and his daily communication through writing; the grandmother's letter from the airport to Oskar, which runs throughout the novel; her letters written when she was a child to Turkish prisoners; the letter her grandmother wrote to her; Oskar's letters to pen pals like Hawking and Jane Goodall; A. R. Black's one-word-definition note cards; even the last Mr Black's father's letters to loved ones, written while he was dying. Acts of language also bonded Oskar to his father: he remembers his admiration for his father by recounting his dad's habit of circling with a red pen mistakes in the *New York Times*; this trait further links Oskar's father to his own father, when we encounter a letter between them full of red marks—Oskar's father's close attention to language, signaled by all those marks, constitutes the only evidence we have that he ever read a letter from his father. The last interaction between father and son also indicates, on multiple levels, love and connection through acts of language: Oskar's father created for him the story of the sixth borough, in which a boy and girl, deeply in love but separated from each other as Central Park floats away, build an ever-lengthening line between them through which they communicate via tin-can phone. When the line reaches its breaking point, she says to him, "I love you," and he keeps her frozen, material love in a can on a shelf floating over Antarctica (220).

These stories within stories, letters within letters, pictures within journals within a novel that amalgamates all of these acts of language, not only represent the theme of language's ability to mean and connect people, but they also ask us to consider *how* language and even the novel itself create meaning and connection. That is, this fractured novel, made up of three distinct narrating voices (Oskar, grandma, grandpa), and filled with numerous other voices, forces us as readers to do exactly what Oskar first does by digging in Central Park, and then repeats in his quest to find a lock for his key: we must assemble the pieces, connect the dots, follow the clues, and see what kind of whole results from the gathering together of all the parts. The novel quietly underscores this idea with its final embedded picture: as Oskar describes the communal effort (the limo driver gamely doing most of the hard work) of digging up his father's empty coffin, the book offers, without textual comment, an image of the night sky (318). It thus identifies this moment in the graveyard as an act of creation and meaning-making, a connecting of dots into image, and a shorthand for Oscar's journey from the crazy Central Park constellations—asking, what is true?—to his new way of reading light and dark matter that asks, what do I depend on, what do I believe?

Just as Oskar's quest never satisfyingly ends, the novel never properly ends for us: the first events Oskar narrates actually occur after the events of the last chapter. Such an almost-circular, or defiantly uncircular, narrative structure, notably common in contemporary fiction (as we have seen in *Infinite Jest* and *House of Leaves*), speaks to a trend in literature to resist the novel's traditional implication that everything ends neatly, bows tied, lessons fully learned. These formal devices of fragmentation and recursiveness are the novel's way of reminding us of the *work* involved in making it all make sense, and that that work never ends—whether we are reading a novel or living our lives. Birth to death, beginning to end is a stacking of turtles, unsupported by bedrock, but still an act of gravity requiring all of us and holding all of us together in relation to each other. As in *The Road*, *ELIC* aims to pluck us out of the "unbearable lightness of being," asserting the existence, importance, and welcome weight of matter, and that matter makes meaning by making the world. Foer, though, goes one step further by asking us to consider what it means to think about language itself as one of those things that both matters and is matter.

ELIC's transformation of language into meaningful presence puts into literary practice a theory of literature launched by Hans Gumbrecht nearly simultaneously with the novel. In his *Production of Presence: What Meaning Cannot Convey* (2004), Gumbrecht argues for a return to reading as embodied endeavor—one that acknowledges the importance of the physical realities through which language and interpretation function—rather than the exclusively hermeneutical thing it has, via poststructural ideas about language, become. Working through a tradition reaching back to Walter Benjamin's celebration of the "immediate physical 'touch' of cultural objects," Susan Sontag's declaration in "Against Interpretation" that "in place of a hermeneutics we need an erotics of art" (1964), and even Lyotard and Derrida, Gumbrecht notes that "the main interest in [our] intellectual environment [has] shifted from the identification of meaning . . . to problems regarding the emergence of meaning," and aims to escape the eddy of endless meaning effects by returning our attention to the ways in which language connects us to the tangible world. Reading with attention to the "production of presence," for Gumbrecht, means acknowledging that "any form of communication, through its material elements" (which can include medium, spoken qualities, and physical effects registered on the body) "will 'touch' the bodies of the persons who are communicating in specific and varying ways."[47]

Essentially Gumbrecht argues for a new concept of the aesthetic experience, "as an oscillation . . . between 'presence effects' and 'meaning effects.'" In so doing he espouses, in a strikingly Pater-esque way, an argument for appreciating art, and especially literature, as something that affects the body and impacts the physical world. Such an argument for reading comes as a reaction to the postmodern insistence that all arguments and concepts should be "antisubstantialist" and add to a "meaning culture" whose attention is held by the operations of systems of signs rather than the substances, or space-occupying things, put into relationship by those systems. In making such an argument, Gumbrecht does not abandon the central poststructuralist assertions about problems of language and their accompanying problematizing of belief and certitude. Rather, he locates his ideas within poststructural ideas of language themselves. For example, he reads de Man's perpetual mourning of language's inability to refer to the material world as keeping the material referent ever present, a stick against which the slippery chain of signifiers must always be measured. Further, he grounds his assertion of the need to keep the material present in all aesthetic acts in Heidegger, who may have divorced language from the human but also defined being as fundamentally "being-in-the-world," a revolt against the loss of the world outside human consciousness caused by the Cartesian subject-object split.[48]

Hence, Gumbrecht argues that a "presence culture," in which the dominant self-reference is the body, rather than the mind,[49] is able to quantify things like feelings, or impressions of closeness or absence, of approval and resistance, that a "meaning" culture cannot measure. Such a presence culture operates in *ELIC* when Oskar "invents" a shower whose water would turn colors when it hit one's skin, signifying one's mood; or an ambulance that would flash **"DON'T WORRY!"** or **"GOODBYE! I LOVE YOU!"** (72) as it whisked its passenger down loved ones' streets; or a "reservoir of tears" that would measure, each day, the sorrow pouring out of New York City residents (38). In fact, when we meet Oskar, on page 1, we do so through his desire to orient himself in relation to the bodies and hearts around him: he imagines everyone swallowing little microphones so that "when you skateboarded down the street at night you could hear everyone's heartbeat, and they could hear yours, like sonar" (1). Driving Oskar in his key search and in his inventiveness is a need—like that of Haddon's autistic boy—to read and weigh the feelings of those around him, so that he can know how to be in the world in relation to them. His almost neurotic need to read in these ways simultaneously points to the inherent difficulty of such acts of reading, the unreliability of the systems of signification provided us by the world, and the intensity of our resulting need to strive to read and thus connect with other people in response. *ELIC* then envisions our contemporary world as mind-based meaning culture in which inventive acts of language invoke presence, defiantly making meaning that matters in the world.

In doing so, it radically reconfigures alliances between origins of textual meaning and functions of presence and absences, shattering assumptions that have been in place for centuries and that shape the story we tell about the evolution of literature and meaning from Renaissance humanism, through Romanticism, and into the discomfiting reversal perpetrated by poststructuralism. When charting this series of shifts in textual meaning in his essay on the "Greatly Exaggerated" death of the author, Wallace also does so in terms of a larger shift from presence to absence: he identifies the Romantic belief that textual meaning derived from the intention of a unified author with *presence*; the New Critical reaction to that, which derived textual meaning not from the author but from the text; and then the poststructural reader-response exaggeration of the New Critical stance, which located meaning in the reader and required the *absence* of author as knowable and intentional force, and the absence of determinable meaning.[50] Such a shift implies a wholesale surrender of the text to Gumbrecht's meaning culture. Instead, much contemporary fiction returns to an emphasis on present things and meaning, derived from the text, but still quite apart from any Romantic/Renaissance notion of the unified, intending subject, reversing meaning culture's increasing separation of language from world, word from thing, and sign from meaning. In so doing, texts become increasingly dependent on the reader's participation (as Chapter 5 will argue), constructing presence from the fractured subjects and writer-reader nexuses that arise in a poststructural world.

Ending "In a Beginning": Linguistic materiality in *The Book of Portraiture*

As if looking through the wrong end of a telescope, Steve Tomasula's *The Book of Portraiture*, published in 2006, also marks its contemporariness using the World Trade

Center attacks, but in reverse: it represents their aftermath as not the enormity of the towers' absence but as the absurd atomity to which those attacks reduced so many human bodies. In the novel's final section, a bio-artist works at a lab where thousands of thimble-sized wells contain DNA solutions prepared from fragments of victims, "each a microscopic portrait, each a tiny grave."[51] That such a reduction could constitute portraiture indicates one of the many ways that Tomasula's novel redefines portraiture, or the art of representing the human.

Like *ELIC*, *Portraiture* takes the poststructural position that, given the inadequacy and inaccuracy of all systems of signification, any attempt to represent the human requires consideration and use of multiple forms of language, word, and image. Tellingly, the novel's *tour-de-force* meditation on the limits and possibilities of representation comes from the voice of Diego de Velazquez, historical seventeenth-century Italian painter whom Tomasula employs to develop concepts of representation away from mimetic realism and into more contemporary privileging of perspective. Originally pursuing, like all court painters, the perfection of mimetic representation, Valezquez discovers the inescapability of perspective—that "all acts of seeing are acts of framing" (79)—by paying attention first to a painting's ability to change the viewer's perspective (e.g. of the featured nobility), and then—turning the telescope around, *Endgame*-style—noticing that every painting of an Other also contains the perspective of the painter himself. Representing the culmination of his thinking on representation is his *Las Meninas*, in the novel and in reality a wall-sized painting that displaces its most powerful subjects (the king and queen), places the painter within it, and situates the viewer such that she feels contained by it. Through Velazquez, Tomasula considers art's inability mimetically to represent the human, its insistence on multiple perspective, and the connection between the two: all acts of understanding through art come as a result of an attempt to represent the world; only through attention to the *things* of the world, and our attempts to order them via representation, can we arrive at a perspective through which we can fully consider the human, as a subjective concept and as a thing in the world.

As a whole the novel presents a development of human ideas about representation from the invention of the alphabet to our current poststructuralist, post-9/11 crisis of signification. It opens with a rumination on how written language might have emerged as attempts to mimic in marks the things in the world that shaped human experience: titled "In a Beginning," chapter 1 traces, in an unspecified time and place in ancient Egypt, one man's eureka discovery of visual connections between the things of the world and the symbols used to represent them. By separating the symbols into both their pictorial pieces and their aural phonemes, this man—who reinvents himself as "Moses" to mark the signifying occasion—births himself, the alphabet, and a creation story from what would become an originary biblical system of signification in one cocky swoop. It ends with another chapter titled "In a Beginning," in which a modern-day artist, appropriately named Mary, takes biological building blocks as her canvas, wryly encoding a biblical decree about "man"'s dominion over the world in bacterial DNA. After translation into Morse code and representation via genetic code, the bacterial soup paraphrases Genesis, proclaiming, "LET MAN HAVE DOMINION OVER ALL THE PLANTS AND ANIMALS OF THE EARTH" (318). The art seems to solve the sign-thing gap, the material used to express the message demonstrating the message itself. But by demonstrating that the power to order the world and to use it to create language comes from the human and not from God, the art clearly mocks its biblical source. Then Mary makes the art also mock its own seeming solution: she invites viewers of the art installation to change—and therefore disprove—the decree. With a click of a mouse, anyone anywhere with internet access can trigger a blast of UV light that alters the encoding through mutation. Creating a kind of genetic telephone game, Mary's bio-art demonstrates the domination of the individual and the body over the word, and the perfect randomness of the language that tries to deny that domination.

The three chapters lying between these bookending beginnings, set in seventeenth-century Italy, early twentieth-century Germany, and postmodern America, suggest advances in concepts of representation that allow us to travel from one beginning to another, and witness the ways in which these ideas impact and originate in the body and the world. Chapter 3, for example, comprises the journal entries of an early Freudian analyst as he attempts to treat an attractive young woman whose only malady seems to be an appreciation of her own sexuality that the age would not allow her. As he attempts to "cure" her "nervous tension" while remaining bound to sexist Freudian ideas about women's sexuality (like calling "female orgasm" an "oxymoron," 108) and Puritanical ideas about "proper" sexual expression—and, perhaps more importantly, while denying his own palpable attraction to his patient—the doctor enlists increasingly bold and body-oriented techniques, culminating in administrations of "electromechanical percussors" (138). Results of this treatment are so well-received that the once unwilling therapy patient begins to increase the frequency of her visits. As the doctor buries his own clear attraction to her in sophisticated ponderings of newfangled ideas about representation of emotion and desire in photography and art, his language becomes increasingly sexually charged and phallus-obsessed, so that in the end it is he and not his smart, self-aware patient who strikes us as *hysterical*. Her treatment ends when he receives in the mail from her a magazine ad featuring an "electro-powered vibro-wand . . . facial massager": she has learned to define her "problem" as of the body and self-solvable. The journal entries cleverly demonstrate via language the power of the body to create perspectives through which we stubbornly, and often mistakenly, view the world. Thus it reminds us that, despite recent theorizing about the slipperiness of language, and though we must recognize that the subject makes meaning and resist the solace of the objective, we must not forget the power of the body and of things in the world—and that sometimes a "cigar" really is just a "cigar."

On the other hand, coming after, and perhaps still in, a time when language and even the world itself have been theorized as a system of signs and, worse, of largely ineffective signs, and in the midst of a debate about what language can do and therefore what literature and the study of literature can do in the real world, *Portraiture*'s assertions about the power of language to act materially in the world feel as surprising and risky as they do necessary and optimistic. Perhaps more surprising still is that Tomasula models the biological art in this novel after real twenty-first-century scientific-artistic accomplishments that support his novel's shocking insinuation: language is of the body, writes with and on the body, and therefore changes the world. Certainly Tomasula's work at times takes a more sinister and problematizing tone than does Foer's. Rather than ending with a boy's newfound understanding of what it is to be human in this universe of mostly dark matter, *Portraiture* ends with an ominous image of what the human might have poststructurally become. Mary plans her next creative act to be the making of a viable embryo using her egg, her (rather unloved) boyfriend's sperm, and junk DNA from a third person. She will call it "Trinity," and she entertains the idea of taking its third piece from the relic'd body of a saint.[52] Such contemplation of the complete reduction of the sacred to bodily matter strikes us as sinister enough. But she has made provisions for other "junk DNA"—in case the saint can't be heisted—and the novel ends with a box of this human junk having just arrived, Mary "cradling it against her waist" as she walks out the door (323). In such a moment, with the human having become a synecdoche of itself, it and its creation so reduced and separated from any semblance of love, womb, or fully human experience, Tomasula's novel forces us to consider, *White Noise* style, all that might be lost when we allow representation to dominate the things and especially the humans of the world.

There is a way in which such a "discovery" by recent fiction of the need to return to presence and the body should not come as much of a surprise. Where else was fiction going to go? Unlike *The Names*, its wandering cult literalizing the Lacanian notion that "the symbol manifests itself first of all as the murder of the thing,"[53] *The Road*, *ELIC* and *Book* demonstrate the materiality of language, or language's dependence on the material, to remind us not of the monstrous *threat* to the human posed by acts of signification, but that all acts of signification are determined and executed by bodies in the world; and that only by remembering this experientially undeniable connection between word and thing can we view language not as estranging self from world and other but as the insufficient mechanism we most bountifully have for becoming present in the world and to the other. Far from Jameson's "antigravity of the postmodern"[54] or Kundera's "unbearable lightness of being,"[55] this return to things and our ability to apprehend them through language is a return to the welcome weight of things that matter, and to a view of language not as futile but rather as part of an unkillable system of forces that hold these things, and us, in relation, mapping meanings like points of light, scratching chronicles whose relevance to the earth we carry forward like fire.

Notes

1   *Publisher's Weekly*, in its review of *Extremely Loud & Incredibly Close*, calls Foer "one of the few contemporary writers willing to risk sentimentalism in order to address great questions of truth, love and beauty" (January 31, 2005).
2   Hoberek, "Introduction: After Postmodernism," 237.
3   Foer, *Extremely Loud & Incredibly Close*, 281. Subsequent references will be noted parenthetically.
4   McHale, "When Did Postmodernism Begin?" 400.

5   Interestingly, *No Country for Old Men*, which Cormac McCarthy published one year before *The Road*, ends with "*And then I woke up*," one waking almost seeming to lead into another (New York: Vintage, 2005), 309 (original italics).

6   *Endgame* seems an obvious precursor to *The Road* not only because of their shared contemplation of the fate of the postapocalyptic human, but also because its ever-ending unendingness also mimics the critical sense that postmodernism was born into its sputtering death throes. Indeed, Steven Connor appropriated *Endgame*'s opening line in describing postmodernism as "Finished, it's finished, nearly finished, it must be nearly finished" in *The Cambridge Companion to Postmodernism* (Cambridge: Cambridge University Press, 2004), 1.

7   Cormac McCarthy, *The Road* (New York: Vintage International, 2006), 11. Subsequent references will be noted parenthetically.

8   Arguments have been made that the novel ends redemptively, implying a kind of salvation through the saving of the Christlike boy, and I do not disagree that the ending offers us this warm reading. But the very fact that the novel's end continues to generate so much debate, and that the novel as a whole generates such diametrically opposed readings, argues the point that McCarthy chose not to end the novel with any clear sense of direction or purpose. See, for example, Randall Wilhelm's "'Golden chalice, good to house a god': Still Life in *The Road*," and Jay Ellis's "Another Sense of Ending," in *Cormac McCarthy Journal* 6 (2008): 129–46 and 22–38.

9   Mitchell's novel also literalizes this creed, moving from the cannibalism of the "uncivilized" tribes in the Pacific islands of the nineteenth century to a futuristic "civilization" on the eve of world apocalypse that feeds the murdered bodies of its genetically engineered working class to those still in service. As in *Cloud Atlas*, cannibalism in *The Road*—the charred remains of the newborn baby on a spit— provides the book's most shocking evidence of the intensity of the self's solipsistic voraciousness, not as a result of an overabundance of images, but as a result of a dearth of things.

10 Such trinities abound in the novel, and I would go so far as suggesting that McCarthy adds strength to the subtle infusion of trinities by favoring trinity in the meter of his prose, often using trisyllabic spondees such as "dull glass bell" (4), "poor meal cold" (10), "gray day break" (11)—to list just a few in early pages—which, in combination with these triple-adjective descriptions, underscores the Christian imagery occurring throughout the novel.

11 I think of Thomas Pynchon's bawdy songs and set pieces in *The Crying of Lot 49* (New York: J. B. Lipincott, 1966) and *Gravity's Rainbow* (New York: Viking, 1973), the pervasively wry—but not quite black—humor in Donald Barthelme's "At the End of the Mechanical Age" and other stories (New York: E. P. Dutton, 1976), even the Pynchonesque absurdity of early Don DeLillo, as in *Ratner's Star* (New York: Vintage, 1976).

12 See, for example, page 280:
    He closed his eyes and talked to him and he kept his eyes closed and listened. Then he tried again.
    He woke in the darkness, coughing slowly. He lay listening.

13 Tomasula, "Three Axioms," 100.

14 Brown, "Thing Theory," 14, 11.

15 Distinctions between the "object" and the "thing," meaningful in thing theory but not in the broad sign/thing opposition I am enlisting here, will be explored below.

16 Later published in *Critical Inquiry* 30 (Winter 2004): 225–48.

17 See *The Spirit of Terrorism: And Requiem for the Twin Towers* (New York: Verso, 2002).

18 Latour, "Why Has Critique Run out of Steam?," 227, 231 (original italics).

19 Tomasula, "Three Axioms," 102. This concern is central to Wallace's diagnosis in the 1993 interview with McCaffery of the failure of ironic, "crank-turning" postmodern fiction in the 1990s as well, and to the thesis of his argument about television in "E Unibus Pluram," as discussed in Chapter 2.

20 Susan Sontag, "Against Interpretation," *Against Interpretation and Other Essays* (New York: Picador, 196), 17.

21 Such as Bill Brown and Hans Gumbrecht, discussed below.

22 Brown, "Thing Theory," 4–5, 6.

23 Ibid., 16.

24 Ibid., 14.

25 Ibid., 3.

26 Ibid., 15. Brown's reading here is strikingly reminiscent of Christopher Lasch's notion, detailed in Chapter 2, of the late twentieth century's narcissistic culture resulting in a "longing to be free from longing" (*The Culture of Narcissism*, 241). Deeply Freudian, Lasch's assessment amounts to accusing contemporary American culture of enacting a kind of death drive that it transmits, like smallpox, to every nation that gobbles up its much-demanded cultural products. Peter Schwenger also connects the object's discreetness from the totality of the thing it represents with the death drive, when he associates the object's inability to be what we desire, or what we would like to read it as, with Lacan's reading of the *fort-da* game in which the point and the thing desired is not really the object lost (*fort*) but the experience of loss that is always there (*da*) apart from the object and unassuageable by the object: "Lacan identifies the death drive with a shortfall in representation" ("Words and the Murder of the Thing," *Critical Inquiry* 28 (2001): 109). I also see an interesting change in our contemplation of things as they relate to the death drive between a modernist text like Roberts's *The Time of Man* (1926), whose main character views stones in a field as being as irrepressibly alive as her young self, and the very different claim by an apocalypse-courting character in DeLillo's 2010 *Point Omega* that "we want to be stones in a field" (53).

27 Donald Judd, "Specific Objects" (1965), *Complete Writings, 1959–1975* (New York, 1975): 189; quoted in Brown, "Thing Theory," 14.

28 In what might be a complete reversal of this assertion of mere objecthood via art, a recent exhibit at the Museum of Modern Art in New York illustrates the extremes to which we have taken this anthropomorphizing of objects today, striving not just to allow them to represent us and our feelings but to put them in *conversation* with us, and therefore granting them a kind of selfhood and consciousness that has been imagined for years but never so fully realized. The desire to collapse the human/object divide works in the opposite way, too, in devices and art projects that use humans and/or human work to take the place of the machine. Examples include devices that communicate to human ears the sounds made by trees, a film of a man performing the job of a computer, a video of two men acting as analog clock by constantly sweeping trash into the moving shapes of its hands, technologies that become human- or animal-like companions to humans, and many more. See *Talk to Me: Design and the Communication between People and Objects*, which ran from July 24–November 7,

2011 and was also represented in a book by the same name published by MOMA in New York City.

29   Brown, "Thing Theory," 3.

30   Ibid., 14.

31   Ibid., 16.

32   Sontag, "Against Interpretation," 13.

33   Ibid., 14.

34   Boswell notes that Wallace viewed the relationship between texts and reading similarly, believing "fiction is changed by the reader as much as the reader is changed by the fiction." See *Understanding David Foster Wallace*, 125.

35   Sontag's thinking explicitly opposes this reasoning. Urging the integration of form and content, she criticizes as wholly distorting the practice of equating meaning only with content, calling such form-denying acts of interpretation "the revenge of the intellect upon art" (7), and claiming that "to interpret is to impoverish, to deplete the world—in order to set up a shadow world of 'meanings.' It is to turn the world into this world. ('This world'! As if there were any other.)" (7), and asserts the irrelevance of authorial intention: "It doesn't matter whether artists intend, or don't intend, for their works to be interpreted" (10). Also: "'Never trust the teller, trust the tale,' said Lawrence" (9).

36   Vincent P. Pecora, "Words, Words, Mere Words, No Matter from the Heart . . .," *American Literary History* 19 no. 1 (2007): 236–7.

37   Ibid., 243.

38   Waters, "Literary Aesthetics: The Very Idea," *The Chronicle Review* 52 no. 17 (December 16, 2005): B6.

39   While I am not interested in connecting postmodernism to a particular historical/ political event, in this way I sympathize with Brown's declaration in 2005 that postmodernism began not in 1967 but on September 11, 2001.

40   Walter Benn Michaels, *The Shape of the Signifier* (Princeton: Princeton University Press, 2004), 1.

41   See Michel Faber's review for the *Guardian* on June 4, 2005 (www.guardian.co.uk/ books/2005/jun/04/featuresreviews.guardianreview22). That Faber later completely misreads the Tomoyashu interview in the novel's middle chapter, however, renders his judgment of the book questionable. See my argument on the chapter titled "Happiness, Happiness," below.

42   See "Extremely Cloying & Incredibly False," a review of the novel by Harry Siegel in *New York Press* on April 20, 2005, among others (http://nypress.com/ extremely-cloying- incredibly-false). When I led a book group discussion on this novel at the Ellenville Library (in November 2009), a group made of smart senior readers for whom "novel" meant "traditional realism" and who were complaining about the *ELIC*'s multiple plots and narrators before we had even sat down, I heard many vociferous versions of these same complaints. But by the end of the discussion, all but one of the members admired the book, suggesting that many objections arise not because of the book itself but because of a lack of tools with which productively to read the book.

43   My thanks to Steve Florczyk for pointing out to me this history of illuminated texts.

44   For example, Steve Tomasula's *The Book of Portraiture* (Tallahassee: FC2, 2006); W. G. Sebald's *Austerlitz* (New York: Random House, 2001); Mark Danielewski's second novel, *Only Revolutions* (New York: Pantheon Books, 2006); and, through

the use of one drawing of a stapler that mocks this oncoming trend, Dave Eggers's *A Heartbreaking Work of Staggering Genius* (New York: Vintage, 1999).

45   Among a plethora of examples of ekphrastic twenty-first-century literature—perhaps more prevalent in British literature than in American today—are Ian McEwan's *Atonement* (New York: Doubleday, 2002), David Mitchell's *Cloud Atlas* (New York: Random House, 2004), John Banville's *The Sea* (New York: Knopf, 2005), and Don DeLillo's *Point Omega* (New York: Scribner, 2010).

46   Eliot, "The Metaphysical Poets," 65, 60.

47   Gumbrecht, *The Production of Presence*, 10, 13, 17.

48   Ibid., 18, 81–3, 66.

49   Ibid., 80.

50   David Foster Wallace, "Greatly Exaggerated," in *A Supposedly Fun Thing I'll Never Do Again* (New York: Little, Brown and Company, 1997), 138–45.

51   Tomasula, *The Book of Portraiture*, 293. Subsequent references will be noted parenthetically.

52   Mary's DNA translation of Genesis reprises a bio-art work called *Genesis* by Eduardo Kac (1999). In 2000 Kac produced *GFP Bunny*, a rabbit named "Alba" whose genetic manipulation allowed it to glow fluorescently green. *Specimen of Scenery about Marvelous Discoveries*, exhibited in 2004 and 2006, recast *Genesis* by creating works of art made of "living pieces that changed during the exhibit in response to internal metabolism and environmental conditions." And his 2003/2008 piece, *The Natural History of the Enigma*, seems to reverse the influence of art and book by enacting a version of Mary's final work of art in Tomasula's *Portraiture*, which she called "'Trinity'": Kac's *Natural History* is a "genetically engineered flower that is a hybrid of Kac and Petunia." At least no saints were involved. See "Bio Art," accessed April 8, 2011. www.ekac.org/transgenicindex.html.

53   Lacan, *Écrits*, 140.

54   Jameson, *Postmodernism*, 101.

55   Milan Kundera, *The Unbearable Lightness of Being* (New York: Harper Perennial, 1984).

5

"Set . . . softly down beside you": Poststructural Realism in "Octet" and *Everything Is Illuminated*

When *The Road* asserts the primacy of real, present things in order to point to the meaningful absence of all that has been lost and cannot be accurately made present through signification; when *ELIC* materializes language in order to lead its young hero to the truth of his father's empty coffin; when *The Book of Portraiture* offers atoms, DNA, and electro-powered vibrawands to name and salve the human, literature charts a shift away from twentieth-century poststructuralism worth exploring. The pendulum swings. After bearing for decades with a poststructurally minded literature asserting—at first with the *jouissance* of release, but then with the grimness or apathy of having no idea where things could go from there—that the world is made of the gap (between sign and thing; between truth and truth), of all that cannot be represented or understood, novels in the twenty-first century draw a world made of real things and materially effective and affective language that are all we have for articulating, understanding, and salving the gap. Made themselves of language, though, novels know they have no access to the real real in order to make this point. And so the need for a poststructural realism arises, the need for a method of representation via language that can invoke the real we miss and need in order to reconnect literature to the world we live in, rather than just to the one we theorize.

The undying longing for connection via language explored in even the linguistically murderous, suffocatingly ironic, and fatally narcissistic novels examined in the first half of this book attests to the fact that literature never lost its humanist desires, even during its to-date most antihumanist emanation. I have argued that such longing, however repressed, is characteristic of even this late twentieth-century phase of solipsistically meta fiction, and that whether we read in it the solipsism or the longing for empathetic connection depends on how we choose to read these complicated texts that struggle against themselves as much as they struggle against the humanism they aimed to break away from. One example of such a self-divided, or double text is John Ashbery's famously self-reflexive poem, "Paradoxes and Oxymorons" (1980):

This poem is concerned with language on a very plain level.
Look at it talking to you. You look out a window
Or pretend to fidget. You have it but you don't have it.
You miss it, it misses you. You miss each other.

The poem is sad because it wants to be yours, and cannot.
What's a plain level? It is that and other things,
Bringing a system of them into play. Play?
Well, actually, yes, but I consider play to be

A deeper outside thing, a dreamed role-pattern,
As in the division of grace these long August days
Without proof. Open-ended. And before you know
It gets lost in the steam and chatter of typewriters.

It has been played once more. I think you exist only
To tease me into doing it, on your level, and then you aren't there
Or have adopted a different attitude. And the poem
Has set me softly down beside you. The poem is you.

Read through the lens of antihumanistic language terminally reflecting on itself, this poem is a testament to language's ability to empty itself of meaning: in defining what the poem "is" (1), the poem retreats ever further from meaningful specificity, equating the poem first with "language" (1) and then with "play" (7), itself enigmatically defined as "A deeper outside thing . . . Open-ended" (9–11), then relegated to an undefined "it," and finally resorting to that quintessentially postmodern thing, a tautology: "It has been played once more" (13). Meanwhile, from first to last stanza, the poem asserts that it and its reader "miss" each other. What meaningful thing has been communicated here, from poem to reader? And yet, the poem is also full of affect and appeals for empathy: first it is "concerned"; then it is "sad," morphing the connotation of "miss" from one of absence—reader and poem are not there for each other—to one of longing that keeps both text and reader present for each other, while assuming a present empathy between them. By the last line, when the poem has "set me," the author, "softly down beside you," the intimacy between reader and writer is clear: the poem has manifested the author, in all gentle companionship and present proximity, for the reader. Finally, the poem enacts complete intimacy, identity, between reader and text—"the poem is you"—leaving reader and writer together in the company of, and inhabiting, the poem. The author has made himself present for the reader, the text present in the reader, and has thus reached the reader herself.

Still possibly invoking that tautologic that has so notably plagued the self-reflexive thinking of postmodern literature,[1] this identification-replete ending harnesses such intense personification, and such a tender tone, that one feels left more in the presence of a caring author and/or text than in their snide disaffection. Metafiction always has this choice to make: to construct an onanistic game that leaves the reader out, or to invoke the presence of text and/or author precisely in order to build through them a longing toward something meaningful and shared that needs the reader to occupy the other end of that longing.[2] Readers always have the choice to read the onanism, or the empathy, or both. After decades of largely solipsistic metafiction and critical readings of metafiction, literature of the twenty-first century quite baldly employs metafiction toward the humanist, and formerly "realist" goal of making the author and text feel intimately present for a reader whose participation in that act of humanism the text depends on. This chapter will examine specific formal and thematic ways in which literature of the early twenty-first century accomplishes these goals, turning poststructural metafiction to the ends of traditional realism and humanism.

By the early twenty-first century, society has absorbed into itself the cultural gestures of postmodernism (such as irony, as Wallace demonstrates in *Infinite Jest*) and the signifying tricks of poststructuralism (such as self-reflexivity and metanarrative, seen in the recent flurry of metanarrative in movies like *Synecdoche, NY*; *Adaptation*; *Memento*; and film adaptations of metanarrative novels, like *Atonement*—to name a very few[3]) that were originally intended to work against mainstream culture and concepts of both reality and representation, or art. In such a society, producing "reality effects"—pointing to what feels "real" to us—*requires* antirealism; that is to say, realism in the twenty-first century, born of poststructural notions of language, and into a culture steeped in irony and winking metamoments, harnesses traditionally antirealist tools like nonlinear, nonchronological, and multiple narration, hypertext, self-reflexivity, and metafiction, in order to represent a highly signification-oriented textual world that feels as real to us, and—in the hands of the best contemporary writers—as warm and fuzzy, as did, for the nineteenth-century reader, the muddy streets of *Middlemarch*.[4]

An appeal to realism, to finding ways to encounter, invoke, or return to the real through current poststructural artistic and literary practices, appears in many of the critical calls for a new and newly productive way of reading and understanding literature in the postmodern age, though not yet expressed in relation to literary attempts to enact them. Most often-cited is Hal Foster's 1996 *The Return of the Real*, which defines a meaningful difference between historical avant-garde art in relation to neo (post-1960) avant-garde art, and between postmodernism in relation to modernism. One of his key ways of characterizing that difference is in the return of the real in art as essentially traumatic, and art's methods for representing the real as what he calls "traumatic realism." Following Lacan's (also 1960s era) understanding of the real, especially in "The Unconscious and Repetition," as inherently traumatic, the traumatic as a missed encounter with the real, and so the real as unrepresentable, Foster theorizes postmodern representations of traumatic events in two ways: the first type, similar to Lacan's "*automaton*," simply repeats the "symptom" of the trauma without being able meaningfully to contain it; but the second, like Lacan's *tuché*, is a repetition of the repressed traumatic real, screened by the first repetition but "nonetheless returned, accidently and/or obliquely, in this very screening." Thus representations of traumatic events function both as a defense against the felt trauma of the event and as an invocation of it; the repetition of the trauma via representation "is both a draining of significance and a defending against affect"[5] and an "obsessive fixation on the object in melancholy," and therefore on the melancholy itself. Reading several of Andy Warhol's silkscreens[6] as evidence of traumatic realism in action, Foster asserts that "somehow in these repetitions . . . several contradictory things occur at the same time: a warding away of traumatic significance *and* an opening out to it, a defending against traumatic affect *and* a producing of it." Essential to this understanding of trauma and the real is Lacan's notion that the real is that which always resists interpretation, so that the real is never the thing being represented, even via traumatic realism; rather, all representation can do is invoke the real by illustrating the impossibility of making it present in representation: "Repetition serves to *screen* the real understood as traumatic. But this very need also *points* to the real."[7]

This reading of the real as that which can only be represented via neurotic and poorly apprehended returns of repressed affect (often narcissistic fear for the self or suffering at the self's unfulfillment, less often fear for the loss of the loved one) provides another useful framework for explaining the hamstrung humanism that characterizes the fiction discussed in the first half of this book. For characters in DeLillo's *The Names* and *White Noise*, Wallace's *Infinite Jest*, and Homes's *Music for Torching*, language and representation operate as methods of defending themselves against the real and the traumatic, and the novels—up until Homes's recuperative acts of sacrifice and reinvocations of conventional realism—invoke these repressed elements of affect, meaning, the real, and the human connection they enable, only by pointing to the absence of these things, rather than representing the things themselves. Foster registers a similar repression operating in postmodern art and theory, and blames it for the traumatic nature of this return of the real:

> Why this fascination with trauma, this envy of abjection, today? To be sure, motives exist within art and theory. As suggested, there is dissatisfaction with the textualist model of culture as well as the conventionalist view of reality—as if the real, repressed in poststructuralist postmodernism, had returned as traumatic.[8]

Citing the same "dissatisfaction" with a "textualist model" of the world that motivates theorists like Latour, Waters, Sontag, Brown, and Gumbrecht to call for a new model that privileges the real or the thing over (or at least in intimate relationship with) the sign, Foster connects the traumatizing of the real to its repression by the sign.

Further, he notes, citing trends in post-1960 visual art toward representing the abject, sick, and wounded, that another result of such repression of the real has been that "for many in contemporary culture truth resides in the traumatic or abject subject, in the diseased or damaged body."[9] Certainly late twentieth-century literature suggests a similar conclusion about the relationship between efforts at representing the real and the abject: consider the confluence of earnestness and attempts at human connection in *Infinite Jest* with the diseased, malformed, and outcast, as we see in softheaded Mario, legless (and Canadian) Marathe, and the sweat-licking Lyle. Worse, *The Names* and *White Noise* ominously imagine their seekers of "truth" via language and representation as murderous men in caves, or a man who is noxiously diseased and waiting for death, while acting murderously. Their innocent extralinguistic truth lies in the child, and, in the case of *White Noise*, one whose muteness is as inexplicable and marginalizing as is his hours-long crying jag, and who is nearly killed at novel's end. In *Music for Torching*, affect, meaning, and the potential for novelistic wholeness reside only within the head-shot body of a boy-murdered boy—but the narrative dies with this disclosure. In a literature under the trance of late twentieth-century poststructural ideas about language, the sign manifesting itself as murder of the thing, it seems that attempts to say something true often become traumatic acts, inflicting injury and social exile on their tellers, as well as stalling out their narratives.

But while I do see this idea of traumatic realism—the return of the real as traumatic repetition of the unrepresentable real—as characteristic of late twentieth-century postmodern fiction, I do not think it describes twenty-first-century fiction, in which truth now could be said to lie less *in* the diseased and damaged body and more in the wake of, and in causal proximity to it. Johnny Truant finds his way to peace, understanding of self, and final clarity about his past and his formative relationship to his mother, because of the beastly death of the unredeemingly mad Zampanò: by passing the book to Johnny with his death at the beginning of the novel, Zampanò becomes the sacrifice required for Johnny's healing and enlightenment. Similarly, Oscar's journey to self-knowledge, a new belief, and a rediscovery of his love for and meaningful dependence on his mother comes in the wake of, and prompted by, his father's death, which precedes the novel's opening. In *The Book of Portraiture*, the young female analysis patient "heals" her own malady by coming to a fuller sense of self in contrast to and through experiencing her doctor's own anxiety-denying repression.[10] In this way, all of these novels offer answers to the question of what comes at the empty end of *Music for Torching*: they convert sacrifice of the diseased or abject into meaning, affect, and human connection, thus no longer representing the real only by pointing to its absence, but instead pointing to everything that exists necessarily around the absent real, around and in the wake of trauma, as meaningful and productive in the human experience.

Foer's first novel, *Everything Is Illuminated* (2002), exemplifies well this shift from absence to presence, and from trauma as a stalling-out point to narrative-generating proximity to trauma. This novel also implies, in several thematic ways, that truth and self reside not, untranslatably, "in the traumatic or abject subject," but rather around it and in the narrativized wake of it. Enlisting three different narratives, the novel ostensibly gives the story of an author, named Jonathan Safran Foer, who searches for the true history of the destruction of his grandfather's shtetl during World War II, which he then fictionalizes into his own novelistic account of the long history of that shtetl.[11] But the novel becomes the story of fictional Foer's Ukrainian translator, Alex, as he comes to terms with the gruesome truth of his own grandfather's unheroic act of betrayal in a nearby shtetl. On the largest thematic level, all self-knowledge in these stories comes directly out of encounters with (if not full understandings of) not traumatic atrocity itself but stories about it.[12] And at the heart of this novel—in its novel within the novel—lies a creation story that also attributes to proximity of the abject, diseased, and traumatic the genesis of self, family, and community. Acting as origin for that internal novel, for fictional Foer's entire ancestry, and for the town, Trachimbrod, that is birthed along with novel and ancestry, is Brod, born slick-backed from the waters that will open and close both the novel of fictional Foer and the novel of Foer himself. And Brod, origin of all things, becomes so because of her intimacy with a man who—with an errant sawblade embedded in his head, increasingly mad, and walled off from her for her own safety—epitomizes the generative possibility of the disfigured, traumatized, and abject.

The method and symbol of their intimacy also exemplify what I see as a shift from an earlier postmodern traumatic realism—which cannot represent the real but can only imply it by representing its absence, the ever-present gap—to a new kind of realism that endeavors, earnestly, to represent the real through the *things that exist around the gap*, understanding that the absence can only exist *in relation* to a presence that defines it. For Brod and her husband the Kolker (whom she renames Safran, and who will become the great-great-great-great grandfather of fictional Foer), the significant absence is a hole that they cut in the wall between them so they can communicate with each other, make love, and conceive Jonathan's ancestor. Thus absence becomes origin and medium for the birth of everything with which this embedded novel, and the novel *Everything Is Illuminated* around it, concerns itself. Foer (and Foer) elevates this absence to creative significance when describing the hole:

> They lived with the hole. The absence that defined it became a presence that defined them. Life was a small negative space cut out of the eternal solidity, and for the first time, it felt precious—not like all of the words that had come to mean nothing, but like the last breath of a drowning victim.[13]

Here, absence is equated with reality and life, rather than with the ephemeral, unreal word. After the Kolker dies, Brod cuts a circle around the hole and wears the resulting "pine loop" on her necklace, to "remind her of the second man she had lost in her eighteen years, and of the hole that she was learning is not the exception in life, but the rule. The hole is no void; the void exists around it" (139). By opposing rather than equating hole and void, hole and absence, and defining the hole as the rule of life, the stuff of life itself, Foer explodes (or implodes) the binary opposition of absence and presence, representation and real, implying that the realest, most present and powerful thing we have is the hole itself. The hole is not what eludes us: it is what defines us. When Brod wears the pine loop around her neck, a loop that signifies not the loop but the hole defined by it in relief, she asserts that the hole is the thing that matters most though it depends on the thing around it to signify it.

Fittingly, the Kolker does not stop mattering in death. Bronzed, with his "perfectly perpendicular saw blade" stuck handily in place (139), the Kolker becomes sundial and talisman for the community, so that in becoming a thing he accrues the power to measure and shape the lives of others—until, like all gods, he becomes remade in his worshippers' images:

> So many visitors came to rub and kiss different parts of him for the fulfillment of their various wishes that his entire body had to be rebronzed every month. He was a changing god, destroyed and recreated by his believers, destroyed and recreated by their belief.
>
> His dimensions changed slightly with each rebronzing. Over time, his arms lifted, inch by inch, from down at his sides to high above his head. . . . His face had been polished down so many times by so many beseeching hands, and rebuilt as many times by as many others, that it no longer resembled that of the god to whom those first few prayed. For each recasting, the craftsmen modeled the Dial's face after the faces of his male descendants—reverse heredity. . . . Those who prayed came to believe less and less in the god of their creation and more and more in their belief. The unmarried women kissed the Dial's battered lips, although they were not faithful to their god, but to the kiss: they were kissing themselves. And

> when the bridegrooms knelt, it was not the god they believed in, it was the kneel;
> not the god's bronzed knees, but their own bruised ones. (140)

Like the pine loop that signifies him, the bronzed dead Kolker signifies not in spite of but because of the absence at its center, the dissolution of the body enabling the birth of all the things the people need to derive from it, primarily faith and belief. So, also like the pine loop, the absent center can only be defined and signify because of the real thing(s) around it. Thus, the Kolker revises the famously German-spitting nun at the end of DeLillo's *White Noise*, with a crucial reversal of tone: unlike the wry, somewhat bitter, pathetic critique of the nun's proclamation—"Fools, idiots, those who hear voices, those who speak in tongues. We are your lunatics. We surrender our lives to make your nonbelief possible" (319)—the description of the Kolker as faithless symbol of faith is respectful, more reverent than funny in an often achingly funny book. Foer depicts the belief inspired by and surrounding the absenting Kolker, though totally separate from him and anything he might have intentionally signified, as neither sacrilege nor cause for ridicule or pathos.

Just as *House of Leaves* greets us as a novel whose world is already a product of mediation, rather than suffering the loss of the primary or the painful discovery of that loss, so does *Everything Is Illuminated* generate its belief from the hole that is not the void but the rule—not to mock these things but to empower them. In fact, the novel seems to birth its generative babe from language itself, the words "*I will . . . I will . . .*" accompanying Brod up from the river of her birth, as they later, in another narrative altogether (a letter from Alex's grandfather to fictional Foer), enact the novel's end (8, 276). All of the novel we hold in our hands is contained in those words that begin one internal novel and end another: just as language is insufficient but all we have, so is belief the same, and yet we must use both to get through the world, as the characters in this novel gamely do. And unlike Warhol's art, which can point to the real only by representing its total absence, the bronzed Kolker and the pine loop point very consciously to the *presence* of all that is signified by the absent center—belief, faith, individual and communal heredity—and to all the present, real things in the world necessary to define the absence that signifies. Those things, as the bronzed Kolker, might be irrelevant and/or constantly changing, and yet they are crucial: here, the hole can't exist without them, and neither can meaning or belief.[14]

It makes sense that we see a resurgence of interest in things in theory just as we see new literary techniques for pointing to presence rather than absence. These techniques are not a naïve reversal of poststructuralism—narrative strategies designed to repress or cover up absence, discontinuity, and uncertainty by constructing a comfortingly definitive world—but are rather a new way of seeing the gap as defining, in relief, a present world that is our only way of knowing the real—both the Lacanian real that is always inaccessible, in both our life experience and in representation, and the real thing as represented in but never fully present in art. Essentially I am arguing that with such a shift in representing the relationship between the real and the gap, we are seeing a fundamental change in perspective, in the way in which literature comes at the dual problems of representing that which is always unrepresentable (trauma, the real and the self in Lacanian theory) and of representing real things that are never real in representation. Rather than eddying in the crisis of representation, in the unrepresentable gap, as late twentieth-century novels such as the ones discussed in earlier chapters seem to do, more recently novels seem to be searching for and finding ways of using the gap—always there, never denied—to generate meaning and belief, and grounding us once more in real things by characterizing the gap as defined by these things.

Art as the real and the real-est art:
"Lost in the Funhouse" and "Octet"

Before developing through postmodern literature and theory this notion of a return to the real, and representing the real, from within poststructuralism itself, I want to differentiate the concept of poststructural realism I am proposing from two other current ideas about new realism in twenty-first-century literature. Both of them stand in opposition to my concept of a twenty-first-century method of representation that employs metafiction to invoke the real, and the empathy, community, critique, and communication that come along with the real in literature. One, called "dirty realism," has come to describe writing done within the historical postmodern period that is formally and generically traditionally realist, however interested it is in the problems of postmodern culture. Bill Buford, in a 1983 *Granta* issue titled "Dirty Realism: New Writing in America," characterizes dirty realism as realism that is "particularized," "informed by discomforting and sometimes elusive irony," and primarily concerned with "the belly-side of contemporary life." But it is "not self-consciously experimental."[15] Best known for writing dirty realism is Raymond Carver, and perhaps we might consider A. M. Homes working somewhat in that vein as well.[16] In his *Hicks, Tribes, and Dirty Realists*, Rebein also refers to dirty realism as a return to traditional realism, though somewhat (and vaguely) informed by the cultural lessons of postmodernism. Toth and Brooks, in their introduction to *The Mourning After*, describe dirty realism as being "in direct contradistinction to both traditional forms of realism and the metafictional devices of postmodernism,"[17] acknowledging that dirty realism is doing something different in comparison to traditional realism, but that what it is *not* doing is metafiction.

"Neorealism" presents a more complicated comparison but likewise is defined in opposition to metafiction. In fact, Toth cites several critics[18] to back his assertion that neorealism arose specifically in response to the "failure" of metafiction.[19] For him, metafiction "failed" because it ultimately asserts its own grand narrative, implies a "latent belief" in only one "true" version of reality, and is "haunted by the very specter [it] attempted to exorcise: the specter of a telos, the specter of a positivism, the specter of humanism."[20] "Neorealism," on the other hand, he describes as "explicitly embracing *and* deferring the possibility of the referent of mimesis," "identifying *both* itself *and* metafiction as equally contingent and equally relevant 'language games.'" Following Kristiaan Versluys in her introduction to *Neo-Realism in Contemporary Fiction* (1992), he asserts that the defining characteristic of neorealism is its "acceptance of realism *as a contingent narrative act.*"

Setting aside the question of exactly how this "neorealism" "accepts" narrative "as a contingent narrative act" better, or, say, less hegemonically, than does metafiction, and the thornier question of whether any narrative act can proceed without asserting *a* version of truth and so in some way subscribing to *a* grand narrative—a fixation that I think postmodern criticism in general needs to let go of it is going to be able to proceed at all—we might ask *how* "neorealism" proposes to move beyond metafiction. Toth answers this question by repeatedly asserting that neorealism "*relaxes the rules*" of postmodernism "and returns to realist forms that openly negotiate the mimetic impulse that postmodern metafiction could never truly abandon."[21] In proposing that literature in the twenty-first century enacts specifically a poststructural, and metafictional realism, rather than a return to traditional forms of realism, I am disagreeing with this version of metafiction espoused by Toth and others, and perhaps more specifically with the notion that any narrative act can proceed free from the "mimetic impulse" which they chastise metafiction for retaining. I am also proposing a different explanation for *how* much of twenty-first-century literature escapes the problems of language described by poststructuralism—which is, after all, most essentially an awareness of the problems, the disjunction between word and world, inherent in the inescapable mimetic impulse. First, my readings of the fiction in this chapter and in Chapter 4 reveal not a "latent belief" in only one version of reality, but rather these novels' concerted efforts to construct worlds in which the idea of one true reality makes no sense at all. Any "truth claims" contained in their narratives are always subject to the competing "truth claims" of their multiple authors and perspectives, so that they explicitly reject *the* grand narrative while also pursuing moments of contingent truth. Finally, I have to agree that such metafiction continues to contain the pursuit of telos and of humanism, but I object to the negative implication that this pursuit constitutes a "haunting," as, in my reading of this fiction, such retained striving for truth and humanism is not an unfortunate undead recurrence to be feared but is rather a vibrant and welcome part of its point. Instead, I will argue for a return to the real, and a way of representing the real in twenty-first-century literature, that evolves specifically out of our poststructural ideas about language and the world, and manifests *through* the metafiction that best demonstrates those ideas—in part because metafiction is most aware of and upfront with its need to negotiate the "mimetic impulse" at the heart of acts of fiction.

One way to read literature as participating in and enabling this shift back toward the real is in itself becoming the solid, present thing through which we can encounter the gap at the heart of both reals. This is exactly the kind of return to the real—viewing art as itself the real, rather than as simply vehicles for representation—that Susan Sontag calls for in her "Against Interpretation," another theorizing of the nature and functioning of art in the postmodern period that centers itself on how postmodern and especially poststructural art evokes the real. Indeed, she begins her essay by identifying our central mistake in theorizing art, repeated over millennia since the Greeks, as viewing it as "necessarily a 'realism,'" thus bracketing off form from content, denying its "incantatory, magical" origins, and converting it by definition into the unreal, the less-than-real, a shadow to the real world and therefore in need of external justification. Instead, Sontag argues, we need to theorize ways to experience art as the real itself: "The aim of all commentary on art now should be to make works of art—and, by analogy, our own experience—more, rather than less, real to us. The function of criticism should be to show how it is what it is, even that it is what it is, rather than to show what it means."[22] While clearly opposing nineteenth-century realism—art as invoking the real from its position of total detachment from the real—Sontag's early postmodern advice for critics and appreciators of art actually describes the relationship between art and the real in exactly the ways that I see realism working in literature in the early twenty-first century.[23]

When *House of Leaves*, *ELIC*, and *The Book of Portraiture* mix fonts, page and ink colors, and textual layouts in ways that require us to read them through their physical details, they assert to us the significance of their real physical properties; further, when they, as well as highly footnoted texts like *Infinite Jest*, require us to turn back and forth through hundreds of pages in order to follow footnotes and story lines, to rotate the book in order to follow text set at varying angles in corners of pages (as in *House of Leaves*), or, as in the case of Danielewski's *Only Revolutions*, to flip constantly from one end of the book to the other, while rotating the book 180 degrees, in order to read the dual narratives that move from cover to cover toward their meeting in the book's center, these texts never let us forget that reading is an embodied interaction with another physical object in the world. Foer's latest work takes this physicality of art into the third dimension, not simply using textual tricks lying flatly on pages but carving the book out of the pages themselves, excising words selectively to convert his favorite childhood novel, Bruno Schulz's *The Street of Crocodiles*, into his own "novel," *Tree of Codes* (2010). Its collection of diecut pages—somewhat reminiscent of Oscar's looking "through the story of the turtles" to his quizzical fourth-grade classmates in *ELIC*—is a kind of textual sculpture, its "meaning" and artfulness coming at least as much, if not more so, from its status as a sculptural object than from its linguistic content.[24] In this way, I see these novels at the "end" of the postmodern period asking, even requiring us to read them exactly as Sontag urged us to read art at the period's beginning. Drawing attention to their formal aspects, these novels come to us as works of art to be reckoned with through all of the ways in which they are physically present in the world.

Another way that novels are enacting a new realism, attention to the real, is through innovations not just in their physical forms but also, and perhaps more conventionally meaningfully, in their innovations in narrative form—uses of language to evoke the real—in a new kind of literary realism that arises out of poststructural notions of language, knowledge, and matter. On the other side of postmodernism, Latour, like Sontag, also framed his call for a shift away from postmodernism's hopeless enmirement in unknowability in terms of a return to realism, but a different kind of realism than Sontag's. Rather than urging us to consider art as a thing, Latour advised us to reconsider how we represent thingness in art, and in critique: "The critical mind, if it is to renew itself and be relevant again, is to be found in the cultivation of a *stubbornly realist attitude* . . . but a realism dealing with what I will call *matters of concern*, not *matters of fact*."[25] Central to this shift for him is our recognition that the world, and reality, is not made up of concrete, finally knowable, universal truths, that "facts" instead are gross reductions via politics and polemics of "matters of concern." Once the powerful innovation of the Enlightenment, in the wake of their debunking via the (perhaps equally powerful) poststructuralist period, "matters of fact" have become not only impotent to launch critique, but also, more damningly, unable to describe the world to us: facts have become unreal.

Closely related to Latour's definition of the fact as untrue and unreal is his definition of the thing as inherently multiple and unbounded: "A thing is, in one sense, an object out there and, in another sense, an *issue* very much *in* there, at any rate, a *gathering*."[26] For Latour, things are gatherings of objects and of attitudes, interpretations, and intentions of and for the objects that result in heterogeneous things, whose known, decided reductions are their insufficient objects: "All objects are born things, all matters of fact require, in order to exist, a bewildering variety of matters of concern." The object is what we master and simplify in order inadequately to grasp the thing. Critique, then, must move "not *away* but *toward* the gathering, the Thing."[27] One way of making this move is to move toward and through a realism that is not a return to pre-poststructuralism realism, itself in part a mechanism for converting the spread of things into meticulously rendered objects, but that seeks to preserve the thingness of things—their multiplicity and indeterminacy, their comprising, but not being reducible to, intention, interpretation, and attitude:

> It is not the case that there would exist solid matters of fact and that the next step would be for us to decide whether they will be used to explain something. It is not the case either that the other solution is to attack, criticize, expose, historicize those matters of fact, to show that they are made up, interpreted, flexible. It is not the case that we should rather flee out of them into the mind or add to them symbolic or cultural dimensions; the question is that matters of fact are a poor *proxy* of experience and of experimentation and, I would add, a confusing bundle of polemics, of epistemology, of modernist politics that can in no way claim to represent what is requested by a realist attitude.[28]

Realism today requires attention to a contemporary reality and perception of reality that are multiplicitous, changing, always already read, and populated by similarly understood things (Things).

Left for art and literature is the task of translating critique's Thing-based realist attitude into a literary realism that preserves this notion of thingness as a gathering, an "assembling." As Latour seeks critique that can be "associated with *more*, not with *less*, with *multiplication*, not *subtraction*,"[29] so must literature craft a realism that represents the gathering of thingness, the endless multiplicity of reality, rather than paring it down to the contained objecthood drawn by the variations of narrative authority, singular perspective, and moral order of traditional realism. And as we have seen from Bill Brown's theorizing of the thing, and from the struggle to invoke thingness via language in the novels examined in Chapter 4, in which every thing in literature and critique is a thing read and represented, this new realism in literature must recognize the dependence of the Thing on representation, in that, in literature, every thing is itself an act of representation, of representing matters of fact—or of matters of fact representing the Thing. Either way, thingness in literature illustrates how considered things cannot exist outside of systems of signification, and that any realism that recognizes this must be made of, and, more importantly, *know* it is made of, systems of representation. One way to preserve the Thing in realism is through a self-conscious realism, a metafictive realism: poststructuralism turned toward the ends of realism.

David Foster Wallace sought to transform American fiction away from postmodern language games and into a method for generating meaningful critique and empathy in exactly this way, with increasing success over the course of his fiction. In Chapter 2 I argued that Wallace's masterwork *Infinite Jest*—in process at the time of his interview with Larry McCaffery and published just three years after it—does not fully enact the agenda for fiction he set forth there, primarily because its world is so steeped in irony and, worse, an uncombatted infantile narcissism and solipsism, that its characters cannot manage the kind of empathy that Wallace wants for them and for us. His fiction before *Infinite Jest* seems to fall even further from this mark, amounting to, in his words, a "trap" in which he caught himself "trying to expose the illusions of metafiction the same way metafiction had tried to expose the illusions of the pseudo-unmediated realist fiction that had come before it."[30] Here he is describing the "horror show" of "Westward the Course of Empire Takes Its Way," the hundred-plus page novella that anchors *Girl with Curious Hair* (1989) with a patricidal critique of Barth's "Funhouse" that does not manage to escape from its own labyrinthine critique into meaningful fiction. Also collected in *Girl* is "Little Expressionless Animals," his best example of what he calls, in "E Unibus Pluram," "image fiction." Referred to as "post-postmodernism" by some critics and "hyperrealism" by others, image fiction is for Wallace "a natural adaptation of the hoary techniques of literary realism to a nineties world whose defining boundaries have been deformed by electric signal." Such fiction represents one step away from traditional realism, in that it addresses *themes* of hyperreality and post-postmodernism, using "transient received myths of pop culture as a *world* in which to imagine fictions about 'real,' albeit pop-mediated, public characters."[31]

His work in *Infinite Jest* and after, however, moves increasingly away from traditional realism in structure and theory, toward a recuperation of the things he criticized early metafiction for destroying. I read his work as a whole as providing one of the strongest and earliest models we have of how poststructural fiction in general, and metafiction specifically, can allow the reader the pleasures and meaningful products of realist fiction.[32] Indeed, part of Wallace's legacy to American letters must be that he became one of the first postmodern American fiction writers consistently to reestablish language as a mechanism for communicating affect and meaning—not by ignoring the poststructuralist turn either in his novels' concepts of language or in their own linguistic structures, but through the mechanisms of mediation and irony that have long seemed to substitute language tricks for meaningfulness. In reassessing Wallace's work as turning old postmodern tricks to new ends, we can begin, as Hoberek suggested, to think about where literature today is going, and how we have come, thankfully for most of us, to a literary landscape that looks and feels considerably different than the postmodern tradition Wallace inherited.

But Wallace was not the first to reach for affect and meaning through poststructuralism. Rather, one of the goals of this book is to posit a way of reading postmodern literature that registers how postmodern writers have been experimenting with methods of using poststructural narrative techniques to fashion a new kind of realism throughout the period, in fact, in generations of attempts that have spawned and fed and fruitfully reacted to each other. One of the most prominent and influential examples of such synergy between writers in search of poststructural methods of realism is that of John Barth and Wallace.[33] And the work of both of these authors reminds us that at the center of the crises of language, authority, belief, and communication that characterize postmodernism lies the fate of the family in fiction and culture.

John Barth's "Lost in the Funhouse" (1968) offers an excellent example of a, or perhaps the, formative metafictional text of the early postmodern period that knows from the start that a threat to the family and to interpersonal bonds that create families lay at the heart of its explosion of realistic narrative structures. It also provides an early illustration of how metafiction works on the reader to create empathy.[34] The title story contains two competing narratives: one is a traditional *bildungs roman* in which an adolescent boy, Ambrose, discovers that the true purpose of the funhouse is to allow space for the sexual play whose aesthetic attractions he can't fathom in his innocent hurry to skip to the part where he becomes the loving parent he himself lacks. The other presents the voice of the author writing the story and exposing along the way not only his narrative methods but also his consuming anxiety about his ability successfully to use those methods in constructing the story of Ambrose. One facile reading of this story views the metafictive voice as prohibiting the progress of the affect-oriented *bildungs roman*, and, in conjunction with ancillary pieces of the text, reducing the collection's figures of mothers and fathers to writing machines or, worse, superfluousness.[35]

But we also see in the title story how the anxieties of this mediating authorial voice overlap those of the character Ambrose, the former doubting his abilities and identity as an author in the same pages in which the latter suffers his adolescent crisis of identity while confronting his fragmented, infinitely multiplied reflection in the hall of funhouse mirrors. In this way the funhouse comes to represent the author's struggle as much as it also more blatantly stands for the boy's *bildungs roman* and the reader's frustrated wandering through the labyrinthine story built by the integration of one into the other. Each amplifying the other's existentialist anxiety, when narrator and character overlap in the "he" that contains them both on the last page, our empathy with their anxieties, and our identification with them, grows, and the reader appreciates how narrative and metanarrative work together to create identification and empathy between the characters, rather than opposing each other, as they seem to in the beginning of the story. But even more intense empathy comes from this *opposition* of narrative and metanarrative: set next to the clearly fictive story of Ambrose, the author's self-conscious ruminations feel immediate and real. We feel we are not empathizing with an unreal literary character—which is fun, and satisfying, in the way that Western art first satisfied via cathartic transference—but that we are empathizing with an author, even (when we read sloppily) with a real person, John Barth. In this way, the "reality effects" of traditional realism, the ability of fiction to make the real seem present, pales in comparison to those of such blatant metanarrative, which can create realist spaces that harbor a text's real-est things.

It is this irresistible urge to identify authorial voice with real author in "Lost in the Funhouse" that speaks to the self-reflexive story's humanity and to its humanistic interests. For this use of authorial construction to invoke real author appeals to us quite earnestly—despite the story's clever killing off of mother and father in various ways in its preface and appendix, despite its mockery of Ambrose's earnest vision of himself as a father—by creating an authorial voice that floats just a hair above the page. And it is this gesture that Wallace repeats and intensifies in his "Octet," while also intensifying the appeal to empathy by changing his themes from the family estrangement or mockery of *Lost in the Funhouse* to questions of family and interpersonal devotion in "Octet."

The central piece in Wallace's 1999 short-story collection *Brief Interviews with Hideous Men*, itself a complex system of unfinished framing devices requiring readerly intervention to make sense,[36] "Octet" immediately demands interaction between reader and text by requesting the reader's responses to the text and even participation in constructing it. The "story" comprises a series of pop quizzes on moral and ethical dilemmas involving friend and family relationships, all ending in questions requiring the reader's judgment, but does not clarify the terms in which the reader must make such judgments (one long quiz ends with the vague demand, "Evaluate"), or ask the questions the reader is prepared to answer (after a scenario involving two "terminal" drug addicts: "Which one lived?"). Thus the reader must not only answer but also interpret each quiz. As in *Jest*, the story's footnoted footnotes also require the reader's concerted engagement, both reminding the reader of the text's constructedness, and literally moving her across the page and between pages, from main text to subtext, as Danielewski does during the action scenes of *House of Leaves*. The footnotes' "excised" quizzes likewise allow the text to sprawl beyond our traditional sense of the text proper, as if to place the reader in intimate cahoots with a writer whose editor has held him insufficiently apart from his audience.

Further bringing the reader into relationship with the writer, Wallace deploys the second-person point of view to impose a direct shoe-swapping of reader and writer: "You are, unfortunately, a fiction writer," pop quiz 9 begins,[37] then proceeds to obliterate realism's fourth wall by telling us with "queer *urgency*" (146) about the need for "100% candor" (148) in "interrogating the reader" (151) "sincere[ly]" and "naked[ly]" (154) that plagues said fiction writer—which is to say, us, the readers. By the end of the piece, Wallace has collapsed even these distinctions, making the "you" ultimately "more like a reader, in other words, down here quivering in the mud of the trench with the rest of us, instead of a *Writer*, whom we imagine to be clean and dry and radiant of command presence as he coordinates the whole campaign from back at some gleaming abstract Olympian HQ" (160). He articulates the power-defined reader-writer binary only to collapse it as reader becomes a writer who is herself asked to make the imaginative empathetic identification back with the reader in whose position she began. Doing so allows him to accomplish the goals he set for himself in the 1993 interview: it is the literary equivalent of that unthinkable act that Wallace imagines in the story for his reader/writer, "addressing the reader directly and asking her straight out whether she's feeling anything like what you feel" (154). Only, he never does ask her outright. Instead he mediates the question by placing it in the mouth of a character-writer who addresses the reader supremely indirectly, in that he has already asked the reader to imagine herself as the writer.

Wallace also creates empathy between reader and writer structurally, in a manner similar to Barth's: "Octet"'s metafictive narrative strategies intensify the fictitiousness of its stories, throwing into relief an authorial voice that feels intensely real in comparison. In this way, Wallace revises realism, creating the feeling of reality not by allowing the reader to absorb herself into another world through the illusion of verisimilitude, but by creating a world so obviously false, constructed, *written*, that the voice responsible for writing that world, the man behind the curtain, seems to be sitting next to us here, in our world—seems to have been "set . . . softly down beside you" us. Baudrillard famously said of Disneyland that

> Disneyland is there to conceal the fact that it is . . . all of "real" America, which *is* Disneyland. Disneyland is presented as imaginary in order to make us believe that the rest is real, when in fact all of Los Angeles and the America surrounding it are no longer real, but of the order of the hyperreal and of simulation.[38]

Wallace converts this idea of the simulacra, which felt so threatening to human connection and even our notions of humanity in the 1980s and 1990s and in novels of that era, like *White Noise,* into a method for sculpting through fiction a powerful human presence whose insistent engagement with the reader makes her feel, in her own life, less alone.[39] His invocation of real presence via intensification of linguistic absence—conjuring a new realism by emphasizing the constructs of fiction—is also a way of ironizing irony, to turn it back toward earnestness: Evidence from my teaching indicates that these attempts at mediating immediacy, at creating empathy between reader and writer, do work, on readers far beyond the language-obsessed ones who study and write criticism on metafiction. Students at all levels love Wallace much of the time, and if they do not they feel passionate dislike or intense frustration with him, and I think the prevalence of book-throwing alone that goes on when my students read Wallace attests to the fact that he really moves them, and moves them to move him right back.

That Wallace, like Barth, Ashbery, Danielewski, and Foer (as I will discuss below), invokes such a strong sense of a real, present author via the multiplying, antirealist devices of poststructuralism marks another seeming reversal of poststructuralism from within poststructuralism itself. For these authors enact not the "death of the author," as Roland Barthes and Michel Foucault diagnosed near the beginning of the poststructural period, but rather a concerted invocation of the author, and, in the cases of "Octet," *House of Leaves, ELIC, Everything Is Illuminated*, and *The Book of Portraiture*, the massive proliferation of authors, in the interest of not only representing the real but also implying the reader's responsibility and participation in that representation, and in relationship to the newly present author.[40] That is, whereas for Barthes, antirealism meant that "the birth of the reader must be at the cost of the death of the Author"[41] and for Foucault "the author is . . . the ideological figure by which one marks the manner in which we fear the proliferation of meaning,"[42] for these poststructuralist novelists, the author is precisely the thing whose presence must be invoked in order also to imply the reader, the reader's sense of the real, and the empathetic relationship between reader and writer that allows the still proliferative poststructural narrative to be in the service of things that matter.[43] Wallace states his own opinion about the "question" of the "death of the author" quite clearly in his 1997 essay, well-titled, "Greatly Exaggerated": "For those of us civilians who know in our gut that writing is an act of communication between one human being and another, the whole question seems sort of arcane."[44]

Wallace's formal and structural methods for creating author, reader, empathy, and meaning in relation to each other are becoming characteristic of metafiction in the twenty-first century, fiction that invokes empathy and authorial presence specifically by invoking a sense of the real. His methods, and other poststructural narrative devices that have grown alongside and out of them, rely on a strategy that is very much akin to what Latour recommended for reattaching meaning and the real to critique: *multiplying* and making visible, rather than streamlining and hiding, the mechanisms of fiction at work in creating that sense of reality. These strategies for fiction shatter traditional realism's binary axis of thing/sign, real world/ representation, freeing the representation from the mimetic economy that relegates it to the shadow of the real. Instead, metafictive realism creates a world of multiple planes and perspectives, in which it is impossible to locate an origin or original in relation to which the representation can be deemed unreal, or a center against which it can be measured as outlying. So this explosive decentering of the structures of mimetic fiction does not destroy or obfuscate the real, to make the sign primary over it or even its substitute (as Baudrillard argued during late twentieth-century postmodernism), but rather it makes a space in which the real might be or seem present within representation—in order to make the representation itself invoke, make present, the real.

Writing readers writing worlds: *Everything Is Illuminated*

By intensifying the invocation of the real earlier enacted by Barth, in order to conjure not only the author's presence but also his empathy and earnest desire to connect with his reader, Wallace's 1999 "Octet" serves as a model for the multiple directions and further lengths to which writers of the twenty-first century have begun to take the increasingly productive tool of metafiction. We can see these writers, like Wallace, employing poststructuralist narrative techniques and specifically metafiction to represent the real in at least three distinct ways. One, explored above, involves constructing multiple planes of reality such that one of them emerges as "most real," communicating the uncanny sense that a "real" character, narrative, or world exists at the heart of the more obviously written ones surrounding it; often this "real-est" plane also contains the text's author, who suddenly feels very present to the reader, in a striking reversal of the "death of the author" that defined early poststructural ideas about reading and writing. Another, similarly multiplying technique mixes and/or blurs several points of view in order to prevent any sense of a central, originating perspective or being that authors or controls the fiction. A third emphasizes the role of the reader—whether a fictional reader contained in the narrative or the actual one holding the book, sometimes both—in constructing the novel, making the actual reader register his or her own centrality in and continuity with the fictional world, a different way of immersing the reader in the world of the novel. When Wallace constructs empathy between writer and reader via mediation, he makes all of the work required by both writer and reader present, visible, and inevitably part of the reading process. Such work, required by the text in order for it to be "read" at all, makes the demanding author feel palpably present to the reader, and suggests the power of reading to affect the real world. Ultimately, this assertion of the power of reading and writing, long missing from much postmodern fiction, marks perhaps the most radical break from twentieth-century postmodern fiction, and the most important way in which twenty-first-century poststructural fiction begins to achieve humanist goals for fiction neglected by irreverent postmodern and über-aesthetic modernist fiction alike.

Like Foster, Latour, and Sontag, Bill Brown contemplates new ideas about representation and the real as he reconsiders our notions of things. As he does so in "Thing Theory," he also gestures toward the first type of new realism identified above. Paraphrasing an early postmodern theorist, Cornelius Castoriadis, Brown writes, "Representation does not provide 'impoverished "images" of things'; rather, 'certain segments' of representation 'take on the weight of an "index of reality" and become "stabilized," as well they might, without this stabilization ever being assured once and for all, as "perceptions of things"'."[45] As I have discussed in Chapter 4, Brown is trying to get at something here other than notions of realism per se, but the fact that his exploration of the relationship between things and how we represent them leads to the notion of an "index of reality" points to the way in which representation is, of course, always not anathema to but necessary to the production of the real in literature. Brian McHale makes a similar observation about the ability, or even insistence, of representation-obsessed postmodern literature to create spaces for the real when he posits the idea of "paraworlds," or alternate realities, as a dominant trend in science fiction literature.[46] In light of this abiding attention to the real by so many theorists of poststructural methods of representation, the adroitness of twenty-first-century literature that is so explicitly interested not just in representation but in multiple layers of representation to create such reality effects begins to make sense.

Jonathan Safran Foer's *Everything Is Illuminated* employs all three of these metafictive methods of poststructural realism. First, it follows the "paraworld" pattern of constructing a novel around another novel whose fictionality in the context of the fiction creates a space, even the seeming requirement, of a corresponding nonfictionality. An intensification of John Barth's technique in "Lost in the Funhouse," this strategy essentially makes manifest Barthes's and Culler's concept of "reality effects,"[47] and Hal Foster's theory of "the return of the real" in art via traumatic realism—art becoming so wholly representation, surface, and sign that its very insistence on the impossibility of making the real present points to the absence of the real and therefore to the existence of the real. Foer signals a "real" presence by building it around a super-unreal narrative in *Everything*—much as he does in his later *ELIC*—not only, like Barth, by inserting himself into the text as author of the novel within the text, but also by exaggerating that embedded novel's fictionality in several ways. Most obviously, the embedded novel announces itself as a novel through liberal use of magical realism: Trachimbrod is a world in which baby Brod, her crib filled with name-bearing paper slips, refuses to choose her own parent by remaining statue-still for two days; the light generated by all the sex acts inspired by Trachimbrod Day can be seen from space; and, in the moment before the bombing that will obliterate Trachimbrod, "the [bronzed Kolker-turned-sundial] tiptoed across the cobblestones like a chess piece and hid himself under the breasts of the prostrate mermaid" (271). And that is not to mention the sawblade, much less the generative hole. Further, the embedded novel points structurally to its own fictionality, even metafictionality, when its narrative inexplicably transforms for several pages into a play (173–6).

The Trachimbrod novel also exaggerates its fictionality by perseverating thematically on the untruthfulness, even apocryphalness, of all acts of writing. Foer opens the embedded novel, and begins the history of the shtetl, with a wholly indeterminate statement: "It was March 18, 1791, when Trachim B's double-axle wagon either did or did not pin him against the bottom of the Brod River" (8). Then, as the novel tells the story of the shtetl, it accumulates fictionalized histories, such as that of Yankel, who composed letters to himself from Brod's "mother"—a woman he never knew and in fact, given that Brod seems to have been birthed from the Brod River (in a symbolic act of tautological self-generation), never even existed; then he reads them to his adopted daughter to instill in her a sense of her own, totally untrue, history. Even Yankel is not only Yankel but was once Safran, having, after a shameful trial that ruined his good name, "changed his name to Yankel, the name of the bureaucrat who ran away with his wife" (47). These are only a few examples of the many fictions of not only the histories drawn by this embedded novel, but also of the sources of those fictional histories.

Truth, and its ability to be rendered through language, remains at issue in Alex's "real" account of the journey that inspired the novel, too. Immediately and repeatedly we encounter the frametale as a product of translation—first through the hysterically spotty English of its Ukrainian narrator, and once again through distortions introduced via Alex's letters about that frametale, and about the embedded novel, addressed to the fictional author Foer. Alex admits to changing, inventing, or omitting aspects of the journey,[48] whether to aid his grandfather's understanding (62), make the somewhat hapless and anxiety-prone Jonathan look better in print (142), or cover up his grandfather's tragic and shameful past (153). And even these distortions sometimes receive further distortion from the linguistic frameworks housing them: when reporting what his grandfather said to the sole survivor of the shtetl, Alex writes, "'You should have died with the others,' he said. (I will never allow that to remain in the story.)" (153). But remain it does. At the same time, Alex also alludes to changes in his text he has reluctantly made at Jonathan's insistence—changes we never see, implying yet another authorial intervention that has gone past or happened after Alex's own. But however much it continues the novel's theme of the questionability of all acts of writing, Alex's account of the journey asserts its status as the "real" portion of the novel throughout, and Alex as the "real" character reaching real insight and growth through reading fiction. Further, in all of these levels of remediation, the question of what "really happened," both during the destruction of Trachimbrod and during Alex and Jonathan's meaningfully shared experience of researching that destruction, becomes paramount, as it becomes totally unknowable: the multiply framing fictionalities insist on the presence of a real and a truth, in the process of exposing the impossibility of both.

In creating these multiple planes of reality, and raising the issue of authorship in each of them, Foer also employs a second technique of invoking the real via multiplicitous poststructuralism: creating varying uses of point of view, such that one of them or one outside all of them emerges as most "real." For not only do we read Alex's journey account and letters to Jonathan from the first-person point of view, but we also find, if we pay close attention, the same first-person point of view in the embedded *novel*. Most disorienting is the relative scarcity of signals of this perspective: in nearly a hundred pages of embedded novel, a first-person pronoun appears only three times,[49] each coming as a shock to the reader who (especially given the rampant magical realism) otherwise feels she is reading an omniscient third-person narrator. Who is this "I"? It is fictional Foer, of course, inserting himself into his novel just as actual Foer is inserting himself into the larger book. The reality-invoking implications of this double (or really triple, once we count the grandfather's letter to Jonathan) first-person perspective multiply further when we consider that *all* of these first-person narrators lie outside the novel when taken as a whole: who authors the novel, *Everything Is Illuminated*? Which of these three figures—all of whom strike us as "real" in comparison to the fictionality of the sawblade-headed Kolker and the dead-armed Safran—assembled the pieces in the order that comprises the book we hold in our hands? Not the grandfather, who is dead by suicide at the end of the book. Probably not Alex, whose many requests to omit damning information about his family go unheeded. Perhaps Jonathan, who, after all, would have had access to all of the materials contained in it—though, as he appears via first person only in the novel within the novel, never within the "real" frametale that contains it, he feels by far the least present narrator in the book. Nothing suggests his authorial intervention beyond the embedded novel at its heart. But the fact of the triple narrators (Alex, Jonathan, and the grandfather, in his final letter) and triple narratives (Alex's account of the journey in search of Trachimbrod, his letters to Jonathan, and Jonathan's novel about Trachimbrod) raises unavoidably the question, whose hand and eye bring all of these fragments together? Who is the novel's creative force? Thus this tripled authorial perspective becomes another way of making the real present: conjuring a real author—setting him softly down beside you—on whose existence apart from the fictional ones the novel depends.

Other novels that employ this multiply narrated, planed, and pieced structure, like *ELIC* and *House of Leaves*, invoke the real author in a similar way, raising the question of what ordering force constructed the textual container that holds all the pieces.

And *Everything* and *House* share another innovative structural feature that invokes a real author: as Danielewski places a simple check in the bottom right corner of a page to create an Escher-like hypertextuality among his multiple narrators, Foer creates wormholes throughout his novel that connect his narratives through time while implying that each in some way writes the other. In 1803, Brod sees through a telescope Jonathan's 1943 photo of his grandfather with Augustine (87–9); in 1969, Jonathan's mother and grandmother witness, in footage of the first moon walk, the glow seen from space of lovers on Trachimbrod Day (95); during the journey to find Augustine, Alex reads in Jonathan's diary a paragraph his grandfather will write months later in his last letter to Jonathan (160). And the words that end the book—"*I will*" and "*I will*" (276)—written by the grandfather in his 1998 letter to Jonathan, open the Trachimbrod novel written by Jonathan long before ("*I will . . . I will . . .*" 8). Such suggestions of narratives writing each other imply either that the book has no other author beyond the book's own narratives, or that it *must* have another, separate author to assemble the narrative pieces. Danielewski cheekily foregrounds this authorial ambivalence and multiplicity when he leaves his own name off the title page of *House of Leaves*, crediting the novel instead to the character Zampanò, and relegating himself to an outlying facing page. Here we find another clear reality effect of such poststructural narrative techniques: not the death of the author but the massive proliferation of authors in a way that also serves to make present the real author of the proliferation.

Other recent novels accomplish a similar invocation of the real author through less pervasive, more subtle multiplication of point of view and narrative. In *The Road*, for example, it is often hard to tell whether the narrative proceeds from the point of view of an unnamed third-person narrator, who seems to dictate much of the story, or from the first-person point of view of the father. McCarthy's trademark minimalist style, relying on the kinds of vaguenesses in nouns and pronouns that Hemingway used to such evocative advantage, and the resulting flat, evasive tone, work brilliantly here to elide even the owner of the story at any particular point. The approach heightens the allegorical feel of the book: this is every person's tale, or could be; and the tale signifies something deep and powerfully true, though one must plumb beyond its simple surfaces to read it. It also renders the father palpably present in the odd moments in which he bursts forth in first person:

> He lay listening to the water drip in the woods. Bedrock, this. The cold and the silence. The ashes of the late world carried on the bleak and temporal winds to and fro in the void. Carried forth and scattered and carried forth again. Everything uncoupled from its shoring. Unsupported in the ashen air. Sustained by a breath, trembling and brief. If only my heart were stone.[50]

Such few and startling uses of insightful first person, coming unmarked and unremarked upon in a sea of flat, objective narration, combine with the similarly few and startling uses of second-person reader address[51] to make the unnamed father feel much more present and real to us than any sustained, traditionally realistic first-person or omniscient third-person narrator might.

Don DeLillo achieves a similar reality effect via the infrequent self-reflexivity of his narrator in *The Names* (as discussed in Chapter 1); in fact DeLillo, whose novels appear to be much more structurally conventional than do these wildly poststructural works by Foer, Danielewski, and Tomasula, often uses slippage and shifting of point of view to construct fiction that is anything but traditionally realistic. For example, in *Underworld*, he mixes entire sections written in first person with others narrated via third person; in *Ratner's Star*, he sometimes allows perspective to float without warning from character to character, stream-of-consciousness style, alongside sudden fixed first-person accounts by Billy and others that remain unowned; most daringly, and piercingly, he ends the book with a long narration that seems to come from the point of view of an alien being unsubject to the falsifying effects of perspective itself. In doing so, DeLillo draws attention to the author required both to imagine such diversity of perspective and to sew them together into a meaningful whole. Even Homes accomplishes something similar with her much more subtle invocation of the second person in *Music for Torching*, creating strange metamoments that signal another dimension seeming to contain an author.[52]

As we see in "Lost in the Funhouse" and "Octet," one important effect of this proliferation of authors via self-reflexivity and shifting point of view is the text's ability to project the power of reading and writing, and of the empathetic relationships between readers and writers negotiating those challenging metafictional devices, to affect the real world. Similarly, Foer generates many of the reality effects of *Everything* by implying ways in which acts of reading, writing, and speaking make "real" things happen outside of the "fiction" in the novel. Late in the novel, Alex stops translating the tragedies of Trachimbrod reported by the survivor of the massacre, as if the absence of that report in the story will keep the truth behind it absent as well (186). Later he begs Jonathan to stop reading his account of the massacre, as if not-reading the truth of his grandfather's betrayal of his best friend Hershel is the same as not-knowing the truth (which is impossible, as Foer already knows it), or even the same as that truth's not-existing at all (224). In a world where fictional spaces carve out, in relief, the existence of real ones—the present acts of signification pointing to and therefore manifesting the absent real—it is precisely acts of signification, and of reading them, that create both fictional and real worlds. Foer demonstrates this connection between reading, writing, and the real most powerfully by constructing the novel such that acts of reading determine the complex form of the entire text: we encounter pieces of fictional Foer's novel at the same pace at which Alex reads them, each piece followed by his reaction to it communicated in a letter to Foer. These letters reveal Alex's clear growth as a character, out of a false, selfish bravado born from innocence and insecurity, and into the resolve to act and change his life that can only come from self-knowledge acquired via knowledge of the world's tragedies. By shaping the novel according to the pace of Alex reading Jonathan, and by integrating Alex's growth as a character into his reader's accounts of Jonathan's novel, Foer implies that it is Alex's acts of reading that create and shape his acts of writing (his account of the journey), his growth into self-awareness, and the structure of the novel, *Everything Is Illuminated*.

Indeed, the *only* meaningful growth in the novel comes from Alex, and it comes, tellingly, directly out of his reactions to, and rejection of, the beliefs and principles espoused by the book (the embedded novel) he is reading. Ultimately, Alex, and the novel *Everything Is Illuminated*, grows in empathy and understanding of himself and others by rejecting cynical twentieth-century postmodern ideas about language and the real, represented by the world of the embedded novel. Likewise, both Alex and *Everything* move increasingly toward an understanding of poststructural notions of language and knowledge, and of belief, that does not see them as being mutually exclusive from each other. While the embedded novel is a kind of example, perhaps even spoof, of a poststructuralist representation of atrocity that can neither redeem its characters nor make up for their suffering, Alex—who is both reader and writer in this book—attains the redemptive goals of humanist fiction, specifically by reading and writing. And what he learns in doing so charts a reversal of tired postmodern assumptions about how things signify, how words mean.

We know that fictional Foer, the novel's embedded novelist, does not share Alex's humanist understanding of the tragedy they have uncovered via their journey to find Augustine, or his *bildungs-roman* growth, because of the novel he writes after that journey. That embedded novel tells us how Jonathan processes the trio's ultimate inability to find Augustine, and the gruesome discovery about Alex's grandfather that they find in her stead. Rather than prompting an act of redemptive writing, the absent signifier of Augustine leads Foer to write a novel that ultimately privileges absence, depicting it as ubiquitous, formative, and insurmountable.[53] Jonathan's morbidly fanciful history of Trachimbrod asserts these views in its depictions of things, language, and love: Brod emerges as a poster girl for pessimistic poststructuralist ideas about signification, and the absolute schism between the pleasure and meaning of the sign, and the dull, irrelevant thing:

> Brod's life was a slow realization that the world was not for her, and that for whatever reason, she would never be happy and honest at the same time. She felt as if she were brimming, always producing and hoarding more love inside her. But there was no release. Table, ivory, elephant charm, rainbow, onion, hairdo, mollusk, Shabbos, violence, cuticle, melodrama, ditch, honey, doily. . . . None of it moved her. She addressed her world honestly, searching for something deserving of the volumes of love she knew she had within her, but to each she would have to say, *I don't love you.* Bark-brown fence post: *I don't love you.* . . . Physics, the idea of you, the laws of you: *I don't love you.* Nothing felt like anything more than what it actually was. Everything was just a thing, mired completely in its thingness. (79–80, original italics)

Yearning for that thing beyond the thing which is surplus, the surplus that is, according to structuralist ideas about the sign like those of Lévi-Strauss, the catalyst for acts of signification themselves—the surplus that *is* signification[54]—Brod's inability to love the thing itself is a model of the deconstructive dilemma that has plagued fiction for half a century. The world of the embedded novel holds tight to its inescapable dilemma:

"[Brod and Yankel] reciprocated the great and saving lie—that our love of things is greater than our love for our love of things" (83). And they pass down that privileging of the farther-flung steps on the signifying chain to a future generation that will turn this love of love into a love of the simulacrum:

> The Double House revealed every aspect of its owners' new affluence. . . . But Menachem was most proud of the scaffolding: the symbol that things were always changing, always getting a little better. He loved the skeleton of makeshift beams and rafters more and more as construction progressed, loved them more than the house itself, and eventually persuaded the reluctant architect to draw them into the final plans. Workers, too, were drawn into the plans. Not workers, exactly, but local actors paid to look like workers. . . . (The blueprints themselves were drawn into the blueprints, and in those blueprints were blueprints with blueprints with blueprints . . .) (162)

The "Double House" is a thing that symbolizes a symbol, thereby eclipsing itself. It is also, in the tradition of *House of Leaves* and *Music for Torching*, a house that cannot *be* a home but only *signifies* the house as the site of the crisis of signification. This elevation of the sign surfaces as well in the next generation—a "real" generation in the context of the whole novel, contemporaneous with the writing of the embedded novel—as the bitter lesson expressed by Alex's grandfather in the aftermath of not finding Augustine: "'We were stupid,' he said, 'because we believed in things'" and "there are not things to believe in" (245).

For Brod, yearning for the magical sign makes her "a genius of sadness. . . . She was a prism through which sadness could be divided into its infinite spectrum" (78), unable to love another real, excessively thing-y being: "So she had to satisfy herself with the *idea* of love—loving the loving of things whose existence she didn't care at all about." It also isolates her from the rest of the world, in that she lives "in a world once-removed from the one in which everyone else seemed to exist" (80). Brod's loving "love itself," and living in a "once-removed" world, is thus akin to the dark postmodern model of narcissistic representation found in early DeLillo, in Jack's fear of fear itself (*White Noise*), and Singh's terrifying proclamation that "the world has become self-referring" (*The Names*). Brod transmits this once-removed love through the generations along with her contempt for things, as we see in Lista's explanation for her love of dead-armed Safran several generations later:

> It was not the death that had so attracted her to it, but the unknowability. The unattainability. He could never completely love her, not with all of himself. He could never be completely owned, and he could never own completely. Her desire had been sparked by the frustration of her desire. (237)

Prefiguring the narcissism born of the twentieth-century industrial media machine and its accompanying consumer culture, Lista's desire for endless desire recapitulates the death drive that Lash identifies as the result of a postmodern "longing to be free from longing" (241). Brod, Yankel, Safran, and all the women who "love" him exemplify the twisted and sad consequences of loving the gap, and despising the thing.

One other consequence of this privileging of the gap, the signifier, and the symbol—as we have seen in novels operating from this antihumanist concept of language—is the disastrous inability of language, thoroughly cut off from the real world, to be meaningful. As in *ELIC*, Foer signals the direness of the problem of language by connecting it to the problem of communicating love, implying a causality between the impotence and unreality of them both. *Everything* makes this connection when Safran, descendant of Brod, realizes the emptiness of being loved out of women's desire for desire and not for him: "Women had said *I love you* without his ever speaking. *The more you love someone*, he came to think, *the harder it is to tell them*. It surprised him that strangers didn't stop each other on the street to say *I love you*" (234, original italics). Whereas *ELIC* recognizes this problem in language and then solves it with language—"How can you say I love you to someone you love?" asks Oscar's grandmother, before signing her letter to him, "I love you" (314)—the novel within *Everything* does not: "*I don't love you*," he and his beloved say to each other, before he marries another (234).

Indeed, *Everything*'s embedded novel delights in examples of futile, even ridiculous attempts to understand and preserve through language the intimacies and histories of the people and shtetl of Trachimbrod. *The Book of Recurrent Dreams* attempts to understand citizens' waking lives through narcissistic examinations of their dreams, instead only exposing their endless loops of self-reflection (36–41). The novel's other text-within-a-text-within-a-text, *The Book of Antecedents*, comprises attempts to understand the future by "reconciling with the past," by recording every quotidian happening of the citizens, and updating the book "continually," so that "when there was nothing to report, the full-time committee would report its reporting, just to keep the book moving, expanding, becoming more like life: *We are writing . . . We are writing . . . We are writing . . .*" (196). Such attempts to preserve the real through meaningless acts of signification culminate in two pages covered with only that repeated self-aware declaration of the act of language (212–13). As the desire to preserve Trachimbrod against the Nazi attack that is sure to come in 1942 peaks, citizens' attempts to record Trachimbrod in language reach a fever pitch, until "Memory begat memory begat memory" (258), the entire shtetl eddying in the recursivity of endless representation.

The story of the shtetl, and of its author's ancestors, ends with an account of the Jewish inhabitants of Trachimbrod drowning themselves in the river Brod to escape the death delivered by Nazi bombs, or being shot in the head by Nazis cleaning up after the bombs, or being burned alive in their synagogue along with their sacred books. The novel's final record of these deaths comes by way of a page of *The Book of Recurrent Dreams* as it flutters to rest, and, one assumes, to later burn, on "a child's burnt face" (272). In this dreamed account of the massacre, the final words fictional Foer provides, periodlessly, for the history of his family are these: "this is what we've done we've killed our own babies to save them" (273). Appearing in the description of a dream, recorded on a burning page, and delivered, impossibly, through the voice of the Brod river, this "historical" account not only ends in unimaginable horror, but it adds insult to injury by recording the horror through multiple layers of mediation so unreal, tenuous, and transient that the report of the horror serves only to underscore its absolute inability to transmit or record anything truthful or lasting about the horror. In providing such a bleak and unresolving ending to a novel that struggles with such weighty topics as truth, belief, community, family, and, most essentially, how to be human in a world in which such horrors can happen, fictional Foer delivers on the promise of futility offered by antihumanist models of language that see it as incapable of providing meaningful record, much less heartening redemption, for the sufferings of the real world.

The novel *Everything Is Illuminated*, however, does not end at that point. Instead, it closes with a letter written by Alex's grandfather, addressed to Jonathan, and translated for him by Alex. The letter describes the triumphant stand Alex has taken against his oppressive father, sending him away for good and thereby freeing himself and, more importantly for him, his little brother Iggy from their father's physical and psychological abuse, creating for them both a space in which to mature uncontorted. We know that Alex will fulfill the promise allowed him by this act of bravery because of the sentiments he expresses in his final letter to Jonathan, which marks the last chronological moment in the story of the novel as a whole. In it, Alex articulates his stern rejection of the cynical worldview expressed by the novel Jonathan has written, in terms of both its attitude toward love, and its investment in the "once-removed" and self-referring, rather than in present things and people:

> *You are a coward, Jonathan, and you have disappointed me. I would never command you to write a story that is as it occurred in the actual, but I would command you to make your story faithful. You are a coward for the same explanation that Brod is a coward, and Yankel is a coward, and Safran is a coward—all of your relatives are cowards! You are all cowards because you live in a world that is "once-removed," if I may excerpt you. I do not have any homage for anyone in your family, with exceptions of your grandmother, because you are all in the proximity of love, and all disavow love.* (240, original italics)

When Alex distinguishes here between two kinds of truth—things as they "occurred in the actual" and what is "faithful"—he draws a distinction that is very similar to Latour's concepts of "matters of fact" versus "matters of concern." Alex knows, and often acknowledges in his letters to Jonathan, that stories cannot, and perhaps should not, slavishly recount "facts" as they happened ("*We are being very nomadic with the truth, yes?*" he writes to Jonathan when he has read about half of Jonathan's novel. But he continues, "*if we are to be such nomads with the truth, why do we not make the story more premium than life? It seems to me that we are making the story even inferior,*" 179, original italics). But still he feels increasingly strongly that stories can and should remain true to their matters of concern, which is to say that stories should do more than represent irredeemable suffering; they should imagine and represent growth out of that suffering as surely as they must represent the suffering itself. And what happens *after* the suffering—the growth out of it—is meaningful.

Alex describes what he has learned about love, truth, and making active choices to pursue and protect both, especially in relation to one's family,[55] in terms of what he has *read* about Brod, Safran, and Augustine; we watch Alex approach these lessons at the pace of his reading Jonathan's novel. These framings in terms of reading allow the novel *Everything* to argue that acts of reading have powerful, positive effects on people in their real worlds—while physically shaping acts of writing. It is an argument for the productiveness of language, and that acts of representation can and do capture and affect real things, quite unlike what Jonathan "attempt[ed] to perform" with his irredeemably tragic novel. Rather than representing language as mediating the real to the point of invisibility, as does the multiply mediated account of the shtetl's end, Alex represents language as flawed yet productive, able to communicate and create empathy between people even in the absence of perfect understanding. Alex relates this positive view of language early in the novel, with his characteristic blend of humor and pathos. In the middle of their grim journey, he and his grandfather watch one of the two potatoes belonging to the hungry vegetarian Jonathan fall onto the dirty floor of a decidedly un-veg-friendly Ukrainian restaurant:

> "Welcome to Ukraine," Grandfather said to him, and punched me on the back, which was a thing I relished very much. Then Grandfather started laughing. "Welcome to Ukraine," I translated. Then I started laughing. Then the hero started laughing. We laughed with much violence for a long time. . . . I witnessed that each of us was manufacturing tears at his eyes. It was not until very much in the posterior that I understanded that each of us was laughing for a different reason, for our own reason, and that not one of those reasons had a thing to do with the potato. (67)

"Very much in the posterior" of that moment, after finishing the journey but, more importantly, after reading Foer's novel about the failed journey, Alex understands that even if the fallen potato means something different to them all, what matters is the shared feeling it generates, and the resulting bond that does mean something similar to all of them.

Matters of concern and the matter of choice

By novel's end we find that Alex has also communicated his belief in the productiveness of language by becoming a reader and writer who makes a difference in the real world using language, experiencing through both the kind of empathy that leads to affect and in turn causes real change. In one of his late letters to Jonathan, Alex writes, "*Do you know that I am the Gypsy girl and you are Safran, and that I am Kolker and you are Brod, and that I am your grandmother and you are Grandfather, and that I am Alex and you are you, and that I am you and you are me?*" (214, original italics). Given his later admission that if his father knew "*who I desire to love, he would kill me, and this is no idiom*," we can read this expression of identification, and its comparison of Alex and Jonathan to pairs of lovers in the embedded novel, also as an expression of romantic love, and an expression of "guileless" empathy that knows no equal in the novel's novel: "*This is about choosing. Can you understand? Please attempt to. You are the only person who has understood even a whisper of me, and I will tell you that I am the only person who has understood even a whisper of you*" (218). It is acts of real empathy such as these, experienced between Alex and Jonathan by way of and because of acts of reading and writing, that teach Alex another lesson that is core to this book: "*you will write very many more books than I will*," he tells Jonathan, "*but it is me, not you, who was born to be the writer*" (145). Thus *Everything Is Illuminated* defines a "writer" not as simply one who puts clever words on a page, but as one who uses language out of and to enact empathy between human beings, which can lead to positive growth out of the sufferings that are inevitable in the world.

A "writer," in this case, and in the case of all the empathy-building metafiction examined in this book, is also one who writes with a visible awareness of his writing, an awareness of his reader, and a goal of enabling both to meet through the text. To enable this meeting, the text must be visible as text; the reader must encounter its structures and strictures, must slog through its devices and at times rearrange its chaotic pieces into sensible shapes, earning her both a sense of intimacy with the text and author and a sense of having participated in the making of the text. Thus these metafictive devices of multiple narrators and narratives, self-conscious and hypertextual structures, shifting point of view, nonchronological narrative, footnotes and other formal oddities, and collapsing of boundaries between writer and reader (and text) are not curious anomalies to mainstream fiction but rather are fundamental to how twenty-first-century fiction achieves humanist goals for literature, and demonstrates what we have long been missing, the continued power of acts of reading and writing, and the ability of literature to mean and act in the world.

But as late postmodern fiction has shown, always self-reflexivity carries the risk that it might slip into navel-gazing, that self-referentiality might die into tautology. Fundamental to all metafiction is the both/and problem/potential of multiplicity that can explode into meaningless indeterminacy as easily as it can gather Things into meaningful matters of concern. Implicit in some of the novels examined here, as in the three views of language as identified by James in *The Names*, and explicit in others, such as Foer's, is the idea that where metafiction goes and what it does—antihumanist nihilism or humanist quest for meaning—results from the choices we make not only in how we write it but also in how we read it. Alex lobbies overtly for reading and writing the latter. Standing up to his father at last, Alex learns not only to grow out of suffering, but also that the only way to do that is by *paying attention* to the things and concerns of his real world, and by learning through discipline to *choose* to put his attention onto the good:

> We all choose <u>for</u> things, and we also all choose <u>against</u>, but like Safran, and like you, I discover myself choosing this time and the next time against what I am certain is good and correct, and against what I am certain is worthy. I choose that I will not, instead of that I will. (241, original emphases)

The novel is a journey from Alex's early choosing of "I will not" to the choice of "*I will*" that opens the embedded novel dubiously but ends the novel as a whole with great power and efficacy: *Everything* enacts this positive choice for its hero and for fiction itself. In offering the stale pessimism of the embedded novel's views and uses of language, and a "real" character who chooses *against* the old saw represented by Brod's unlove of the Kolker and *for* a retro investment in love, belief, and commitment to family—all discovered and articulated through language—*Everything* enacts the both/ and multiplicity of poststructural ideas about language and truth, and points to the fact that such multiplicity forces us to choose. It also suggests, somewhat radically still, that we are free to choose *for* rather than *against* those things we value and have missed, like language as an avenue to meaning and connection. When Alex takes his impassioned stand for choosing "that I will," Foer the real novelist seems to echo Wallace's critique of postmodern fiction and goal for changing it in his 1993 interview. Alex "understands" what fictional Foer is trying to do—depict the challenges of love and of, at times, acting humanely, and of language in capturing that troubled love and inhumanity. But he rejects Jonathan's project as an effective one, as Wallace rejects the solipsistic project of late postmodern fiction. Instead, Alex asserts clearly what he believes—"*I do not believe in Augustine*" and "*I told my father exactly what I thought, as I will now tell you, for the first time, exactly what I think*" (241, 242)—and offers Jonathan in his sign-off, for the first time, his "Love."

In this way, *Everything Is Illuminated* reveals another essential piece of the problem of language, and the key to translating language into its own solution, not much recognized by literary criticism or theory. Poststructuralism, so insistent on the illogic of singular truths, of equating words and things or signs and precise meanings, has been for decades a hypocritical opportunity to insist stubbornly on a singular reading of poststructuralism. In this grand narrative, we critics and theorists and readers have often equated it with antihumanism, unrepresentability, and meaninglessness. The writers and theorists examined in this book expose the contradiction inherent in that insistence, and point instead to the fact that the multiplicity of narratives, narrators, authors, worlds, meanings, and readings necessarily generated in literature by poststructural literary techniques and ideas about language create unavoidably multiplicitous ways of understanding the principles that inform those texts, and how those principles affect our readings of them. A great, arguably the greatest, innovation of modernism, intensified to the point of defining the period and culture of postmodernism, has been the shift to subjectivity as a dominating framework for understanding the world and how we understand the world. One way to react to such a radical shift in worldview has been fear: that no guarantee of shared perspective means nothing shared or meaningful can exist, and that multiple possibilities for truth and belief kill the categories altogether, leaving us alone in our solipsistic simulacra of them. It has taken us decades to see that reaction as one possibility among many, to acknowledge that we can choose how we read and react to poststructural ideas about language and all the things that language constructs and conveys. It is this multiplicity of ways of reading and using poststructuralism itself, and the importance of choosing to read language as once again meaningful, that I see these writers of late postmodernism struggling to convey, and writers of the early twenty-first century depicting with increasing passion and conviction.

Modeling for his readers this choice of empathy through fiction, specifically metafiction, was the life's project of David Foster Wallace. At the end of his life, even when he was suffering in a way imaginable perhaps only to his similarly plagued characters in *Infinite Jest*, Wallace was writing, for years, an enormous project, *The Pale King*, from the perspectives of characters doing the most boring work he could conceive: IRS auditing. Enacting empathy with a way of being in the world wholly outside his own experience,[56] the novel aims to bring the reader into that space of stillness and void of stimulus in which one must decide where to place one's attention, in which one must *make choices*, as he forces us to do in "Octet," about how to use one's intellect and feelings—for the self, and for the self via the other. This core idea of extending the self out to the other, as the most crucial (but often difficult) thing that one can do in one's life, provided the foundation of a speech Wallace gave to the graduating class at Kenyon College in 2005.[57] At the thematic heart of the speech is the fish joke that Wallace first deployed in *Infinite Jest*, but to a slightly different end. There, Wallace used the image of invisible immersion to suggest the twin addictions of drugs and cultural irony, both fueled by our constitutive and culturally fed narcissism, as well as our frustrated attempts to recognize and resist those harmful addictions. In his speech to the graduates at Kenyon College, however, Wallace revised the joke, allowing it to signify positively by associating water with everything around us that we miss when we get stuck in that narcissism. His advice that day to the graduates, all poised and about to spring like his adolescent boy on the diving board in "Forever Overhead,"[58] was the same lesson he seems to hope he and we can learn from empathizing with the painful struggle of a mind yoked to the most numbing work Wallace could imagine: "*choose* what you pay attention to and . . . *choose* how you construct meaning from experience." The engagement with fiction as fiction demanded by humanist-minded metafiction—not a pleasing escape from the demands of people and language in the real world, but a coming to terms with both—was for him the only way "to keep from going through your comfortable, prosperous, respectable adult life dead, unconscious, a slave to your head and to your natural default setting of being uniquely, completely, imperially alone, day in and day out."[59] Metafiction as practiced by Wallace and writers like him is exactly not the disaffected language games that some have tended to accuse it of being, or that twentieth-century postmodernism popularized. It is language's best solution to the problem of language, and a model for being present, to the self and the other, in an endlessly constructed world.

Notes

1   Pynchon constructs a tautology that encompasses an entire novel: disclosing nothing concerning the mystery of the Tri/ystero, *The Crying of Lot 49* instead leaves us with Oedipa to "await" the thing we've been waiting for all along, "the crying of lot 49" (152).

2   This reading of "Paradoxes and Oxymorons" as invoking both the text's ability to create empathy and its inescapable solipsism echoes that of another famously metafictional Ashbery poem, "Self-Portrait in a Convex Mirror," around which Wallace based the first piece of his 1989 *Girl with Curious Hair* (New York: W. W. Norton and Company, 1989), a short-story collection that explores the same textual

conundrum. For a brief account of Wallace's use of Ashbery in "Little Expressionless Animals," see Boswell's *Understanding David Foster Wallace* (Columbia, SC: University of South Carolina Press, 2003), 3–4.

3   I do not mean to suggest that metafictive film is an invention of recent years. Indeed, one can easily read *Synecdoche, NY* (2008) as a more consistently postmodern (though less provocative) revision of Fellini's 1963 *8 ½*, for example. What might be new is the prevalence of metafictive and self-reflexive strategies in both popular film and television, as in television series like *The Simpsons*, *Lost*, *The Office*, and *Arrested Development*, and mainstream films like *The Last Action Hero* (1993), *Fight Club* (1999), and even crossing into the normally schlocky horror genre in *Funny Games* (1997). Also, we might say that the intensity of such metafictive strategies of remediation has intensified, and/or that we as a mass audience are more accepting of and interested in stories that tell the metastory of their making than we have been in the past. *Adaptation* (2002), for instance, a self-conscious, metafictive film about the adaptation of the nonfiction book *The Orchid Thief*, took its metaturn as writer Charlie Kaufman struggled to write a straightforward film version of the book. One imagines that his resulting metafictive film pleases its postmodern audience much more than any rote translation of the book would have, by asking the question of what rote translation of one genre to another even means. Today, we as a mass audience are educated and curious about problems of genre, form, translation, and representation.

4   Wallace made a similar claim during his March 1996 interview with David Lipsky (see *Although*, 291) and in 1993: "[E]very two or three generations the world gets vastly different, and the context in which you have to learn how to be a human being, or to have good relationships . . . become [*sic*] vastly different. And the structures with which you can communicate those dilemmas or have characters struggle with them seem to become appropriate and then inappropriate again and so on" (see Burn, *Conversations*, 18).

5   Hal Foster, *The Return of the Real* (Cambridge: MIT Press, 1996), 138, 131.

6   These images include *White Burning Car III* and *Ambulance Disaster*, both from 1963, and both using "*galling*" repetitions of crashed automobiles to both obscure the real tragedy of the event and make it, via image, "pop" (Foster, 134). Such visual art by Warhol is fundamental to understanding the mutual disgust and glee of J. G. Ballard's early, machine-meets-body work in *The Atrocity Exhibition* (San Francisco: Re/Search, 1990 [1970]) and *Crash* (New York: Farrar, Straus, and Giroux, 1973).

7   Foster, *The Return of the Real*, 132 (original italics).

8   Ibid., 166.

9   Ibid.

10 Other examples of such meaningful focus in the wake of trauma abound in this novel. In the novel's fourth and most formally scattered section, the text gathers itself structurally while formerly fragmented characters gather themselves mentally and geographically in the wake of one character's trauma-induced suicide. And the book's final "In a Beginning" contrasts Mary's cradling of the inhuman makings of a human—the DNA at her hip—with the very real loss of a daughter as token in a political grievance, so that not just we but also the narrative remains conscious of the loss of the human.

11 Adding a layer of "paraworlding" (see discussion of McHale, below) to this novel is the fact that it was born out of its author's own (inconclusive) journey in search of his grandfather's past.

12 In this way—and I am only gesturing generally to a complex topic that deserves and will likely soon receive concerted critical attention—Foer's novels, grounded in World War II and the Holocaust as they are, offer one productive way out of the eddying language traps of de Manian trauma theory from the 1990s, as developed by Cathy Caruth in *Unclaimed Experience: Trauma, Narrative and History* (Baltimore: Johns Hopkins University Press, 1996) and *Trauma: Explorations in Memory* (Baltimore: Johns Hopkins University Press, 1995).

13 Jonathan Safran Foer, *Everything Is Illuminated* (New York: Mariner, 2002), 135. Subsequent references will be noted parenthetically. This hole in which Brod and the Kolker live prefigures the "Something" and "Nothing" places of Oskar's grandmother and grandfather in *ELIC*, taking on the same sinisterness and cynicism once we read *Everything* in its entirety, as I do below, as a critique of Brod's choice to live via the hole.

14 As my student Jennifer Gutman pointed out, Foer repeats this image of presence (loop/bronzed Kolker) signifying and being made possible by absence (hole/dissolved body) when Oskar looks at his classmates through the story of the turtles in *ELIC*: by cutting out the letters, as the atomic bomb obliterated all dark matter, Oskar draws our attention not simply to the light matter that remains but to its ability to keep present the shapes of the missing dark matter.

15 Bill Buford, "Dirty Realism," *Granta* 8 (1983): 4.

16 She does so, however, with an eye toward the metafictive interrogation of *how* narrative accomplishes its realist tricks that I see as characteristic of poststructuralist realism. See my "A Lamb in Wolf's Clothing," in *Critique* 53 no. 3 (2012): 214–37.

17 Neil Brooks and Josh Toth, eds, *The Mourning After: Attending the Wake of Postmodernism* (New York: Rodopi, 2007), 4.

18 See Robert McLaughlin, "Post-Postmodern Discontent: Contemporary Fiction and the Social World," *Symploke* 12 no. 1–2 (2004): 53–68; Kristiaan Versluys, "Introduction," *Neo-Realism in Contemporary Fiction* (Amsterdam: Rodopi, 1992), 7–12; and Winifried Fluck, "Surface and Depth: Postmodernism and Neo-Realist Fiction," *Neo-Realism in Contemporary Fiction*, ed. Kristiaan Versluys (Amsterdam: Rodopi, 1992).

19 Dirty realism and neorealism share this belief in the "failure" of metafiction: Rebein asserts that everything useful that could be done using self-reflexive narrative had been done by the 1980s, a claim I will dispute in this chapter.

20 Toth, *The Passing of Postmodernism*, 137.

21 Ibid., 119 (original italics). Further complicating matters is the fact that Clayton Crockett, in an essay contained in *The Mourning After*, seems to be describing "neorealism" as something that needs to be *resisted*, and offering, via Deleuze and Zizek, theoretical methods for doing so.

22 Sontag, "Against Interpretation," 4, 3, 14.

23 Interestingly, even ideology-defending Michaels relates his defense of content-driven reading in terms of the text's ability to conjure the real, but in such a way as to divorce that ability from meaning-making: "It's when the mark becomes meaningless that it becomes most 'real'" (*The Shape of the Signifier*, 8).

24 Despite Foer's enormous success and devoted audience, there is little evidence to suggest that people have read this "novel." Its form, however, has generated attention. See Wagner, "Jonathan Safran Foer Talks *Tree of Codes* and Conceptual Art," *Vanity Fair*, November 10, 2010, accessed June 3, 2011, www.vanityfair.com/

online/daily/2010/11/jonathan-safran-foer-talks-tree-of-codes-and-paper-art and Heller, "Jonathan Safran Foer's Book as Art Object," *New York Times*, November 24, 2010, accessed June 3, 2011, http://artsbeat.blogs.nytimes.com/2010/11/24/ jonathan-safran-foers-book-as-art-object/. Michel Faber's review of the book does praise the novel for its "poignant" reworking of Schulz's original text, but even this review spends more time considering the book's form than a reading of it (*Guardian*, December 18, 2010, accessed June 3, 2011, www.guardian.co.uk/books/2010/dec/18/ tree-codes-safran-foer-review).

25 Latour, "Why Has Critique Run out of Steam?," 231 (original italics).

26 Ibid., 233 (original italics).

27 Ibid., 247, 246 (original italics).

28 Ibid., 245 (original italics).

29 Ibid., 246, 248 (original italics).

30 A. O. Scott, "The Panic of Influence," *The New York Review of Books* 47 no. 2 (2001): 39–43, accessed July 13, 2012, www.nybooks.com/articles/archives/2000/feb/10/ the-panic-of-influence.

31 Wallace, interviewed by McCaffery, "An Interview with David Foster Wallace," 172, 171 (original italics).

32 In "The Salon Interview" in 1996, Wallace declares, "I've always thought of myself as a realist" (Burn, *Conversations*, 60).

33 For a fuller exploration of the ways in which Barth's and Wallace's fiction influenced each other through a variety of texts—most notably Wallace's early "Westward the Course of Empire Takes Its Way" (1989)—see chapter 1 of Burn's *Jonathan Franzen at the End of Postmodernism* (New York: Continuum, 2008). Here I want to focus specifically on Wallace's expansion of Barth's early metafictive construction of empathy and reality effects.

34 Recent criticism has begun to read Barth's collection in just this way: see Marjorie Worthington's "Done with Mirrors: Restoring the Authority Lost in Barth's Funhouse," *Twentieth-Century Literature* 47 no. 1 (2001): 114–36.

35 See John Barth, "Seven Additional Author's Notes," in *Lost in the Funhouse* (New York: Anchor, 1988), 202.

36 For a reading of Wallace's deployment of metafictive narrative strategies in the interest of empathy in this collection as a whole, see my chapter on *Brief Interviews* in *A Companion to David Foster Wallace Studies*, ed. Marshall Boswell and Stephen J. Burn (New York: Palgrave MacMillan, 2013).

37 David Foster Wallace, *Brief Interviews* (New York: Little, Brown, and Company, 1999), 145. Subsequent references will be noted parenthetically.

38 Jean Baudrillard, *Simulations* (New York: Semiotext(e), 1983), 25.

39 Wallace expresses his desire to use metafiction in exactly this way in his interview with David Lipsky: "There's stuff that really good fiction can do that other forms of art can't do as well. And the big thing . . . seems to be, sort of leapin' over that wall of self, and portraying inner experience. And setting up . . . a kind of intimate conversation between two consciences" (*Although*, 289).

40 Adam Kelly reaches a similar conclusion about the new importance of reader and author in relation to each other when he argues that Wallace constructs with his fiction a "new sincerity," invested with intent but not with selfish motive, and requiring "a particular kind of listener" or reader in order to confirm the fiction's resulting sincerity. See "David Foster Wallace and the New Sincerity in American

Fiction," *Consider David Foster Wallace*, ed. David Hering (Los Angeles: Sideshow Media Group, 2011), 141. I find it curious, then, that he reads the "you" of "Octet"'s quiz 9 as the voice of the author addressing himself, rather than addressing the reader.

41 Roland Barthes, "The Death of the Author," *Image, Music, Text*, ed. and trans. Richard Howard (New York: Farrar, Straus, and Giroux, 1981).

42 Foucault, "What Is an Author?," *Textual Strategies: Perspectives in Post-Structural Criticism*, ed. Josué V. Harari (Ithaca: Cornell University Press, 1979 [1969]).

43 Though, as Kelly points out in "The New Sincerity" (145), and Zadie Smith implies in *Changing My Mind* (New York: Penguin, 2009), 287, my reading of "Octet" as an enactment of empathy and identification between writer and reader actually signals my "choice" (Kelly) to "have faith" (Smith) in the sincerity of that speaker. Were the narrative to demand that reading, it would abandon poststructuralism altogether for the easy comfort of traditional realism. As is a humanist view of language in *The Names*, sincerity and empathy in "Octet" must be in part constructed by the reader through her conscious choice of them in order to continue to function within the context of poststructuralism.

44 Wallace, *Supposedly*, 144. Foster also points to the "rebirth of the author" in his *The Return of the Real*, positing its "absentee authority" as what happens when "trauma discourse magically resolves two contradictory imperatives in culture today: deconstructive analyses and identity politics" (168). Perhaps it is a testament to how deeply involved in trauma discourse much of twenty-first-century fiction is—which is why Freudian/psychological/narcissism-based readings work so well with the texts examined here—that what Foster posits for trauma discourse seems to hold true for all of the metafictive texts discussed in this book.

45 Brown, "Thing Theory," 8; Brown paraphrases Castoriadis, *The Imaginary Institution of Society*, trans. Kathleen Blamey (Boston: MIT Press, 1998): 331, 332.

46 McHale, "When Did Postmodernism Begin?," 410.

47 See Roland Barthes's "The Reality Effect," *French Literary Theory Today*, ed. Tzvetan Todorov (London: Cambridge University Press, 1982) and Jonathan Culler's "Convention and Naturalization," *Structuralist Poetics: Structuralism, Linguistics, and the Study of Literature* (Ithaca: Cornell University Press, 1975).

48 In this way, Alex closely resembles the reading/writing narrator of *House of Leaves*, Johnny Truant.

49 "And the baby? My great-great-great-great-great grandmother?" (16); "I've imagined her many times" (76); "But he didn't know that then, and neither did they, just as none of them knew that I would one day write this" (93).

50 McCarthy, *The Road*, 11.

51 See Chapter 4.

52 Homes, *Music*, 312: "think of bag ladies, men living on steam grates, the Montgomery boy."

53 In reading the thing-symbol, presence-absence metaphor of the generative hole between Brod and the Kolker as evidence of a positive shift in our ability to find meaning around the gap, and in the wake of trauma, I am pointing out the embedded novel's subtle awareness of the multiple readings available for the absences and losses that make up our lives. Ultimately, the book argues that that multiplicity confers the necessity of making a choice in how we will read it, as I discuss at the end of this chapter; the embedded novel and the novel as a whole make different choices.

54 See Chapter 1, p. 25–6.

55 When Alex writes his grandfather narrating his best friend Herschel's murder, the account centers on the grandfather's understanding that family means everything. When he begins to narrate the unthinkable moment in which he points out Herschel as a Jew, thereby condemning him to death, he does so by differentiating him not as a Jew but as not-family (see 248–51). The embedded novel soon repeats this total devotion to family, specifically to one's offspring, when the Dial explains why Safran would marry Zosha while loving the Gypsy girl by telling him, "*you love the baby in Zosha's belly*" (263–4, original italics).

56 With the exception of the time he spent auditing advanced tax courses as research for writing his last novel. See Charles B. Harris, "David Foster Wallace: 'That Distinctive Singular Stamp of Himself,'" *Critique* 51 no. 2 (2010): 171.

57 Published posthumously as *This Is Water: Some Thoughts Delivered on a Significant Occasion, about Living and a Compassionate Life* (New York: Little, Brown, and Company, 2009).

58 In *Brief Interviews with Hideous Men*, 1999.

59 Wallace, *This Is Water*, 56, 60.

Metamodernism

There's a certain set of magical stuff that fiction can do for us.... One of them has to do with the sense of ... capturing what the world feels like to us, in the sort of way that I think that a reader can tell "Another sensibility like mine exists. Something else feels this way to someone else." So the reader feels less lonely. ...

The history of fiction represents this continuing struggle to allow fiction to continue to do that magical stuff. As the ... cognitive texture of our lives changes.... And as the different media by which our lives are represented change. And it's the avant-garde or experimental stuff that has the chance to move the stuff along. And that's what's precious about it.

David Foster Wallace[1]

One of my favorite book titles is Joan Didion's *We Tell Ourselves Stories in Order to Live*. This is the truest thing we can say about writing because that is what all stories do: they take strings of otherwise unrelated experience and order and shape them into storylines with beginning, middle, and end, with arc, with moral, with meaning. As the ancient Greeks did for the points of light in the night sky, stories gather the scattered events of real and imagined lives and make them into meaningful portraits. We tell ourselves stories all the time, every day, and we come to know and relate to others by listening to theirs: whatever trivial or untrivial thing someone is talking about in a moment, one can always ask, what story is she telling? Consider all of Beckett, or Tom Hanks's beloved "Wilson" in *Cast Away*, which really amount to the same thing: the struggle to escape monologue, through storytelling.[2] Say what you like about grand narratives, Lyotard. Undeniably, they simultaneously govern our lives and are what our lives produce.

The primary goal of this book has not been to declare the end of postmodernism, or necessarily to refute that claim, or even to postulate the nature of the movement that will dethrone postmodernism, as inevitably something must, or to name that movement. The pun in the book's title is intended to allow me to engage with these territories of inquiry without offering an eclipsable decisiveness that would only wrest attention from readers who know better than to put their faith in it: now is not the time to do hastily and with too little information what will surely be done with more evidence and staying power many years hence. Rather, its goal has been simply to characterize some crucial new formal and thematic developments in early twenty-first-century literature, namely empathy, presence, and connection via poststructural language; to consider how this literature compares to what has come before in postmodern literature; and to begin to chart a through-line between the centuries while understanding intervening changes. That is to say, it has aimed to offer one story about the relationship between humans and language and literature at the end of one century and as the next begins, knowing its usefulness lies in its being one among many.

The story I have proposed goes something like this: poststructural theories about language in the mid- to late twentieth century resulted in literary uses of and attitudes about language that often veered toward futility; from the 1990s forward, and especially in the early twenty-first century, writers and theorists have been rethinking these ideas about language and trying new ways of enlisting poststructural narrative techniques toward humanist ends of meaning-making, communication, and empathy in and between characters, readers, writers, and texts. Its logic is simple and rests on certain assumptions about the literary periods relevant to it: if (and all of this could be, is being, and ever will be debated in all sorts of ways) the essential change marked by postmodernism amounts to intense antifoundationalism, particularity, and subjectivity of truth and belief, then the literature we are seeing in the nascent twenty-first century is still fundamentally postmodern, rather than something wholly beyond postmodernism. If the essential change marked by poststructuralism amounts to the arbitrariness of language and resulting multiplicity of possibility of meaning, then this literature remains resolutely poststructural. If central, abiding goals of fiction, as we have understood them at least since the humanist shift of the Enlightenment, are to contemplate the nature of the human and the ways in which human beings know the world and connect with each other to live well and with empathy in the world, then this postmodern, poststructural fiction continues the humanist goals of literature in ways that earlier postmodern literature did not clearly or primarily do.

Given these assertions, which the book has aimed to make and prove, one more might be made, with far less pointed argument and more of a spirit of catalyzing wonder. If the essential change insisted upon by modernism out of traditional realism is one of discontinuity, subjectivity, and reflexivity, then we should also acknowledge that this newly humanist postmodernism also participates most concertedly in the continued project of modernism—as most current theorists acknowledge is true for postmodernism in general—but with a difference, or via new methodology: the intensification of poststructural narrative techniques developed in the postmodern period. In this way we can see literature of the twenty-first century as modernism achieved through the literary techniques of poststructuralism, self-consciousness of form, narrative voice, and textuality primary among them.

Perhaps one way of thinking about the striking continuity (though increasing intensity) in innovative technique among all of these phases of literature, in conjunction with the equally striking changes in mood—from lamenting modernism, to the early *jouissance* of postmodernism, to late postmodernism's disaffected irony, to twenty-first-century literature's return to belief and earnestness—is in seeing all of these phases as moods of literary modernism's contribution to the larger Enlightenment project that Habermas called "modernity."[3] In this view, which Habermas articulated in his 1980 essay "Modernity—an Incomplete Project," modernism participates in the newly rational, individual-centered project of repudiating tradition and inherited ways of being by breaking with literary tradition in the form of traditional realism, and using its innovations in form and technique to mourn "a lost sense of purpose, a lost coherence, a lost system of values." To Habermas, poststructuralism amounted to a "repudiation of this kind of Enlightenment 'modernity,'" an attack on "the ideals of reason, clarity, truth, and progress."[4] Seen in this framework, twenty-first-century literature, with its clear evocation of truth, belief, and knowledge, however much confined to the chaotic uncertainty of poststructuralism, and with its attitude of sincerity and care over irony and apathy, could represent a poststructural attainment of Enlightenment/modernist goals for fiction that earlier postmodernism could not approximate.

Essentially, such a narrative maintains that twenty-first-century literature be read as not separate from the project of modernity or of modernism, or from the project of postmodernism, but as a reorienting of postmodernism and its attending linguistic concepts of poststructuralism, turned toward the Enlightenment project of modernity. But it reorients itself in a way that is—because it is inherently and essentially poststructuralist in its assumptions about language, knowledge, and the world—always conscious of the *struggle*, and specifically the struggle *through language and representation*, necessary to access any version of truth. This narrative also asserts that without making transparent that struggle—the degree to which every act of reading, writing, even thinking and knowing is mediated and remediated, technologically or not—all that is disclosed is power, and the ability invisibly to express/wield it. In other words, without such transparency, what we express is bias, more than truth or knowledge, which instead lie in the struggle, in the indeterminacy, in the dialectic between presence and absence, word and thing, in the tension of the both/and that is postmodernism. Inflected with the twenty-first-century mood of possibility for connection within self-conscious acts of language, this truthful tension is also a kind of poststructural, metafictional version of modernism.[5] But it is modernism that is crucially self-aware, literature that is aware of being literature operating in a modernist vein, through postmodernist literary techniques turned toward modernist goals: metamodernism.

A point of light in a crowded sky, this reading of postmodern and twenty-first-century literature is offered in the hope that it will help all of us interested readers and critics begin to flesh out a fuller picture of what literature today is, what it means to us, and what it says about who we are as human beings that we have created it as such, in this moment of our long chronicling history. Surely gazers far in the future will look at the constellations we map today and see different animals altogether, given the same points of light, but the urgency, I think, is to remember to recognize each point as meaningful, and so worthy of inclusion in our plotting. For too long, many readers of late twentieth-century literature have not properly placed postmodern literature among those points, have not included it in our plots that connect literature of the Enlightenment spirit with literature today; in many ways the literature itself did not invite such reading. Literature today, however, once again asserts its status as meaningful points of light, and reminds us to look back at what came before and find its place in the stories and plottings we use to make sense of the world through language. Literature as constellation, sextant, chronicle, or key: we can connect its dots to say almost anything, but the point is in the connecting, and in registering the gravity generated between bodies that holds them and all of us together.

Notes

1   Wallace, interviewed by David Lipsky, *Although* (New York: Broadway Books, 2010), 39.
2   I am indebted to James Goodwin for what I still find the most meaningful insight I've encountered on Beckett. The *Cast Away* analogy is my own and I have always found it allows new students of Beckett to grasp the essence of his dark, heartfelt work immediately.Such a reading of Beckett opposes the usual reading of his work as a recapitulation of the drive toward silence undertaken by French symbolists like Mallarmé, which reading allows a reader like Josh Toth to use Beckett as an exemplar of a postmodern quest for paralysis, as he does in *The Passing of Postmodernism* (Albany: State University of New York Press, 2010), see especially page 180. But instead I would argue that Beckett exemplifies how postmodernism encapsulated *from the start* this simultaneous drive toward solipsism and silence, and struggle to escape both through connection and communication—as do the novels examined in this book.
3   Barry expresses wonderfully clearly in his *Beginning Theory* this larger view of modernity as essentially an Enlightenment project, and I think it does much to enable us to think productively about the normally vexing ways in which modernism, postmodernism, and any possible "post-postmodernism" can seem to be all shades of the same color. Therefore, I think his concept of modernism and postmodernism as separate "moods" of the project of modernity works well; to his two moods of modernism's nostalgia and postmodernism's *jouissance* I have added what I consider to be two more recent moods: late postmodernism's ironic apathy and twenty-first-century literature's sentimental gravity.
4   Barry, *Beginning Theory*, 86.
5   Boswell points out that Wallace described himself as being a "nervous member of some still-unnamed (and perhaps unnameable) third wave of modernism." See *Understanding David Foster Wallace* (Columbia, SC: University of South Carolina Press, 2003), 1.

Works Cited

8 ½. Film. Directed by Frederico Fellini. Rome: Cineriz, 1963.

Abrams, M. H. "How to Do Things with Texts." In *Doing Things with Texts: Essays in Criticism and Critical Theory*, edited by Michael Fisher. New York: W. W. Norton and Company, 1989.

Adam, Barbara and Stuart Allan, eds. *Theorizing Culture: An Interdisciplinary Critique after Postmodernism*. London: University College of London Press, 1995.

Adaptation. Film. Directed by Spike Jonze. Los Angeles: Columbia Tristar, 2002.

Albee, Edward. *A Delicate Balance*. New York: Penguin Books, 1997.

Alter, Robert. *The Pleasures of Reading in an Ideological Age*. New York: Simon and Schuster, 1989.

Altieri, Charles. *Act and Quality: A Theory of Literary Meaning and Humanistic Understanding*. Amherst: University of Massachusetts Press, 1981.

American Beauty. Film. Directed by Sam Mendes. Los Angeles: Dreamworks, 1999.

Amis, Martin. *London Fields*. New York: Vintage Books, 1991.

Appiah, Kwame Anthony. *Cosmopolitanism: Ethics in a World of Strangers*. New York: W. W. Norton and Company, 2006.

Ashbery, John. "Paradoxes and Oxymorons." In *Shadow Train*. New York: Penguin, 1981.

Atonement. Film. Directed by Joe Wright. London: Focus Features, 2007.

Auerbach, Erich. *Mimesis: The Representation of Reality in Western Literature*. Translated by Willard Trask. Princeton: Princeton University Press, 1953.

Bakhtin, M. M. *The Dialogic Imagination: Four Essays*. Edited by Michael Holquist. Translated by Caryl Emerson and Michael Holquist. Austin: University of Texas Press, 1981.

Ballard, J. G. *The Atrocity Exhibition*. San Francisco: Re/Search Publications, 1990.

— *Crash*. New York: Farrar, Straus, and Giroux, 1973.

Banville, John. *The Sea*. New York: Knopf, 2005.

Barry, Peter. *Beginning Theory: An Introduction to Literary and Cultural Theory*. New York: Manchester University Press, 1995.

Barth, John. *Lost in the Funhouse*. New York: Anchor, 1988.

Barthelme, Donald. "At the End of the Mechanical Age." In *Amatuers*. New York: E. P. Dutton, 1976.

Barthes, Roland. *Camera Lucida: Reflections on Photography*. Translated by Richard Howard. New York: Farrar, Straus, and Giroux, 1981.

— "The Death of the Author." In *Image, Music, Text*. Edited and translated by Stephen Heath. New York: Hill, 1977.

— "The Reality Effect." In *French Literary Theory Today*. Edited and translated by Tzvetan Todorov. London: Cambridge University Press, 1982. 11–17.

Bataille, Georges. *The Accursed Share*. Vol. 1. Translated by Robert Hurley. New York: Zone Books, 1991.

— *Visions of Excess: Selected Writings, 1927–1939*. Translated by Allan Stoekl. Minneapolis: University of Minnesota Press, 1985.

Battersby, James L. *Paradigms Regained: Pluralism and the Practice of Criticism*. Philadelphia: University of Pennsylvania Press, 1991.

Baudrillard, Jean. *Simulations*. Translated by Paul Foss, Paul Patton, and Philip Beitchman. New York: Semiotext(e), 1983.

— *The Spirit of Terrorism: And Requiem for the Twin Towers*. Translated by Chris Turner. New York: Verso, 2002.

Bauman, Zygmunt. *Intimations of Postmodernity*. New York: Routledge, 1992.

Beckett, Samuel. *Endgame*. New York: Faber, 1976.

Bell, Bernard Idding. *Postmodernism and Other Essays*. New York: Morehouse, 1926.

Berger, Peter and Hansfried Kellner. "Marriage and the Social Construction of Reality." *Diogenes* 12 no. 46 (1964): 1–24.

"Bio Art." Eduardo Kac. Accessed June 3, 2011. www.ekac.org/transgenicindex.html.

Blue Velvet. DVD. Directed by David Lynch. Wilmington, NC: MGM/United Artists, 1986.

Bonca, Cornel. "Don DeLillo's *White Noise*: The Natural Language of the Species." *College Literature* 23 no. 2 (1996): 25–44.

Bookchin, Murray. *Re-enchanting Humanity: A Defense of the Human Spirit Against Anit-humanism, Misanthropy, Mysticism, and Primitivism*. London: Cassell, 1995.

Boswell, Marshall. *Understanding David Foster Wallace*. Columbia, SC: University of South Carolina Press, 2003.

Bosworth, David. "The Fiction of Don DeLillo." *Boston Review* 8 no. 2 (1983): 29–30.

Bourne, Randolph. *Youth and Life*. Freeport, NY: Books for Libraries Press, 1967.

Bowen, Deborah. "Preserving Appearances: Photography and the Postmodern Realism of Anita Brookner." *Mosaic* 28 no. 2 (1995): 123–49.

Brooks, Neil, and Josh Toth, eds. *The Mourning After: Attending the Wake of Postmodernism*. New York: Rodopi, 2007.

Broude, Norma and Mary D. Garrard, eds. *Reclaiming Female Agency: Feminist Art History after Postmodernism*. Berkeley: University of California Press, 2005.

Brown, Bill. "Thing Theory." *Critical Inquiry* 28 (2001): 1–22.

Bryant, Paula. "Discussing the Untellable: Don DeLillo's *The Names*." *Critique: Studies in Modern Fiction* 29 no. 1 (1987): 16–29.

Budick, Ariella. "Beyond Appearances in Suburbia." *Los Angeles Times* July 10, 2002: F4.

Buford, Bill. "Dirty Realism: New Writing in America." *Granta* 8 (1983): 4–5.

Burn, Stephen. *David Foster Wallace's* Infinite Jest: *A Reader's Guide*. 2nd edn. New York: Continuum, 2012.

— *Jonathan Franzen at the End of Postmodernism*. New York: Continuum, 2008.

Burn, Stephen, ed. *Conversations with David Foster Wallace*. Jackson: University Press of Mississippi, 2012.

Camus, Albert. "The Fact of Absurdity." In *The Myth of Sisyphus and Other Essays*. Translated by Justin O'Brien. New York: Knopf, 1955.

Carmichael, Thomas. "Lee Harvey Oswald and the Postmodern Subject: History and Intertextuality in Don DeLillo's *Libra*, *The Names*, and *Mao II*." *Contemporary Literature* 34 no. 2 (1993): 204–18.

Carter, Cynthia. "Nuclear Family Fall-out: Postmodern Family Culture and the Media." In *Theorizing Culture: An Interdisciplinary Critique after Postmodernism*. Edited by Barbara Adam and Stuart Allen. New York: New York University Press, 1995. 186–200.

Caruth, Cathy. *Trauma: Explorations in Memory*. Baltimore: Johns Hopkins University Press, 1995.

— *Unclaimed Experience: Trauma, Narrative and History*. Baltimore: Johns Hopkins University Press, 1995.

Cast Away. Directed by Robert Zemeckis. Universal City, CA: Dreamworks, SKG, 2000.

Cavanaugh, Tim. "Ironic Engagement: The Hidden Agenda of the Anti-Ironists." *Reasononline*. 2001. Accessed July 25, 2003. http://reason.com/0112/co.tc.rant.shtml.

Cheal, David. *New Poverty: Families in Postmodern Society*. London: Greenwood Press, 1996.

Cohen, Samuel S. *After the End of History: American Fiction in the 1990s*. Iowa City: University of Iowa Press, 2009.

Connor, Steven. Introduction to *The Cambridge Companion to Postmodernism*. Edited by Steven Connor. Cambridge: Cambridge University Press, 2004.

Crockett, Clayton. "Postmodernism and the Crisis of Belief: Neo-Realism vs. the Real." In *The Mourning After: Attending the Wake of Postmodernism*. Edited by Neil Brooks and Josh Toth. New York: Rodopi, 2007.

Culler, Jonathan. "Convention and Naturalization." In *Structuralist Poetics: Structuralism, Linguistics, and the Study of Literature*. Ithaca: Cornell University Press, 1975. 131–60.

Danielewski, Mark. *House of Leaves*. New York: Pantheon Books, 2000.

— *Only Revolutions*. New York: Pantheon Books, 2006.

DeCurtis, Anthony. "'An Outsider in This Society': An Interview with Don DeLillo." In *Introducing Don DeLillo*. Edited by Frank Lentricchia. Durham: Duke University Press, 1991.

DeLillo, Don. *The Names*. New York: Vintage Books, 1989.

— *Players*. New York: Vintage Books, 1989.

— *Point Omega*. New York: Scribner, 2010.

— *Ratner's Star*. New York: Vintage, 1976.

— *Underworld*. New York: Scribner, 1997.

— *White Noise*. New York: Penguin Books, 1985.

Derrida, Jacques. *Of Grammatology*. Translated by Gayatri Chakravorty Spivak. Baltimore: Johns Hopkins University Press, 1976.

— "Structure, Sign, and Play in the Discourse of the Human Sciences." 1970. Translated by Richard Macksey and Eugenio Donato. In *The Critical Tradition: Classic Texts and Contemporary Trends*. Edited by David H. Richter. New York: St. Martin's Press, 1989. 959–71.

Díaz, Junot. *The Brief Wondrous Life of Oscar Wao*. New York: Riverhead Books, 2007.

Didion, Joan. *We Tell Ourselves Stories in Order to Live: Collected Nonfiction*. New York: Everyman's Library, 2006.

Domanska, Ewa. *Encounters: Philosophy of History after Postmodernism*. Charlottesville: University Press of Virginia, 1998.

Durkheim, Emile. *The Elementary Forms of Religious Life*. Translated by Karen E. Fields. New York: Free Press, 1995.

Eggers, Dave. *A Heartbreaking Work of Staggering Genius.* New York: Vintage Books, 2001.

Eliot, T. S. "The Metaphysical Poets." In *Selected Prose of T. S. Eliot*. Edited by Frank Kermode. New York: Farrar, Straus, and Giroux, 1975.

Ellis, Jay. "Another Sense of Ending." *Cormac McCarthy Journal* 6 (2008): 22–38.

Eraserhead. DVD. Directed by David Lynch. Los Angeles: Libra Films, 1976.

Eshelman, Raoul. *Performatism, or, the End of Postmodernism*. Aurora, CO: Davies Group Publisher, 2008.

"*Extremely Loud & Incredibly Close*." *Publishers Weekly*. January 31, 2005. Accessed July 12, 2012. http://publishersweekly.com/978–0-618–32970–0.

Faber, Michel. "*Extremely Loud & Incredibly Close*: Review." *The Guardian.* June 4, 2005. Accessed June 3, 2011. www.guardian.co.uk/books/2005/jun/04/featuresreviews. guardianreview22.

— "*Tree of Codes* by Jonathan Safran Foer—Review." *The Guardian*. December 18, 2010. Accessed June 3, 2011. www.guardian.co.uk/books/2010/dec/18/tree-codes-safran-foer-review.

Fight Club. DVD. Directed by David Fincher. Los Angeles: Fox 2000 Pictures, 1999.

Fluck, Winfried. "Surface and Depth: Postmodernism and Neo-Realist Fiction." In *Neo-Realism in Contemporary Fiction*, edited by Kristiaan Versluys. Amsterdam: Rodopi, 1992.

Foer, Jonathan Safran. *Everything Is Illuminated*. New York: Mariner, 2002.

— *Extremely Loud & Incredibly Close.* New York: Houghton Mifflin, 2005.

— *Tree of Codes*. London: Visual Editions, 2010.

Foster, Dennis A. "Alphabetic Pleasures: *The Names*." In *Introducing Don DeLillo*. Edited by Frank Lentricchia. Durham: Duke University Press, 1991. 157–73.

Foster, Hal. *The Return of the Real: The Avant-Garde at the End of the Century*. Cambridge: MIT Press, 1996.

Foucault, Michel. "What Is an Author?" In *Textual Strategies: Perspectives in Post-Structuralist Criticism.* Edited by Josué V. Harari. Ithaca, NY: Cornell University Press, 1979.

Freud, Sigmund. *Beyond the Pleasure Principle.* 1920. Translated and edited by James Strachey. New York: W. W. Norton and Company, 1961.

— "Mourning and Melancholia." In *The Standard Edition of the Complete Psychological Works of Sigmund Freud.* Edited and translated by James Strachey. Vol. 14. London: Hogarth Press, 1953.

— "On Narcissism." In *The Standard Edition of the Complete Psychological Works of Sigmund Freud.* Edited and translated by James Strachey. Vol. 14. London: Hogarth Press, 1953.

— *The Psychopathology of Everyday Life.* In *The Standard Edition of the Complete Psychological Works of Sigmund Freud.* Edited and translated by James Strachey. Vol. 6. London: Hogarth Press, 1953.

— "Remembering, Repeating, and Working Through." In *The Standard Edition of the Complete Psychological Works of Sigmund Freud.* Edited and translated by James Strachey. Vol. 12. London: Hogarth Press, 1953.

— *Studies in Hysteria.* In *The Standard Edition of the Complete Psychological Works of Sigmund Freud.* Edited and translated by James Strachey. Vol. 2. London: Hogarth Press, 1953.

Funny Games. DVD. Directed by Michael Haneke. New York: Halcyon Pictures, 2007.

Fussell, Paul. *The Great War and Modern Memory.* Oxford: Oxford University Press, 1975.

Gardner, Helen. *In Defence of the Imagination.* London: Oxford University Press, 1984.

Gass, William H. *Willie Masters' Lonesome Wife.* Normal, IL: Dalkey Archive Press, 1989.

Gates, Jr., Henry Louis. *The Signifying Monkey: A Theory of African-American Literary Criticism.* New York: Oxford University Press, 1989.

Giles, Paul. "Sentimental Posthumanism: David Foster Wallace." *Twentieth-Century Literature* 53 no. 3 (2007): 327–44.

Goffman, Erving. *The Presentation of Self in Everyday Life.* New York: Doubleday, 1959.

Gordon, Fran. "Suburban Inferno: The Divine Comedy of A. M. Homes." *Poets and Writers.* July–August 1999: 24–9.

Green, Jeremy. *Late Postmodernism: American Fiction at the Millennium.* Gordonsville, VA: Palgrave Macmillan, 2005.

Gribble, James. *Literary Education: A Re-evaluation.* London: Cambridge University Press, 1983.

Gumbrecht, Hans. *In 1926: Living at the Edge of Time.* Cambridge: Harvard University Press, 1997.

— *The Production of Presence: What Meaning Cannot Convey.* Stanford: Stanford University Press, 2004.

Haddon, Mark. *The Curious Incident of the Dog in the Night-Time.* New York: Vintage, 2003.

Hagedorn, Ann. *Savage Peace: Hope and Fear in America, 1919*. New York: Simon and Schuster, 2007.

Harris, Charles B. "David Foster Wallace: 'That Distinctive Singular Stamp of Himself.'" *Critique* 51 no. 2 (2010): 168–76.

Harris, Jonathan, ed. *Value, Art, Politics: Criticism, Meaning and Interpretation after Postmodernism*. Liverpool: Liverpool University Press, 2007.

Harrison, Thomas. *1910: The Emancipation of Dissonance*. Berkeley: University of California Press, 1996.

Hayles, N. Katherine. *How We Became Posthuman: Virtual Bodies in Cybernetics, Literature, and Informatics*. Chicago: University of Chicago Press, 1999.

— "The Illusion of Autonomy and the Fact of Recursivity: Virtual Ecologies, Entertainment, and *Infinite Jest*." *New Literary History* 30 no. 3 (1999): 675–97.

— "Saving the Subject: Remediation in *House of Leaves*." *American Literature* 74 no. 4 (2002): 779–806.

— *Writing Machines*. Cambridge: MIT Press, 2002.

Hegel, Martin. *Introduction to Aesthetics*. Translated by T. M. Knox. Oxford: Clarendon, 1979.

Heidegger, Martin. *Poetry, Language, Thought*. Translated by Albert Hofstadter. New York: HarperCollins, 2001.

Heller, Steven. "Jonathan Safran Foer's Book as Art Object." *New York Times*. November 24, 2010. Accessed June 3, 2011. http://artsbeat.blogs.nytimes.com/2010/11/24/jonathan-safran-foers-book-as-art-object.

Hoberek, Andrew. "Introduction: After Postmodernism." *Twentieth-Century Literature* 53 no. 3 (2007): 233–47.

Holland, Mary K. "A Lamb in Wolf's Clothing: Postmodern Realism in A. M. Homes's *Music for Torching* and *This Book Will Save Your Life*." *Critique: Studies in Contemporary Fiction* 53 no. 3 (2012): 214–37.

— "Mediated Immediacy: On *Brief Interviews with Hideous Men*." In *A Companion to David Foster Wallace Studies*. Edited by Marshall Boswell and Stephen J. Burn. New York: Palgrave Macmillan, 2013.

Homes, A. M. "Adults Alone." In *The Safety of Objects*. New York: William Morrow and Company, 1990.

— "A Conversation with Amy Adler and A. M. Homes." Hammer Museum. Los Angeles, California. July 24, 2002.

— *Music for Torching*. New York: HarperCollins, 1999.

— *This Book Will Save Your Life*. New York: Penguin Books, 2006.

Hutcheon, Linda. *A Poetics of Postmodernism: History, Theory, Fiction*. New York: Routledge, 1989.

Inchausti, Robert. *The Ignorant Perfection of Ordinary People*. New York: State University of New York Press, 1991.

Jacobs, Timothy. "American Touchstone: The Idea of Order in Gerard Manley Hopkins and David Foster Wallace." *Comparative Literature Studies* 38 no. 3 (2001): 25–31.

Jameson, Fredric. *Postmodernism, or, The Cultural Logic of Late Capitalism*. Durham: Duke University Press, 1999.

Joyce, James. "The Dead." *Dubliners*. New York: Penguin, 1991. 183–236.

Judd, Donald. "Specific Objects." *Complete Writings, 1959–1975*. New York: Press of the Nova Scotia College of Art and Design, 1975.

Kac, Eduardo. *Kac*. Accessed June 3, 2011. www. ekac.org.

Kakutani, Michiko. "The Age of Irony Isn't Over After All." *New York Times*, October 9, 2001: C9.

Katz, Jack. "Families and Funny Mirrors: A Study of Social Construction and Personal Embodiment of Humor." *American Journal of Sociology* 101 no. 5 (1996): 1194–238.

Kelly, Adam. "David Foster Wallace and the New Sincerity in American Fiction." In *Consider David Foster Wallace: Critical Essays*. Edited by David Hering. Los Angeles: Sideshow Media Group Press, 2011.

Kirby, Alan. *Digimodernism: How New Technologies Dismantle the Postmodern and Reconfigure Our Culture*. New York: Continuum, 2009.

Kundera, Milan. *The Unbearable Lightness of Being*. New York: Harper Perennial, 1984.

Lacan, Jacques. *Écrits, A Selection*. Translated by Alan Sheridan. New York: W. W. Norton and Company, 1977.

— *The Seminar of Jacques Lacan, Book XI: The Four Fundamental Concepts of Psychoanalysis*. Edited by Jacques-Alain Miller. Translated by Alan Sheridan. New York: W. W. Norton and Company, 1981.

— "The Unconscious and Repetition." In *The Seminar of Jacques Lacan, Book XI: The Four Fundamental Concepts of Psychoanalysis*. Edited by Jacques-Alain Miller. Translated by Alan Sheridan. New York: W. W. Norton and Company, 1981.

Lasch, Christopher. *The Culture of Narcissism: American Life in an Age of Diminishing Expectations*. New York: W. W. Norton and Company, 1979.

The Last Action Hero. DVD. Directed by John McTiernan. Los Angeles: Columbia Pictures, 1993.

Latour, Bruno. "Why Has Critique Run Out of Steam? From Matters of Fact to Matters of Concern." *Critical Inquiry* 30 (2004): 225–48.

LeClair, Thomas. "An Interview with Don DeLillo." *Contemporary Literature* 23 no. 1 (1982): 19–31.

— "The Prodigious Fiction of Richard Powers, William Vollmann, and David Foster Wallace." *Critique: Studies in Contemporary Fiction* 38 no. 1 (1996): 12–37.

Lévi-Strauss, Claude. *Introduction to the Work of Marcel Mauss*. Translated by Felicity Baker. London: Routledge and Kegan Paul, 1987.

Lipsky, David. *Although of Course You End Up Becoming Yourself: A Road Trip with David Foster Wallace*. New York: Broadway Books, 2010.

Lopez, Jose and Gary Potter, eds. *After Postmodernism: An Introduction to Critical Realism*. New York: Continuum, 2005.

Maltby, Paul. "The Romantic Metaphysics of Don DeLillo." *Contemporary Literature* 37
  no. 2 (1996): 258–77.
McCaffery, Larry. "An Interview with David Foster Wallace." *Review of Contemporary
  Fiction* 13 no. 2 (1993): 127–50.
McCaffery, Larry and Sinda Gregory. "Haunted House—An Interview with Mark Z.
  Danielewski." *Critique: Studies in Contemporary Fiction* 44 no. 2 (2003): 99–135.
McCarthy, Cormac. *No Country for Old Men*. New York: Vintage International,
  2005.
— *The Road*. New York: Vintage International, 2006.
McEwan, Ian. *Atonement*. New York: Doubleday, 2002.
McHale, Brian. "1966 Nervous Breakdown; or, When Did Postmodernism Begin?"
  Modern Language Quarterly 69 no. 3 (2008): 391–413.
— *Postmodernist Fiction*. New York: Methuen, 1987.
McLaughlin, Robert. "Post-Postmodern Discontent: Contemporary Fiction and the
  Social World." *Symploke* 12 no. 1–2 (2004): 53–68.
McPherson, Tara, ed. *Digital Youth, Innovation, and the Unexpected*. Cambridge, MA:
  MIT Press, 2008.
Memento. Film. Directed by Christopher Nolan. Altadena, CA: Newmarket Films. 2000.
Meynell, Hugo. *Postmodernism and the New Enlightenment*. Washington, DC: Catholic
  University Press, 1999.
Michaels, Walter Benn. *The Shape of the Signifier: 1967 to the End of History*. Princeton:
  Princeton University Press, 2004.
Mitchell, David. *Cloud Atlas*. New York: Random House, 2004.
Morris, David. "Lived Time and Absolute Knowing: Habit and Addiction from *Infinite
  Jest* to the *Phenomenology of Spirit*." *Clio* 30 no. 4 (2001): 375–415.
Morris, Matthew J. "Murdering Words: Language in Action in Don DeLillo's *The Names*."
  Contemporary Literature 30 no. 1 (1989): 113–27.
Nichols, Catherine. "Dialogizing Postmodern Carnival: David Foster Wallace's *Infinite
  Jest*." *Critique: Studies in Contemporary Fiction* 43 no. 1 (2001): 3–16.
"Nielsen Media Research." Accessed December 31, 2003. www.nielsenmedia.com.
Nietzsche, Friedrich. *The Birth of Tragedy*. Translated by Francis Golffing. New York:
  Doubleday, 1956.
North, Michael. *Reading 1922: A Return to the Scene of the Modern*. New York: Oxford
  University Press, 1999.
Olson, Kirby. *Comedy after Postmodernism: Rereading Comedy from Edward Lear to
  Charles Willeford*. Lubbock: Texas Tech University Press, 2001.
Orlean, Susan. *The Orchid Thief*. New York: Trafalgar Square, 2007.
Osteen, Mark. *American Magic and Dread: Don DeLillo's Dialogue with Culture*.
  Philadelphia: University of Pennsylvania Press, 2000.
Ott, Michael R., ed. *The Future of Religion: Toward a Reconciled Society*. Boston: Brill,
  2007.

Pecora, Vincent P. *Self and Form*. Baltimore: Johns Hopkins University Press, 1989.

— "Words, Words, Mere Words, No Matter from the Heart. . . ." *American Literary History* 19 no. 1 (2007): 232–50.

Pinsker, Sanford. "Imagining the Postmodern Family." *Georgia Review* 48 no. 3 (1994): 499–515.

Pynchon, Thomas. *The Crying of Lot 49*. New York: J. B. Lippincott, 1966.

— *Gravity's Rainbow*. New York: Viking, 1973.

Rebein, Robert. *Hicks, Tribes, and Dirty Realists: American Fiction after Postmodernism*. Lexington, KY: University of Kentucky Press, 2001.

Riding, Laura and Robert Graves. *A Survey of Modernist Poetry*. New York: Haskell House, 1927.

Roberts, Elizabeth Maddox. *The Time of Man*. Lexington, KY: University Press of Kentucky, 2000.

Roth, Michael S. *The Ironist's Cage: Memory, Trauma, and the Construction of History*. New York: Columbia University Press, 1995.

Ruch, Allen B. "Book Review: *House of Leaves*." 2000. *The Modern World*. Accessed June 8, 2003. http://themodernworld.com/review_house_of_leaves.html.

Said, Edward. *Humanism and Democratic Criticism*. New York: Columbia University Press, 2004.

Samuels, Robert. *New Media, Cultural Studies, and Critical Theory after Postmodernism: Automodernity from Zizek to Laclau*. New York: Palgrave MacMillan, 2010.

Sarup, Madan. *An Introductory Guide to Post-Structuralism and Postmodernism*. Athens: University of Georgia Press, 1993.

Schwenger, Peter. "Words and the Murder of the Thing." *Critical Inquiry* 28 (2001): 99–113.

Scott, A. O. "The Panic of Influence." *The New York Review of Books* 47 no. 2 (2000): 39–43. Accessed July 13, 2012. www.nybooks.com/articles/archives/2000/feb/10/the-panic-of-influence.

Sebald, W. G. *Austerlitz*. Translated by Althea Bell. New York: Random House, 2001.

Shklovsky, Victor. "Art as Device." *Theory of Prose*. Translated by Benjamin Sher. Normal, IL: Dalkey Archive Press, 1991.

Shorter, Edward. *The Making of the Modern Family*. New York: Basic Books, 1975.

Siegel, Harry. "Extremely Cloying & Incredibly False: Why the Author of *Everything Is Illuminated* Is a Fraud and a Hack." *New York Press*. April 20, 2005. Accessed June 3, 2011. http://nypress.com/extremely-cloying-incredibly-false.

Sin, Lena. "Hey Pop Culture Mags—We Still Need You." *Thunderbird: UBC Journalism Review* 4 no. 1 (2001). Accessed July 25, 2003. www.journalism.ubc.ca/thunderbird/2001–02/october/magazines.html. [currently unavailable]

Smith, Zadie. "Brief Interviews with Hideous Men: The Difficult Gifts of David Foster Wallace." In *Changing My Mind: Occasional Essays*. New York: Penguin, 2009.

Sontag, Susan. "Against Interpretation." In *Against Interpretation and Other Essays*. New York: Picador, 1961.

Spirited Away. DVD. Directed by Hayao Miyazaki. Japan: Studio Ghibli, 2002.

Stacey, Judith. *Brave New Families: Stories of Domestic Upheaval in Late Twentieth Century America*. New York: HarperCollins, 1990.

— *In the Name of the Family: Rethinking Family Values in the Postmodern Age*. Boston: Beacon Press, 1996.

Stansky, Peter. *On or about December 1910: Early Bloomsbury and Its Intimate World*. Cambridge: Harvard University Press, 1996.

Steiner, George. *Real Presences: Is There Anything in What We Say?* New York: Faber, 1989.

Stierstorfer, Klaus, ed. *Beyond Postmodernism: Reassessments in Literature, Theory, and Culture*. New York: W. de Gruyter, 2003.

Synecdoche, NY. DVD. Directed by Charlie Kaufman. New York: Sony Pictures Classics, 2008.

Talk to Me: Design and the Communication Between People and Objects. Museum of Modern Art, New York. July 24, 2011. Paula Antonelli, Senior Curator.

Tomasula, Steve. *The Book of Portraiture*. Tallahassee, Florida: FC2. 2006.

— "Three Axioms for Projecting a Line (or Why It Will Continue to Be Hard to Write a Title sans Slashes or Parentheses)." *Review of Contemporary Fiction* 16 no. 1 (1996): 100–8.

Toth, Josh. *The Passing of Postmodernism: A Spectroanalysis of the Contemporary*. Albany: State University of New York University Press, 2010.

Verslyus, Kristiaan. Introduction to *Neo-Realism in Contemporary Fiction*. Amsterdam: Rodopi, 1992. 7–12.

Wagner, Heather. "Jonathan Safran Foer Talks *Tree of Codes* and Conceptual Art." *Vanity Fair.* November 10, 2010. Accessed June 3, 2011. www.vanityfair.com/online/daily/2010/11/jonathan-safran-foer-talks-tree-of-codes-and-paper-art.

Wallace, David Foster. *Brief Interviews with Hideous Men*. New York: Little, Brown and Company, 1999.

— *Consider the Lobster and Other Essays.* New York: Little, Brown and Company, 2005.

— "E Unibus Pluram: Television and U.S. Fiction." *Review of Contemporary Fiction* 13 no. 2 (1993): 151–95.

— *Girl with Curious Hair*. New York: W. W. Norton and Company, 1989.

— *Infinite Jest*. Boston: Little, Brown and Company, 1996.

— *The Pale King*. New York: Little, Brown and Company, 2011.

— "Shipping Out, or the (Nearly Fatal) Comforts of a Luxury Cruise." *Harper's Magazine* January 1996: 33–56.

— *A Supposedly Fun Thing I'll Never Do Again: Essays and Arguments*. New York: Little, Brown and Company, 1997.

— *This Is Water: Some Thoughts, Delivered on a Significant Occasion, about Living a Compassionate Life.* New York: Little, Brown and Company, 2009.

Waters, Lindsay. "Literary Aesthetics: The Very Idea." *The Chronicle Review* 52 no. 17 (2005): B6.

Watson, George. *The Certainty of Literature: Essays in Polemic.* New York: Harvester, 1989.

Watt, Ian. *The Rise of the Novel: Studies in Defoe, Richardson, and Fielding.* Berkeley: University of California Press, 2001.

Wilhelm, Randall. "'Golden Chalice, Good to House a God': Still Life in *The Road.*" *Cormac McCarthy Journal* 6 (2008): 129–46.

Wilson, H. T. *Capitalism after Postmodernism: Neo-Conservatism, Legitimacy, and the Theory of Public Capital.* Boston: Brill, 2002.

Wittmershaus, Eric. "Profile: Mark Z. Danielewski." 2000. *Flakmagazine.* Accessed June 18, 2003. www.flakmag.com/features/mzd.html.

Worthington, Marjorie. "Done with Mirrors: Restoring the Authority Lost in John Barth's Funhouse." *Twentieth-Century Literature* 47 no. 1 (2001): 114–36.

Zalewski, Marysia. *Feminism after Postmodernism: Theorising Through Practice.* London: Routledge, 2000.

Index

8 ½ 194n.3

Abrams, M. H. 5, 12, 19n.10
Adam, Barbara 18n.2, 19n.12, 20n.27
Adaptation 167, 194n.3
Albee, Edward 92, 93, 97, 124n.3
  A Delicate Balance 92
Allan, Stuart 18n.2, 19n.12
Alter, Robert 19n.12
Althusser, Louis 4, 6
Altieri, Charles 4, 5, 12, 19n.9
American Beauty 93
Amis, Martin, *Time's Arrow* 52n.15
antihumanism 3–8
  and metafiction 191
  in *The Names* 24, 29, 30
  and poststructuralism 35, 131, 166,
    188–9, 192
  in twentieth-century literature 2, 10,
    15, 28, 165, 188
antirealism *see* realism
Appiah, Kwame Anthony,
    Cosmopolitanism 3, 5, 6, 8, 19n.13
Ashbery, John, "Paradoxes and
    Oxymorons" 165, 179, 193–4n.2
Atonement 163n.45, 167
author
  death of 156, 179, 180, 181, 184
  invocation of 8, 21n.38, 166, 178–83
avant-garde 15, 142, 167, 199

babble
  in *Infinite Jest* 61
  in *The Names* 31, 39, 45
  in *White Noise* 50
Babel 25, 28, 31, 35, 50, 61
Bakhtin, M. M. 42, 54n.34
Ballard, J. G., *Crash*, *The Atrocity
    Exhibition* 194n.6
Banville, John, *The Sea* 163n.45

Barry, Peter 18n.8, 202n.3, 202n.4
Barth, John 12, 13, 196n.33
  "Lost in the Funhouse" 177–9, 196n.34,
    196n.35
Barthelme, Donald 13, 20n.6
  "At the End of the Mechanical
    Age" 160n.11
Barthes, Roland 19n.18, 112, 126n.32, 179,
    180, 181, 197n.41, 197n.47
Bataille, Georges 25, 123n.2, 142
Battersby, James L. 19n.12
Baudrillard, Jean 4, 6, 135, 139, 179, 180,
    196n.38
Bauman, Zygmunt 20n.27
Beckett, Samuel 20n.36, 136, 199,
    202n.2
  Endgame 131
  Not I 144
belief
  and David Foster Wallace 58, 60, 156,
    177
  in *Everything Is Illuminated* 170–3, 186,
    189, 190, 192
  in *Extremely Loud & Incredibly
    Close* 149, 150, 151, 155
  in *House of Leaves* 121, 123
  and humanism 4, 6, 9, 11, 18n.5,
    18n.7, 28
  in *Infinite Jest* 70, 74, 85n.15
  and language 31, 37
  in *The Road* 131, 135, 138
  in twenty-first century literature 200,
    201
  in *White Noise* 50–1, 171
Bell, Bernard Idding 20n.30
Bellow, Saul 10
Benjamin, Walter 1, 85n.4, 139, 142, 155
Blake, William 148
Bloom, Harold 5, 122
Blue Velvet 93

Bonca, Cornel 51n.5, 54n.37
Bookchin, Murray 19n.11
Boswell, Marshall 86n.23, 87n.43, 162n.34,
　　194n.2, 196n.36, 202n.5
Bosworth, David 54n.33
Bourne, Randolph 127n.43
Brooks, Neil 13, 14, 16, 21n.46, 172,
　　195n.17
Broude, Norma 17n.2
Brown, Bill 16, 139, 141–4, 147, 160n.14,
　　161n.26, 162n.39, 168, 175, 181
Bryant, Paula 51n.2, 54n.37, 55n.39
Budick, Ariella 124n.7
Buford, Bill 172
Burn, Stephen 12–15, 20n.30, 20n.34,
　　21n.46, 85n.1, 87n.42, 87n.44,
　　88n.51, 194n.4, 196n.32, 196n.33,
　　196.316
Butler, Judith 142
Byatt, A. S. 141

Camus, Albert, "The Fact of
　　Absurdity" 52n.17
Carmichael, Thomas 51n.3, 55n.41
Carter, Cynthia 20n.27
Carter, Graydon 119
Caruth, Cathy 195n.12
Carver, Raymond 20n.36, 172
Cast Away 199, 202n.2
Cavanaugh, Tim 120, 126n.39
Cheal, David 20n.27, 96
choice
　　and belief in *Infinite Jest* 70
　　and David Foster Wallace 193
　　and humanism in *The Names* 34, 40–5
　　and hypertext 124n.13
　　and love in *Everything Is
　　　Illuminated* 190–2, 197n.53
　　and meaning in *Extremely Loud &
　　　Incredibly Close* 151
　　and metafiction in "Paradoxes and
　　　Oxymorons" 165–6
　　and postmodernism 15, 16
　　and sincerity 197n.43
Cohen, Samuel 13, 14
constellations 12, 151, 154, 201
Crockett, Clayton 195n.21
Culler, Jonathan 19n.18, 181, 197n.47

Danielewski, Mark Z. 2, 15, 16
　　House of Leaves 7, 91–128, 130, 148,
　　　178, 179, 184, 185
　　Only Revolutions 162n.44, 174
de Man, Paul 4, 145, 155, 195n.12
deconstruction 2, 5, 18n.5, 35, 51, 141,
　　186, 197n.44
DeCurtis, Anthony 53n.20
DeLillo, Don 15, 60, 93, 96, 120
　　The Names 6, 23–45, 47, 50, 51n.3,
　　　52n.7, 53n.24, 57, 61, 92, 121, 134,
　　　144, 159, 168, 185, 187, 191, 197n.43
　　Players 126n.40
　　Point Omega 161n.26, 163n.45
　　Ratner's Star 160n.11, 185
　　Underworld 185
　　White Noise 6, 45–51, 51n.5, 55n.45,
　　　55n.47, 57, 61, 85n.4, 88n.52, 92, 93,
　　　96, 99, 120, 121, 124n.6, 159, 168,
　　　171, 179, 185, 187
Derrida, Jacques 4, 6, 14, 27–8, 35, 40, 41,
　　43, 52n.15, 52n.16, 53n.22, 54n.35,
　　54n.37, 121, 122, 134, 139, 155
Díaz, Junot, *The Brief Wondrous Life of
　　Oscar Wao* 18n.6
Dickens, Charles 148
Didion, Joan 199
dirty realism *see* realism
Domanska, Ewa 17n.2
Durkheim, Emile 25

Eggers, Dave, *A Heartbreaking Work of
　　Staggering Genius* 130, 163n.44
Eliot, George, *Middlemarch* 167
Eliot, T. S., 149
　　The Waste Land 130
Ellis, Jay 160n.8
empathy
　　in *Brief Interviews with Hideous
　　　Men* 196n.36
　　and *Everything Is Illuminated* 186,
　　　190–3
　　and *House of Leaves* 123
　　and humanism and antihumanism 3,
　　　17, 141
　　and *Infinite Jest* 60, 62, 75–7, 176, 181
　　and "Lost in the Funhouse" 177–8
　　and metafiction 166, 172, 177

and "Octet" 179–80, 197n.43
and "Paradoxes and Oxymorons" 166, 193n.2
and twentieth-century fiction 15
and twenty-first century fiction 51, 200
Enlightenment, the 3, 6, 16, 17, 140, 141, 175, 200, 201
Eraserhead 52n.15
Eshelman, Raoul 13, 14, 20n.34

Faber, Michael 19n.12, 162n.41, 196n.24
family
    and crisis of signification 8–11
    and *Everything Is Illuminated* 169, 183, 188, 189, 192, 198n.55
    and *Extremely Loud & Incredibly Close* 150
    and *House of Leaves* 7, 99–109, 124n.6
    and *Infinite Jest* 70–1, 76–7, 82–5
    and "Lost in the Funhouse" 177–8
    and *Music for Torching* 91–8
    and *The Names* 25, 29, 30, 32, 35, 36, 39–45
    and "Octet" 178
    and *The Road* 138
    and *White Noise* 47, 51, 55n.42, 82–5, 88n.51
Fight Club 194n.3
Fish, Stanley 5
Fluck, Winifred 195n.18
Foer, Jonathan Safran 15
    Everything Is Illuminated 7, 169–72, 179–93
    Extremely Loud & Incredibly Close 7, 18n.7, 53n.25, 129–30, 147–56, 159
    Tree of Codes 174, 195n.24
form
    in *Book of Portraiture* 157, 194n.10
    and/versus content 4, 129–30, 140, 144, 145, 145–7, 162n.35, 173–4
    in *Everything Is Illuminated* 185
    in *Extremely Loud & Incredibly Close* 147–9, 154
    in *House of Leaves* 98–9, 101, 121–3
    and metafictional film 194n.3
    narrative form 174–5
    and point of view 41–3

and poststructural realism 167, 172, 180, 191, 200–1
and poststructuralism 18n.6, 28
and *Tree of Codes* 195n.24
Foster, Dennis 39, 53n.21, 53n.27
Foster, Hal 141–2, 167–8, 181, 194n.6, 197n.44
Foucault, Michel 4–6, 121, 133, 179–80
freeplay 27, 40, 53n.22, 54n.37
Freud, Sigmund 4, 7, 13, 19n.12, 26, 31, 35, 62–3, 67, 79, 86n.21, 86n.23, 109–10, 140, 158, 161n.26, 197n.44
Funny Games 194n.3
Fussell, Paul 120

Gardner, Helen 19n.12
Garrard, Mary D. 17n.12
Gass, William H., *Willie Masters' Lonesome Wife* 148
Gates, Jr., Henry Louis 19n.23
Giles, Paul 81
glossolalia
    in *The Names* 30–4, 44–5
    in *White Noise* 50
god, God
    in *The Book of Portraiture* 157–9
    in *Everything Is Illuminated* 170–1
    in *Extremely Loud & Incredibly Close* 151
    in *The Names* 23, 25, 26, 31, 45
    in *The Road* 133, 134–7
Goffman, Erving 87n.43
Graves, Robert 20n.30
gravity 133, 150, 154, 159, 202
Green, Jeremy 12, 14, 20n.27
Gregory, Sinda 125n.16, 125n.22, 126n.27
Gribble, James 19n.12
Gumbrecht, Hans 16, 21n.42, 141, 147, 155–6, 161n.21, 168

Habermas, Jürgen 201
Haddon, Mark, *The Curious Incident of the Dog in the Night-Time* 148, 156
Hagedorn, Ann 21n.42
Harris, Charles B. 198n.56
Harris, Jonathan 17n.2
Harrison, Thomas 21n.42

Hawking, Stephen, *A Brief History of Time* 149–51, 153, 154
Hayles, N. Katherine 8, 68, 78, 82, 83, 88n.48, 88n.50, 89n.55, 104, 112, 124n.12, 124n.14, 125n.16, 126n.25, 126n.28, 127n.50
Hegel, Martin 35, 43, 121
Heidegger, Martin 4, 26–8, 51n.5, 56n.48, 100, 134, 139, 155
Heller, Steven 196n.24
Hemingway, Ernest 184
    "Big Two-Hearted River" 135
    "A Clean, Well-Lighted Place" 63
Hoberek, Andrew 11, 14, 15, 129, 176
Homes A. M. 46
    "Adults Alone" 93, 97
    Music for Torching 7, 10, 15, 51n.4, 91–9, 100, 102, 103, 123n.2, 124n.6, 124n.11, 168, 172, 185, 186, 187, 197n.52
    This Book Will Save Your Life 124n.11
humanism
    and deconstruction 27, 40, 41, 43
    liberal humanism 3, 8
    and neorealism and dirty realism 172–3
    post-1945 3–8
    and poststructuralism 131, 147, 156, 165, 167, 168
Husserl, Edmund 4
Hutcheon, Linda 85n.5, 120–2
hyperreal 4, 46, 139, 176, 179
hypertext 7, 98, 99, 103, 124n.13, 148, 167, 184, 191

Inchausti, Robert 20n.27, 96
infant 28, 52n.15, 65, 82, 84
    infantile desire 7, 48, 50, 79
    infantile narcissism *see* narcissism
    infantilization (in *House of Leaves*) 125n.24; (in *Infinite Jest*) 61–4, 66–8, 80, 84, (in *Music for Torching*) 94, (in *White Noise*) 46, 47, 55n.42,
irony
    and antihumanism 1
    and dirty realism 172
    and disaffection 1, 7, 9, 55n.47, 200, 201

    in *House of Leaves* 99, 106, 118–23
    in *Infinite Jest* 57–9, 62, 66, 68, 73, 78, 80, 81, 83, 84, 85n.4, 176, 193
    in "Octet" 179
    and postmodernism 11, 17, 167

Jacobs, Timothy 87n.43
Jameson, Fredric 18n.5, 28, 35, 116, 119, 120, 121, 126n.36, 138, 140, 159
Jencks, Charles 11, 12
Johnson, Samuel 149
Joyce, James, "The Dead" 55n.47
Judd, Donald 161n.27

Kac, Eduardo 163n.52
Kakutani, Michiko 120, 126n.37, 126n.41
Kang, Minsoo 11, 12, 21n.46
Katz, Jack 123n.1
Kelly, Adam 196n.40, 197n.43
Kirby, Alan 13, 14, 18n.2, 20n.34, 20n.37, 21n.38
Klein, Melanie 67
Kojève, Alexandre 121
Kundera, Milan, *The Unbearable Lightness of Being* 159

Lacan, Jacques 4, 6, 30–1, 35, 62, 84, 86n.23, 134, 139, 142, 159, 167, 171
    fort-da game 26–7, 86n.21, 161n.26
language
    as addiction 60–1
    antihumanist 3–8, 25, 26–9, 30, 35, 166, 188, 189
    and disaffection (in *The Names*) 30–4 (in *White Noise*) 49–51, 168
    and family 8–11
    and the gap 32, 43, 136, 138, 165, 170–2, 173, 187–8, 197n.53
    humanistic 3–8, 16–17, 24, 35, 40–5
    invoking the real 174, 186, 190, 191, 193
    materiality of 18n.7, 21n.38, 129 (in *The Road*) 131–8, 138–47 (in *Extremely Loud & Incredibly Close*) 153–6, (in *The Book of Portraiture*), 157–9
    natural 24
    poststructural 15–16, 18n.5, 46, 52n.16, 54n.37, 135, 167, 168, 200–1

prelapsarian 32, 48
problems and limits of 2, 17, 20n.34, 30, 42, 43, 51n.3, 91–2, 98, 139–40, 173, 188, 192, 193; (in *Infinite Jest*) 59–62; (in *Extremely Loud & Incredibly Close*) 151–3, and 165
self-conscious, self-referring 23, 41–3, 54n.33, 72, 109, 166, 176–7, 191, 200, 201
as solution to problem of language 2, 3, 129, 137–8, 153, 188, 192, 193
as surplus 25–6, 32, 51n.4, 186
and the symbolic order 31, 53n.21, 62, 81, 84
and things 142–4, 175, 186
and Wittgenstein 59–60
Lasch, Christopher 7, 20n.27, 47, 53n.17, 55n.42, 65–7, 72, 82–3, 86n.23, 92, 94, 96, 161n.26
The Last Action Hero 11, 194n.3
Latour, Bruno 16, 139–41, 147, 168, 174, 175, 180, 181, 189
LeClair, Thomas 53n.20, 56n.48, 78, 82, 86n.17, 87n.43, 88n.54, 89n.55
Lévi-Strauss, Claude 25, 28, 43, 52n.16, 186
Lipsky, David 85n.1, 87n.42, 194n.4, 196n.39
Lopez, Jose 17n.2
Lyotard, Jean-Francois 6, 138, 140, 155, 199
grand/master narrative 6, 138, 140, 172, 173, 192, 199

McCaffery, Larry 12, 20n.33, 57–9, 66, 73, 83, 87n.32, 125n.16, 125n.22, 126n.27, 131, 176
McCarthy, Cormac 184
No Country for Old Men 160n.5
The Road 7, 15, 131–8, 143, 160n.8, 160n.10
McEwan, Ian, *Atonement* 163n.45
McHale, Brian 11–12, 14, 21n.39, 21n.42, 181, 194n.11
McLaughlin, Robert 195n.18
McPherson, Tara 17n.2
Mallarmé, Stephen 99, 144, 202n.2
Maltby, Paul 55n.41

Mauss, Marcel 142
mediation
and connection 2, 62, 66, 98, 176, 181
and disaffection 10–11, 47, 51n.3, 91, 188
and family 9–11
and irony 57–8, 68
and narcissism 67–8, 71, 81
and postmodern culture 10, 18n.5, 23–5, 45, 47, 65, 67, 93, 96, 100, 188
remediation 102–23, 126n.25, 183, 188, 194n.3
and subjectivity 25, 35, 43, 65, 71
Memento 167
metafiction 7, 10, 11, 20n.33, 165, 166, 177
in *Brief Interviews with Hideous Men* 196n.37
and choice 191
and dirty realism, neorealism 13, 172–3, 195n.19
and empathy 177, 180, 192–3, 196n.39
in *Everything Is Illuminated* 181–5, 191
and film 194n.3
in "Lost in the Funhouse" 177–8
in *Music for Torching* 195n.16
in "Octet" 178–80
and poststructuralism 176, 201
and realism 172, 173, 176, 179, 180, 181
and trauma 197n.44
metamodernism 201
metanarrative 109, 167, 177–8
Meynell, Hugo 19n.12
Michaels, Walter Benn 145–7, 152, 195n.23
Mitchell, David, *Cloud Atlas* 131, 160n.9, 163n.45
modernism 11, 12, 14, 15, 130, 142, 147, 149, 167, 192, 200–1, 202n.3, 202n.5
modernity 139, 140, 201, 202n.3
Morris, David 89n.55
Morris, Matthew 38, 54n.36, 54n.37

Nabokov, Vladimir, *Pale Fire* 106, 126n.27
narcissism
cultural 7, 64, 82–4, 88n.50, 88n.53, 110, 187, 193
and Freud 7, 67, 110–11, 161n.26, 197n.44

in *House of Leaves* 102
in *Infinite Jest*: primary/infantile 72–81,
    84, 87n.42, 176; secondary/adult 59,
    68–71, 77, 88n.45
and Lasch 55n.42, 65–7, 161n.26
and *White Noise* 47
neorealism *see* realism
Nichols, Catherine 62, 86n.17, 86n.22,
    87n.43
Nielson Media Research 124n.6
Nietzsche, Friedrich 4
    The Birth of Tragedy 34–5
North, Michael 21n.42

Oldenburg, Claus 142–4
Olson, Kirby 18n.2
Orlean, Susan, *The Orchid Thief* 194n.3
Osteen, Mark 26, 53n.24, 54n.37, 55n.47,
    56n.48
Ott, Michael R 17n.2

Pecora, Vincent 55n.47, 145–7
performatism 13, 20n.34
Pinsker, Sanford 8–10, 138
posthumanism 8
postindustrial 7
postmodernism
    end of 1, 11–17, 21n.46, 145–6, 199
    success of 15–17
"post-postmodernism" 12, 13, 14, 20n.34,
    141, 176, 202n.3
poststructuralism 1–3, 8, 13, 15–17,
    19n.12, 20n.34, 25, 28, 43, 46–7, 51,
    99, 118–19, 129, 132, 135, 139–42,
    145–8, 155–7, 165, 167–8, 171–5,
    186, 192, 197n.43, 200–1
    and antihumanism 3–8
    and digimodernism 21n.38
    and empathy, affect 177, 200
    and family 8–11
    and humanism 6, 18n.7, 123, 129, 131,
        138, 147, 181
    and realism 7, 165, 167, 172, 173, 176,
        181, 183, 185, 195n.16, 201
    narrative techniques 130, 177, 179, 180,
        184, 200
    versus postmodernism 18n.5
potlatch 25, 92, 95, 97, 123n.2, 124n.9
Potter, Gary 17n.2

psychoanalysis 3, 7, 121, 123, 138
    and Freud 62–3
    and Lacan 31
    and "working through" 98–9, 109–18
Pynchon, Thomas 13
    The Crying of Lot 49 148, 160n.11,
        193n.1
    Gravity's Rainbow 130, 160n.11

reader
    constructing the text 61–2, 107,
        124n.13, 148, 156, 178, 181
    in relationship with text 58, 66, 97, 135,
        141, 145, 162n.34, 166–7, 177, 184,
        191, 200
    in relationship with writer 8, 14, 58, 60,
        66, 156, 178–81, 185, 191, 196n.40,
        197n.43
real, the
    and *fort-da* game 27
    and Foster, "The Return of the
        Real" 141, 167–8, 197n.44
    and the gap 136, 138, 165, 170–3,
        187–8, 197n.53
    in *Everything Is Illuminated* 169–72,
        180–90
    in *House of Leaves* 112, 123
    in *Infinite Jest* 62, 85
    in *Music for Torching* 94
    and poststructuralism 7, 129, 172–80,
        195n.23
    and representation 11, 16, 27, 144, 165
    and *The Road* 131–6, 138
    in *White Noise* 45, 48–51, 51n.3,
        55n.47, 88n.52
realism
    antirealism 11, 167, 179–80
    "aural realism" 61
    and cosmopolitanism 5
    dirty realism 13, 172, 195n.19
    hyperrealism *see* hyperreal
    magical realism 182–3
    and metafiction, and
        poststructuralism 7, 20n.35, 131,
        144, 165, 167, 172–81
    neorealism 13, 20n.35, 172–3, 195n.19
    "radical realism" 88n.54
    "reality effects" 7, 144, 167, 178, 181,
        184–5, 196n.33, 197n.47

and theater of the absurd 65–6
and things/thingness 175–6
traditional realism 3, 7, 20n.36, 144,
    147, 157, 162n.42, 167–8, 172–6, 178,
    180, 197n.43, 200–1
traumatic realism 167–70, 181
social realism 10
Rebein, Robert 13, 14, 172, 195n.19
remediation *see* mediation
Riding, Laura 20n.30
Roberts, Elizabeth Maddox, *The Time of
    Man* 161n.26
Roth, Michael S. 85n.5, 121–3
Roth, Philip 10
Ruch, Allen B. 123n.1

sacrifice
    in *House of Leaves* 169
    in *Music for Torching* 7, 96–7, 102,
        123n.2, 168–9
    in *The Names* 25–6, 51n.4
Said, Edward 3, 5, 6, 8
Samuels, Robert 17n.2
Sarup, Madan 1, 5
Schwenger, Peter 161n.26
Scott, A. O. 196n.30
Sebald, W. G., *Austerlitz* 162n.44
Serres, Michael 142
Shakespeare, William, *Hamlet* 80
Shklovsky, Victor 87n.32
Shorter, Edward 20n.27
Siegel, Harry 162n.42
signification, crisis of 7, 9, 41, 61, 91,
    99–102, 115–18, 123, 157, 171–2, 187
Sin, Lena 126n.28
Smith, Zadie 197n.43
solipsism
    and infantile narcissism 52n.15, 64, 76,
        84, 176
    in *Infinite Jest* 61–2, 68, 76–7, 80–2,
        88n.54
    and irony 58
    and language 59
    and metafiction 165–6, 193n.2
    in *The Names* 43, 53n.24
    and postmodernism 6–7, 17, 78, 192,
        202n.2
Sontag, Susan 16, 65, 140, 144–7, 155,
    162n.35, 168, 173–4, 181

Spirited Away 52n.15
Stacey, Judith 20n.27
Stansky, Peter 21n.42
Stein, Leo 142
Steiner, George 19n.12
Stierstorfer, Klaus 18n.2
structuralist, structuralism 4, 186
Synecdoche, NY 167, 194n.3

*Talk to Me: Design and the Communication
    Between People and Objects* 161n.28
tautology 3, 152, 166, 191, 193n.1
textuality 13, 129, 130, 147, 200
thing, the, and signification 129, 146–7,
    197n.53
thing theory 139–43, 160n.15, 175–6
    in *The Book of Portraiture* 157–9
    in *Everything Is Illuminated* 161n.26,
        168–72, 186–7, 191–3
    in *The Names* 24, 26–7, 31, 37, 42, 159
    in *The Road* 131–7
    in *White Noise* 46
Tomasula, Steve 1, 139
    The Book of Portraiture 7, 15, 129–30,
        156–9, 162n.44, 163n.52, 185
Toth, Josh 13–16, 21n.46, 172–3, 202n.2
trauma, and "working
    through" *see* psychoanalysis
traumatic realism *see* realism
Twain, Mark 148

Updike, John 10

Versluys, Kristiaan 172, 195n.18

Wagner, Heather 195n.24
Wallace, David Foster 8, 12–13, 15, 18n.5,
    20n.33, 46, 51, 99, 111, 119, 123,
    126n.27, 129, 131, 146, 161n.19,
    162n.34, 176, 177, 181, 192–3,
    194n.4, 196n.32, 196n.33, 196n.39,
    196n.40, 199, 202n.5
    Brief Interviews with Hideous Men 178,
        196n.36
    Consider the Lobster 130
    "E Unibus Pluram" 12, 16n.19, 176
    "Forever Overhead" 193
    Girl with Curious Hair 176, 193n.2
    "Greatly Exaggerated" 156, 180

Infinite Jest 7, 52n.15, 57–89, 91,
    110–11, 121, 126n.35, 154, 167, 168,
    174, 176, 178, 193
"Octet" 7, 178–80, 185, 193, 197n.40,
    197n.43
The Pale King 193, 198n.56
"Shipping Out" 63–8, 86n.27
*A Supposedly Fun Thing I'll Never Do
    Again* 18n.5, 63, 79
This Is Water 193, 198n.57
Warhol, Andy 46, 167, 171, 194n.6

Waters, Lindsay 145–6, 168
Watson, George 19n.12
Watt, Ian 1, 2
Wilhelm, Randall 160n.8
Wilson, H. T. 18n.2
Wittgenstein, Ludwig 59–60
Wittmershaus, Eric 124n.12, 125n.23
Wolfe, Tom 20n.36
Worthington, Marjorie 196n.34

Zalewski, Marysia 17n.2